KU-428-615

INVERNESS IV4 1DL

TAXATION

FOR

EXECUTORS AND TRUSTEES

TAXATION

FOR

EXECUTORS AND TRUSTEES

By

ANTHONY R. MELLOWS, T.D., B.D., Ph.D., LL.D.

Solicitor of the Supreme Court;
Fellow of King's College London;
Professor of the Law of Property in the University of London

FIFTH EDITION

LONDON

BUTTERWORTHS

1981

ENGLAND:	BUTTERWORTH & CO. (PUBLISHERS) LTD. LONDON: 88 Kingsway, WC2B 6AB	
AUSTRALIA:	BUTTERWORTH PTY. LTD. SYDNEY: 271-273 Lane Cove Road, North Ryde, NSW 2113 Also at MELBOURNE, BRISBANE, ADELAIDE and PERTH	
CANADA:	BUTTERWORTH & CO. (CANADA) LTD. TORONTO: 2265 Midland Avenue, Scarborough M1P 4S1	
NEW ZEALAND:	BUTTERWORTHS OF NEW ZEALAND LTD. WELLINGTON: 33-35 Cumberland Place	
SOUTH AFRICA:	BUTTERWORTH & CO. (SOUTH AFRICA) (PTY.) LTD. DURBAN: 152/154 Gale Street	
U.S.A.:	BUTTERWORTH & CO. (PUBLISHERS) INC. BOSTON: 10 Tower Office Park, Woburn, Mass. 01801	

First Edition	*August 1967*
Reprinted	*February 1968*
Second Edition	*September 1969*
Third Edition	*January 1972*
Fourth Edition	*October 1976*
Fifth Edition	*August 1981*

©

BUTTERWORTH & CO. (PUBLISHERS) LTD.

1981

All rights reserved. No part of this publication may be reproduced or transmitted in any form or by any means, including photocopying and recording, without the written permission of the copyright holder, application for which should be addressed to the publisher. Such written permission must also be obtained before any part of this publication is stored in a retrieval system of any nature

ISBN 0 406 62395 3

This book is sold subject to the Standard Conditions of Sale of Net Books and may not be re-sold in the U.K. below the net price fixed by Butterworths for the book in our current catalogue

Reproduced from copy supplied, printed and bound in Great Britain by Billing and Sons Limited, Guildford, London, Oxford, Worcester

Preface

The general pattern of this edition follows that of the previous four. Thus, it follows chronologically the phases in which an executor and trustee may be concerned with income tax, capital gains tax, development land tax and capital transfer tax, namely:

(a) settling the deceased's personal tax liability;
(b) administering the estate;
(c) administering the trust; and
(d) distributing the trust fund.

A section is also included on the creation of a trust in lifetime.

In many respects the treatment of income tax and capital gains tax has been expanded, and there are new chapters on income which is treated as that of the settlor, and on general considerations affecting the taxation of trusts as a whole. The statement of the law generally has been brought up to date.

I continue to hope that this book will be useful for executors and trustees who are not lawyers, as well as for their professional advisers. I have, therefore, endeavoured to explain the basic concepts and principles as they occur, and in so doing I hope that non-lawyers will find the book readable. For the lawyer and accountant, I hope that I have given sufficient authority without making the text too disjointed and indigestible.

In order to keep this book to a compact size, I have had to be selective. The types of transaction which attract liability to income tax, capital gains tax and development land tax, and in many respects capital transfer tax, are essentially the same whether they are effected by an individual or by executors or trustees. The first section of the book, dealing with settling the deceased's personal tax position, is, therefore, less detailed than the rest, but the principles with which it deals are of general application throughout the book.

The law is stated as at 1 May 1981, but the provisions of the Finance Act 1981 are included.

ANTHONY R. MELLOWS
203 Temple Chambers
Temple Avenue
London EC4

Contents

Contents

Part III: *The Administration of the Estate*

Contents

Contents

Part VII: The Administration of a Trust

Contents

Contents

Table of Statutes

Table of Statutes

Table of Statutes

Table of Cases

Table of Cases

Table of Cases

Table of Cases

Settling the Deceased's Personal Tax Liability

Chapter 1

General Considerations

A EXECUTOR'S LIABILITY

As soon as possible after death, and certainly before completing the administration of the estate, the executor must agree with the Inspector of Taxes the deceased's personal liability to tax to the date of death, and he must pay any outstanding tax or obtain for the benefit of the estate any repayment of tax due. If he distributes all the deceased's assets without settling the tax position, he can expect to be both pestered by the Revenue until the position is dealt with, and to be called upon to pay any tax due out of his own pocket. If he does not obtain any tax repayment due to the estate, he may be sued personally for the amount which could have been obtained.

Further, where the total value of the deceased's assets exceeds the figure at which capital transfer tax is payable, before the winding up of the estate is completed, any income tax and capital gains tax payable or repayable must be taken into account in the final assessment to capital transfer tax. Although it is often not possible to ascertain the amount of tax payable or repayable until some time after the death, once the figure is known it is regarded, as appropriate, as a debt or an asset of the deceased as at the date of death. As in the case of income tax and capital gains tax, the executor is personally responsible to see that capital transfer tax is paid, so that he must not distribute all the assets until it is finally established that no further liability for capital transfer tax exists.

B ADMINISTRATION

To ascertain the deceased's personal liability for income tax for the period ending at the date of his death, it is usual to make returns to the Inspector of Taxes to whom the deceased made his returns. The address and reference of the appropriate Inspector will usually appear from the deceased's papers. If these papers do not assist, the address of the appropriate inspector may be ascertained in one of two ways. If the deceased was employed, or, usually, self-employed, the appropriate Inspector will be the one for the area in which the deceased worked. If the deceased was retired or unemployed, the Inspector will usually be the one for the area in which the deceased had his principal residence.

Alternatively, the address of any Inspector of Taxes may be obtained by writing to: — The Secretary, Board of Inland Revenue, Somerset House, Strand, London WC2, or by telephoning 01 – 438 6622 and asking for "Income Tax Enquiries".

C EXECUTOR'S INITIATIVE

It is useful to remember that there is no automatic process by which the Inspector is notified of the deceased's death as soon as it occurs. He will, of course, find out ultimately, but this may not be for several months. As it often takes a considerable time to agree the tax position, to avoid the administration of the estate being delayed, the executor is advised himself to notify the Inspector of the death, and to request the Return form so that the procedure is set in motion.

D TIME FOR MAKING ASSESSMENTS

It will usually be in the executor's interest to agree the tax liability as quickly as possible, so that he may ensure that he will not be under any outstanding personal liability. The Revenue are, however, bound by certain time limits for making assessments upon the personal representatives in respect of the tax liability of the deceased. (Administrators of the estates of persons who died without making a will are in the same position as executors for tax purposes, and both executors and administrators are known as "personal representatives".) The time limits are:

a   an assessment may be made upon personal representatives not later than three years from the end of the tax year in which the

2

death occurs (TMA 1970, s. 40 (1)). The tax year runs from 6 April in each year. Thus if the deceased died on 10 June 1980 (in the tax year ending 5 April 1981) the assessment may be made at any time before 5 April 1984.

b   an assessment made within this time may relate to any year of assessment which ended within six years of the date of the *assessment* (TMA 1970, s. 34 (1)). So that an assessment made on 5 April 1984 in respect of the income of a person dying on 10 June 1980 cannot refer to an earlier tax year than that ended 5 April 1978.

c   where, however, any tax has been lost to the Revenue due to the wilful default, neglect, or fraud of the deceased, an assessment made within the appropriate time may relate to any tax year which ended not earlier than six years prior to the date of *death* (TMA 1970, s. 40 (2)). (Under rule *b* the period runs from the date of assessment.) Thus, where this present rule applies, if the deceased died on 10 June 1980 and the assessment is made by 5 April 1984, it may relate to the tax year ended 5 April 1975, or any subsequent year.

The scope of rule *c* is wide, for "neglect" includes failure to make any return, or to give any information required by the Income Tax Acts.

These rules apply also to govern the time within which the Revenue can make capital gains tax assessments (TMA 1970, s. 40 (3)).

The time limits here discussed relate to assessments in respect of income arising or chargeable gains occuring during the lifetime of the deceased: they do not relate to income received by, or chargeable gains realised by, the personal representatives in respect of the period after the date of death.

Chapter 2

The Deceased's Personal Tax Liability: Income Tax

A THE PRINCIPLES

The Return of Income will cover the income received by the deceased in the period from the preceding 6 April to the date of the death. Against this may be set personal allowances, details of which are given at p. 34, *post*. Although the amounts of personal allowances are intended to cover a complete tax year, the whole of the relevant allowances, and not merely a proportion, may be claimed in respect of the period from the previous 6 April to the date of death. An element of tax planning is therefore involved in dying as well as in marrying and having children!

If the deceased did not make a Return of Income for the tax year ending on the 5 April before the date of death, a separate Return will be required for that tax year.

In making the Return, the executor has to have regard to:

a the deceased's sources of income, that is:

    (i) the various sources;

    (ii) the method of assessment appropriate to those sources; and

    (iii) whether or not tax was deducted at source on payment;

b charges on income, such as payments of mortgage interest; and

c personal allowances which may be claimed.

It is necessary to consider separately each source of income.

B HEADS OF CHARGE

If income is to be chargeable to tax, it must fall within one of the Schedules or Cases of those Schedules. There is no simple provision which says that all income is to be taxed. The structures of the

Schedules are often vaguely understood, without their inter-relation being appreciated, and therefore the following Table may be useful. With regard to the column dealing with the bases of assessment, there are, broadly, two possible bases. The first, the "current year basis", charges to tax in one year the actual income of that year. By contrast, the "preceding year basis" charges to tax the income of one tax year but it is calculated on the actual income of the previous tax or accounting year.

TAXABLE INCOME

Schedule/Case	Income charged	Basis of assessment	Method of payment	Remarks
Schedule A	Rents and certain other receipts from land	Current year basis	Direct assessment	Considered at p. 15, *post*
Schedule B	Occupation of commercial woodlands	Current year basis	Direct assessment	Not considered in this book
Schedule C	Interest or dividends from Government and similar securities	Current year basis	Deduction at source	Considered with Schedule F, p. 19, *post*
Schedule D Cases I & II	Profits of trade profession or vocation	Preceding accounting year basis. Special rules for opening and closing years	Direct assessment	Considered at p. 8, *post*
Case III	UK interest not within Schedule C, annuities and other annual payments not taxed at source	Preceding year basis. Special rules for opening and closing years	Direct assessment	Considered with Schedule F, p. 19, *post*
Cases IV & V	Dividends and interest from securities outside UK; income from other possessions abroad	Preceding year basis. Special rules for opening and closing years	Direct assessment	See p. 25 for position where tax only payable on income remitted to UK

Case VI	Income from miscellaneous sources; and income from furnished lettings	Current year basis	Direct assessment	Considered at p. 16, *post*
Tax deducted	Annuities and other annual payments other than interest	Current year	Deduction at source	
Schedule E Case I	Emoluments of resident	Current year basis	Deduction at source under PAYE	Considered below
Case II	UK emoluments of non-resident	—	—	Not considered in this book
Case III	Foreign emoluments outside Case I	Generally, current year basis	Direct assessment	Considered at p. 22, *post*
General charge	Pensions and some National Insurance benefits	Current year basis	Deduction at source under PAYE, or direct assessment	Considered with Schedule E Case I
Schedule F	Dividends, etc., from UK companies	Current year basis	Deduction at source	Considered at p. 19, *post*

CAPITAL GAINS

Capital gains tax	Chargeable gains	Current year basis	Direct assessment	Considered at p. 39, *post*

DEVELOPMENT GAINS

Development land tax	Realisation of development value from land	Current year basis	Direct assessment	See Ch. 4, p. 57, *post*

GIFTS; ASSETS OWNED AT DEATH

Capital transfer tax	Gifts; assets put into settlement; assets owned on death	Current year basis	Direct assessment	Considered at p. 64, *post*

C WAGES, SALARIES AND PENSIONS

1 *Wages and Salaries*

The taxation of wages, salaries and pensions is governed by Schedule E. The deceased will usually have received before his death most, if not all, of what he was entitled to by way of wages, salary and pension, but there will often be a proportion from the last pay day to the date of death owing to the estate. If this is so, this proportion should be added to the amounts already received by the deceased. Tax is deducted at source on these payments under the PAYE system, so that the employer or ex-employer will be able to give details of the total amount paid to the deceased, and the tax deducted therefrom, for the period from the previous 6 April to the date of death. These figures should include any proportionate payments due to the date of death.

The PAYE system makes provision for the allowances due to the deceased in calculating the amount of tax to be deducted. In effect, the benefit of these allowances is spread over each of the payments for the whole tax year which the deceased would have received. By the time of his death, therefore, the deceased will not have received the benefit of a whole year's allowances, and some overpayment of tax will therefore almost invariably have been made.

It is not only actual money which is taxable. Tax is also payable on other benefits which are derived from the employment. If the deceased was provided with accommodation which he was *required* to occupy to perform his duties, he is not taxable on its value, but he is taxable if he was only *entitled* to occupy it. If he was restricted by the terms of his employment in the use which could be made of the premises, and if they were used for his employer's benefit, an apportionment of the benefit could be made, so that he is not taxable on that part of the value of the premises from which his employers derived benefit. Presents or other benefits convertible into money are taxable as is expenditure made by the employer on the employee's behalf. Directors, whatever their earnings, and other employees earning £8,500 or more, are subject to the more stringent provisions of FA 1976, ss. 60 – 67 (as amended).

2 *Earnings abroad*

Earned income arising abroad is considered later (p. 22, *post*).

3 *"Golden handshakes"*

Within certain limits, "golden handshakes", i.e., substantial payments to an employee on the termination of his employment, are taxable. TA 1970, s. 187 provides a general charge to tax on all payments whith are made directly or indirectly in connexion with the termination of an employment, but the first £25,000 of most of such payments is exempt from tax (TA 1970, s. 188 (3); FA 1981, s. 31). The charging provision does not apply to terminal payments arising on death, so personal representatives are only concerned with such payments arising before the death of the deceased, and not upon his death, and in respect of which tax has not been paid (TA 1970, s. 188 (1)).

A form of "top-slicing" relief is available. There is calculated:

a   the amount of tax which would otherwise be chargeable for the year in which the payment is made; and

b   the amount of tax which would be chargeable for that year of the payment were not made.

There may then be deducted from the amount of tax which would otherwise be payable one half of the difference between *a* and *b* (TA 1970, Sch. 8, para. 7; FA 1981, s. 31).

D   BUSINESS PROFITS – DECEASED SELF-EMPLOYED

The taxation of profits of any trade or business comes within Case I or II of Schedule D, whether the deceased was a sole trader, or carried on business in partnership.

1   Profits

Accounts of the business will have to be prepared to cover the period from the time when accounts of the business were last prepared to the date of death, and this is so even if the business is continued by someone else after the death (TA 1970, s. 118). It often happens that there is a delay of one or two years in preparing accounts of a business. In this case, as well as the accounts for the period to the date of death, intermediate accounts for the year or years since the last accounts were in fact prepared will be necessary.

Tax is, of course, payable not on the amounts actually received by the trader, but on his profit. The profit is arrived at by deducting from his gross receipts all expenses wholly and exclusively incurred in connexion with the business during the period to which the accounts relate. Where accountants prepare accounts of the business, they will also prepare a separate statement for tax purposes. This is because certain items, particularly depreciation, for which an allowance is normally made when preparing accounts, are not deductible for tax purposes, but see p. 10, *post*.

To understand the method of assessing profits upon death, it is necessary first to consider the normal method of assessment while the business is continuing. The assessment is on the preceding year basis, so that the amount of tax payable in one year is calculated on the profit shown in the trader's accounts, adjusted as already mentioned, made up to some date in the previous tax year. Suppose therefore that Sidney has his own business as a builder, and he makes up his accounts annually to the 5 July in each year. His liability in the tax year 6 April 1980 to 5 April 1981 will be based on his profits for his accounting year ended 5 July 1979.

When a sole trader dies, the tax for the year of assessment in which he dies is always calculated on the actual profit made during the period from the beginning of the year of assessment to the date of death. Consider Sidney's business further. Suppose that Sidney dies on 5 October, 1981. Suppose also that his accounts show the following profits:

year ended 5 July 1978	:	£1,900
5 July 1979	:	£1,500
5 July 1980	:	£1,800
5 July 1981	:	£2,000
period 6 July 1981 to 5 October 1981	:	£400

The recent assessments will have been as follows:

1979/80 preceding year ended 5 July 1978	£1,900
1980/81 preceding year ended 5 July 1979	£1,500
	£3,400

The assessment for the final year will be on the actual profits.
1981/82 (6 months to 5 October 1981, date of death)

6 April 1981 to 5 July 1981 3/12 × £2,000	=	£500
6 July 1981 to 5 October 1981 3 months		£400 £900

Where, as in this case, it is necessary to make an apportionment of a whole year's accounts, this apportionment is usually made on a time basis.

The Revenue have, however, the option to calculate tax for the two years of assessment previous to that in which the death occurred on the actual profit earned in those years, and not on the preceding year basis (TA 1970, s. 118 (1) (*b*)). If the Revenue exercise this option the assessments on the actual profits would be:

Part I: Deceased's Personal Tax Liability

1979/80	6 April 1979 to 5 July 1979 3/12 × £1,500	=	£375	
	6 July 1979 to 5 April 1980 9/12 × £1,800	=	1350	1,725
1980/81	6 April 1980 to 5 July 1980 3/12 × £1,800	=	£450	
	6 July 1980 to 5 April 1981 9/12 × £2,000	=	1500	1,950
				£3,675

Although the Revenue have the "option" to calculate the assessments for the two years preceding the death on the actual profit earned, they will invariably exercise this option where this increases the assessments. They cannot revise one year only: both years must be taken together.

Where a business passes on death to the trader's husband or wife, the discontinuance provisions are not enforced unless claimed (Extra-statutory concession A8).

2 Capital allowances

A trader is not entitled to deduct from his profits for tax purposes the depreciation on his plant and equipment. Instead, he is given certain capital allowances.

The types and amounts of these allowances are altered from time to time. In respect of expenditure after 21 March 1972 on machinery or plant there is a first year allowance equivalent to the whole of the expenditure (FA 1972, s. 67). Where the expenditure was incurred previously, a smaller first year allowance was usually given, but additional allowances, called "writing down allowances" were given in subsequent years. Expenditure after 12 November 1974 on thermal insulation to an industrial building qualifies for a first year allowance (FA 1975, s. 14).

Expenditure on certain industrial buildings also qualifies for capital allowances in the form of initial allowances and writing down allowances (CAA 1968, s. 1). Where the expenditure is incurred between 12 November 1974 and 10 March 1981, the initial allowance is one half of the cost of the building (FA 1975, s. 13). Where the expenditure is incurred after 10 March 1981 the initial allowance is 75% of the cost (FA 1981, s. 73) 100% allowances are available in respect of small workshops (FA 1980, s. 75).

Capital allowances are intended to amount ultimately to the actual loss caused by depreciation. Where a business is discontinued on death, or is treated as being discontinued, it is necessary to ascertain the "sale, insurance, salvage or compensation moneys" of the assets at that time. If the assets are in fact sold, the figure is the net proceeds of sale. If they are destroyed, or demolished, the figure is the amount received for salvaged materials, less the cost of demolition. If the assets are sold at less than the market value, or given away, the figure is the market value at that time.

If the cost of the assets, less the total of capital allowances granted is greater than the "sale, insurance, salvage or compensation moneys", a balancing allowance for the difference can be claimed. If, however, the cost of the assets, less those allowances, is less than the "sale, insurance, salvage or compensation moneys", a balancing charge is made to cover the difference. The trader will be charged to tax on this difference, up to a maximum of the allowances already granted to him.

Special provisions apply to capital allowances for motor cars. No first-year allowance may be obtained for a private motor car and if its cost exceeds £8,000 the writing-down allowances are limited to £2,000 p.a. (FA 1976, s. 43, F (No. 2) A 1979, s. 14).

Where a motor car, or any other item of plant or machinery, is used partly for the purposes of trade, and partly for private purposes, there is an apportionment of the capital allowances. Most frequently, this apportionment will be made according to the extent of the use of the asset for business purposes, but all relevant circumstances are taken into account.

3 Losses

If the accounts are prepared in accordance with the principles already discussed, and they show that a loss was sustained in the last twelve months of the trade, the loss can be carried back for the three years of assessment before the year in which the deceased died if that loss is not all used up in the year in which the death occurred (TA 1970, s. 174). The latest profits are relieved first. The effect of this will be to provide a repayment for the estate.

Suppose, then, that Angela has a business as a beautician. Her accounts are made up to 31 December in each year, and she died on 5 October 1980.

Her profits are as follows:

Accounts for year ended	Adjusted profit	Year of assessment	Capital allowances
31 December 1976	£3,000	1977/78	£400
31 December 1977	£2,000	1978/79	£520
31 December 1978	£ 400	1979/80	£660
31 December 1979	£ 840		
9 months to 5 October 1980	Loss: £600	6 months – 1980/81	£300

Part I: Deceased's Personal Tax Liability

In this case the Revenue would not revise the 1978/79 and 1979/80 assessments to actual. The terminal loss for the last 12 months is as follows:

(a) 1980/81 loss 6 April 1975 to 5 October 1975 6/9 × £600	£400
(b) 1980/81 capital allowances 6 months	300
(c) 1979/80 loss 6 October 1979 to 5 April 1980	

3/12 × £840 profit	£210	
3/9 × £600 loss	200	
profit	£ 10	treated as nil

(d) 1979/80 capital allowances	
6/12 × £660 = £330, but £400 already used	260
Terminal loss	£960

Loss relieved as follows:

		Original assessments	Deduct terminal loss relief	Net assessments
1979/80	Profit	£400		
	Less: Capital allowances	400	nil	nil	nil
1978/79	Profit	£2,000		
	Less: Capital allowances	520	1,480	£960	£520

4 Foreign profits

Profits from a trade or business carried on abroad are considered later (p. 24, *post*).

E BUSINESS PROFITS – DECEASED IN PARTNERSHIP

1 Generally

The profits of a partnership are assessed on the normal preceding year basis. So that if a partnership makes up its accounts to 31 December in each year, the profit for the year ended 31 December 1979 will form the basis of assessment for the year 1980/81. It is then necessary to ascertain the liability of each partner. The total amount due to each partner from the partnership is calculated irrespectively of the name given to those payments. Suppose that Peter and Paul are in partnership, and the partnership deed provides that they shall

12

each be entitled to a "salary" of £1,000, and "interest" at £5 per cent on their partnership capital; and that the "profits" will then be divided as to 2/3rds to Peter and 1/3rd to Paul. If this profit sharing arrangement exists throughout 1980/81, the assessment for that year will be split on this basis, even though it is based on the profits of an earlier year when the profit may have been much greater or less, and the sharing arrangements may have been very different. No part of the sum received from the partnership will be treated as unearned, even if it is described as "interest", so that it will not be subject to the investment income surcharge (p. 37, *post*).

Each partner is then entitled to personal allowances and the tax on each partner is then computed. The tax payable by the firm is the total of the tax payable by each of the partners.

If there has been some change in the members of the partnership, or the profit sharing arrangements, during the year of assessment, the assessment is apportioned. This apportionment takes into account the length of time for which the arrangements were in force during that year of assessment (TA 1970, s. 154 (3)).

2 Notice of election for continuing basis

Where one partner dies, the general principle is that the partnership comes to an end at the date of death. However, all the surviving partners, and the personal representatives of the deceased partner, may elect that the partnership is to be regarded as continuing for income tax purposes. This election must be made within two years of the death (FA 1971, s. 17).

If the partnership is regarded as coming to an end, the method of assessment will be the same as in the case of the death of a sole trader (p. 8, *ante*). Thus, for the period from 6 April to the date of death, the tax will be calculated on the actual profit made in that period. Further, the Revenue will have the option to assess the two preceding years also on an actual basis. Where the partnership is treated as continuing, the assessment for the year in which the death occurs is on the preceding year basis.

There will be an apportionment, usually on a time basis, of the profits of that year between the deceased partner and the surviving partners.

The notice exercising the option to treat the partnership as continuing must be sent to the Inspector of Taxes within two years from the date of death, and it must be signed by all interested parties, including the deceased's personal representatives. In deciding whether or not to sign this notice, the personal representatives must be guided solely by the aim of reducing so far as possible the tax payable by the estate. They have no legal duty to consider the other partners. If for the welfare of the estate they do not wish to sign a notice, they would nevertheless be justified in doing so if they took an indemnity from the surviving partner or partners to make good to them the difference in the tax between that which would have been payable by the deceased if the election had not been made, and the tax which was actually payable. As a general principle, if the profits of the practice are steadily rising and are likely to continue to do so, it is advantageous for the option to be exercised.

Suppose that Peter, Paul and Percy are partners, making up their accounts to 5 January. Suppose also that Percy dies on 5 October 1980 and the profits are:

year ended 5 January 1978		£6,800
year ended 5 January 1979		£5,000
year ended 5 January 1980		£6,400
9 months 6 January 1980 to 5 October 1980	£4,500	
3 months 6 October 1980 to 5 January 1981	2,000	£6,500

Suppose further that the likely profit for the year ending 5 January 1982, is £8,000. If the partnership is treated as coming to an end, assessments on the partnership as a whole for 1980/81 and 1981/82 will be as follows:

1980/81:	6 April to 5 October 1980: 6/9 × £4,500		£3,000
	6 October 1980 to 5 January 1981:	£2,000	
	6 January to 5 April 1981: 3/12 × £8,000	2,000	4,000
1981/82:	6 October 1980 to 5 January 1981	£2,000	
	6 January 1981 to 5 October 1981 9/12 × £8,000	6,000	8,000
			£15,000

In this case the Revenue would not wish to adjust the 1978/79 and 1979/80 assessments of £11,800 to actual profits, these being only £11,650.

If election is made for continuation, the assessments will be:

1980/81	Year ended 5 January 1980 split as to old partnership: 6 April to 5 October 1980	£6,400	
	and new partnership: 6 October 1980 to 5 April 1981		£3,200
1981/82	Year ended 5 January 1981		3,200
			6,500
			£12,900

It thus pays the partnership as a whole to elect for continuation: the total assessments are £12,900 instead of £15,000. However, the personal representatives of Percy are only concerned with the period up to 5 October 1980 and an election for continuation would increase that assessment from £3,000 to £3,200. They should not sign the election unless they are indemnified against any extra tax.

3 Losses

Losses are apportioned in the same way as profits between the partners. Even if because of death a partnership is treated as discontinued, losses of partners continuing in the business can nevertheless be carried forward. Terminal loss relief cannot be claimed unless a partnership is treated as permanently discontinued (TA 1970, s. 154 (3)).

4 Administration

Returns of partnership income are the responsibility of the "precedent partner", that is, the first person named in the partnership agreement, provided he is an acting partner and resident in the United Kingdom (TMA 1970, s. 9).

F BUSINESS PROFITS—LIMITED COMPANY

If the deceased carried on business by means of a limited company, albeit a "one-man company", that company is regarded as a separate legal entity from him. He will be employed by the company, and the income which he has received from it will be by way of salary and/or directors' fees, which are taxable under Schedule E (p. 6, *ante*), and possibly dividends on his shares, which are taxable under Schedule F (p. 19, *post*).

G INCOME FROM LAND

1 Generally

The primary charge to tax on profits from land arises under Schedule A.

The possible sources of income from land are:

(a) rents under leases, or tenancies (TA 1970, s. 67 (1));

(b) rent charges;

(c) certain receipts of an income nature receivable by a person by virtue of his ownership of an interest in land; and (*d*) in certain cases, premiums on leases granted after 4 April 1963 (TA 1970, s. 80).

It is proposed to consider only premiums and rents.

2 *Premiums on leases*

Where a premium is taken on the grant of a lease for a period which does not exceed 50 years, it is necessary to reduce the premium by 1/50th for each complete period of twelve months other than the first for which the lease is granted. The balance is treated as rent received in the year in which the lease is granted.

If, therefore, a lease is granted for twenty-one years at a premium of £2,500, one deducts from the premium $\dfrac{21 - 1}{50} \times$ £2,500, which equals £1,000. The remaining £1,500 is treated as rent. If a lease is granted for 50 years at a premium of £2,500, there is deducted $\dfrac{50 - 1}{50} \times$ £2,500, giving £2,450. In this case the remaining £50 is treated as rent.

A premium taken on a lease of over 50 years does not attract liability to income tax (unless the lease were granted by a dealer in property, when the dealer would be taxed in the usual way on the profits of that business). Liability to capital gains tax may, however, arise (see pp. 53–55).

Income from land outside the United Kingdom is not within these provisions (TA 1970, s. 67 (1)).

Complex provisions (TA 1970, Sch. 3) enable an individual owner to treat the chargeable premium as payable by equal amounts over the length of the term of the lease.

In certain circumstances, a premium taken on the grant of a lease may give rise to a liability to development land tax. This is considered later (p. 57, *post*).

3 *Rents*

There is no charge to tax on rents as such, but there is a charge on *profits* from rents. This means that expenses can be set against rents to arrive at the profit. These expenses must, however, be broadly of a recurring nature, or for the maintenance or repair of the property rather than for its improvement. The landlord who provides central heating, for example, can clearly deduct the running cost in calculating his profit. Again, a landlord who repairs damaged slates in the roof can deduct that cost but a person who purchases a derelict house will not be able to deduct the cost of large scale improvements.

Subject to certain limits, the owner is taxed on the income which is receivable, even if it is not actually received.

Where the tenant is entitled to the use of furniture supplied by the landlord, the normal charge to tax arises under Case VI of Schedule D. The landlord, or his personal representatives, can, however, elect by notice to the Inspector of Taxes within two years after the end of the year of assessment, that part of the rent shall be assessed under Schedule A. This will often make no difference, but whether or not such election is desirable will depend on whether the landlord is entitled to deduct more expenses under Schedule A. This really requires professional advice, and the facts of each particular case have to be considered.

4   Deductible expenses

From the sums receivable, there may be deducted payments actually made (but not liabilities incurred but not paid) in respect of the following:

(*a*) expenditure necessary to maintain the value of the property by repairs, decorations, etc. Subject to what has already been said, expenditure on improvements is not deductible;

(*b*) insurance;

(*c*) management of the property;

(*d*) services provided under the lease, for which the lessee does not reimburse the lessor;

(*e*) general and water rates, and similar charges;

(*f*) rent, or ground rent, or similar periodical payments payable by the owner.

The position with regard to mortgage interest is considered at p. 30.

5   Deficits

Where the deductible expenses exceed the rent for the period in question, it is important to know whether the deficit can be set against rents arising under subsequent leases of the same property, or rent arising under leases of other properties owned by the same landlord, In this connexion it is necessary to distinguish between:

a   a lease not at a "full rent". A "full rent" is a rent which is sufficient, taking one year with another, to meet the outgoings and under which a profit is envisaged:

b   a lease at a full rent which is a "tenant's repairing lease", that is, a lease where the tenant is under an obligation to maintain and repair the whole, or substantially the whole of the premises comprised in the lease;

c   a lease at a full rent which is not a tenant's repairing lease.

A deficit on a lease not at a full rent may be carried forward, but only set off against profits arising under the same lease. The deficit cannot be set off against other profits, or against profits arising under a future lease of the same property.

A deficit on a lease at a full rent, whether or not a tenant's repairing lease, can be carried forward and set off against future profits arising in respect of that property, either under the same lease, or under a future lease, except that there can be no carry forward to a future lease if in the meantime the property has been occupied by the owner, or let at a rent which is not a full rent.

Alternatively, a deficit on a lease at a full rent can be set off against profits arising in respect of other property owned by the same landlord if the profits arise under a lease which is not a tenant's repairing lease (TA 1970, s. 72 (4)).

The Revenue accept accounts which are prepared for each property, or which are prepared for each of the three types of property. They will not accept block accounts covering different types of property.

If the deceased owned a large house which he occupied as his residence on 5 April 1963, as well as other properties, he would have been entitled to add the outgoings on his residence to those of other properties let at a full rent and managed as one estate, and to set off the aggregate expenditure against rents from the rest of the properties, provided he had accepted liability to tax on the up to date annual value of the properties which were not let, or not let economically (TA 1970, s. 73 (2)).

The assessment is on a current year basis. Thus for 1980/81 the tax is assessed on the actual profit made during that period. To enable this to be done, a provisional assessment is made based on the previous year's profits, and this is then adjusted after the end of the year.

The tax for a tax year is usually payable on 1 January of that year. If, therefore, a person dies between 6 April and 31 December, he will not usually have paid any tax in respect of his profits in that year. An account must be prepared on the lines mentioned, and the liability agreed. If, however, a person dies between 1 January and 5 April, the tax for that full year under the provisional assessment will probably have been paid, so that when the final accounts have been prepared, only some adjustment may be necessary.

6   *Profits arising from the disposal of land*

A profit made on the disposal of land or buildings may give rise to liability to development land tax. This is considered later (p. 57, *post*). Apart from this there may be a liability to income tax. The position depends on the circumstances in which the profit was made. The deceased might have been a trader or dealer in land or buildings. There is no single test of what a dealer is, but if the deceased bought and sold a number of properties, other than those in which he lived, it is likely that he will be regarded as a trader, unless he bought these properties mainly with a view to deriving an income from them. The deceased might also be regarded as a trader even if he bought only one of these properties, if, at the time when he bought it he intended to dispose of it at a profit according to a clear plan or policy. If he was a trader, his trading profit is calculated according to the same principles as any other profit from self-employment (p. 8, *ante*).

If the deceased was not a trader or dealer in land it is then necessary to consider whether he purchased the land or buildings, or developed them, with the sole or main object of realising a gain from their disposal. If this was the case, there is a liability to income tax on the profit under Case VI of Schedule D. In any other situation the liability to tax, if any, is to capital gains tax. This is considered later (p. 39, *post*).

H INVESTMENT INCOME

Dividends and similar distributions by United Kingdom companies are chargeable under Schedule F. Interest from United Kingdom Government and similar securities is chargeable under Schedule C. Other UK dividends and interest which are not taxed at source are assessable under Schedule D Case III. It matters little to the recipient which of these Schedules applies.

1 Dividends

(a) *Received before death* Dividends will have been paid with the benefit of a tax credit, so that for most purposes the result is as if the amount actually paid represents a larger sum from which income tax at the basic rate has been deducted. Interest on debentures and on Government and similar securities will in fact have been paid subject to deduction of income tax at the basic rate in force when the payment was made. In either case there will, therefore, be no further income tax at the basic rate payable though higher rate tax may be payable (see p. 36, *post*). In addition, the investment income surcharge may also be payable (see p. 37, *post*). If the total income of the deceased for the period from the previous 6 April to the date of death was sufficient to keep his income below the level at which he is required to pay tax, a repayment claim can be made. This depends on his "total income", a concept discussed at p. 25, *post*.

(*b*) *Received after death* Where a dividend is received after death for a period wholly before the deceased died, for the purpose of determining the person entitled to that amount, it is treated as having arisen before the death. The personal representatives therefore add it to the capital of the estate even though it was a receipt of an income nature. Similarly, where a dividend is received after death for a period partly before and partly after the death, the dividend is apportioned (Apportionment Act 1870, s. 3) and the part representing the period before death is added to capital. As regards tax, however, no apportionment is made. If the payment is made after death, this will affect the position of the personal representatives making a return of the income arising *after* the date of the death (p. 142, *post*) but no part of the payment should be included in a return of the deceased's income to the date of death (*I.R. Comrs. v Henderson's Executors* (1931), 16 T.C. 282). The only exception is if the company had declared the dividend before the death, so that it was actually due to the deceased before his death: in this case the whole of it is regarded as income of the deceased and should be included in his return. If, however, the resolution for payment provided that it should be made after the date of death, the dividend will be the income of the personal representatives (*Potel v I.R. Comrs.*, [1971] 2 All E.R. 504).

2   *Interest payments not subject to deduction of tax*

The interest on certain Government securities, of which 3½% War Loan is the most common, may be paid without deduction of tax (see p. 393, *post*). Further, loan interest paid by individuals and bank deposit interest, is usually paid gross. Where these sums have been received before death, or have become due before death, tax will be payable on them.

Assessments to income tax in respect of interest are related to each "source" of that interest. Strictly, each deposit account, even with the same bank, is treated as a separate source, although in practice the taxpayer is permitted to treat all accounts with the same bank as comprising one source.

Except for the first two years in which interest is derived from a source, the liability is on a preceding year basis. Thus, the assessment for the year 1980/81 will be based on the actual interest for the year ended 5 April 1980. Special rules apply where the taxpayer ceases to possess the source. He will actually do so when an account is closed, and he is deemed to do so when he dies (TA 1970, s. 121 (5)). Under these rules, the tax for the year in which the source ends is based on the actual interest for that year (s. 121 (1)); and the Revenue can adjust the assessment for the preceding year to that on the actual interest which arose in that year.

3 Building Society interest

By special arrangement with the Revenue, Building Society interest is not subject to income tax in the hands of the recipient. It must, however, be included in the return, as the recipient may be liable to income tax at the higher rate upon the grossed up amount of building society interest.

4 National Savings Bank and Trustee Savings Bank interest

The first £70 of interest from the National Savings Bank, and from the Trustee Savings Bank (other than interest from special deposits and investment deposits) is exempt from income tax (TA 1970, s. 414 (1), (4); FA 1977, s. 29).

I ANNUITIES

1 "Purchased life annuities"

All annuities are taxable under Schedule D Case III. Usually income tax at the basic rate is deducted at source, so that no assessment is necessary. If the deceased was in receipt of an annuity, it is important to establish whether or not it was a "purchased life annuity". A "purchased life annuity" is, broadly, an annuity for the life of an individual granted in exchange for a capital sum by a company, usually an insurance company, in the ordinary course of business (TA 1970, s. 230). Among the annuities excluded from this definition are retirement annuities or superannuation pensions, and annuities purchased in pursuance of a direction in a will.

Where an annuity is within this provision, each payment is treated as being made up partly of a return of capital, and partly a payment of interest, and only the interest part is taxable. The interest part is in fact paid subject to deduction of tax, and there is, of course, no tax payable on the capital element. Although tax is deducted at source, by special arrangement the rate of tax may have been less than the basic rate. This arrangement will operate where the Revenue are satisfied that the recipient has a small income, and would not be liable to pay tax at the basic rate.

2 *Other annuities*

The whole of the payments received in respect of other annuities will be regarded as income, from which tax will have been deducted at source upon payment. In the case of annuities provided in con-nexion with a former employment or occupation, the deceased will not normally be subject to the investment income surcharge upon the receipts. Where the deceased had a small income only, some repay-ment may be due.

3 *Payment after death*

Where after death the personal representatives receive the final payment of an annuity which terminated on death, that should not be included in the deceased's tax return: the personal representatives themselves are chargeable to tax on it. (*Stewart's Executors* v *I.R. Comrs.* (1952), 33 T.C. 184).

J INCOME RECEIPTS FROM TRUSTS

1 *Where the deceased was a life tenant*

Where the deceased was a life tenant under a trust, the income tax position is broadly the same as in the case of dividends. So that if the trustees made a payment after death covering the period both before and after death, though for purposes of general administration it must be apportioned, no part of the payment should be included in the deceased's tax return.

2 *Other cases*

Where income is paid to a discretionary beneficiary, the trustees are required to deduct income tax at a rate which equals the basic rate (1981/82 30%) and the investment income surcharge (1981/82 15%). In this case, a beneficiary who is not liable to pay income tax in excess of the basic rate on his total income, including the gross amount of the trust income paid to him, may make an income tax repayment claim. This is considered further at p. 248.

Any capital payments will not be subject to income tax, although where payments of an income nature are made from capital, the trustees will have been liable to tax in respect of them (p. 148).

K FOREIGN INCOME

It is outside the scope of this book to consider the tax position of a person who at his death was not resident in the United Kingdom. It is, however, appropriate to consider the position of a person who was resident in the United Kingdom at the time of his death, and who received or was entitled to receive earned income or unearned income from abroad.

1   *Foreign earned income*

(*a*) *Income liable to tax*   The general rule is that where a person who is an employee is resident and ordinarily resident in the United Kingdom (these concepts are considered at p. 369, *post*) he is liable to income tax under Case I of Schedule E on the total amount of his earnings, whether or not he performs his duties in the United Kingdom (FA 1974, s. 21(1)). However, to this general rule there are certain exceptions.

(i)   where the duties of the employment are performed wholly or partly outside the United Kingdom, and the employee is absent from the United Kingdom for a continuous period of 365 days, there is, in effect a total exemption from liability to tax under Schedule E (FA 1977, Sch. 7, para. 8). The exemption is also available in certain circumstances where the employee visits the United Kingdom for short periods;

(ii)   where the duties of the employment are performed wholly or partly outside the United Kingdom, and the employee is absent from the United Kingdom for 30 or more qualifying days, there is a liability under Schedule E, but only on 75% of the earnings (FA 1977, Sch. 7, para. 2). Broadly, qualifying days are days of absence from the United Kingdom for the purposes of work, and days of travel for such purposes;

(iii)   where the duties of the employment are performed *wholly* outside the United Kingdom, and the employer is resident outside and not resident within the United Kingdom, the Schedule E liability is restricted to that on 75% of the earnings, whether the period of absence is more or less than 30 days (FA 1977, Sch. 7, para. 3).

Where the deceased was employed by the Crown on duties of a public nature, and he was paid out of the public revenue of the UK, he is regarded as performing his duties in the UK. Thus a Foreign and Commonwealth Office official or an Army officer serving abroad will be taxable in the same way as if they in fact performed their duties in England.

(*b*) *Expenses* A person performing his duties either wholly or partly abroad is, broadly, entitled to deduct from his income expenses which would be allowable as deductions if the duties were performed in England. The expenses of travelling from the United Kingdom to take up the employment, and back on the termination of the employment are deductible (FA 1977, s. 32 (2)).

(*c*) *Basis of assessment* In general, the whole of the emoluments of an employment which are taxable under Schedule E are taxable in the year of assessment in which they are earned (TA 1970, s. 181 (1)). In some cases, particularly where the employer is in the UK, the tax will have been deducted in the normal way under the PAYE system. Where this has not been done, a direct assessment will be raised.

2 Foreign trading income

Where a trade or business is carried on abroad the general principle is that the taxpayer is liable to income tax under Case I or Case II of Schedule D, in exactly the same way as if the trade or business had been carried on in the UK but on only 75% of the profit (FA 1974, s. 23). The liability is, therefore, in no way dependent upon the profits being remitted to the UK. If the taxpayer is not domiciled or ordinarily resident in any part of the UK, he is only liable to tax under Schedule D on income remitted to the UK (TA 1970, s. 122 (1); FA 1974, s. 23 (1)).

In this case, the tax is calculated on the amount remitted to the UK in the preceding year of assessment, and not, as in the case of income from employment, in the year of assessment in which the remittance is made.

3 Foreign visits by self-employed

If the deceased carried on, either as a sole trader or as a partner, a trade, profession or vocation in the United Kingdom, from the year 1978/79 relief is available in certain circumstances where he made visits abroad for business purposes. Provided that the deceased spent at least 30 days in the year of assessment working abroad, 25% of the net profits which relate, on a time basis, to the period of absence are exempt from tax (FA 1978, s. 27 and Sch. 4).

4 Foreign pensions

In general, 90% of a foreign pension is taxable in the UK, whether or not it is remitted here (FA 1974, s. 22 (1)). However, only 50% of pensions paid to victims of National-Socialist persecution by German or Austrian governmental agencies is taxable (s. 22 (2)).

The remittance basis applies to foreign pensions paid to a taxpayer who is not domiciled or is not ordinarily resident in any part of the UK.

5   Other foreign income

Other foreign income, such as income from securities or possessions, or from a foreign trust fund, is taxable under Schedule D Case IV or V on the actual amount of income which arises, whether or not any part of it is remitted to the UK, unless the taxpayer is domiciled outside the UK, when the remittance basis applies. The assessment is on the preceding year basis. Special provisions apply where, by virtue of provisions of the country in which the income arises, it cannot be remitted from that country.

Where the deceased was entitled to bonus shares under a foreign trust, they will be treated as capital unless they represent a series of recurrent payments over a substantial period of time. Where they are capital, no liability to income tax can arise (*Baron Inchyra* v. *Fennings,* [1966] Ch. 37; *Lawson* v. *Rolfe,* [1970] Ch. 612).

6   Double taxation

In order to prevent, or to reduce the burden of, taxation both in the UK and abroad, relief or exemption may be obtained under a Double Taxation Convention and reference will have to be made to the Convention which applies in any particular case. Where no Double Taxation Convention or similar agreement is in force, and tax is chargeable on an arising basis, the foreign tax paid may be deducted from the gross income in calculating the net amount of income upon which the tax is assessed.

L   SHORT TERM GAINS

Until 5 April 1971 there were two sets of rules which governed the taxation of capital gains. The first related to short term gains, which were gains made where the disposal occurred before or within twelve months after the acquisition of the asset. The second set related to capital gains tax gains. As from 6 April 1971 this distinction has been abolished, and all gains are now subject to capital gains tax (FA 1971, s. 56). These are dealt with in Chapter 3 (*post,* pp. 39 *et seq.*).

M   THE CONCEPT OF TOTAL INCOME

When all the sources from which the deceased received income have been identified, it is then possible to calculate his total income for the period from the preceding 6 April to the date of death. A similar calculation will have to be made for any previous year of assessment for which the total tax liability has not been agreed. The total income is calculated so that any reliefs due to the deceased can be ascertained, and so that his highest rate of tax can be calculated.

It is, therefore, necessary to

a   add together the taxable income from each source;

b   where appropriate, aggregate the income of certain other members of the family;

c   deduct "charges" on income;

d   calculate the amount due in respect of personal reliefs; and

e   calculate the income tax due on the balance.

The aggregate of *a* and *b* is known as the gross statutory income. The gross statutory income less *c* is known as the net statutory income. The net statutory income less *d* is known as the taxable income or total income.

The sources of income which lead to the total income have been considered. It not remains to consider the remaining factors.

N   AGGREGATION

There may be aggregated with the income of a man that of his wife and that of his children.

1   Wife

a   General rules

The general rule is that the income of a married woman is treated as the income of her husband for all tax purposes (TA 1970, s. 37 (1)). This does not apply if the spouses are separated by a court order or by a separation agreement; nor if the spouses are in fact living apart in such circumstances that the separation is likely to be permanent (TA 1970, s. 42). Except in these cases, the general rule has the effect that the husband is assessed on both his own and his wife's income. Where, however, the husband has not paid the tax, the Revenue may recover it from the wife, or, if she is dead, from her personal representatives (TA 1970, s. 40). The Revenue must, however, take action within six years (*Johnson* v. *I.R. Comrs.*, [1978] 2 All E.R. 65).

The spouses may elect to be separately assessed. The reliefs and allowances are then apportioned between them and the parties are then assessed as separate persons (TA 1970, s. 38). However, election for separate assessment only affects the machinery for recovery of tax, and it does not affect the total amount which both pay.

Where the wife dies, her husband, or, if he also is dead, his personal representatives, may disclaim liability for unpaid tax arising in respect of the wife's income. The disclaimer must be made by notice given both to her personal representatives and the Inspector within two months of the date of the grant of probate of her will or letters of administration to her estate (TA 1970, s. 41). The effect is, then, broadly, as if the husband and wife had been separately assessed during their lifetime. It is always desirable to consider whether this disclaimer should be made. The effect of doing so is to make the liability for the payment of the tax that of wife's estate, and so it is deductible in the calculation of her net asset value for capital transfer tax purposes.

b Separate taxation of wife's earnings

In respect of the year 1972/73, or any subsequent year, a husband and wife or their personal representatives may jointly elect that the earnings of the wife shall be charged to tax as if she were a single person with no other income. In general, the election must be made not earlier than 6 months before the beginning of the year of assessment to which it relates, and not later than 6 months after the end of that year. Once it has been made for one year of assessment, it remains in force for subsequent years unless it is revoked (FA 1971, s. 23).

In contrast to an election for separate assessment, where this election is given, the total tax payable is altered; the effect is that:

i   the notice applies to only the earned income of the wife;

ii it applies to all her earned income, except (a) pensions and certain other payments which she receives in respect of her husband's past employment; and (b) family allowances and National Insurance benefits which are treated as earned income for tax purposes and are not payable by virtue of the wife's own contributions;

iii other income of the wife is ignored for the purposes of *her* assessment; and,

iv she is treated as a single person, and, therefore, obtains the single person's allowance. She is entitled to earned income relief on the total of her income.

27

So far as the husband is concerned

    i   the unearned income of the wife continues to be aggregated with his; and

    ii he too is assessed as a single person, and therefore only receives the single person's allowance.

This election is not advantageous unless there is a substantial liability to income tax at the higher rates or the wife has substantial earnings. An election for separate assessment can still operate but it still does not reduce the total tax payable and would apply to the wife's unearned income only.

2   Children

Since 6 April 1972 the income of an infant unmarried child has not been aggregated with that of his parents (FA 1971, s. 16 (1)).

O CHARGES ON INCOME

Certain types of payment made by an individual are known as charges on his income. These payments are all made in pursuance of a legal obligation, which is either a deed or agreement concluded between the payer and the payee; or an order of the Court. The legislation treats the gross amount paid as forming part of the total income of the recipient, not as forming part of the income of the payee. If, therefore, a person has an actual income of £2,000 p.a., and he pays £500 p.a. to his former wife under a court order, the payments under that order are deducted from his total income, so that his ultimate tax position is as if he had received only £1,500 p.a., with no liability under the order.

Charges on income fall into two categories:

    a those which the deceased paid gross; and,

    b those in respect of which the deceased was entitled to deduct income tax when paying.

Where the deceased made the payment gross without being entitled to deduct tax, he is entitled to recover the tax which he has suffered on a sum equivalent to the gross payment. If he deducted tax when making the payment, then provided this was made out of taxed income, he is entitled to keep for himself the tax deducted. The final result is the same. This can be shown by two examples, in each of which the deceased had an income of £2,000, from which tax at the rate of 30% was deducted when he received it. There is a charge on his income of £500.

Example 1: Payment made gross

	£
Gross income	2,000.00
Tax deducted at 30%	600.00
Net amount received	1,400.00
Charge on income: paid gross	500.00
	900.00
Repayment due to payee (tax at 30% on £500)	150.00
Final net position	£1,050.00

Example 2: Payment made subject to deduction of tax

		£
Gross income		2,000.00
Tax deducted at 30%		600.00
		1,400.00
Gross charge on income	£500.00	
Tax deducted on payment	150.00	350.00
		£1,050.00

In either case the result is the same as if the deceased had in the first instance only received £1,500 and had had no charge on his income. The tax on £1,500 at 30% is £450, and the net amount is £1,050.

The gross amount of all charges on income ranks as a deduction from the total income. This has the effect that personal reliefs may only be granted on the total income, less the gross amount of the charges (TA 1970, s. 25).

The charges on income are:

1 *Payments under non-charitable covenant*

Payments made under deed of covenant which can have a life of more than 6 years are charges on income for the purposes of income tax at the basic rate but generally not at the higher rates (TA 1970, ss. 434 and 457). The only payments under non-charitable covenant which are allowable as a charge for higher rate purposes are those, within limits, for the acquisition of a partnership interest, or an interest in a business (TA 1970, s. 457 (1), (2)) or where the covenant was entered into for full consideration (*Bulmer* v. *I.R. Comrs.*, [1967] Ch. 145).

The payer is entitled to deduct tax when making the payment (TA 1970, s. 52).

2 Payments under charitable covenant

In respect of the years 1981/82 and thereafter gross payments of up to £3,000 made under covenants to charity are treated as charges on income for both basic and higher rates of tax if the covenants last for four years or more (FA 1980, ss. 55, 56).

3 Mortgage interest

Mortgage interest (including interest paid to a building society) ranks as a charge on income in certain circumstances. Unsecured loan interest also ranks as a charge on income where the loan was applied for the purchase or development of land or buildings.

a There are three basic conditions which must be satisfied. These are:

i the person making the payment must own freehold or leasehold land in the UK or the Irish Republic at the time when the payment of interest is made;

ii the purpose of the loan must have been (1) to purchase that land; or (2) to develop or improve that land or its buildings; or (3) to pay off a loan effected for either of these purposes; and

iii the money raised by the loan must have in fact been applied within a reasonable time for the specified purpose, and it must not have been applied for any other purpose before being applied for the specified purpose (TA 1970, s. 57).

Where these basic conditions are satisfied, further conditions must be satisfied, according to whether the property is the taxpayer's residence, or is investment property.

b The following conditions must be satisfied where the property is the taxpayer's residence.

i where the loan was taken out before 27 March 1974, the total interest, without limit on the amount of the loan, is a charge on income to the extent that it is payable before 6 April 1982 (FA 1974, s. 19 (4), F (No. 2) A 1979, s. 10). In this case *none* of the following conditions need be satisfied.

ii where the loan was taken out after 26 March 1974, and in any case where the interest is payable after 5 April 1982, the interest only ranks as a charge on income to the extent that the following conditions are satisfied:

(a) the property is the only or main residence of the tax-payer; or of a dependent relative; or of a former or separated spouse. There is no general relief for interest paid on loans for the purchase of "second homes";

(b) the loans on which the interest is payable does not exceed £25,000. The limit of £25,000 is reduced where in respect of loans for some other purposes taken out before 27 March 1974 interest is eligible for relief. These purposes are, broadly, bank loans and loans for second homes (FA 1974, Sch. 1, para. 5).

c The following conditions must be satisfied where the property is an investment property.

i As in the case just mentioned, where the loan was taken out before 27 March 1974, the total interest, without limit on the amount of the loan is a charge on income to the extent that the interest is payable before 6 April 1982, and in this case *none* of the following conditions need be satisfied (FA 1974, s. 19 (4)).

ii Where the loan was taken out after 26 March 1974, and in any case where the interest is payable after 5 April 1982, the interest only ranks as a charge on income to the extent that the following conditions are satisfied:

(a) the property must be let at a commercial rent for more than 26 weeks in any period of 52 weeks; and when it is not let it must either be available for letting or it must not be capable of being let as a result of works of construction or repair (FA 1974, Sch. 1, para. 4); and

(b) the interest paid can only be set off against income from the property let, or against income from other property (para. 7). An excess of interest over income can be carried forward and offset against income from property in future years.

d A special rule applies where interest is paid by personal representatives. If the condition in *b* were satisfied in the deceased's lifetime, then if the property is used after his death as the only or main residence of the deceased's widow, or of a dependent relative, interest paid by personal representatives is eligible for relief (FA 1974, Sch. 1, para. 8). Likewise interest paid by

31

personal representatives where the conditions in *c* were satisfied during the deceased's lifetime is eligible for relief (*ibid*).

e Mortgage interest in respect of a loan taken out before 27
March 1974 for any purpose which satisfies the basic conditions
in *a* is a charge on income provided it is payable before 6 April
1982 (FA 1974, s. 19 (4)).

4 Other loan interest

In certain other circumstances, interest is a charge on income.
Briefly, these circumstances are:

a Where the loan was used in acquiring shares in a close company, or for re-lending to a close company, if the taxpayer
owns at least 5% of the share capital of the company (FA 1974,
Sch. 1, para. 9, FA 1980, s. 28).

b Where the loan was used in acquiring a share in a partnership,
or for re-lending to the partnership (para. 11), provided the
interest of the deceased was not that of a limited partner (FA
1981, s. 25).

c Where the loan was used to pay estate duty or capital transfer
tax in respect of the deceased's personal property prior to the
grant of probate or letters of administration (para. 17;
FA 1975, Sch. 12, para. 19).

d Where the loan did not exceed £25,000, and at least 90% of it
was used to purchase an annuity (para. 24). This only applies
where the taxpayer was 65 or over at the time when the loan
was taken out; and where the loan is secured on land owned
by the taxpayer.

e Generally where the loan was taken out before 27 March 1974,
in respect of interest payable until 1982. In the case of a bank
loan replacing an overdraft, the interest only qualifies for
relief to the extent that the amount of the loan does not exceed
the amount of the overdraft on 26 March 1974 (FA 1974,
s. 19 (4), (5)).

5 General conditions

In each case relief is only given if the rate of interest is a "reasonable commercial rate". This expression is not defined, but almost
certainly it extends to a rate substantially in excess of a normal
building society lending rate. Where the interest is in excess of the
reasonable commercial rate, only the excess is excluded from that
relief.

In the case of all loan interest, other than that paid to a foreign resident, payment must be made without deduction of tax. It is then for the payer to satisfy the Inspector of Taxes that the conditions are satisfied, and a repayment is then made.

6 Bank interest

To be eligible for relief, bank interest must satisfy the conditions stated above for loan interest. Where they are satisfied, and the interest is actually paid, relief will be given. If, however, the bank merely debits an overdrawn account with interest and no credits are paid in, no tax relief may be claimed. It is said that there is no "real payment of interest" in this case (*Paton* v. *I.R. Comrs.* (1938), 21 T.C. 626). To obtain relief, it is necessary to obtain from the bank a certificate 38E which shows the amount of that interest.

Payment of bank interest is made without deduction of tax (TA 1970, s. 54 (2)).

7 Payments for wife and/or children

a Voluntary payments If the deceased was a married man separated from his wife, and he maintained her by voluntary contributions, he is not entitled to deduct the amount of those contributions in assessing his total income. (If he "wholly maintained" her, which probably means if he was paying her enough for her living expenses, even though she had other income, he is, however, entitled to a married man's personal allowance (p. 34, *post*).)

b "Small maintenance payments" If the deceased had been making weekly payments under a court order not exceeding £33 a week or £143 a month to his wife, or former wife, or payments of £18 a week or £78 a month for the education maintenance or benefit of a child under 21, these sums will have been paid without deduction of tax, and are a charge on income (TA 1970, s. 65; Income Tax (Small Maintenance Payments) Order 1980). The deceased would not, however, have been entitled to a married man's personal allowance in respect of such payments to this wife.

c Payments under Court Order or Separation Deed Payments for the maintenance of a wife or children under a court order, which were not "small maintenance payments", and payments made under a separation deed, will have been made subject to deduction of tax, and the position is as if the payments were made under a covenant (*supra*).

8 *Payments for pension*

Premiums paid by the deceased under any approved retirement annuity scheme, and contributions paid by him to an approved superannuation fund are deductible in computing his total income.

Apart from the payments listed in paras. 3, 4, 5, 6, 7 and 8, payments made by the deceased from which he is *not* entitled to deduct tax when making the payments are not deductible when calculating his total income.

P SPECIAL RELIEFS FOR ELDERLY TAXPAYERS

A special age allowance is given to a single taxpayer who is 65 or over by the end of the year of assessment, or to a married couple where either or both is over 65 by the end of the year of assessment. Where this age condition is satisfied a single taxpayer receives an allowance of £1,820 and a married couple £2,895 (TA 1970, s. 8 (1A); FA 1980, s. 22) in place of the ordinary rates of allowance.

These allowances are only given where the total income (see p. 26, *ante*) for the year does not exceed £5,900. If it does exceed £5,900 the allowance is reduced by £2 for every £3 of income over £5,900, until it is reduced to the ordinary single person's or married person's allowance.

Where a wife has earned income, she is entitled to the wife's earned income allowance in addition to this age allowance.

Q PERSONAL RELIEFS

1 *Generally*

Each person is entitled to certain personal reliefs, according to his own circumstances. These reliefs are expressed as a deduction from the tax payable and effect is given to reliefs by deducting them from the total income. Tax is calculated on the net income after all reliefs have been deducted.

The deductions are:

Relief	*Amount to be deducted from total income*
	£
Personal—married man	2,145
Personal—single man	1,375
Wife's earned income	1,375 (or, if less, amount of wife's earned income)
Single person looking after child or children	770

Dependent relative	
(other than single woman)	100
(single woman)	145
Daughter's services	55
Blind person	360
Blind allowance for a married couple	
who both are blind	720

2   Child allowances

In general, child allowances are no longer given. They are, however, available in certain circumstances where the child is living abroad (FA 1977, s. 25) and, until 1980/81, in certain circumstances where the child is over the age of 19 and undergoing a course of full-time education or training (FA 1977, s. 26).

3   Life assurance

A form of relief is given in respect of premiums paid on most policies of the life assurance. The taxpayer is, in general, permitted to deduct from the amount which he pays to the insurance company until 5 April 1981, 17½% of the premiums and thereafter 15% of the premium (TA 1970, s. 21 (4), FA 1980, s. 29). However, the total amount of the premiums on which relief is given does not exceed £1,500, or one-sixth of the taxpayer's total income, whichever is the greater (TA 1970, s. 21 (1)). Where the limit is exceeded, the taxpayer is required to refund the excess to the Revenue.

4   Widow's bereavement allowance

From 6 April 1980 onwards a widow, but not a widower, is entitled to a bereavement allowance of £770 for the year of assessment in which her husband dies (FA 1980, s. 23). This is in addition to any other personal allowance that may be due to her.

R   THE RATES OF TAX

Income tax is charged on the amount of taxable income after deducting charges on income and also after deducting the amount of personal reliefs. The tax is calculated in three stages:

1 applying the basic rate to the total of the net taxable income up to £11,250,

2 applying higher rates instead of the basic rate where the total income exceeds £11,250; and

3 applying *in addition* an investment income surcharge in respect of certain unearned income.

Part I: Deceased's Personal Tax Liability

1 The Basic Rates

At present (1981/82) the basic rate of income tax is 30% (FA 1981, s. 19).

2 The Higher Rates

a Taxable income for higher rate purposes

Where the net taxable income of an individual exceeds £11,250, he is liable to income on that excess at the higher rates. However, it may be necessary to re-calculate his total net taxable income because certain items have to be brought into account which do not have to be brought into account for basic rate purposes. Thus, for higher rate purposes it is necessary to bring into account the grossed up equivalent of building society interest received (FA 1971, Sch. 6, para. 40, and Sch. 14; FA 1972, Sch. 24, para. 22). This is calculated by the formula:

$$\text{Interest received} \times \frac{100}{100 - \text{Basic Rate}}$$

Thus, if the basic rate is 30%, the grossed-up equivalent of building society interest of £50 is

$$50 \times \frac{100}{100 - 30} = \frac{100}{70} = £71.42$$

Secondly, payments under most deeds of covenant are allowable in calculating the net statutory income for basic rate purposes, but not for higher rate purposes.

b The rates

The basic and higher rates for 1981/82 are:

Slice of Income	Cumulative Income Total at top of slice £	Rate on slice %	Tax on slice £	Cumulative Tax Total at top of slice £
The first £11,250	11,250	30	3,375	3,375
The next £2,000	13,250	40	800	4,175
The next £3,500	16,750	45	1,575	5,750
The next £5,500	22,250	50	2,750	8,500
The next £5,500	27,750	55	3,025	11,525
The remainder		60		

3   The Investment Income Surcharge

a   What is Investment Income?

For the purposes of the investment income surcharge, investment income is *all* income except (FA 1971, s. 32 (3)):

i   wages and salaries (TA 1970, s. 530);

ii   pensions in respect of past employment (*ibid*);

iii the taxable part of "golden handshakes" and similar payments (*ibid*; see p. 7, *ante*);

iv   profits of a trade, profession or vocation where the taxpayer was self-employed, providing that he was actively engaged in it, and not just a sleeping partner (*ibid*);

v   certain rental and other income which is immediately derived by the taxpayer from his employment (*ibid*);

vi   maintenance payments (FA 1974, s. 15, FA 1978, s. 21);

vii annuity payments made by partners to their former partner or his widow or dependant (FA 1974, s. 16). In general terms, if the annuity payments exceed 50% of the earnings of the outgoing partner in the best three out of the last seven years in which he was working in the partnership, that excess *is* treated as investment income.

b   Charges on income and reliefs

Where there are charges on income, such as payments under covenant or mortgage interest, they are deductible from investment income before being deductible from earned income (FA 1971, s. 34 (2)). Reliefs, however, are deducted first from earned income, and only any excess of reliefs over earned income can reduce the investment income (s. 34 (4)).

At present (1981/82), the investment income surcharge is not payable on the first £5,500 of investment income. Thereafter, it is' payable at 15% (FA 1981, s. 19).

S   POST WAR CREDITS

Personal reliefs were drastically reduced by the Finance Act 1941, and the reduced reliefs applied for the years 1941/42 to 1945/46. It was provided that the additional tax paid by the taxpayer by virtue of some of these reductions was to be credited to the taxpayer, and "post war credit" certificates were issued for the amount of that credit. It was intended that the taxpayer should be repaid at the end of the war, but general repayment was not authorised until 1972 (S.I. 1972, Nos. 374, 1840).

A claim for repayment of the certificates is made to the tax office which issued the certificates, which is not necessarily the same as the office to which returns are currently made. The application must be accompanied by the certificates, and since 31 December 1978 it has not been possible to reclaim certificates (The Post-War Credit (Income Tax) Order 1978, S.I. 1978 No. 662).

Chapter 3

The Deceased's Personal Tax Liability: Capital Gains Tax

A INTRODUCTION

The object of capital gains tax is to impose a charge on the increase in the value of an asset between the date of its acquisition and the date of its disposal. The assets which a person owns at the date of his death are not deemed to be disposed of on death, so that no charge arises on death (CGTA 1979, s. 49 (1) (*b*)). This chapter is concerned with the position where the deceased disposed of assets in the period between the preceding 6 April and the date of death, or in any previous year for which the liability has not been agreed.

B EXEMPTIONS AND RELIEFS

1 *Generally*

Capital gains tax may not be payable on a gain which is realised on the disposal of an asset because

a   the asset is not a chargeable asset; or

b   the gain is not a chargeable gain.

It will be convenient to consider first both types of exemption.

2 *Exempt assets*

The following types of property are the most common which do not give rise to a claim for tax:

a   Most types of tangible movable assets having a predictable life not exceeding 50 years (CGTA 1979, s. 127).

b   National savings certificates, premium bonds, defence bonds, and national development bonds (CGTA 1979, s. 71).

c   Gains on the disposal of currency acquired for personal expenditure abroad (CGTA 1979, s. 133).

d Betting winnings, and winnings from prizes (CGTA 1979, s. 19 (4)).

e Life insurance policies, in most cases. Generally, whether they represent surrender values, or payments on the maturity of the policy, sums received under a life policy are not taxable (CGTA 1979, s. 143). There is an exception to this rule where the person disposing of the asset is not the original beneficial owner of the policy, *and* he acquired the interest under the policy for money or money's worth. Where this is the case, the tax is calculated on the difference between the aggregate of the premiums paid and any capital sum paid on acquiring the interest on the one hand, and the capital sum received on the other hand.

f Deferred annuity contracts. These are contracts with an insurance company providing for the payment of an annuity at some future date. The rules are the same as for life policies. Where the exception applies, so that the contract gives rise to a claim for tax, the tax is calculated by taking as the disposal value the capitalized value of the right to receive the annuity at the point of time when the first of these payments is made (CGTA 1979, s. 143 (4)).

g Private dwelling-houses. No capital gains tax is payable on gains accruing on the disposal during the lifetime of the deceased or on his death of his only or main private residence, together with gardens and grounds up to one acre, or such larger area as is appropriate to the particular house (CGTA 1979, s. 101). This exemption is based not on the mere owner-ship of the house, but on the owner's *use* as his private residence. Thus, unless one of the special rules noted below applies, the exemption is restricted to that proportion of the period of ownership during which the owner occupied the house, although in all cases for the last two years of ownership he is deemed to have occupied the property (CGTA 1979, s. 102 (1); FA 1980, s. 80). This exemption applies only where the acquisition of the house was not made for the purpose of making a gain from its disposal (CGTA 1979, s. 103 (3)).

He is also entitled to exemption for any or all of the following periods if both before and afterwards he used the house as his only or main residence:

i any periods of absence for any purpose which do not amount in the aggregate to more than three years;

ii any period of absence during which the owner had to live away because he was working abroad;

iii any periods of absence not exceeding in total four years during which the owner lived away from home but elsewhere in the United Kingdom because of his job (CGTA 1979, s. 102 (3)); and in any period after 30 July 1978 during which the deceased resided in other, so-called, job-related accommodation but intended in due course to residence in the property disposed of (CGTA 1979, s. 101 (8)).

Partial exemption may be obtained if the periods mentioned above are exceeded. Thus, suppose a house bought in 1967 is owned for six years, and sold at a profit of £1,200. Suppose also that the owner lived in the house for the first and last years of this period. He can claim exemption for those two years, and the first three years of the absence under rule (i) above. Only the gain in respect of one year will therefore be taxable, i.e., $1/6 \times £1,200 = £200$.

A special rule applies where the property has been partly owner occupied and partly let, and the property is disposed of after 5 April 1980. In this case it is necessary to calculate first what would be the amount of the gain which would be chargeable by reason of the letting. This will depend both on whether the whole or only part of the property was let, and on the period for which the property was let. It is then necessary to calculate the amount of the gain which is not chargeable by virtue of the ordinary private residence exemption. The amount of the gain attributable to the part of the property which has been let is restricted to the excess over the lower of (i) the gain which is exempt and (ii) £10,000 (F (No. 2) A 1980, s. 80).

In addition to the exemption which the owner can claim for his own house, he can also claim exemption for a house occupied by a dependent relative. A "dependent relative" means any relative of the owner, or of his spouse, who is incapacitated by old age or infirmity from maintaining himself, or the mother of the owner or of his spouse, if the mother is widowed, separated or divorced. The exemption applies only if the residence was provided rent free (CGTA 1979, s. 105).

A similar exemption applies where the house was owned by trustees, and the deceased occupied it as his main residence in accordance with the terms of the trust (CGTA 1979, s. 104).

h   Chattels worth less than £2,000.

A gain on the disposal of a chattel is not taxable if the value at the date of disposal does not exceed £2,000. There is a limited relief where the value of the chattel is somewhat in excess of £2,000 (CGTA 1979, s. 128).

If a number of articles constitute a set — and that is a question of fact in each case — and they are sold separately but to the same person, the separate transactions are treated as one (CGTA 1979, s. 128 (4)). There are further provisions which apply where there is a series of gifts to the same person (CGTA 1979, s. 151).

i   Works of art. In certain circumstances, works of art, including manuscripts and scientific collections, may be exempt if they are of appropriate importance, and are given or bequeathed for national purposes, or to a university or local authority. Exemptions may also be claimed if they are given or bequeathed to a person who undertakes to keep them in the United Kingdom and available for inspection. Further exemptions apply in the case of land given to the public and in the case of assets transferred to a maintenance fund for a historic building (CGTA 1979, ss. 147, 148).

j   Interests under trusts. Interests under trusts are not taxable unless the interests were acquired by purchase (CGTA 1979, s. 58).

k   Decorations for valour. These are exempt, unless acquired by purchase (CGTA 1979, s. 131).

l   Gains made on disposals of certain Government securities are exempt from capital gains tax. These are listed at p. 283. The gains are exempt only if the securities are disposed of more than one year from the date of their acquisition (CGTA 1979, s. 67).

3   Small gains

Even where the asset is not exempt the gain may fall within one of two provisions by which it is exempt because of its size.

There are two provisions under which gains which could otherwise be chargeable are exempt because of their size.

a   Gains accruing on the gift of assets not exceeding in total £100 in the year of assessment are exempt (CGTA 1979, s. 6).

b   The first £3,000 of gains on any type of asset, and which arise on any type of disposal, are not chargeable (CGTA 1979, s. 5;

FA 1980, s. 77). In respect of the year of assessment 1979/80, and previous years, only the first £1,000 of gains was not chargeable.

4 Rolling over gains

In certain circumstances, it is possible for a gain to be rolled-over. The effect is that the acquisition value of an asset is reduced by what would otherwise have been the amount of the chargeable gain, with the result that the tax is deferred. These circumstances are:

a *Gifts after 5 April 1980* Where an individual disposes of an asset after 5 April 1980 by way of gift, or by way of sale at a deliberate under-value, both he and the disponee can elect that no chargeable gain shall accrue to the disponor but that the acquisition value to the disponee shall be reduced by what would have been the amount of the chargeable gain accruing to the disponor (FA 1980, s. 79).

b *Settlement after 5 April 1981* A similar provision applies where an individual disposes of an asset to a settlement, save that only he need elect (FA 1981, s. 78).

c *Gifts prior to 6 April 1980* In respect of gifts made before 6 April 1980, a similar relief was available, but only where the subject matter of its gift was, broadly, business assets, shares in a family trading company, or agricultural land (CGTA 1979, s. 126).

d *Incorporation of a business* Where a person transfers a business as a going concern to a company, and he receives in exchange shares in that company, what would otherwise be the amount of the chargeable gain is deducted from both the value of the business assets transferred and the value of the shares acquired (CGTA 1979, s. 123).

e *Replacement of business assets* Within certain limits, where a business asset is sold and replaced by a new asset, the gain which arises on the disposal of the old asset can be rolled over into the new asset (CGTA 1979, s. 115).

5 Retirement relief

Where the deceased in his lifetime disposed of certain business assets, then, if at the time of the disposal he had attained the age of sixty, he could have been entitled to relief (CGTA 1979, s. 124). Although the relief is generally known as retirement relief, it is not necessary for the deceased to have retired in order to obtain it.

The relief depends both on the age of the deceased at the time of disposal and the period for which the asset disposed of had been used for business purposes. Where the deceased had attained the age of sixty-five and the asset had been used for business purposes for ten years, the relief is on £50,000 of gains.

The assets in question are an unincorporated business, and shares or securities in a family trading company.

C DISPOSAL

1 Actual disposals

The charge to tax arises when the asset has been disposed of, and "disposal" covers disposal in any way, e.g. sale, gift or exchange. It also includes the part disposal of an asset, such as the creation of an interest in or a right over the asset. Thus a premium taken on the grant of a lease gives rise to liability to tax under complicated provisions, but the part of the premium which is chargeable to income tax under Schedule A (p. 16, *ante*) or to development land tax is excluded from liability to capital gains tax. Even wider, there is deemed to be a disposal if a capital sum is received from an asset, even if that asset is retained in full, and even if the person making the payment does not thereby acquire an asset (CGTA 1979, s. 20). The following payments are, then (subject to what is said below) included:

  a   capital sums received by way of compensation for any kind of damage or injury to assets, or for the loss, or destruction of assets. This includes sums paid for infringement of copyright, for infringement of ancient lights, or for damage or destruction to a physical asset;

  b   sums received under an insurance policy against the risks of any kind of damage or injury to property;

  c   sums received in return for forfeiture or surrender of rights, or for refusing to exercise rights. This includes payments received for relieving another person from a contract or restrictive covenant;

  d   sums received as consideration for the use or exploitation of assets. This includes a premium for a lease of land, for the right to use machinery or plant, and for the right to exploit copyrights.

Where the sum received is used for the restoration of the asset, instead of giving rise to a charge to tax, it can be treated as reducing the expenditure on that asset. The effect is to defer the tax which will ultimately be payable. Similarly, if a lost asset is replaced, any gain can be deducted from the cost of the replacement, unless it is a wasting asset.

Where property is given away, or sold at less than its market value at that time, the market value is nevertheless taken as the value on disposal.

Special rules apply to the disposal of options. Where the option is to take shares which are dealt with on a stock exchange, the abandonment or disposal of the option is treated as the disposal of a chargeable asset (CGTA 1979, ss. 137 (4), 139). The same principle applies where there is the abandonment or disposal of an option to acquire assets for use in a business (CGTA 1979, s. 137 (4) (b)). Apart from this, in general the abandonment of an option is not generally regarded as the disposal of a chargeable asset (CGTA 1979, s. 137 (4)).

2 Deemed disposals

Although no liability can arise to capital gains tax unless there is a disposal, certain events are deemed to be disposals. Where there is a deemed disposal, the capital gains tax consequences are the same as in the case of an actual disposal.

The main circumstances in which there is a deemed disposal, apart from these which relate to settled property and which are considered later (see p. 254, *post*), are as follows:

a where a capital sum is derived from an asset (CGTA 1979, s. 20);

b where a person who has control over a company uses that control to pass value out of shares (CGTA 1979, s. 25 (2));

c where a person appropriates an asset held by way of investment to trading stock, or *vice versa* (CGTA 1979, s. 122);

d where there is the entire loss or extinction of an asset (CGTA 1979, s. 22 (1)); and

e where an asset comes to have negligible value (CGTA 1979, s. 22 (2)).

D CALCULATION OF THE GAIN

1 Generally

The gain is calculated by deducting from the disposal value the following items:

a   the acquisition value of the asset, or, where, as in the case of goodwill or a business or a copyright, it was created, the expenditure incurred in creating the asset (CGTA 1979, s. 32 (1) (*a*));

b   expenditure wholly and exclusively incurred by the person who owned the asset for the purposes of enhancing its value (CGTA 1979, s. 32 (1) (*b*)). To be allowable, the expenditure must be reflected in the state or nature of the asset when it is disposed of, so that ineffective or wasted expenditure is not allowed;

c   expenditure wholly and exclusively incurred in establishing or defending the owner's title to the asset *(ibid)*; and

d   certain expenditure incurred wholly and exclusively for the acquisition or disposal of the asset (CGTA 1979, s. 32 (2)). The types of allowable expenditure under this head are:

   i legal fees, including stamp duty;

   ii fees paid to a surveyor, valuer, auctioneer, agent or accountant, but a fee for calculating the gain or loss is not incurred for the purposes of the disposal;

   iii costs of advertising to find a buyer or seller; and

   iv in the case of a disposal, the cost of valuation required for the purpose of calculating the gain or loss on the asset.

While the expenses directly attributable to the sale or purchase are allowable, costs of financing the purchase are not. So, for example, the expenses of a mortgage are not allowable in calculating the gains on the disposal of land.

The gain is calculated in terms of the face value of the money involved, and no allowance can be claimed for depreciation in the value of the proceeds of sale as a result of inflation (*Secretan* v *Hart*, [1969] 3 All E.R. 1196).

There are specifically excluded premiums paid under an insurance policy, and sums paid by the Crown or any public or local authority. Thus, for example, although the cost of capital improvements to a house would normally be allowed, if they were paid for by means of an improvement grant from the local authority, they would not be allowed (CGTA 1979, s. 42). There are also excluded payments of an income nature (CGTA 1979, s. 33).

An apportionment will be made if there is disposal of only part of an asset.

2 *Acquisition and disposal values*

The acquisition and disposal values of assets will be calculated in one of four ways.

a   *The actual consideration*   In the case of a disposal which is
made in a transaction at arm's length between "non-
connected" persons, the actual consideration adopted by the
parties constitutes the value for capital gains tax purposes.
There is no general rule which permits the Revenue to
substitute some other value, such as the market value of the
asset in question.

b   *The market value*   In certain circumstances, the actual
consideration adopted by the parties is ignored, and the transaction is deemed to have taken place at the open market value
of the asset in question. The main circumstances where this is
so are:

   i   where the transaction is not at arm's length (CGTA 1979,
       s. 29A; FA 1981, s. 90);

   ii where the transaction is between "connected persons'
       (CGTA 1979, ss. 62 (2); 29A);

   iii where the asset is appropriated to or from trading stock
       (CGTA 1979, s. 122); and

   iv where the asset comes to have negligible value (CGTA
       1979, s. 22 (2)).

The rule applies in the case i and ii only where there is a corresponding disposal, and where consideration in money or money's worth
equivalent to the market value was given.

c   *No gain, no loss*   In the case of most dispositions between one
spouse and the other, the disponor is treated as disposing of the
asset for a consideration which will give rise neither to a gain
nor a loss (CGTA 1979, s. 44).

d   *Special values*   There are a number of special rules prescrib-
ing special values. These include:

   i. where a set of assets is acquired (CGTA 1979, s. 151); and

   ii. where a value has been determined for capital transfer tax
       purposes (CGTA 1979, s. 153).

3 Part disposals

A liability to capital gains tax can arise where there is only a part
disposal of an asset. There is a part disposal where the disposal is of
part only of a physical asset, such as the sale of part of an area of land
owned by the taxpayer, or where the disposal is of part of the rights
of ownership in respect of an asset, such as the grant by a freeholder
of a lease of his land. The principle is widened so that where any type

of property is derived from an asset which is disposed of, that disposal is a part disposal (CGTA 1979, s. 19 (2) (*b*)).

Where there is a part disposal, the acquisition value is apportioned according to the formula $\dfrac{A}{A + B}$, where:

A is the value of the interest disposed of; and
B is the value of the interest retained (CGTA 1979, s. 35).

Having apportioned the aquisition value, an ordinary capital gains tax computation is made. No adjustment is made to the disposal value.

4 Assets owned on 6 April 1965

Where the asset was owned on 6 April 1965, there is liability to capital gains tax only in respect of the gain from 6 April 1965 to the date of disposal. Special rules, which are noted below, apply to stock exchange securities. In other cases, generally a "time apportionment" basis is adopted, under which the gain is regarded as having accrued at a uniform rate from the date of acquisiton. If, therefore, an asset was acquired on 5 April 1960, for £4,000 and sold on 5 April 1975 for £7,000, the gain of £3,000 would be regarded as arising at the rate of £200 p.a for each of the 15 years. Therefore, only 10/15ths of the gain would be chargeable, i.e. £2,000 (CGTA 1979, Sch. 5, para. 11).

Alternatively, the taxpayer, or his personal representatives, may elect that the actual value of the asset at 6 April 1965 shall be taken, and the chargeable gain is calculated, as if the asset had been acquired at that price on that date (Sch. 5, para. 12). If, by taking the April 1965 value, a loss results, relief is restricted to the actual loss suffered if smaller, and if there is an actual gain, there is deemed to be neither gain nor loss.

E SPECIAL TYPES OF ASSET

1 Shares and other stock exchange securities

There are a series of complicated rules which govern the calculation of the gain on a disposition of shares and other stock exchange securities. These rules, in general terms, are as follows:

a Each holding of shares of the same class in the same company is regarded as constituting the asset for capital gains tax purposes (CGTA 1979, s. 65 (2)). Thus, each individual share is not an asset.

b   Where shares were held on 6 April 1965, any chargeable gain or allowable loss is calculated on the basis of the market value of those shares on that day. This value is the higher of:
  (i) a figure halfway between the two prices in the quotation in the Stock Exchange Official Daily List; and
  (ii) a figure halfway between the highest and lowest prices of recorded bargains.

The Council of the Stock Exchange, has published a list of these values, known as the "Blue Book", and other lists are produced by other publishers. Similar rules apply for unit trust holders in any unit trust scheme the units of which are purchased directly by the managers of the scheme.

Where special circumstances exist which make the quoted price an inaccurate measure of the price which the shares would fetch, an alternative basis of valuation is adopted (CGTA 1979, s. 150 (3); *Hinchcliffe* v. *Crabtree*, [1971] 2 All E.R. 104).

c   This primary rule is adjusted, however, so that the assessable gain is not larger than the actual gain which the owner makes from the date when he in fact did acquire the asset (CGTA 1979, Sch. 5, para. 2). So that if the shares were acquired before 1965 for £120, stood at £100 on 6 April 1965, and were disposed of for £150, the assessable gain is limited to £30, although the actual gain over 1965 values is £50.

d   If there has been a loss by reference both to the 6 April 1965 price and the acquisition value, the allowable loss is the lower figure.

e   Where there is a loss by reference to the value of the shares at 6 April 1965, but an overall gain, or a gain by reference to the same value but an overall loss, the disposal of the asset is treated as if it had given rise to neither gain nor loss. For example, if shares were purchased for £100, stood at £150 on 6 April 1965, and were sold for £130; or if shares were purchased for £150, stood at £100 on 6 April 1965, and were sold for £130, there is neither gain nor loss (CGTA 1979, Sch. 5, para. 2 (1)).

f   Where shares of the same class in the same company have been acquired at different prices and on different occasions before 6 April 1965, it is necessary to identify shares being disposed of with those which were acquired. The "first in, first out" rule

49

applies, so that the first shares acquired are treated as being the first shares sold (Sch. 5, para. 2 (2)).

g   Where shares of the same class are acquired after 6 April 1965, and part of the holding is then sold, to ascertain the acquisition value of the shares sold, the shares are "pooled". Suppose, therefore, that 400 shares are purchased after 6 April 1965 for £450, that later a further 500 shares are acquired for £600, and lastly 600 shares are sold for £750. The acquisition value of the 600 shares sold is calculated:

400 shares cost	£450
500 shares cost	600
900 shares cost	£1,050
so:		
600 shares cost	£700

On the facts of this example, then, there will be a chargeable gain of £50.

h   In respect of any disposal made after 19 March 1968, the taxpayer may elect that in respect of all securities in either or both the following categories:

i fixed interest securities and preference shares; and
ii equities and other quoted securities not included in (i)

pooling shall apply (CGTA 1979, Sch. 5, para. 4). Where an election is made to this effect, the actual acquisition cost is disregarded, and the market value at 6 April 1965 is taken. Suppose, therefore, that the deceased had a holding of 400 shares on 6 April 1965, with a market value at that date of £400; that he acquired a further 200 shares after that date for £250 and sold 300 shares in 1969 for £450. If the election has been made, the calculation is:

Holding at 6 April 1965	400	£400
Subsequent acquisition	200	250
	600	650
sale of 300 produces		£450
acquisition value	$\dfrac{300}{600} \times £650$	325
chargeable gain		£125

An election may be made within two years of the end of the year of assessment in which the first disposal is made, but once made, the election will cover all securities in the class covered by the election, whenever a disposal occurs.

Even where the deceased did not himself make the election, his personal representatives may make it on his behalf.

i   In principle, the issue of bonus shares does not give rise to a chargeable gain, but there will be a chargeable gain (or an allowable loss) when those shares are sold. If there is a part disposal, pooling will again be necessary. Suppose:

100 shares are purchased in 1966 for £120; and
50 shares are issued in 1967 as a bonus

if the whole 150 shares were sold for £150, the chargeable gain would be £30. If only 40 shares were sold, for £35, the chargeable gain would be:

disposal price	£35
acquisition price (pooling)	
100 shares cost	£120
50 shares issued free	
150 shares cost	£120

so:

$$40 \text{ shares cost} \quad \frac{40}{150} \times £120 = \underline{32}$$

therefore chargeable gain = £3.

The position where stock or share dividends are issued is considered later (p. 272, *post*).

j   Where gilt-edged securities are disposed of, and there has been more than one dealing with the same stock, so far as possible securities disposed of are treated as having been acquired within the previous twelve months (CGTA 1979, s. 68). This is so that the exemption for disposals of gilt-edged securities (CGTA 1979, s. 67) will have as limited an application as possible. The position where Government securities are issued upon the compulsory acquisition of other shares after 6 April 1976 is considered below.

k   If there is a conversion of capital, or takeover bid, as a result of which one block of shares is received in exchange for another block, and no money passes, then this transaction is not treated as a disposition for capital gains tax purposes. The new holding is equated with the old (CGTA 1979, s. 78). Thus, capital gains tax will be payable if the new holding is sold for a higher price than the acquisition cost of the old holding, but no tax will be payable until that sale occurs.

l   If on the reorganization or take over, the shareholder receives a cash sum as well as a block of new shares, he is treated as if he had disposed of part of his old holding. For this purpose, an appropriate part of the cost of the old holding is attributed to the cash sum received. The new holding is then treated as the residue of the old holding. If on a conversion of capital (but not a take over) a sum is received which is less than 5 per cent of the value of the securities, the sum may be treated not as a part disposal, but as a deduction from the original expenditure (CGTA 1979, s. 83 (2)).

m   Where a "rights issue" is made, no liability to capital gains tax arises merely because the issue is made. For calculating the gain on a disposal, the amount paid for the rights shares is treated in the same way as the amount paid for any other shares of the same class as the original holding. If the rights are sold, a liability to capital gains tax may arise.

n   Where there is a rights issue, or any other reorganisation of the share capital of a company, any consideration given by the taxpayer is allowable only to the extent that the value of his holdings immediately after the reorganisation exceeds the value immediately before it (CGTA 1979, s. 79 (1); FA 1981, s. 91).

o   A special rule applies in respect of "compensation stock", namely Government stock which is issued in exchange for other shares acquired compulsorily after 6 April 1976. In this case no liability to tax arises at the time of the exchange, but, broadly, the amount of the gain to the date of exchange is carried forward and tax on it becomes payable at the time when the Government stock is disposed of (CGTA 1979, s. 84).

p   Where shares in a company which is not quoted on a stock exchange were acquired prior to 7 April 1965, the capital gains tax liability will normally be calculated on a time-apportionment basis, but the taxpayer may elect to have his liability determined according to the value of the shares on 6 April 1965 (see p. 48, *ante*). This, however, is subject to two qualifications. First, if there was a reorganization of the share capital of the company after the date when the taxpayer acquired his shares, but before 6 April 1965, his holding will be valued as at 6 April 1965. Secondly, if there is a reorganization after 6 April 1965, the holding is valued at the date of reorganization. When the shares are subsequently disposed of, the taxpayer may elect to have the gain for the period up to the date of reorganization calculated on the time-apportionment basis, and for the period from that date to the date of disposal, the chargeable gain is the actual gain made (CGTA 1979, Sch. 5, para. 14).

2 Land reflecting development value

In many cases, where the asset is an interest in land which has development value, a liability will arise to development land tax, and the liability to capital gains tax will be restricted (see p. 62, *post*).

Where land reflecting development value was owned on 6 April 1965, the market value at that date must be adopted, and the taxpayer will not have the right to elect for time-apportionment, if the land is disposed of for a consideration in excess of the current use value, or if material development has been carried out after 17 December 1973 (CGTA 1979, Sch. 5, para. 9).

3 Leases

Where a lease is granted at a premium, that premium will be subject to capital gains tax but the premium is set against only a part of the acquisition value of the land. The basic formula for ascertaining that part is (CGTA 1979, Sch. 3):

$$\text{Acquisition cost of land} \times \frac{\text{Amount of premium}}{\text{Amount of premium} + \text{market value of reversion}}$$

Thus, suppose a house is purchased in 1969 for £6,000; that a lease is granted in 1971 for 60 years at a premium of £6,250; and that the value of the reversion after the grant of the lease (including the right to receive the rent under the lease) is £1,250. The chargeable gain is calculated as follows:

$$£6,250 - \left(£6,000 \times \frac{£6,250}{£6,250 + £1,250} = £5,000 \right) = £1,250.$$

However, special rules relate to leases having 50 years or less to run and which are referred to as short leases. The expenditure incurred in acquiring a short lease is deemed to waste away over the remainder of the duration of the lease in accordance with the following table:

Part I: Deceased's Personal Tax Liability

Years	Percentage	Years	Percentage
50(or more)	100	25	81.100
49	99.657	24	79.622
48	99.289	23	78.055
47	98.902	22	76.399
46	98.490	21	74.635
45	98.059	20	72.770
44	97.595	19	70.791
43	97.107	18	68.697
42	96.593	17	66.470
41	96.041	16	64.116
40	95.457	15	61.617
39	94.842	14	58.971
38	94.189	13	56.167
37	93.497	12	53.191
36	92.761	11	50.038
35	91.981	10	46.695
34	91.156	9	43.154
33	90.280	8	39.399
32	89.354	7	35.414
31	88.371	6	31.195
30	87.330	5	26.722
29	86.226	4	21.983
28	85.053	3	16.959
27	83.816	2	11.629
26	82.496	1	5.983
		0	0

The table applies both to the acquisition and disposal of all the premises comprised in a lease, and also to the grant of a sub-lease out of a short lease. Two examples may assist. First, suppose that Adam acquired for £5,000 a lease with 30 years to run and sold it nine years later for £5,100. He would not be able to deduct the full £5,000 from the disposal value: his deductible figure would be £5,000 × $\frac{74.635}{87.330}$ = £4,273, and his capital gain would therefore be £827 not £100. The property is deemed to have depreciated by £727 while he had the use of it.

Secondly, suppose that Benedict also acquired for £5,000 a lease with 30 years to run but that after five years, when the lease had only 25 years to run, he granted a sub-lease out of it for 7 years at a premium of £1,000. The proportion of the £5,000 which Benedict may deduct from the £1,000 is calculated as follows:

$$£5,000 \times \frac{81.100 - 68.697}{87.330} \text{ or } \frac{12.403}{87.330} = £710$$

so that the capital gain is £290. In this calculation the figure of 81.100 is that appropriate to the grant of the sub-lease (the original lease having 25 years to run) and the figure of 68.697 is that appropriate to the end of the sub-lease, by which time the original lease will have 18 years left to run.

Relating the provisions governing capital gains tax on leases to liability under Schedule A (see p. 16, *ante*) the position is as follows:

a The part of a premium for a lease which is chargeable to income tax as rent under Schedule A is exempt from capital gains tax;

b Where a lease is granted out of an interest in land which is not a short lease, the part of the premium receivable which is taxed under Schedule A is excluded from the numerator but not from the denominator of the fraction. Suppose, therefore, that a house is purchased in 1969 for £10,000; that in 1970 a lease is granted for 21 years at a premium of £2,500; and that the value of the freehold after the grant of the lease is £9,500. The Schedule A liability is assessed on:

Premium   £2,500

Reduced by $\dfrac{21 - 1}{50} \times$ £2,500 =   1,000

_____

"Rent" chargeable under Schedule A = £1,500 (See p. 16, *ante*).

The capital gains tax computation is therefore:

Proceeds £2,500 less already taxed £1,500 =   £1,000

Deduct appropriate part of cost of acquisition:

£10,000 $\times$ $\dfrac{£2,500 - £1,500}{£2,500 + £9,500} = \dfrac{£1,000}{£12,000} =$ 833

_____

Chargeable gain =   £167

c Where a sub-lease is granted out of a short lease the amount of the chargeable gain is calculated without taking into account the Schedule A liability. The part of the premium which has been charged under Schedule A is *then* deducted from the gain, and capital gains tax paid on the difference. It is, however, provided that no capital loss may be created in this way.

F LOSSES

Where the value of an asset on disposal is less than its acquisiton value, within certain limits relief can be obtained in respect of that loss (CGTA 1979, s. 29). This loss relief is primarily offset against chargeable gains which accrue in the same year of assessment. If there is still a balance of the loss outstanding it is carried forward and deducted from subsequent gains as they occur. Capital losses may not be offset from liability to income tax.

The position where a capital loss is incurred in the year in which a person dies is dealt with at p. 160, *post*.

G PAYMENT OF TAX

After giving relief for any losses, tax is chargeable on the net capital gains for the year of assessment at the basic rate of 30 per cent (CGTA 1979, s. 3).

The tax is based on the actual gains made in each year of assessment, and is payable as a result of direct assessment.

Chapter 4

The Deceased's Personal Tax Liability: Development Land Tax

A GAINS PRIOR TO 1 AUGUST 1976

In certain circumstances, where development value was realised on the disposal of land after 17 December 1973 and before 1 August 1976, a liability to development gains tax could have arisen under the provisions of the Finance Act 1974. Except in one case, noted later (p. 63, *post*) the charge to development gains tax does not apply where the disposal occurs after 31 July 1976, and this tax is not considered further in this book.

B DEVELOPMENT LAND TAX

1 Introduction

The provisions of the Development Land Tax Act 1976, are some of the most complex of all in the tax legislation, and in most cases where a problem arises it will be necessary to refer to a specialist work on the subject. It is intended here only to give an outline of the tax, and this will also serve as an introduction to the special provisions of the tax which relate to personal representatives and trustees and which are considered in a later chapter (p. 162, *post*).

2 Interests in land

Development land tax is payable as a result of the disposal not of land or buildings as such, but of an interest in land or buildings (s. 1 (1)). Where separate interests exist in land, as where there is a freehold subject to a lease, it is necessary to make the calculations in respect of the separate interests.

3 Circumstances giving rise to tax

Development land tax may be payable whenever there is an actual or deemed disposal of an interest in land. The disposal may be of the whole interest, or part; and it may be in respect of the total area of land to which the interest relates, or part.

a   Actual disposal

There is an actual disposal whenever an interest in the property is disposed of for valuable consideration. Thus, a sale or exchange, or the grant of a lease will amount to a disposal for this purpose. However, no liability arises as a result of the devolution of property on death (DLTA 1976, s. 9) nor on the making of a lifetime gift of property (s. 10).

b   Deemed disposals: I

In certain circumstances a person is deemed to make a part disposal of his interest even although in reality there is no disposal. In general, these circumstances are where a capital sum is received in respect of the land (s. 3). Examples are where a sum is received in respect of compensation for damage to the land, or where a sum is received for the use or exploitation of the land.

c   Deemed disposals: II

The other situation in which a person is deemed to dispose of his interest is where a project of material development is commenced (s. 2). A project of material development consists, very broadly, of the carrying out of building works or the making of a change in the use of land for which planning permission is required (Sch. 1).

C   EXEMPTIONS AND RELIEFS

The main exemptions and reliefs are as follows:

1   *Gifts, death*   It has been seen above that there is no liability to development land tax when a gift is made, or when the owner dies.

2   *The first £50,000*   The first £50,000 slice of development value realised in a financial year is exempt (s. 12; F (No. 2) A 1979, s. 24 (2)). A financial year ends on 31 March. This exemption is considered further later (p. 62, *post*).

3   *Owner-occupiers*   No development land tax is payable when development value is realised by an individual on the sale or development of his main residence (s. 14). This exemption applies to the house itself and to its gardens or grounds up to

an area of one acre, inclusive of the site of the house, or, in certain circumstances, a larger area. Partial relief is available where only part of the house is occupied as the main residence.

4 *Building a family house* Where a person owned land on 12 September 1974, there will not be a deemed disposal of the land by virtue of the carrying out of a project of material development if the development consists solely of the building of a single dwellinghouse, and if at the time when the development is begun, the owner of the land, or an adult member of his family, intends to occupy the house as his sole or main residence (s. 15).

5 *Land held as stock-in-trade* Where a builder owned land on 12 September 1974, and it had the benefit of planning permission on that date, no development land tax is payable on an actual or deemed disposal of the land (s. 16).

6 *Industrial land* If an industrialist develops land for his own industrial use, no liability to development land tax arises when the development takes place (s. 19). A liability in respect of that development will, however, arise at the time when the land is disposed of, or at the time when it ceases to be used for industrial purposes.

D REALISED DEVELOPMENT VALUE

1 *Generally*

Development land tax is payable when development value of land is realised. Realised development value is (s. 4):

a   the amount of the proceeds of the disposal;

b   less: the costs of the disposal; and

c   less: the relevant base value.

There are three methods of calculating the relevant base value, and these values are known as Base A, Base B and Base C. It is necessary for each possible base value to be calculated. The relevant base value is the highest of the three (s. 5).

2 *Base A*

Base A is the aggregate of (s. 5 (1) (a)):

a   the acquisition cost of the interest which is disposed of;

b   the incidental fees and expenses incurred on the acquisition;

   c the expenditure, if any, which has been incurred in enhancing the value of the interest which is disposed of, provided that it is reflected in the physical state of the land, or in the market value of the interest, at the time of disposal (Sch. 3, para. 1 (a)). If the current use value of the interest has increased as a result of the expenditure, the amount by which the current use value has been increased is deducted from the expenditure (para. 2);

   d the expenditure, if any, which has been incurred in establishing, preserving or defending title to the land (para. 1 (b));

   e the amount by which the current use value of the interest at the time of disposal exceeds the current use value of that interest at the time of its acquisition, or on 6 April 1965, whichever is the later;

   f (i) if the interest disposed of was held on 12 September 1974, the cost of acquisition is increased by 15% for each year for which the interest has been owned, up to a maximum of 4 years (s. 6 (2));

       (ii) if the interest disposed of was acquired after 12 September 1974 but before 1 May 1977, the cost of acquisition is increased by 10% for each year for which the interest has been owned, up to a maximum of 4 years (*ibid*).

3 Base B

Base B is the aggregate of (s. 5 (1) (b); FA 1980, s. 116)):

   a 115% of the current use value of the interest at the time of disposal;

   b any enhancement expenditure, less the amount by which the current use value at the time of disposal has been increased as a result of the expenditure; and

   c any expenditure on establishing, preserving or defending title.

4 Base C

Base C is 115% of the aggregate of (s. 5 (1) (c)):

   a the acquisition cost of the interest which is disposed of;

   b the incidental fees and expenses incurred on the acquisition;

   c any enhancement expenditure (without any reduction for an increase in the current use value as a result of the expenditure);

   d any expenditure on establishing, preserving or defending title.

5 Example

The method of calculating the realised development value can best be shown by an example. Suppose that a property was acquired in 1968 for £100,000 and that the current value use of the property at that time was also £100,000. The expenses of acquisition were £2,000. Enhancement expenditure of £75,000 was incurred, and as a result the current use value at the time of disposal was increased by £30,000. The property is disposed of in 1977 for £375,000, and the expenses of disposal amount to £5,000. At the time of disposal the current use value is £250,000 (including the £30,000 increase which resulted from the enhancement expenditure).

1	Net proceeds of disposal		
	Sale price		£375,000
	less: expenses of disposal		£5,000
			£370,000
2	Base A		
	Acquisition cost		£100,000
	Expenses of acquisition		£2,000
	Total cost of acquisition		£102,000
	Enhancement expenditure	£75,000	
	less: increase in CUV as a result	£30,000	£45,000
	Expenditure on establishment of title, etc.		nil
	CUV at disposal	£250,000	
	less: CUV at acquisition	£100,000	£150,000
	Special addition		
	4 × 15% × £102,000		£61,200
	Thus Base A is		£358,200
3	Base B		
	CUV at disposal		£250,000
	Add: 15%		£37,500
			£287,500
	Enhancement expenditure	£75,000	
	less: increase in CUV as a result	£30,000	£45,000
	Expenditure on establishment of title, etc.		nil
	Thus Base B is		£332,500

4 Base C

Acquisition cost		£100,000
Expenses of acquisition		£2,000
Enhancement expenditure		£75,000
Expenditure on establishment of title, etc.		nil
		£177,000
add: 15%		£26,550
	Thus Base C is	£203,550

5 The relevant base value

The highest of Base A, Base B, and
Base C
i.e. Base A   £358,200

6 Realised Development Value

Net proceeds of disposal		£370,000
less: relevant base value		£358,200
	RDV	£11,800

E   RATES OF TAX

1   *First £50,000 of Realised Development Value*

No development land tax is payable on the first £50,000 of development value realised by a person during a year ended 31 March (s. 12). Husband and wife are treated as separate persons, so that where they dispose of an interest in land jointly owned, the first £100,000 of development value realised is not subject to development land tax.

If the exemption is not used in one financial year, it cannot be carried forward to a subsequent year.

2   *Generally*

Chargeable realised development value is taxed at the rate of 60% (s. 1 (2); F (No. 2) A 1979, s. 24).

F   INTER-RELATION WITH OTHER TAXES

Rules which are very complicated indeed govern the relationship of development land tax to other taxes (Sch. 6). In general, the liability to development land tax should be ascertained first, and any part of the gain remaining is then subject to capital gains tax or, in certain circumstances, to income tax.

A charge to development gains tax may still arise in the case of development commenced before 1 August 1976 if that development was begun after 17 December 1973, or the interest in land was acquired after that date (DLTA 1976, ss. 36, 37).

Chapter 5

The Deceased's Personal Tax Liability: Capital Transfer Tax

A INTRODUCTION

Capital transfer tax is a tax payable:

1 in respect of certain gifts and other transactions entered into by the deceased in his lifetime;

2 in respect of property owned by the deceased on his death; and

3 in respect of property comprised in a settlement in certain circumstances.

The position where capital transfer tax is payable on death, and in respect of property comprised in a settlement is described in some detail in chapters 6 and 14 respectively. It is proposed here to give an outline only of the liability which might be outstanding in respect of events which occurred during the lifetime of the deceased. Many of the provisions which apply on death also apply to lifetime events.

B EVENTS PRIOR TO 27 MARCH 1974

No liability to capital transfer tax could have arisen at the time by virtue of a gift made, or transaction entered into, by the deceased before 27 March 1974 (FA 1975, s. 20 (5)). Gifts made before that date, but within seven years from the death of the deceased may, however, give rise to liability on his death (p. 83, *post*).

C EVENTS AFTER 26 MARCH 1974

In respect of events occurring after 26 March 1974, it is necessary to determine whether there has been a "transfer of value", and, if so, whether that was a "chargeable transfer".

1 Transfer of value

A transfer of value is any disposition made by a person as a result of which the value of his estate immediately after the disposition is less than it would be but for the disposition (FA 1975, s. 20 (2)). The word "disposition" is not usefully defined in the legislation, but it probably means the giving up of some asset or proprietary right. For the purposes of this definition, the concept of a person's estate has nothing to do with a landed estate, but, broadly, means the total value of a person's assets, after deducting most liabilities (s. 23 (1); Sch. 10, para. 1 (1)). In most cases, however, a future interest under a settlement is left out of account (p. 96, *post*); and special rules apply where property is situated abroad, and is owned by a person domiciled abroad (p. 387, *post*).

Because of the wide meaning of the word "disposition", in principle after every lifetime disposition, of whatever nature, it is necessary to calculate the net asset value of the transferor before and after the disposition, and if there is any reduction in that net asset value, there is a transfer of value.

2 Chargeable transfer of value

A chargeable transfer of value is a transfer of value made by an individual, or in some circumstances by a private company, made after 26 March 1974, other than a transfer which comes within one of the exemptions (ss. 20 (5), 39; p. 76, *post*).

D LIFETIME CHARGEABLE TRANSFERS

The circumstances in which events in a person's lifetime can constitute chargeable transfers of value, and so give rise to liability to capital transfer tax, as follows.

1 Gifts

Any gift which is made after 26 March 1974, is a chargeable transfer, unless it comes within one of the exemptions (p. 76, *post*).

2 Sales

a For full value

A sale at full value is not a transfer of value because although it is a disposition, it does not bring about a reduction in the net asset value of the seller. Thus, no capital transfer tax is payable on a sale at full value, even if the purchaser is a close relative. The only situation in which a sale at full value can give rise to liability is where it forms part of a series of events which are known as "associated operations" (p. 68, *post*).

b For less than full value

If a transaction takes the form of a sale, but the purchase price is less than the full value because the seller wishes to confer a benefit on the purchaser, the transaction falls within the definition of a transfer of value, and tax is payable. If, however, there is no intention to confer a benefit on the purchaser, there is no liability to tax if the buyer and seller are not related in some way, or if the terms of the transaction are those which would be expected in an arms length transaction (s. 20 (4)). There is, therefore, no tax liability merely because the seller makes a bad bargain.

3 Leases

In general, the grant of a lease or tenancy will be a transfer of value even if it is granted at a full rent if the value of the grantor's estate is reduced. This will not be so however, in the case of a commercial transaction in certain circumstances (FA 1975, s. 20 (4)) or in the case of the grant of a tenancy of agricultural property for full consideration (FA 1981, s. 97).

4 Deliberate failure to exercise a right

If a person who has any right against another person fails to exercise that right, then he is treated as making a gift if the net asset value of the other person is increased as a result of that failure (s. 20 (7)). If, therefore, a person who owns land allows someone else to acquire a squatters title to part of the land by occupying it for twelve years, then the owner is treated as making a gift of that land to the squatter. The gift is regarded as being made at the last point of time at which the right could be exercised, which, in the case just considered, would be just before the twelve year period runs out. This provision does not apply, however, if the failure to exercise the right was not deliberate.

5 Interest-free loans

In general, where prior to 6 April 1981 a person made a loan of money at less than a commercial rate of interest or allowed another person to have the use of property at less than a commercial rate of interest, an annual charge to tax arose (FA 1976, ss. 115, 116). This rule has been abolished from 6 April 1981 (FA 1981, s. 106).

6 *Transactions by private companies*

If a "close company" — an expression which covers most private companies — makes a transfer of value, the company itself is liable to pay tax (s. 39 (3)). The amount of tax payable, however, is ascertained by assuming that the amount of the transfer is apportioned out among the shareholders and certain other persons having rights in the company, and by making individual calculations according to their own circumstances (s. 39 (2); FA 1976, s. 118).

7 *Other events*

There are certain other situations in which a transaction is treated as a gift. They include some transactions involving the simultaneous grant of an annuity and a life policy (s. 42), and those involving payment after an asset has been disposed of (s. 40). These situations are not considered further.

8 *Mutual transfers*

Special rules deal with the position where the transferor makes a transfer of value to the transferee, and subsequently the transferee makes a transfer of value to the transferor (FA 1976, ss. 86, 87). If Alfred makes a transfer to Brian of £20,000, a subsequent transfer by Brian to Alfred of up to £20,000 will be exempt (s. 86 (2)). If Brian's transfer exceeds £20,000, then on the facts of this example the first £20,000 is exempt. This will also be the case if the transfer made by Brian is to Alfred's wife, or, where the transfer is made within two years after the death of Alfred, if it is to his widow. Generally, these provisions apply only where there are actual transfers of value, and not to transactions which are treated as if they were transfers of value (s. 86 (3)).

The transferor can also take action. To continue the same example, within six years of the transfer from Brian to Alfred, Alfred can claim that the value transferred by him is cancelled to the extent of the value transferred back by Brian (s. 87 (1), (3)). If Brian transferred £15,000 to Alfred, Alfred's claim would cancel the top £15,000 of his transfer (s. 87 (3)).

Where more than 12 months have elapsed between Alfred's transfer and Brian's transfer, the value of Brian's transfer is reduced by 4% for each complete period of 12 months in determining the extent to which value has been re-transferred to Alfred (s. 87 (3) (b)). If, therefore, Alfred transferred £20,000 to Brian in 1976, and Brian transferred £15,000 to Alfred in 1981, Brian would be treated as transferring £12,000 to Alfred and Alfred's claim would be restricted to the top £12,000 of his transfer.

Part I: Deceased's Personal Tax Liability

Where the original transferor, that is, in the terms of the example, Alfred, makes the claim he is entitled to repayment of the tax, and to interest on that repayment. Any transfers of value made by Alfred after the *claim* is made are taxable as if Alfred had never transferred the value which is cancelled, but no adjustment is made in respect of intermediate chargeable transfers of value (s. 87 (1) (b)).

If Alfred dies within the six year period without making a claim, his personal representatives may do so (s. 87 (2)).

9 Transfers set aside

Where a transfer of value is made by a disposition, and that disposition is subsequently set aside, the transferor may claim a repayment of the tax paid in respect of that disposition (FA 1976, s. 88).

10 "Associated operations"

There is a very complicated provision dealing with "associated operations" (s. 44). This provision is intended to cover the position where there are a series of transactions which as a whole have the effect of conferring a benefit, but where there is no gratuitous element in any one transaction. Suppose that a man owns a house, which he really wishes to give to his son. He might seek to achieve this result by, in the first instance, allowing his son to become a tenant. Even if the son pays a market rent for the tenancy, if he gains the protection of the Rent Acts the market value of the house will be materially reduced. The son might then buy the house at its value subject to the tenancy. The rent might be the full rent under a tenancy, and the purchase price might be the full value for a house subject to a tenancy. But the result is to leave the son in the same position as if he had in the first instance acquired the house with vacant possession, but at less than the full value. There is an element of gift in the transaction.

This is just one example of "associated operations". Whenever there are associated operations, the Revenue can roll them all together, look at the overall effect, and if there is an element of gift, then charge tax as a result.

The legislation is drawn in terms which are extremely wide indeed. It may be, however, that the provision applies only where the operations were conducted in pursuance of a previously agreed plan designed to confer an element of bounty on one of the parties; or where at least one of the parties to the transactions is under a moral obligation to join in steps which another requires (see also p. 76, *post*).

There are two restrictions on the scope of the provision. First, an operation which occurred before 27 March 1974 cannot be associated with an operation after that date (s. 44 (2)). Secondly, where the operations consist of the grant of a lease, and a subsequent dealing with the property subject to the lease, the lease and the subsequent dealing are not associated if the lease was granted at a full rent, *and* there is an interval of at least three years between the grant of the lease and the subsequent dealing (*ibid*).

E VALUE OF LIFETIME TRANSFERS OF VALUE

1 *Generally*

Capital transfer tax is, in general, payable by reference to the amount by which the transfer of value caused a reduction in the net asset value of the deceased (s. 20 (2)). To this general rule there are two qualifications.

a   Certain types of asset, and assets generally in certain situations have to be valued on a special basis. Most of the rules in this respect which are considered in respect of property owned on death (p. 88, *post*) apply in respect of lifetime transfers of value.

b   In some cases, it is necessary to increase the reduction in net asset value by taking into account the tax payable (*infra*).

2 *Loss to estate*

Usually, and subject to the rules just referred to, the gift of an asset by the deceased in his lifetime will have caused a reduction in his net asset value equivalent to the value of the gift itself. The reduction in net asset value may, however, have been much larger where the deceased gave away part, but not the whole, of an asset which he owned. This may be particularly so in the case of a controlling shareholding in a private company. Suppose that a private company has net assets of £500,000 and that there are 100 shares in issue. Suppose also that the value of 51 shares is £300,000, that the value of 49 shares is £200,000, and that the value of 2 shares is £6,000. If the deceased had 51 shares, and gave away 2 shares, the recipient would receive an asset worth £6,000, but the reduction in the deceased's net asset value would have been £100,000, and the tax would have been calculated by reference to that £100,000.

F GROSSING UP

1 *Tax paid by recipient*

Where the tax in respect of a lifetime gift or other transfer of value is paid by the recipient, the tax is calculated by reference to the amount of the reduction in net asset value without further adjustment (Sch. 10, para. 1 (1), (2), (3)).

2 Tax paid by deceased

Where the tax in respect of a lifetime gift or other transfer of value was paid or was payable by the deceased, the capital transfer tax has to be calculated upon the basis that the reduction in the deceased's net asset value was not only the value of the gift, but the amount of the tax payable on it. It will be seen (*infra*) that if a person who has made no chargeable transfers of value within the previous ten years gives away £61,818, the tax payable on that sum amounts to £1,818, leaving £60,000. If, therefore, the deceased actually gave to the recipient £60,000, he would be treated as having given away the grossed up equivalent of £60,000, namely £61,818, from which the tax applicable to that gross gift had been withheld. The deceased would therefore have to pay £1,818, representing the tax on that gross gift, to the Revenue. In every case where the recipient did not pay the tax, it is necessary to calculate the grossed up equivalent of the amount actually given to the recipient.

G LIFETIME RATES OF TAX

1 Tables

The following table shows the lifetime rates of tax applicable to transfers after 9 March 1981 (FA 1981, s. 92). A table of rates of tax payable as a result of death is given at p. 128, *post*.

Slice of value transferred	Total at top of slice	Rate on slice	Tax on slice	Total tax at top of slice	Grossed up equivalent at top of slice	Tax payable at top of slice
		Position where transferor deducts tax on making transfer; or where transferee pays tax			*Position where transferor does not deduct tax on making gift and transferee does not pay tax*	
First £50,000	£50,000	nil	nil	nil	£50,000	nil
Next £10,000	£60,000	15%	£1,500	£1,500	£61,818	£1,818
Next £10,000	£70,000	17½%	£1,750	£3,250	£74,062	£4,062
Next £10,000	£80,000	20%	£2,000	£5,250	£86,562	£6,562
Next £10,000	£90,000	20%	£2,000	£7,250	£99,355	£9,355
Next £10,000	£100,000	22½%	£2,250	£9,500	£113,103	£13,103
Next £10,000	£110,000	22½%	£2,250	£11,750	£126,207	£16,207

				Total	*Grossed up*	
		Rate	*Tax*	*tax at*	*equivalent*	*Tax pay-*
Slice of value	*Total at top*	*on*	*on*	*top of*	*at top of*	*able at top*
transferred	*of slice*	*slice*	*slice*	*slice*	*slice*	*of slice*
					Position where transferor deducts tax on making transfer; or where transferee pays tax ←→ *Position where transferor does not deduct tax on making gift and transferee does not pay tax*	
Next £10,000	£120,000	25%	£2,500	£14,250	£139,643	£19,643
Next £10,000	£130,000	25%	£2,500	£16,750	£153,929	£23,929
Next £10,000	£140,000	30%	£3,000	£19,750	£168,846	£28,846
Next £10,000	£150,000	30%	£3,000	£22,750	£184,231	£34,231
Next £10,000	£160,000	30%	£3,000	£25,750	£199,616	£39,616
Next £10,000	£170,000	35%	£3,500	£29,250	£215,001	£45,001
Next £10,000	£180,000	35%	£3,500	£32,750	£239,386	£50,386
Next £10,000	£190,000	35%	£3,500	£36,250	£245,771	£55,771
Next £10,000	£200,000	35%	£3,500	£39,750	£261,156	£61,156
Next £25,000	£225,000	35%	£8,750	£48,500	£299,618	£74,618
Next £25,000	£250,000	35%	£8,750	£57,250	£338,080	£88,080
Next £25,000	£275,000	35%	£8,750	£66,000	£376,542	£101,542
Next £25,000	£300,000	35%	£8,750	£74,750	£415,004	£115,004
Next £25,000	£325,000	35%	£8,750	£83,500	£453,466	£128,466
Next £25,000	£350,000	35%	£8,750	£92,250	£491,928	£141,928
Next £25,000	£375,000	35%	£8,750	£101,000	£532,088	£157,088
Next £25,000	£400,000	35%	£8,750	£109,750	£573,755	£173,755
Next £25,000	£425,000	35%	£8,750	£118,500	£615,422	£190,422
Next £25,000	£450,000	35%	£8,750	£127,250	£657,089	£207,089
Next £25,000	£475,000	35%	£8,750	£136,000	£698,756	£223,756
Next £25,000	£500,000	35%	£8,750	£144,750	£740,423	£240,423
Next £10,000	£510,000	35%	£3,500	£148,250	£757,090	£247,090
Next £40,000	£550,000	40%	£16,000	£164,250	£823,757	£273,757
Next £50,000	£600,000	40%	£20,000	£184,250	£907,090	£307,090
Next £50,000	£650,000	40%	£20,000	£204,250	£990,423	£340,423
Next £50,000	£700,000	40%	£20,000	£224,250	£1,079,553	£379,553
Next £50,000	£750,000	40%	£20,000	£244,250	£1,170,462	£420,462
Next £50,000	£800,000	40%	£20,000	£264,250	£1,261,371	£461,371
Next £50,000	£850,000	40%	£20,000	£284,250	£1,352,280	£502,280
Next £50,000	£900,000	40%	£20,000	£304,250	£1,443,189	£543,189
Next £50,000	£950,000	40%	£20,000	£324,250	£1,534,098	£584,098
Next £50,000	£1,000,000	40%	£20,000	£344,250	£1,625,007	£625,007
Next £10,000	£1,010,000	40%	£4,000	£348,250	£1,643,189	£633,189
Next £240,000	£1,250,000	45%	£108,000	£456,250	£2,086,508	£836,508
Next £250,000	£1,500,000	45%	£112,500	£568,750	£2,586,508	£1,086,508
Next £250,000	£1,750,000	45%	£112,500	£681,250	£3,086,508	£1,336,508
Next £250,000	£2,000,000	45%	£112,500	£793,750	£3,586,508	£1,586,508
Next £10,000	£2,010,000	45%	£4,500	£798,250	£3,606,508	£1,596,508
In excess of	£2,010,000	50%				

Part I: Deceased's Personal Tax Liability

This table is intended primarily to show the amount of tax payable where the transferor deducts tax when making the gift or where the transferee makes the gift, but the grossed up equivalents are shown for comparison. The quickest way of making the calculation is:

a ascertain the total gross amount of value transferred by all previous chargeable transfers;

b ascertain the total gross amount of value transferred by this and by all previous chargeable transfers;

c ascertain from the table the total tax payable on the gross amount at *a*;

d ascertain from the table the total tax payable on the gross amount at *b*;

e deduct *c* from *d*.

Suppose that the deceased made gross chargeable transfers in his lifetime, and more than three years before his death, of £50,000, and £20,000, and makes a further transfer of £40,000 also more than three years before his death. Assuming that there are no relevant exemptions, and that the deceased paid the tax on each transfer the computation, using the stages just described is:

a £50,000 + £20,000 = £70,000
b £70,000 + £40,000 = £110,000
c £3,250
d £11,750
e £11,750 − £3,250 = £8,500

Where it is necessary to gross up the amount of the value transferred, and there is only one net transfer, or all transfers have been net, the following table can be used in the same way. If, therefore, there have been no previous chargeable transfers within the previous ten years, and there is a net transfer of £85,000, the computation is:

	Value		*Tax*		*G.U.E.*
First	£82,750	+	£7,250	=	£90,000
Next	£ 2,250	+	£ 653	=	£ 2,903
	(at 29.03%)				
	£85,000	+	£7,903	=	£92,903

The following table shows the rates payable where net transfers of value are made after 9 March 1981.

Slice of net value transferred		Net total at top of slice	Effective rate on slice	Tax on slice	Total tax at top of slice	G.U.E. at top of slice
First	£50,000	£50,000	nil	nil	nil	£50,000
Next	£8,500	£58,500	17.65%	£1,500	£1,500	£60,000
Next	£8,250	£66,750	21.21%	£1,750	£3,250	£70,000
Next	£16,000	£82,750	25%	£4,000	£7,250	£90,000
Next	£15,500	£98,250	29.03%	£4,500	£11,750	£110,000
Next	£15,000	£113,250	33.33%	£5,000	£16,750	£130,000
Next	£21,000	£134,250	42.86%	£9,000	£25,750	£160,000
Next	£227,500	£361,750	53.85%	£122,500	£148,250	£510,000
Next	£300,000	£661,750	66.67%	£200,000	£348,250	£1,010,000
Next	£550,000	£1,211,750	81.82%	£450,000	£798,250	£2,010,000
Over	£1,211,750		100%			

The computation can be complex where there has been a combination of gross and net transfers. The safest course is to make the calculation in the following stages:

a   convert all previous gross transfers into net transfers by deducting the tax payable in respect of them;

b   ascertain the total net amount previously transferred;

c   add the net amount now being transferred;

d   ascertain the total tax on *b*;

e   ascertain the total tax on *c*;

f   deduct *d* from *e* in order to determine the amount of tax now payable;

g   re-convert the total at *c* to gross terms for the purposes of the CTT history.

Suppose that more than three years before his death, the deceased made a gross transfer of £60,000, on which he paid the tax of £1,500, and that he made a net transfer of £20,000. Suppose that he next made a further net transfer of £30,000. Upon the assumption that there are no relevant exemptions, the calculation becomes:

a   £58,500

b   £58,500 + £20,000 = £78,500

c   £78,500 + £30,000 = £108,500

d

	Value		Tax		G.U.E.
First	£66,750	+	£3,250	=	£70,000
Next	£11,750	+	£2,938	=	£14,688
(at 25%)					
	£78,500	+	£6,188	=	£84,688

e

	Value		Tax		G.U.E.
First	£ 98,250	+	£11,750	=	£110,000
Next	£ 10,250	+	£ 3,416	=	£ 13,666
(at 33.33%)					
	£108,500	+	£15,166	=	£123,666

f £15,166 − £6,188 = £8,978 tax now payable.

g £123,666

2 Changes of rates

Since the introduction of capital transfer tax, the rates have changed in respect of transfers of value made after 26 October 1977 and before 26 March 1980, in respect of those made after 25 March 1980 and before 10 March 1981 and in respect of those made after 9 March 1981. Although the calculations just described show the amount of tax presently payable, the amount of tax in respect of the previous transfers for the purposes of the computation will not necessarily accord with the sums which have actually been paid.

H CUMULATION: THE DECEASED'S CTT HISTORY

1 The principle

In the cases of income tax and capital gains tax, a completely new set of calculations is made for each year of assessment. In the case of capital transfer tax, each person is regarded as having a lifetime CTT history, which commences on 27 March 1974, or the date of his birth, whichever is the later. Exempt transfers of value (p. 76, *post*), to the extent that they are exempt, are left out of account, in determining what a chargeable transfer is (s. 20 (6)) but, the amount of each chargeable transfer of value is logged up against the transferor. Suppose that Alexandra makes a gift to Brian of £70,000, on which Alexander pays the tax, and that he then makes a gift to Charles of £20,000 on which Alexander also pays the tax. Suppose also that both gifts are fully chargeable transfers of value. It has been seen (p. 69, *ante*) that it is necessary to ascertain the grossed up equivalents of these gifts as the donor pays the tax on them. By reference to the table, it will be seen that the grossed up equivalent of the gift to Brian is £74,062, leaving Alexander to pay tax of £4,062 The grossed up equivalent is logged up against Alexander.

In order to calculate the tax payable on the next gift the procedure is:

1	take the gross value of the first transfer	£74,062
2	add the gross value of the second transfer	£25,293
		£99,355
3	determine from the table the amount of tax which would be payable on the combined total of *1* and *2*	£9,355
4	deduct the amount of tax shown by the table as payable on the first transfer	£4,062
		£5,293

For the purposes of the calculation, if the recipient pays the tax, the gross value of the transfers is the amount actually paid to the recipient. A comparable calculation if both Brian and Charles paid the tax on their gifts would be:

1	£70,000
2	£20,000
	£90,000
3	£7,250
4	£3,250
	£4,000

It will be seen that the principle of cumulation is carried over in order to determine the amount of tax payable on death (p. 129, *post*).

2 *10 year cumulation*

The cumulation applies only to chargeable transfers made within a period of 10 years (FA 1981, s. 93). When the 10 year period from the making of a chargeable transfer has expired, the value transferred by that transfer is no longer taken into account. Thus, in the example just given, if Alexander's transfer to Brian was more than 10 years before the transfer to Charles, the transfer to Charles would be within the £50,000 nil rate band.

I EXEMPTIONS

In a number of circumstances gifts and other transfers of value are exempt, either totally, or partially. These circumstances are as follows:

1 Transfers between spouses

The general rule is that a transfer of value of any amount from one spouse to another is entirely free of capital transfer tax (Sch. 6, para. 1 (1)). This rule only applies to the extent either that the value transferred is attributable to property which becomes owned by the recipient spouse, or that the value of the recipient spouse's estate is increased (FA 1976, s. 94 (1)).

A person is a spouse for so long as the marriage subsists, but the provision does not apply to former spouses.

The general rule applies if both spouses are domiciled abroad, and also where the transferor-spouse is domiciled abroad, and the transferee-spouse is domiciled in the UK. In the case, however, where the transferor-spouse is domiciled in the UK, and the transferee-spouse is domiciled elsewhere, the exemption only applies up to a cumulative total value of £50,000 (FA 1975, Sch. 6, para. 1 (2); FA 1980, s. 86).

Where the transfer is one step in a series of associated operations, the value transferred from one spouse to another is not deducted from the total value transferred (s. 44 (3)), but the Revenue only invoke this provision in blatant circumstances.

2 Transfers up to £3,000

The first £3,000 of value transferred in each year is exempt (Sch. 6, para. 2 (1); FA 1981, s. 94). Where a larger transfer is made, and grossing up is necessary, the £3,000 exemption is deducted from the actual value transferred, and only the difference is grossed up (*ibid*). Prior to 6 April 1981, the annual exemption limit was £2,000.

Where the exemption is not used, or not totally used, the balance can be carried forward for one year (para. 2 (2)). The Revenue view is that the balance brought forward is utilized after and not before the allowance for the later year. Suppose that in 1981/82 the deceased made gifts of £400, and that he carried forward a £2,600 allowance to

1982/83. Suppose also that in 1982/83 he made a gift of £3,200. The Revenue view is that the gift of £3,200 in 1982/83 absorbs the allowance for 1982/83 and £200 of the balance from 1981/82. There is, therefore, no balance from 1982/83 to carry forward to 1983/84.

Where gifts made in a year exceed £3,000 (and also any balance brought forward from the previous year), the earlier gifts are treated as exempt until the allowance is used up. Where more than one gift is made on the same day, the allowance is spread among the various gifts proportionately to their value (para. 2 (2)).

A husband and wife have this annual allowance each.

3 Small gifts

Transfers of value made by the deceased to the same person are exempt if they do not exceed £250 in any year (para. 4 (1); FA 1981, s. 94).

4 Normal expenditure out of income

A transfer of value, up to any amount, is exempt to the extent that it was made as part of the deceased's normal expenditure out of income (para. 5). For this relief to apply, it is necessary to satisfy three conditions:

a   the expenditure must be "normal" (para. 5 (1) (a)). This is not defined, but if three or more regular payments can be shown, the requirement of normality will generally be satisfied. Even if this cannot be shown, normality will be established if only one payment has been made, provided it can be shown that subsequent payments would have been made had the deceased survived. This will usually be so in the case of payment of a life assurance premium, or payment under a deed of covenant. Normality is considered from the viewpoint of an outgoing of the deceased, so that regular payments, even to different members of the family, can come within the exemption;

b   the expenditure must be out of income (para. 5 (1) (b)). Income for this purpose is not defined, although the Revenue view is that it means income after the payment of income tax. It seems, however, that where the deceased actually paid his income tax out of capital, all pre-tax income is available for the exemption. The capital element of a purchased life annuity is not, however, available as income (para. 5 (3));

c   the deceased must have been left with sufficient income after incurring the expenditure to maintain his usual standard of living (para. 5 (1) (c)).

5 Gifts in consideration of marriage

Within certain limits, a gift will be exempt if:

a made on the occasion of, or prior to and in contemplation of, a marriage;

b if conditional, that the only condition is the marriage taking effect; and

c in the case of a gift into settlement, if it is made to encourage or facilitate the marriage taking place (*Re Park (No. 2), [1972]* Ch. 385).

The limits are (para. 6):

a by a parent of either party to the marriage: £5,000. Each parent can make such a gift, so that, if all parents are living, a total of £20,000 can be given within the exemption;

b by one party to the marriage to the other: £2,500;

c by a grandparent, or remoter ancestor, of either party to the marriage: £2,500;

d by any other person: £1,000.

Where the gift was into settlement, certain further conditions have to be satisfied (para. 6 (3)).

6 Dispositions for family maintenance

A disposition is not a transfer of value if it is made:

a by one party to a marriage in favour of the other party for the maintenance of that other party (s. 46 (1));

b by one party to a former marriage in favour of the other party for the maintenance of that other party, including the variation of a previous disposition (s. 46 (6));

c by one party to a marriage or former marriage for the maintenance, education or training of a child of either party (s. 46 (1) (b));

d in certain circumstances in favour of a child who is not in the care of a parent for his maintenance, education or training (s. 46 (1) (c));

e in favour of a relative of the transferor, or of the spouse of the transferor, who is incapacitated by old age or infirmity from maintaining himself, or who is the widowed, separated or divorced mother of the transferor or his spouse (s. 46 (3), (6));

f in favour of an illegitimate child of the transferor for his maintenance, education or training (s. 46 (4)).

The exemption applies whether the disposition is an outright gift, or is a gift into settlement. In the case of a disposition in favour of a dependent relative, the exemption applies only to the extent that it is a reasonable provision for the care or maintenance of that relative. In other cases, no express limit is set.

7 Gifts to National Institutions, and for the public benefit

A lifetime gift to one of the specified national institutions is exempt if a gift on death would be (p. 106, *post*). The same applies to gifts for the public benefit (p. 107, *post*).

8 Gifts to charities

A gift to charity made by the deceased in his lifetime more than one year from his death will be exempt up to any amount (Sch. 6, para. 10 (a)). If the gift is made within one year from death only the first £200,000 of charitable gifts is exempt (para. 10 (b); FA 1980, s. 86). In that event, the excess over the £200,000 is logged up against the deceased as part of his cumulation (p. 74, *ante*), but the charity alone is liable for the tax on that excess (s. 26 (3)).

9 Gifts to political parties

Gifts to political parties are treated in the same way as gifts to charities, save that gifts made within one year from the date of death are exempt only up to £100,000 (para. 11).

10 Gifts for benefit of employees

A gift by a person of shares in a company is exempt if the gift is made to trustees to hold the shares upon trusts which permit all or most of the employees and office holders of the company to benefit (FA 1976, s. 90). A number of conditions have to be satisfied in order to obtain the benefit of this exemption.

11 Waivers of remuneration or dividends

Most waivers of remuneration or of dividends are exempt (FA 1976, ss. 91, 92).

J DECEASED DYING WITHIN 3 YEARS OF GIFT

Where the deceased dies within 3 years of making a gift or other chargeable transfer of value, tax is payable at the death-time scale (p. 128, *post*)and not the life-time scale (s. 37 (2)). In general, the additional tax which is payable by virtue of the death is calculated by reference to the value transferred by the *inter vivos* transaction. Where, however, the deceased died after 6 April 1976, and the transfer of value was made in the form of a transfer of property, in certain circumstances a revised basis of valuation can be adopted. No adjustment can be made where the property transferred was tangible movable property. (FA 1976, s. 99 (4)), but in other cases, where the property is still owned by the transferee or the transferee's spouse at the date of death of the transferor, the additional tax payable can be calculated by reference to the value of the property at the date of death of the transferor, rather than by reference to its value at the date of the transfer (s. 99 (1), (2)). This revised basis of calculation only applies if the person liable to pay the tax claims that it should.

A similar adjustment can be made if the transferee disposed of the property transferred before the death of the transferor, if the disposal was by means of an arm's length sale between non-connected persons (s. 99 (1), (6)). In this case the additional tax is calculated by reference to the value of the property at the date of sale.

In certain circumstances, where events other than normal market forces have caused the value of the property transferred to be reduced, a reduction in the value upon which the additional tax is calculated can only be made to reflect the ordinary market forces (FA 1976, Sch. 12). Neither the deceased nor his estate are liable for the additional tax which becomes payable as a result (FA 1975, s. 25 (4)). This is not, therefore, a liability which the personal representatives must discharge.

K INTER-RELATION WITH OTHER TAXES

1 Deceased paying CGT

Where the deceased paid, or his personal representatives are responsible for paying, capital transfer tax on a chargeable transfer of value made by the deceased in his lifetime, then if the transfer also gave rise to liability to capital gains tax, that tax is payable in addition (Sch. 10, para. 1 (2)). No deduction is made in calculating the reduction in net asset value by virtue of the capital gains tax liability. In the case of most transfers of value after 5 April 1980, capital gains tax roll-over relief will be available (p. 43, *ante*).

2 Recipient paying CGT

If the recipient pays the capital gains tax due in respect of the gain which accrued to the deceased, the amount of that tax is deducted from the value which is treated as being transferred by the chargeable transfer of value (Sch. 10, para. 4).

3   Development Land Tax

No relief is given from capital transfer tax in respect of an actual or potential liability to development land tax. However, where the interest in land was acquired as a result of a transaction by virtue of which capital transfer tax became payable, and within six years the person who acquired the interest disposes of it in a transaction which gives rise to liability to development land tax, a reduction can be made in the amount of the development land tax which is payable in respect of the capital transfer tax previously paid (DLTA 1976, Sch. 6, para. 18).

L   EXPENSES OF TRANSFER

If the deceased incurred expenses in making the transfer, these expenses are left out of account. If the recipient paid them, the amount of these expenses is deducted from the value transferred (Sch. 10, para. 6).

Capital Transfer Tax Liability on Death

Chapter 6

Capital Transfer Tax on Death

A INTRODUCTION

The amount of capital transfer tax payable by virtue of the death of a person is calculated in the following way:

1 Add together:

  a the capital value, which in some cases has to be ascertained according to special rules (p. 85, *post*), of all assets which the deceased owned at the date of his death, after deducting therefrom:

  i the value of assets which are exempt from tax to the extent that they are exempt (p. 96, *post*);

  ii the amount of those liabilities and expenses which are deductible (p. 119, *post*);

  iii where property is subject to existing obligations, the amount by which the property is reduced in value by virtue of those obligations (p. 121, *post*).

  b the capital value of all settled property in which the deceased had an "interest in possession" at the date of his death. The expression "interest in possession" is explained, at p. 288, *post*.

  c in respect of deaths occurring before 27 March 1981,

  i the value of certain gifts made by the deceased before 27 March, 1974; and ii the value of certain settled property in which the deceased had an interest in possession before but not after 27 March 1974.

2 Apply to the aggregate of all items within para. *1* the death-time scale of rates (p. 128, *post*).

3 Apportion the amount of tax payable between the various items within para. *1*.

Following the initial calculation, further calculations may be necessary during the administration period. These may be due to:

1 further assets or liabilities coming to light which were not taken into account in the original calculations;

2 an alteration in the terms of the will, or in the effect of the intestacy rules as applied to the deceased's estate, as a result of a Deed of Family Arrangement or similar instrument, or of a disclaimer (p. 173, *post*);

3 the sale of certain types of asset at a price lower than their value on death (p. 165, *post*); and

4 the sale of, or the happening of certain other events affecting, property which was conditionally exempt from tax on the deceased's death.

It is proposed to consider each of these matters in turn.

B ASSETS OWNED BY THE DECEASED AT DEATH

1 General principles

The basic principle is that all assets which the deceased owned at the date of his death are to be brought into account (FA 1975, ss. 22 (1), 23 (1)). This includes claims under the Law Reform (Miscellaneous Provisions) Act 1934 in respect of the death itself (*Kandalla* v. *British Airways Board,* [1980] 1 All E.R. 341). Certain assets are exempt, and these are dealt with later (p. 96, *post*) but in respect of assets which are not exempt it is necessary to have regard to:

a certain general principles governing the value of assets; and

b detailed rules governing the valuation of particular types of assets.

2 General valuation principles

In certain cases the basis on which an asset is to be valued is prescribed by legislation, and in other cases it has been left to be inferred from the old practice relating to estate duty. In the result, the following principles can be deduced.

a   Open market value

The fundamental principle is that the property is to be valued at the price which it could be expected to have fetched if sold in the open market at the date of death of the deceased (FA 1975, s. 38 (1)). No reduction is made on the ground that the whole of the property is deemed to have been placed on the market at the same time (*ibid*).

b   Method of notional sale

Although this is not specified in the legislation, it seems that it is necessary to follow the estate duty principles which were to the effect that the valuation is to be made on the basis that the property is to be regarded as being sold in the way which is likely to produce the best result. Accordingly, if an asset would produce a higher price if it were sold in separate lots, that hypothesis is adopted for valuation (*Earl of Ellesmere* v. *I.R. Comrs.*, [1918] 2 K.B. 735; *Duke of Buccleuch* v. *I.R. Comrs.*, [1967] 1 A.C. 506, H.L.). Conversely, if the asset would fetch a higher price if sold as an entity, the valuation will be made on that basis.

c   "Special purchasers"

If any person has a special interest in purchasing the asset, the price which he would pay is to be taken into account. This does not mean that the value is to be taken as the highest price which the so-called "special purchaser" would pay, but only that the presence of the special purchaser in the market is to be taken into account in determining the open market value.

3   Related property

a   The concept   If the deceased owned an asset and another asset or another part of the same asset is owned

i by his spouse; or

ii by the trustees of a settlement which he or his spouse made before 27 March 1974, and in which there was no interest in possession (defined, p. 288, *post*) at the date of his death, but only in the case of transfers made before 10 March 1981 (FA 1981, s. 105); or

iii in the case of some transfers of value made, by a charity, political party, or body established for national purposes or public benefit and the property in question was the subject of a previous exempt transfer made by the deceased or his spouse after 15 April 1976 (FA 1976, s. 103)

then the asset of the deceased will in one circumstance be treated as being "related to" the asset of spouse or of the trustees (FA 1975, Sch. 10, para. 7 (2)). This rule applies if the aggregate of the value of the deceased's asset on the one hand and of the asset of the spouse or of the trustees on the other hand, when separately ascertained, is less than would be the combined value of these assets if valued together. There is no restriction on the type of property to which this rule applies, but it will most frequently apply to any asset which is jointly owned; shares in a private company; adjoining parcels of land; and collections of almost any type of article.

b Calculation of the value of related property Where any property of the deceased was related to any property of his spouse or of trustees it is necessary to calculate the values of

  i the deceased's property (considered alone, and without taking into account the related property);
  ii the related property (considered alone, and without taking into account the deceased's property);
  iii both the deceased's property and the related property, considered together as one unit.

The deceased's property is then to be brought into account at a value produced by the formula (Sch. 10, para. 7 (1), (3)):

$$\text{iii} \times \frac{\text{i}}{\text{i} + \text{ii}}$$

Suppose that Bernard owned certain fields and that his wife Belinda owned adjoining fields. Suppose also that the value of Bernard's land, considered in isolation, is worth £30,000; that Belinda's land, considered in isolation, is worth £7,500 but that because of the "marriage" value, both areas of land, considered together, are worth £50,000. On Bernard's death, his land will not be brought into account at its actual value of £30,000, but at the value determined in accordance with the formula at:

$$£50,000 \times \frac{£30,000}{£30,000 + £7,500} = £40,000$$

c Calculation in respect of shares A similar procedure is followed where the property consists of shares, debentures, or units in a unit trust of the same class. In this case the apportionment is not by value, but by numbers of shares, according to the formula (Sch. 10, paras. 7 (4), (5)):

$$\text{Total value of} \atop \text{combined holding} \quad \times \quad \frac{\text{No. of deceased's shares}}{\text{No. of deceased's shares} + \text{No. of related shares}}$$

Suppose now that Bernard owns 45 out of 100 issued shares in a private company, and that Belinda owns a further 15 of such shares. 45 shares are worth £30,000; 15 shares are worth £7,750; but 60 shares, because of the control which they carry, are worth £50,000. Bernard's shares will be brought into account at:

$$£50,000 \times \frac{45}{45 + 15} = £37,500$$

Shares in a quoted company will not normally give rise to problems of related property. If Bernard has 45 shares in I.C.I. the value of these shares will not be affected by Belinda's holding of 15. The rules governing related property will have to be brought into account, however, if the combined holding would be so large that, if dealt with on a stock exchange, it would command a price higher than the listed price.

4 Joint property

a Husband and wife   Where property was owned jointly by the deceased and his wife, the related property provisions just discussed will apply.

b Other joint owners   Where the deceased had a share in property jointly with one or more persons other than his wife (and other than with the trustees of a pre-27 March 1974 settlement in which no interest in possession subsists), the ordinary open market value will have to be ascertained. However, usually, the open market value of a share in an asset will be less than the corresponding fraction of the total value of that asset. Where the asset is land or buildings, it is customary to reduce the total value by 10% before calculating the appropriate fraction, but this is only a rule of thumb, and if in any case the open market value of the share would produce a greater discount, the open market value is to be adopted.

c Property passing by survivorship   Where the deceased had a share in property, which was held on the basis of a joint tenancy, so that as a result of the death of the deceased his share automatically passes to the survivor, his share in the property nevertheless has to be brought into account at its value calculated immediately before he died (Sch. 10, para. 9 (2)). It seems that if through age or infirmity it was likely that the deceased would die first this fact can be reflected in the value placed on the share, if the deceased was contractually bound not to convert the joint holding into a tenancy in common.

5 Alteration in value as a result of death

Where the value of any property alters as a result of the death of the deceased, it is brought into account at its value as altered (Sch.

10, para. 9 (1)(a)). This applies particularly in the case of policies of assurance which mature on the death of the deceased (p. 95, *post*).

6 Sale within 3 years of death

A special rule applies where related property is sold within 3 years of the death of the deceased. This is described later (p. 171, *post*).

C PARTICULAR TYPES OF ASSET

There are a number of principles governing the value at which particular types of asset are to be brought into account. These relate to

1 Quoted securities

2 Unquoted securities

3 Dividends

4 Business assets

5 Agricultural land

6 Farm cottages

7 Debts due to the deceased

8 Insurance policies

9 Certain freehold property subject to leases.

1 Quoted shares and securities

It seems that the statutory rule which applies for capital gains tax purposes (CGTA 1979, s. 150 (3)) and the corresponding practice which was used for estate duty will be followed for the valuation of quoted securities.

This is to take the lower of

i the lower of the two prices shown in the quotation for the securities in the Stock Exchange Daily Official List for the date of death, together with one quarter of the difference between these two figures; and

ii halfway between the highest and lowest prices at which ordinary bargains were recorded in the securities on the date of death.

If the death occurred on a date on which the London Stock Exchange was closed, the valuation is to be made on either the last trading day before the death, or the first trading day afterwards, depending on which produces the lower value. The open market value is adopted instead of these methods if the deceased's holding was so large that a higher price could have been achieved. In this case it may be necessary to take account of the related property provisions where the deceased's wife had holdings in the same company (p. 85, *ante*). A special rule is adopted where the securities are realised within 12 months from the date of death (p. 165, *post*).

2 Unquoted shares and securities

All unquoted securities are valued at market value for capital transfer tax purposes, and there is no equivalent of the "assets basis" of valuation which was sometimes applied for estate duty. In most cases shares in private companies are subject to prohibition or restriction on transfer, or subject to an obligation that they shall be offered to other shareholders. Where this is so, it has to be assumed that the shares are freely marketable on death, but that the notional purchaser will take them subject to their actual restrictions (*I.R. Comrs. v. Crossman*, [1937] A.C. 26, H.L.; *Holt* v. *I.R. Comrs.*, [1953] 2 All E.R. 1499).

In making the valuation it is to be assumed that the notional purchaser will have available to him all the information which a prudent prospective purchaser would require if he were proposing to purchase the shares from a willing vendor in an arm's length transaction (FA 1975, Sch. 10, para. 13). In addition to these general rules relating to unquoted securities:

i the rules relating to "related property" (p. 85, *ante*) may apply;

ii where the company is a farming company, agricultural valuation relief may be available (FA 1975, Sch. 8, para. 4 (p. 94, *post*)); and

iii where the company is carrying on a trade, business asset relief may be vailable (FA 1976, Sch. 10 (p. 90, *post*)).

3 Dividends; Rights

Where prior to the date of death a dividend had been declared, but not paid, so that, in the case of a quoted security, the quoted price was ex-dividend, the amount of the dividend is to be brought into account as an asset of the estate. A dividend which is declared after the date of death is not brought into account, even though it relates wholly or partly to the period prior to the date of death. Suppose that the deceased held shares in the Megalon Company Ltd., which on 10 June 1981 declares an ordinary dividend in respect of the calendar year 1980, the dividend being payable on 1 July 1981. The stock is first quoted ex-div on 20 June 1981. If the deceased died on 5 June 1981 no part of the dividend would be brought into account. If he died on 15 June, again no part of the dividend would be brought into account, because the right to receive the dividend would be included in the quoted price. If he died on 25 June, the whole dividend would have to be brought into account. If he died on 5 July, no part of it would be brought into account because he would already have received the dividend. If the dividend warrant had not been presented for payment, however, by the time of the deceased's death, that warrant would be a separate asset of the estate, and would have to be brought into account as such. The same rules are followed where a company makes a right issue, and the shares are quoted ex-rights.

The income tax treatment of dividends has been considered (p. 20, *ante*).

4 Business assets

a Introduction Where the deceased died after 6 April 1976 and certain conditions are satisfied, the value of business assets may be reduced by 20%, 30% or 50% (FA 1976, Sch 10; FA 1978, s. 64).

b Assets eligible for relief The relief is not available where the business is that of dealing in stocks, shares, securities or land or buildings, or of making investments (para. 3 (2)). The relief is also not available in the case of a company where the company is a holding company, and the total of its holdings are in companies within these categories (para. 3 (3)). With these exceptions the assets which are eligible for relief and the percentages by which the open market values are reduced are:

 i a business, or an interest in a business: 50%;

 ii shares or securities of a company, whether quoted or unquoted, which in themselves or which together with other shares or securities owned by the transferor, gave the transferor control of the company: 50%;

 iii shares in an unquoted company which did not give the transferor control: 20%; and

 iv land or buildings, or plant or machinery, which was used wholly or mainly for the purposes of a business carried on by a company of which the deceased had control; or by a partnership of which the deceased was a partner: 30%.

The relief is not available where land was owned by an individual outside the business, nor where it was owned by a spouse of the deceased or a former partner.

c Conditions for relief In order to obtain the relief the following conditions must be satisfied:

i the property must have been owned by the deceased throughout the two years ending with his death; or, where if it was acquired within that period, it must have replaced other property (para. 4 (1)). If the property was inherited, the deceased is treated as having owned it from the date of death of the person from whom it was inherited; or earlier where it was inherited from a spouse (para. 4 (4)).

ii the property must either have been used wholly or mainly for the purposes of the business during the period of two years prior to his death, or have been required for future use for those purposes at the date of his death (para. 8 (2)).

d Value of assets for relief Where the assets consist of an unincorporated business, or an interest in an unincorporated business, the relief is restricted to the net value of the business, after deducting its liabilities (para. 5).

In the case of any asset, where it is subject to a specific liability or incumbrance, the amount secured is deducted from the gross value of the asset, and only the balance is available for relief (FA 1975, Sch. 10, para. 2).

Relief cannot be claimed under this provision for the same value in respect of which relief is claimed under the provisions governing the sale of related property (p. 171, *post*), agricultural property (*infra*), or woodlands (p. 101, *post*) (FA 1976, Sch. 10, paras. 9. 10. 11).

5 Agricultural property relief

a Introduction In respect of transfers prior to 10 March 1981, in certain circumstances working farmer relief was available. This has now been abolished, and replaced with the agricultural property relief, under which, if various conditions are satisfied, the open market value of agricultural land can be reduced by 20% or 50% (FA 1981, s. 96, Sch. 14).

b Agricultural property The relief is available only where the value transferred is attributable to the agricultural value of agricultural property. The concept of agricultural value is considered below (p. 92, *post*) but agricultural property means agricultural land and pasture, ancillary woodlands such as shelter belts, and cottages, farm buildings and farm houses (FA 1981, Sch. 14, para. 1 (2)). It includes buildings used for the intensive rearing of livestock or fish, but excludes live and dead stock, cut crops, and plant and machinery. The relief applies only where the property is situate in the United Kingdom, the Channel Islands or the Isle of Man (para. 1 (4)).

   c   Land directly owned by individual   In the case of land owned directly by the deceased, the open market values are reduced by the following percentages:

    i   where the deceased's interest in the property conferred the right to vacant possession, 50% (Sch. 14, para. 2 (2) (a));

   ii   where the deceased's interest conferred the right to vacant possession within 12 months, 50%;

  iii   where the deceased owned land, but it was let, generally 20%; and

  iv   where the deceased had an interest in land which did not confer the right to vacant possession, but where as a result of arrangements made prior to 10 March 1981, he could have claimed full working farmer relief had he made a transfer before that date, 50% (para. 2 (3)). The main example is where the deceased had previously owned the land with vacant possession, and before 10 March 1981 had granted a lease to two or more tenants, of whom he was one.

   d   Conditions   The conditions to be satisfied are, in the case of land with vacant possession, that the deceased occupied the land for the purposes of agriculture for at least two years; or in other cases that he owned the land for at least seven years, and that throughout that period either he or some other person occupied the land for the purposes of agriculture (para. 3).

Further provisions apply where the land in question replaced other land within the two or seven year periods (para. 4).

   e   Agricultural value   The expression "agricultural value" of agricultural property is defined to mean the value which the property would have if it were subject to a perpetual covenant prohibiting its use otherwise than as agricultural property (para. 1 (3)).

Where the property is subject to a mortgage or charge, the amount secured is deducted from the open market value (FA 1975, Sch. 10, para. 2) and only the balance is capable of being relieved.

The effect of the definition is that no reduction in value is given in respect of development or hope value.

Suppose that the deceased owned a farm of 300 acres, which had an open market value of £180,000. Of this, £30,000 represents hope value, and £150,000 the agricultural value. The property is to be valued for capital transfer tax purposes as follows:

Hope value (actual)		£ 30,000
Agricultural value	£150,000	
Less: relief	£ 75,000	£ 75,000
		£105,000

f Limitations on relief   The 50% transitional relief is subject to one of two limitations:

These limitations are:

i the relief is limited to property having an open market value of £250,000, less the open market value of land transferred by the deceased in his lifetime for which the relief was obtained (FA 1975, Sch. 8, para. 5 (1) (a); FA 1981, Sch. 14, para. 2 (3) (a)); or

ii the relief is limited to 1,000 acres, less the extent of land transferred by the deceased in his lifetime for which the relief was obtained (para. 5 (1) (b)). Rough grazing land is counted as being one-sixth of its actual area for this purpose (FA 1976, s. 74 (6)).

Where the land owned by the deceased at the date of his death exceeds these limits, the relief is apportioned among his properties proportionately to their open market value (para. 5 (3)). The exceed may qualify for the business assets relief (*supra*). If business asset relief is not available, the excess qualifies for 20% relief.

There are no corresponding limitations on the 50% relief for land with vacant possession, or the 20% relief for let land.

g Deceased having acquired land by inheritance   Where the deceased acquired the land on the death of another person, he is treated for the purposes of the conditions as having commenced to occupy the land on the death of that other person (para. 6 (*a*)).

If the land was acquired on the death of the deceased's spouse, then if the spouse satisfied the conditions at the date of death, the deceased is treated as having also satisfied the conditions at that date (para. 6 (b)).

h Partnership interest   Where land was owned by a partnership of which the deceased was a partner, 50% relief is available if the conditions are satisfied (para. 2 (6)).

i Shares in farming company If certain conditions are fulfilled, the relief can be claimed in respect of shares in, or debentures of, a company. These conditions are (para. 9):

i the agricultural property must form part of the company's assets;

ii part of the value of the shares or debentures must be attributable to the agricultural value of agricultural property;

iii the shares or debentures must have given the deceased control of the company immediately before his death ("control" is defined in FA 1975, Sch. 4, para. 13 as amended by FA 1978, s. 66);

iv the property must have been occupied by the company for the purposes of farming:

  a immediately before the death of the deceased; and

  b throughout the last two years of the deceased's lifetime. (Further provisions deal with the position where the company changed farms during that period: para. 12).

v alternatively, the property must have been owned by the company:

  a immediately before the death of the decreased; and

  b throughout the last seven years of the deceased's lifetime and it must have been occupied for the purposes of agriculture by some other person throughout the whole of that period.

j Gifts of agricultural property prior to 27 March 1974 If the deceased made a gift of agricultural property before 27 March 1974, but within 7 years of the date of his death, capital transfer tax may be payable on that gift at the date of death of the decreased (p. 123, *post*). In this case, if the agricultural property is still owned by the beneficiary at the date of death of the deceased, the relief which applied for estate duty purposes can still be claimed. This is briefly described later (p. 124, *post*).

6 Farm cottages

Cottages on a farm which are occupied by workers employed on the farm are valued as if they could only be occupied by such persons, even if they are in fact suitable for residential purposes by other persons (FA 1975, Sch. 10, para. 12).

7 Debts due to the deceased

Where the deceased was legally entitled to receive any sum of money, that sum must in principle be brought into account at its face value (Sch. 10, para. 10). To this rule there are two exceptions:

a   a total or partial deduction can be made where the personal representatives can show that recovery is not reasonably practicable, and that recovery has not been made impracticable by any act or omission on their part (*ibid*);

b   if the sum is not payable on demand, and does not fall due until a future date, a discount may be claimed to reflect that fact. In order to claim that discount, it will be necessary to show that the rate of interest payable on the debt is less than a commercial rate of interest payable on debts of that nature.

8 Life policies

A policy of assurance on the life of the decreased, and which therefore matures on his death, must be valued at its maturity value (para. 9 (1) (a)).

9 Certain freehold properties, subject to leases

Where a lease is granted for the life of a person, or determinable only by reference to the death of a person, and the lease was not granted for a full consideration, the grant of the lease would usually have been treated as the creation of a settlement (Sch. 5, para. 1 (3)). If the deceased had granted such a lease, it is necessary to ascertain what would have been the value of a full consideration for the lease at the time when it was granted. The value attaching to the freehold is then taken as such part of the value of the whole property as at the deceased's death as the consideration, if any, actually provided at the time when the lease was granted bore to the value of what would have been the full consideration at that time (Sch. 10, para. 8).

D   THE EXEMPTIONS

1 Generally

The discussion so far has related to the assets which the deceased owned at the date of his death, and the values to be placed upon them. It is now appropriate to consider the exemptions.

The legislation deals with three broad types of exemption:

- *a* exemptions which depend on the nature of the property;
- *b* an exemption which depends on the cause of death; and
- *c* exemptions which depend on the beneficial entitlement to the property under the deceased's will, or under the intestacy rules.

Exemptions in the first category may be either absolute or conditional. It may assist to summarize these exemptions.

a Exemptions depending on the nature of the property

  i Absolute exemptions:

    a most reversionary interests (p. 97, *post*);

    b cash options under retirement annuity schemes (p. 97, *post*);

    c certain overseas pension rights.

  ii Conditional exemptions:

    a objects of national interest;

    b historic land, buildings;

    c timber.

b Exemption depending on cause of death

Death as a result of injury, etc. sustained on active or similar service.

c Exemptions depending on beneficial entitlement

  a gifts to spouses;

  b gifts to charities;

  c gifts for national purposes;

  d gifts for the public benefit;

  e gifts to political parties.

There are other exemptions which apply where there is an overseas element.

E EXEMPTIONS DEPENDING ON THE NATURE OF THE PROPERTY

1 Reversionary interests

Where a person dies, he is treated as transferring his "estate" at the moment before his death (FA 1975, s. 22 (1)). The deceased's estate for this purpose consists of all the property to which he was beneficially entitled immediately before his death (s. 23 (1)) other than excluded property. The most important type of excluded property is reversionary interests, which are any future interests under a settlement, whether vested or contingent (s. 51 (1)). A reversionary interest in settled property is excluded property, unless that reversionary interest has at any time been acquired for a consideration in money or moneys worth, whether by the deceased or someone else (s. 24 (3) (a)); or unless the deceased or his spouse was the settlor (FA 1976, s. 120). In some cases leases are treated as settlements, but even where this is so, the reversion expectant on the determination of the lease is not treated as excluded property (s. 24 (3) (b)).

2 Cash options under retirement annuity schemes

Various retirement annuity schemes have been approved by the Inland Revenue for income tax purposes, under which, upon a person's death an annuity becomes payable to his widow or dependent. In some of these schemes a person is given the right to direct the trustees of the scheme to pay a lump sum to his personal representatives in lieu of paying the annuity to his widow or dependent. Where this so, the right to require a sum to be paid is excluded property and *does not* have to be brought into account for the purposes of the tax (Sch. 7, para. 2).

3 Overseas pensions

The value of any pension payable to the deceased under the Government of India Act 1935, or of certain pensions payable under the Overseas Pensions Act 1973, is left out of account (Sch. 7, para. 4). This exemption covers most pensions payable abroad by the Governments of former British territories.

4 Deceased non-domiciled or non-resident

Certain other types of property are treated as excluded property where the deceased was non-domiciled or non-resident. These are considered later (p. 387, *post*).

F CONDITIONAL EXEMPTIONS BY VIRTUE OF NATURE OF PROPERTY

1 The general principles

In respect of certain types of asset which the deceased owned at the date of his death, the personal representatives are given a choice.

They may either value the asset on the open market value basis, and pay capital transfer tax on that value. If they do this, there will be no further capital transfer tax liability as a result of the deceased's death when that asset is disposed of. Alternatively, the value of the asset may be left out of account in calculating the amount of tax payable as a result of the deceased's death. When, however, the asset is disposed of, then a liability will usually arise at that time.

These principles apply, with variations of detail, to:

a   land, buildings and objects of national interest; and

b   timber.

G   LAND, BUILDINGS AND OBJECTS OF NATIONAL INTEREST

1   *Scope of exemption*

The exemption may be claimed in respect of:

a   any pictures, prints, books, manuscripts, works of art, scientific collections or "other things not yielding income" which are of national, scientific, historic or artistic interest;

b   any land of outstanding scenic, or historic, or scientific interest;

c   any building which, by virtue of its outstanding historic or architectural interest, warrants special steps being taken for its preservation;

d   any land adjoining a building within *c* which is essential for the protection of the character and amenities of the building;

e   any object which is historically associated with a building within *c* (FA 1976, s. 77 (1)).

The question whether land, buildings or objects fall within these categories is for the Treasury to decide. There is no right of appeal against the Treasury's decision.

For the purposes of category *a*, the expression "national interest" includes a regional interest within the United Kingdom (s. 77 (5)). In practice, this means that the object must be acceptable as a gift to a national or regional museum or art gallery.

2   *Undertakings to be given*

a   Category a   Where the object falls within category *a*, the exemption will be given only if an undertaking is given to the Treasury. The undertaking covers the period until the beneficiary who is entitled to the object dies, or until he disposes of it in any way. The terms of the undertaking are that (FA 1976, s. 77 (2)):

i the object will be kept permanently in the UK, and will be sent abroad only for temporary purposes and according to conditions to be prescribed by the Treasury;

ii reasonable steps will be taken for the preservation of the object; and

iii reasonable facilities will be afforded for public access.

The undertaking may be limited in the case of documents where they are confidential.

b Category b In the case of land within category *b* the requisite undertakings are that (s. 77 (4)):

i reasonable steps will be taken for the maintenance of the land and the preservation of its character; and

ii the public will be afforded reasonable access.

c Categories c and d In these cases the requisite undertakings are that:

i reasonable steps will be taken for the maintenance, repair and preservation of the property; and

ii the public will be afforded reasonable access.

d Category e In this case the undertakings are that:

i reasonable steps will be taken for the maintenance, repair and preservation of the object;

ii reasonable steps will be taken for keeping the object associated with the building concerned; and

iii the public will be afforded reasonable access.

3 Tax becoming payable

Where the exemption has been claimed, capital transfer tax becomes payable when the first "chargeable event" occurs (FA 1976, s. 78). The chargeable events are:

a breach of the undertaking in a material respect (s. 78 (2));

b the death of the person beneficially entitled to the property, except where:

i a further conditional exemption is obtained on that death, with an appropriate undertaking given (s. 78 (5)); or

ii the property is left to a National Institution (p. 106, *post*);

99

 c the sale of the property, except in the case of a sale by private treaty, to a National Institution (s. 78 (4) (a));

 d the gift of the property, or disposal otherwise than on sale, and

  i a further conditional exemption is obtained, and an appropriate undertaking given (s. 78 (5)); or

  ii the disposal is to a National Institution (s. 78 (4) (a)); or

  iii the disposal is to the Revenue in satisfaction of a tax liability (s. 78 (4) (b)).

4 Person liable

Where a chargeable event occurs, the person who is liable to pay the tax is the person who would be entitled to receive the proceeds of sale, or income from the proceeds of sale, if the property were sold at the time when the undertaking is broken, or immediately after the death occurs. Where the property is disposed of, the person for whose benefit the disposal occurred is liable for the tax payable (s. 78 (2), (3)).

5 Amount of tax payable

Where tax becomes payable, it is calculated by reference to the value of the property at the time of the "chargeable event" (*supra*). If at the time of that event the transferor is dead, the rate of tax is the rate, on the death-time scale, that would have applied if the value of the property had been added to the value transferred on his death, and had formed the highest part of that value (FA 1976, s. 79 (1)).

In this event, value transferred on the death of the transferor is increased by the amount on which tax has become chargeable on the occasion of the chargeable event (s. 80 (2)).

H MAINTENANCE FUNDS

There is no liability to capital transfer tax in respect of property which becomes comprised in a maintenance fund settlement (FA 1976, s. 84). This is a settlement which exists for the maintenance, repair or preservation of any land or building in respect of which the conditional exemption can be claimed, provided that, under the terms of the settlements, for at least a period of 6 years the fund can only be used for the purposes of maintenance or for the benefit of the National Institutions (p. 106, *post*) or a charity which exists wholly or mainly for the maintenance of land, buildings or objects which are of scientific, historic, architectural or scenic interest (s. 84 (3), (7); FA 1980, s. 88).

The property will only be exempt if the Treasury is satisfied both that the settlement complies with the specified conditions and that the property itself is of a character and an amount which is appropriate for the purposes of the settlement (s. 84 (2)).

I WOODLANDS

1 *The exemption*

The capital transfer tax legislation divides woodlands into two categories:

a woodlands which are ancillary to agriculture, such as shelter belts on a farm. In this case the agricultural property relief can be claimed in respect of the woodlands themselves (FA 1981, Sch. 14, para. 1 (2); p. 91, *ante*);

b woodlands or forests in their own right, to which a special relief applies.

This special relief applies to the value of trees and underwood, but not to the land itself, in respect of which there is no relief at all.

Where the relief is available the personal representatives have a choice. The trees and underwood can be valued at the date of death, and tax paid on that value at that time in the same way as upon any other asset. Alternatively the value of the trees and underwood can be left out of account at the date of death, with tax becoming payable later. In general, it will be appropriate to pay tax at the date of death where the trees are very young, and for the exemption not be to claimed.

2 *Conditions*

In order to claim the exemption, it must be shown that if the deceased purchased the land on which the trees are growing, that he was the beneficial owner of that land throughout the period of five years ending with his death (FA 1975, Sch. 9, para. 5 (1)). If the deceased acquired the land in any way other than purchase there is no minimum period of ownership.

The deceased is treated as acquiring the beneficial interest in the land at the time of contracting to purchase; and if he contracted to sell the land prior to his death, he would not be regarded as being beneficially entitled to the land at the date of his death, unless, perhaps, the purchaser fails to complete the contract through his own fault.

The relief is also available where under a trust the deceased had an

101

interest in possession (p. 288, *post*) in woodlands (Sch. 5, para. 3 (1); Sch. 9, para. 5 (1)).

3 Tax becoming payable

a Sales Where no tax was paid on the death of the deceased on trees or underwood then tax becomes payable when the trees or underwood are disposed of (para. 2 (1)). This is so whether the trees or underwood are sold together with the land, or separately from the land.

The tax is payable on the proceeds of sale of the timber (if it is sold for full value) or the actual value (if it is sold at an undervalue), at the time of the sale, and by deducting therefrom (para. 6 (2)):

  i the expenses of the disposal;

 ii any expenses incurred in re-planting within 3 years (or longer: FA 1976, s. 75) of the disposal to replace the trees or underwood sold; and

iii where there has been a previous disposal of trees, and replanting took place more than 3 years after the disposal, the expenses of replanting to replace the trees or underwood previously disposed of.

The tax is calculated by adding the net proceeds of sale of the timber to the value of the estate taxed at the date of death; recalculating the total amount due; and deducting the amount of tax previously paid.

b Gifts If the trees or underwood are given by the beneficiary to his spouse, no tax will become payable at that time (para. 2 (3)). Any other disposal by way of gift will give rise to a double charge to tax. There will be a liability, based on the net value of the trees and underwood, by reference to the last death, but based upon the value at the date of disposal; and there will a further liability as a gift, at lifetime rates. In this case, the amount of tax payable under the former charge is deducted from the value of the trees in determining the amount payable under the latter charge (para. 4).

> *Example* Suppose that Donald, who has not made any taxable gifts in his life-time, dies. His assets at the date of his death are woodland, valued at £80,000; trees growing on that woodlands, valued at £20,000; and other assets valued at £50,000. He leaves all his assets to his son Edward, who sells the trees when they are worth £100,000.
>
>   i *Relief not claimed*
>
>   If Donald's personal representatives do not claim the relief on the death of Donald, the amount of tax payable is:

(a) On death of Donald:

Value of woodland	£80,000
Value of timber (at date of death)	£20,000
Value of other assets	£50,000
	£150,000
Tax payable at death-time rates on £150,000	£44,500

(b) On sale of trees   nil

Total tax paid   £44,500

ii *Relief claimed*

If Donald's personal representatives claim the relief on Donald's death, the tax payable is:

(a) On death of Donald:

Value of woodland	£80,000	
Value of other assets	£50,000	
(Value of timber left out of account at this stage)		
	£130,000	
Tax payable at death-time rates on £130,000:		£33,500

(b) On sale of trees

Assets taxed on death of Donald	£130,000	
Add		
Value of trees at date of disposal	£100,000	
Less: replanting expenses, say, £10,000	£90,000	
	£220,000	
Tax payable at death-time rates on £220,000:	£86,000	
Less: tax paid at death	£33,500	£52,500
Total tax paid		£86,000

iii *Gift, not sale*

Suppose now that the facts are the same, that relief is claimed on the death of Donald, but that instead of selling the trees, Edward gives them away to Fergus when they have a value, net, of £200,000. Edward has not himself made any taxable gift in his lifetime, and Fergus agrees to pay the tax on the gift. The tax payable is:

(a) On death of Donald:

Value of taxable assets (as before)	£130,000	
Tax payable (as before)		£33,500

(b) On gift of trees, by reference to
   death of Donald

Net value of trees	£200,000	
	£330,000	
Tax payable		£118,500
		£152,000

(c) On gift, as gift

Value of gift (replanting expenses not deducted)	£210,000	
Less: tax payable at (b)	£118,500	
Deemed value of gift	£91,500	
Tax payable by Fergus on lifetime gift of £47,500		£7,588
		£159,588

4. Business asset relief

Woodlands may also qualify for business asset relief, and where this is so, the relief applies both to the land and to the trees.

Where there is an election to pay the tax on the trees at the time of their subsequent disposal, the relief is calculated by reference to the value of the trees at that subsequent time. However, the relief is only available where, had the election not been made, it could have been available on the death of the deceased (FA 1976, Sch. 10, para. 11; FA 1978, s. 65).

If the election is claimed, and the tax becomes chargeable by virtue of a disposal which is a chargeable transfer of value, and if business asset relief is available in respect of that transfer, the 50% reduction of value is made after the deduction of the tax deferred (*ibid*).

J DEATH ON ACTIVE SERVICE

The exemptions so far considered (pp. 96 to 103) are absolute or conditional exemptions which depend on the nature of the property which the deceased owned at the date of his death. The exemption from capital transfer tax where death occurs on active service is granted solely having regard to the cause of death. This is a total exemption from capital transfer tax, in respect of all assets which the deceased owned at the date of his death, of whatever nature.

This exemption can be claimed in respect of the death of a person where the Defence Council or the Secretary of State for Defence certify that:

1 the deceased died from a wound inflicted, or an accident which occurred, or a disease which was contracted;

2 at a time when the deceased was a member of the armed forces of the Crown; or a member of one of the medical, nursing or similar auxiliary forces; or was subject to military law as an accompanying person; and

3 either (a) the deceased was on active service or other service which involved the same risks;

or   (b) the deceased had previously contracted a disease which was aggravated by such service (Sch. 7, para. 1).

The deceased is treated as dying from a wound if the wound was a contributory cause of death, even if it was not the direct cause of death (*Barty – King* v. *Ministry of Defence,* [1979] 2 All E.R. 80).

K   EXEMPTIONS DEPENDING ON BENEFICIAL ENTITLEMENT

1   *Introduction*

In addition to the exemptions which apply according to the nature of the property, and to the cause of death, other exemptions may be claimed by virtue of the identity of the beneficiary under the will or under the intestacy provisions.

It is proposed to:

a   consider the beneficiaries in respect of whom these exemptions may be claimed;

b   describe the conditions which have to be satisfied in order to claim the exemptions; and

c   describe certain rules which may restrict or eliminate apparent exemptions.

2   *Beneficiaries in respect of whom exemptions can be claimed*

a   Generally   The general position is that where under the terms of the will or under the intestacy rules a benefit is conferred upon one or more of the following classes of person, the property which passes to the beneficiary is either totally or partially exempt from capital transfer tax.

105

These beneficiaries are:

- *a* the spouse of the deceased;
- *b* certain national institutions;
- *c* certain other bodies not established for profit;
- *d* other charities;
- *e* political parties.

It is now necessary to elaborate upon this general statement.

b Gifts to spouses The exemption in respect of a benefit conferred upon the deceased's spouse applies whether the spouse takes the property outright, or only acquires a life or lesser interest in it (FA 1975, Sch. 6, para. 1). (The position in respect of the old surviving spouse exemption for estate duty purposes is discussed later: p. 125, *post*).

There is a restriction on the exemption where the deceased was, but his spouse is not, domiciled in some part of the UK (Sch. 6, para. 1 (2)).

c Gifts to National Institutions The institutions are (Sch. 6, para. 12):

- i The National Gallery.
- ii The British Museum.
- iii The Royal Scottish Museum; The National Museum of Wales; The Ulster Museum.
- iv Any other similar national institution which exists wholly or mainly for the purpose of preserving for the public benefit a collection of scientific, historic, or artistic interest and which is approved for this purpose by the Treasury.
- v Any museum or art gallery in the UK which exists wholly or mainly for that purpose and is maintained by a local authority or university in the UK.
- vi Any library the main function of which is to serve the needs of teaching and research at a university in the UK.
- vii The National Trust for Places of Historic Interest or National Beauty; The National Trust for Scotland for Places of Historic Interest or Natural Beauty.
- viii The National Art Collections Fund.
- ix The Friends of the National Libraries.
- x The Historic Churches Preservation Trust.

xi The Nature Conservancy Council.

xii Any local authority.

xiii The National Debt Commissioners; and any Government Department.

xiv Any university or university college in the UK.

d *Bodies for the public benefit* For this exemption to apply:

i the recipient must be a body not establishd or conducted for profit;

ii the Treasury must direct that the exemption shall apply in the particular case (the matters to be taken into account by the Treasury are set out in Sch. 6, para. 13 (3), (4));

iii the property must be within one or more of the following categories:

   a land which in the opinion of the Treasury is of outstanding scenic or historic or scientific interest;

   b a building in respect of which the Treasury consider that special steps should be taken for its preservation because of its outstanding historic or architectural or aesthetic interest, and the cost of preserving it;

   c land used as the grounds of a building within (*b*);

   d an object which is ordinarily kept in, and given with, a building within (*b*);

   e a picture, print, book, manuscript, work of art or scientific collection which in the opinion of the Treasury is of national or historic or scientific interest;

   f property of any nature given as a source of income for the upkeep of any of the foregoing.

Undertakings can be required as to the use, disposal, preservation and access to any of these items.

e *Charities* A charity is only within the exemption if it is established within the UK (TA 1970, s. 360 (3); FA 1975, s. 51 (1); *Camille and Henry Dreyfus Foundation Inc.* v. *I.R. Comrs.,* [1956] A.C. 39, H.L.).

f *Political parties* For the purpose of the exemption, the party in question must at the last general election before the death of the deceased have either:

   a had at least two members elected to the House of Commons; or *b*   had one member elected, and not less than 150,000 votes must have been given to members of the party who were candidates (Sch. 6, para. 11 (2)).

3   Limitations and conditions

The extent to which gifts to such persons and bodies is exempt, and the conditions which must be satisfied in order to obtain the exemptions, may be summarized as follows:

Beneficiary	Extent to which gift exempt	Sch. 6, para.	Standard Conditions (See below)
Spouse, where deceased and spouse both domiciled in UK	*a* No limit in amount	1(1)	B,C,H,I
	b Exemption only to extent that value transferred is attributable to property which becomes the property of the spouse		
Spouse, where deceased domiciled in UK, but spouse not domiciled	Extent to which valued transferred is attributable to property which becomes the property of the spouse, up to maximum of £50,000, less amount of any lifetime exempt transfers	1(2)	B,C,I
National Institutions	No limit	12	A,C,D,E,F,G,H,I
Body not established or conducted for profit	No limit	13	A,C,D,E,F,G,H,I and the property must be of a specified type
Other charities	£200,000	10	A,C,D,E,F,G,H,I
Policital parties	£100,000	11	A,C,D,E,F,G,H,I

4   Standard conditions

The standard conditions referred to in the table are:

    A   The beneficiary must become immediately entitled to the property, and the exemption does not apply if there is an intermediate gift (Sch. 6, para. 15 (1)). If the deceased gave £100,000 to be held for the benefit of his son for 10 years, and then for a charity, or £50,000 to a charity the gift to take effect 3 years after his death, the exemption cannot be claimed on his death, although, it could at the end of the 10 year or 3 year period. (But see FA 1976, s. 95 (3).)

B There must not be an intermediate gift of the type just described, but the exemption is not lost if the gift only takes effect if the spouse survives the deceased for a specified period, such as 28 days or 3 months (para. 15 (1)).

C If the gift is conditional, the condition must be satisfied within 12 months from the date of death (para. 15 (2)). If the condition is capable of being satisfied within that period, a "wait-and-see" approach is adopted to see whether it is in fact satisfied within that period. It is not essential that the will is worded in such a way that the condition must be satisfied, if at all, within the 12 month period.

D The gift must not be defeasible after 12 months have elapsed since the date of death, and it must not in fact have been defeated within that period of 12 months (para. 15 (3) (a), 4 (b)).

E In general, the deceased must have given his whole interest in the property (para. 15 (3) (b)). This does not mean that the deceased must have given the whole property, but rather that he must not have kept back any interest out of the interest which he himself had. Accordingly, if the deceased owned a freehold house, the gift will only be effective if he gave the freehold, and it will not be effective if he created a lease in favour of someone else, and gave the freehold subject to the lease to beneficiary. It will also not be effective if he reserved a lease to himself and gave the freehold subject to the lease (para. 15 (3) (bb), added by FA 1976, s. 95 (2)). If, however, he only had a lease of the house, and he gives that to the beneficiary, the gift comes within the exemption. If the deceased created an interest out of the property which he gives away, and that interest in fact comes to an end within 12 months from the date of death, the gift still comes within the exemption (para. (4) (a)).

F Neither the property which is the subject matter of the gift nor any part of it must be capable of becoming applicable for purposes which are not charitable or for purposes which are not those of one of the national institutions, bodies established for the public benefit, or political parties (para. 15 (3) (c)). This appears to mean that the property must not become so applicable *under the terms of the will.* If the deceased leaves

109

a house outright to a charity, and the charity sells it to a private individual, the gift is exempt even though the house itself has become applicable for non-charitable purposes. If, however, the deceased left the house to a charity for 50 years, and then for it to pass to his son, the exemption would not apply.

G   If the transfer was made after 15 April 1976, and the property given is an interest in possession in settled property, the settlement must come to an end on the making of that gift (para. 15 (3) (ba), added by FA 1976, s. 95 (2)).

H   If after 15 April 1976 a person or body acquired a reversionary interest in settled property for a consideration in money or money's worth, there is no exemption upon the termination of the interest on which the reversionary interest is expectant (para. 15 (4A)).

I   If the transfer is made after 9 March 1981 in consideration of the transfer of the reversionary interest, the transfer will, in general, not be exempt (FA 1981, s. 104).

L   RESTRICTIONS ON AVAILABILITY OF EXEMPTIONS

1   *Purpose of rules*

Some of the most complicated provisions of the capital transfer tax legislation modify the apparent effect of the exemptions just considered where, by virtue of the terms of the will, or of the intestacy rules, or a combination of the two, some beneficial interests are exempt and others are taxable. It will be appreciated that the effect that one gift is exempt from tax will alter the rate of tax suffered by other beneficiaries whose interests are not exempt. Suppose that a testator dies leaving an estate of £400,000 after the payment of debts and liabilities, but before tax; and that he leaves £150,000 to Andrew and £250,000 to Bernard. He directs Andrew and Bernard each to pay the tax out of their respective gifts. On an estate of £400,000 tax will be payable amounting to £194,000 (assuming that the testator made no chargeable transfers of value in his lifetime). Andrew would therefore suffer tax of £72,750 and Bernard tax of £121,250. If, however, the testator left £150,000 to Andrew, on the basis that Andrew pays the tax in respect of it, and £250,000 to the testator's widow, the chargeable value transferred is restricted to £150,000, and the tax payable is £44,500. On this example Andrew benefits because the remaining property is left to the widow rather than to Bernard. The provisions now to be considered:

a determine the amount of the value transferred on death which is chargeable;

b determine the extent to which a gift is exempt, having regard to other provisions in the will;

c where there is a limit as to the amount of an exemption, as in the case of gifts to non-domiciled spouses, and ordinary charities, determine how an excess over the limit is dealt with; and

d prescribe rules as to the manner in which the burden of the tax payable is to be borne by the various beneficiaries (Sch. 6, para. 16; FA 1976, s. 96 (2)).

2 *Deaths after 6 April 1976*

The rules now to be described relate to the position where the death occurred after 6 April 1976 (FA 1976, s. 96 (1)). The position where deaths occurred before that is generally similar, although there are alterations in details, which are not considered in this book.

3 *Gifts totally exempt; or totally non-exempt*

The rules apply only where the value which is treated as being transferred on death is, or might be, exempt as to part but not as to the whole. No adjustments are necessary to the apparent position where it is clear that either the value transferred is totally chargeable, or totally exempt.

4 *Categories of gift*

Where the rules do apply it is necessary first to place into categories the various beneficial interests.

a *Specific and residuary gifts* For the purposes of these rules where a person or body receives some benefit under a will or the intestacy rules, he is said to receive a "gift" (Sch. 6, para. 23 (1)).

Gifts, as to defined, are divided first into two categories, namely:

 i specific, and

 ii residuary.

All gifts which are not residuary are treated as specific for this purpose (para. 23 (1)) even if they would not be so treated for the purposes of the general law. So that where the deceased left a pecuniary legacy, that would be treated as a specific gift.

b *Gifts which do, and do not, bear their own tax* Gifts also have to be divided into those which do, and those which do not, bear their own tax. A gift is said to bear its own tax if the burden of that tax falls upon the recipient of the property, and is not payable out of the general residue of the estate.

The rules are:

i Freehold land, wherever situated, bears its own tax unless the will provides to the contrary. This is also the case in respect of other forms of "realty" (but this provision does not include leaseholds).

ii Property of any nature which is situated outside the UK bears its own tax, unless the will provides to the contrary.

iii Where property was jointly owned by the deceased and another, the deceased's share which devolves upon his co-owner bears its own tax, unless the will provides to the contrary.

iv Assets other than realty which are situated in the UK will only bear their own duty if the will so provides. Accordingly, if the deceased made any gift upon the basis that the beneficiary pays the tax in respect of it, that gift will bear its own tax (para. 23 (2)).

c *Possible situations* It will be appreciated that any case in which the rules apply will fall into one of the following three categories:

i There are specific gifts only, and no gifts of residue;

ii There are no specific gifts, and gifts of residue only; or

iii There are both specific and residuary gifts.

Different rules apply to each of these categories.

5 *Specific gifts only*

a *When arises* In practice, there will be specific gifts but no gifts of residue only where specific gifts were given of an amount greater than the value of the estate. In this case the gifts as given by the will abate according the general law (Sch. 6, para. 17). The rules as to abatement are described later (p. 117, *post*) and the abatement is made without taking into account any tax payable. Thus, if the deceased by his will left £50,000 to his son, and £200,000 to his wife, but on death he was worth only £200,000, the general law would proportionately reduce the legacies to £40,000 for the son and £160,000 for the wife. This is followed for capital transfer tax purposes.

b *Value attributable to gifts* The amount of the specific gifts as appears from the face of the will, subject to abatement where

112

necessary, is often not the same as the value which is treated as being transferred for capital transfer tax purposes. It is necessary to establish first the amount of the value attributable to each gift.

The value attributable to each gift is calculated as follows (Sch. 6, para. 19 (1), substituted by FA 1976, s. 96 (3)):

Circumstance	*Attributed value*
i Gift totally exempt	actual value
ii Gift partially but not totally exempt, and non-exempt part bears its own tax	actual value
iii Gift partially but not totally exempt, and non-exempt part does not bear its own tax	actual value of part exempt, together with grossed up equivalent of remainder
iv Gift totally non-exempt, bearing its own tax	actual value
v Gift totally non-exempt, not bearing its own tax	grossed up equivalent of actual value

c   *Grossing up*   Where the only gifts which are or might be taxable are specific gifts which do not bear their own tax, the grossed up equivalent value is:

i the value actually transferred by the specific gifts which do not bear their own tax; and

ii the amount of tax which would be chargeable if the value transferred was only equal to the value at i (Sch. 6, para. 19 (3), substituted by FA 1976, s. 96 (4)).

The effect of grossing up the values of specific gifts may lead to the result that the total of the value attributed to specific gifts exceeds the total actual value of the estate. In this case further abatement is necessary, and this is described below (p. 117, *post*).

The operation of these rules is illustrated below in conjunction with the effect of gifts of residue (p. 114, *post*).

6   *Gifts of residue only*

Where there are gifts of residue only, these gifts are treated as having their actual values (Sch. 6, para. 20). The total tax payable is therefore calculated by reference to the value of the non-exempt gifts of residue. Thus, if a testator leaves the whole of his property amounting to £200,000 to be divided equally between his wife and his son, the chargeable value transferred will be £100,000.

7   Combined specific and residuary gifts

a   Steps in computation   Where there are both specific gifts and gifts of residue it is necessary:

   i   to calculate "the assumed amount of tax";

   ii   to calculate "the assumed rate of tax";

   iii   to gross up those specific gifts or those parts of specific gifts where grossing up is necessary at the assumed rate of tax;

   iv   to calculate the total value attributable to specific gifts;

   v   to calculate the total value attributable to residuary gifts;

   vi   to calculate the actual rate of tax; and

   vii   to apply that rate to the chargeable value transferred.

b   "the assumed amount of tax"   In order to calculate the assumed amount of tax, it is necessary first to determine the value attributable to specific gifts which do not bear their own tax (Sch. 6, para. 19 (3B) (a) (i)). This value is calculated on the same basis as considered above, namely:

   i   the actual value of such specific gifts; together with

   ii   the amount of tax which would be payable if the only value transferred were represented by the value at i.

Thus, the value at i is grossed up at the ordinary death-time rates.

   The parts of the value transferred attributable to specific gifts and gifts of residue are then determined, with the value not attributable to specific gifts being attributable to residue (para. 20).

   Suppose, therefore, that a testator dies leaving an estate, after the payment of debts and liabilities, of £400,000; that he leaves £100,000 to his son, that legacy not bearing its own duty; and his residue to be divided equally between his widow and his daughter. Upon the assumption that the testator had made no chargeable transfers of value in his lifetime, the legacy of £100,000 would be grossed up at the ordinary death-time rates to £137,777. The total value attributable to residue is, therefore:

Actual value of estate	£400,000
less: value attributed to specific gift	£137,777
	£262,223

The daughter is regarded as taking a gift of £131,111.50 and the widow as taking a gift of £131,111.50.

The assumed amount of tax is the amount of tax which would be payable on the death-time scale on the chargeable value treated as being transferred (para. 19 (3B) (b)). This value is:

Value of son's legacy	£137,777.00
Value of daughter's share of residue	£131,111.50
	£268,888.50

Tax at death-time rates on £268,888.50 is £115,333. This is the "assumed amount of tax".

c *"the assumed rate of tax"* The assumed rate of tax is the rate found by dividing the assumed amount of tax by the chargeable value which is treated as transferred (para. 19 (3B) (a)). On the facts of the example, this is

$$\frac{£115,333.00}{£268,888.50} \times 100 = 42.89\%$$

d *Grossing up* The calculations of the assumed amount of tax and the chargeable value treated as transferred were made solely in order to ascertain the assumed rate of tax, which is the rate to be used for actual grossing up. It is now necessary to go back to the facts of the case and to gross up where necessary. To continue with the same example, the value attributed to the gifts is:

Gift	Calculation		Attributed value
Specific gift to son, not bearing own tax	£100,000 grossed up at 42.89%		£175,100
Total residue	Total estate	£400,000	
	less: specific gift	£175,100	£224,900
One half residue to daughter			£112,450
Total taxable estate	Specific gift	£175,100	
	residue	£112,450	£287,550

The tax applicable to £287,550 at the death-time rates is £126,530.

e *Actual rate of tax* The actual rate is found by dividing the actual amount of tax by the value attributed to the chargeable gifts. In the example this is:

$$\frac{£126,530}{£287,550} \times 100 = 44\%$$

115

f   Incidence of tax   The computation so far only determines the actual rate of tax. The actual amount of tax payable and the incidence of tax is described below, but first it is necessary to consider two further rules.

8   Exemption limits exceeded

In the case of gifts to non-domiciled spouses, ordinary charities and political parties, the gifts are exempt only up to the limits of £50,000, £100,000 or £200,000. Where there are gifts which exceed these limits, it is necessary to determine which gifts are exempt. Suppose, for example, that the deceased, who had not made any charitable gifts within the last year of his lifetime, left legacies of £100,000 to the RSPCA, and £150,000 to the NSPCC. In this case:

  i   if one or more gifts bears its own tax, and one or more gifts does not bear its own tax, the excess above the exemption limit (in this case £200,000) is attributed to the gift or gifts which do not bear their own tax, before being attributed to the gift or gifts which do bear their own tax (para. 19 (2) (a)).

  ii   subject to this, the excess over the exemption limit is attributed to the various gifts proportionately to their values (para. 19 (2) (b)).

If, therefore, in the example just considered, the gift to the NSPCC does not bear its own tax but the gift to the RSPCA does, the determination is:

Total value of gifts to ordinary charities:

RSPCA	£100,000
NSPCC	£150,000
	£250,000
Exempt up to	£200,000
	£50,000

The excess over the limit, namely £50,000, is attributed to the NSPCC gift (which does not bear its own tax). The gift to the RSPCA is therefore treated as being a specific gift totally exempt, and the gift to the NSPCC is treated as being a specific gift exempt up to £100,000, and non-exempt for the remaining £50,000.

If, however, both gifts did not bear their own tax, the excess over the limit, £50,000, would be attributed:

as to $\quad £50,000 \times \dfrac{£100,000}{£250,000} = £20,000$ to the RSPCA,

and as to $£50,000 \times \dfrac{£150,000}{£250,000} = £30,000$ to the NSPCC.

The gift to the RSPCA would therefore be exempt up to £80,000 and non-exempt as to the remaining £20,000; and the gift to the NSPCC would be exempt up to £120,000 and non-exempt as to the remaining £30,000.

9 Abatement of tax

The effect of grossing up the values of specific gifts may lead to the total attributed value being in excess of the total actual value of the estate. In this case the attributed values are treated as abating to the total actual value of the estate (para. 18). The rules as to abatement prescribed by the general law, and which are followed here, are:

i If the deceased indicated in his will the order in which legacies should abate, that indication will be followed (*Sayer* v. *Sayer* (1714), Prec. Ch. 392).

ii If there is no indication, legacies abate in the following order:

    a residue;

    b general and pecuniary legacies, and demonstrative legacies to the extent that the specified property is not sufficient to answer them;

    c specific legacies, and demonstrative legacies to the extent that the specified property is sufficient to answer them.

iii Within each class the deceased may have indicated how the legacies should abate between themselves, and, if so, that will be binding (*A.-G.* v. *Robins* (1722), 2 P. Wms. 23).

iv If there is no indication of this nature, the legacies abate rateably between them (*Clifton* v. *Burt* (1720), 1 P. Wms. 678).

For the purposes of this order of abatement, the concept of gifts of residue, and of specific legacies, are those applicable for the purposes of the general law, and *not* the special meanings which were given earlier (p. 111, *ante*).

10 Incidence of tax

In general, a testator can direct in his will how tax is to be suffered by the beneficiaries. For example, he can direct that a gift which would not otherwise bear its own tax shall bear its own tax. However, there are two statutory rules which will apply even if the will contains contrary directions. These are (Sch. 6, para. 22, substituted by FA 1976, s. 96 (5)):

a to the extent that a specific gift is exempt, no tax shall fall on it; and

b to the extent that a gift of residue is exempt, the whole of the tax payable in respect of residue shall fall upon the remainder of the residue.

To revert to the example considered previously (p. 115, *ante*), the distribution of the estate will be:

Gift		Net benefit	Tax
Specific legacy to son		£100,000	
Tax thereon, calculated at 44% on the attributed value of £175,000			£77,044
Residue:			
Estate	£400,000		
less: specific gift	£100,000		
	£300,000		
less: tax thereon	£77,044		
net residue	£222,956		
One half residue to daughter	£111,478		
less: tax thereon at at 44%		£162,476	£49,052
One half residue to widow		£111,478	nil
		£273,904	£126,096

The operation of these rules leads to confusion because the same gift is treated as having different values at different stages in the calculation. Thus, the gift to the daughter is valued at £131,111.50 in calculating the assumed amount of tax (p. 114); at £112,450 in calculating the actual rate of tax (p. 115); and at £111,478 in calculating the actual amount of tax payable in respect of it (*supra*). It is, however, important to remember that the value of a gift determined for an earlier stage in the calculation has no significance whatever for the final stage.

M   DEDUCTION OF LIABILITIES

The preceding pages of this chapter have been concerned with two main topics, namely, the assets which the deceased owned at the date of his death and the value at which they are to be brought into account (pp. 84 to 95), and the exemptions from tax which might apply having regard to the nature of the property (pp. 95 to 104), the cause of death (p. 104) and the identity of the beneficiary (pp. 105 to 118). The next step is to deduct liabilities which were outstanding at the date of death. While it has been convenient to consider all exemptions together, strictly liabilities are deducted before the exemptions conferred by virtue of the identity of the beneficiary are applied.

The rules as to liabilities are comparatively straightforward.

1   Secured liabilities

Where a debt or liability is secured on an asset, the debt or liability is treated as reducing the value of that asset (FA 1975, Sch, 10, para. 2). If, therefore, agricultural land is mortgaged, the agricultural property relief, if it is available, will be restricted to the net value of the land after deducting the amount outstanding under the mortgage. If the amount of the debt exceeds the value of the asset on which it is secured, the value of the asset itself is treated as being reduced to nil, and the excess ranks as an unsecured debt.

If the debt is secured on more than one asset, the legislation is silent but it seems that the general law as to secured debts will be followed, so that

a   if one asset is charged by way of primary security, and another by way of collateral security, the debt is regarded so far as possible as being charged against the primary security; and

b   if both assets are charged by way of primary security, the debt is regarded as reducing the value of the two assets proportionately.

2   Unsecured liabilities

In general, all unsecured liabilities are taken into account at their value at the date of death, and they reduce the net value treated as being transferred by the deceased accordingly (Sch. 10, para. 1 (1)).

3   Liabilities incurred without consideration

Every liability which was imposed by law can be taken into account (para. 1 (3)). Apart from this, liabilities, whether secured or unsecured, which were incurred by the deceased are to be taken into

119

account only to the extent that they were incurred for a consideration in money or money's worth (*ibid*).

If the deceased acquired an asset subject to a debt or liability, that debt or liability can be taken into account even if it was not originally incurred for a consideration in money or money's worth (*ibid*).

4 Liabilities with right of re-imbursement

Where there is a liability of the deceased's estate, and a corresponding right of re-imbursement or indemnity, the liability can only be deducted if the personal representatives can show that re-imbursement cannot reasonably be expected to be obtained (para. 1 (5)).

5 Future liabilities

Where the deceased was under an obligation to discharge a debt or liability at some time after the date of his death, that debt or liability is valued as at the date of death and is brought into account only at that figure (para. 1 (4)).

6 Foreign liabilities

Where there is a debt or liability due to a person who is resident abroad the rules so far described apply if either the debt or liability was secured on property in the UK or is to be discharged within the UK (para. 3). In other cases, the amount of the debt or liability reduces the value of the deceased's assets outside the UK (*ibid*).

N DEDUCTION OF EXPENSES

1 Generally

The general rule is that any expenses which are incurred after the date of death, whether in the course of the administration of the estate or not, are not deductible in the calculation of the capital transfer tax payable by virtue of the death. To this rule there are two exceptions.

2 Funeral expenses

The amount of reasonable funeral expenses may be deducted (para. 9 (1) (b)) and it is not necessary in calculating these expenses to take account of any death grant paid. The cost of a tombstone is not deductible.

3 Expenses in respect of foreign property

An allowance may be claimed against the value of property situated outside the United Kingdom in respect of such of the

120

expenses which are incurred in administering or realising the property as are attributable to the situation of the property (para. 9 (1) (d)). This allowance is equivalent to the total of such expenses, up to a maximum of 5% of the value of the property itself.

O OBLIGATIONS AFFECTING THE PROPERTY

The deceased may in his lifetime have granted an option in favour of someone else to purchase property at a specified price, or may have restricted his rights of disposal in some other way, such as by the grant of a pre-emptive right. In such circumstances, the restriction on the right of disposal is generally ignored in determining the value of the property on death, and this is so whether the right was created before or after the introduction of capital transfer tax (para. 5 (1), (2)). If, however, the deceased received money or money's worth as consideration for the grant of the right, the existence of the right is taken into account to that extent (*ibid*).

Suppose that when his house was worth £50,000 the deceased granted to someone else for £10,000 an option to purchase the house for £40,000. Suppose also that the option is not exercised until after the death of the deceased, by which time the house is worth £75,000. The Revenue view is that because the option was granted for full consideration, the restriction is taken into account to its full extent, so that the value of the house on the deceased's death is limited to £40,000.

P SETTLED PROPERTY IN WHICH DECEASED HAD INTEREST IN POSSESSION

1 *Introduction*

It will have been seen (p. 83, *ante*) that in addition to property which the deceased owned outright at the date of his death, capital transfer tax is also payable in respect of certain settled property.

2 *Deceased having an interest in possession*

A person who is beneficially entitled to an interest in possession (defined, p. 288, *post*) in settled property is treated as being beneficially entitled to that property itself (Sch. 5, para. 3 (1)). Accordingly, it is to be taken into account in calculating the value of his estate on death (s. 22 (1); 23 (1)). Where this provision applies, the property subject to the trust is valued at the date of the deceased's death. To this general rule, there are a number of exceptions, (*infra*).

3 Deceased as discretionary beneficiary

Where the deceased did not have an interest in possession in settled property, but was the beneficiary under a discretionary trust, no part of the trust fund is brought into account. This is so even if until his death the deceased was receiving income or capital from the trust.

4 Exceptions

Even where the deceased did have an interest in possession in settled property until his death, there are certain circumstances in which that property does not have to be brought into account.

a Interest reverting to settlor Where the deceased was entitled to an interest in possession, and on his death the settled property reverted to the settlor, then provided the settlor himself was still alive at the date of death of the deceased, in general the settled property is exempt from tax on the deceased's death (FA 1975, s. 22 (2)). This does not apply, however, if the settlor himself acquired a reversionary interest in the property for money or money's worth (*ibid*); or where a reversionary interest was transferred into a settlement after 9 March 1981 (FA 1981, s. 104).

b Settlor's spouse becoming entitled Where the deceased was entitled to an interest in possession and on his death the settlor's spouse became entitled to the settled property itself, the general rule is that the settled property is exempt from tax on the deceased's death (s. 22 (3)). This exemption applies where the settlor's spouse became entitled to the settled property itself, and also where she became entitled to a further interest in possession in it. Further, the exemption only applies where two conditions are satisfied. These are:

i the spouse must have been domiciled in some part of the UK at the date of the deceased's death, and resident for income tax purposes in the year of assessment in which the death occurred; and

ii neither the settlor nor his spouse must have acquired any reversionary interest in the property for a consideration in money or money's worth.

This provision also applies where the settlor's widow or widower becomes entitled on the death of the deceased if the deceased died before 1 April 1977 or if the settlor died less than two years before the death of the deceased (FA 1976, s. 110 (1)).

The provision does not apply where the application of it depends on the transfer of a reversionary interest into the settlement after 9 March 1981 (FA 1981, s. 104).

c. Death of spouse before 13 November 1974 When estate duty was in force, s. 5 (2) of the Finance Act 1894, provided that if the first spouse to die left property upon trust for the surviving spouse for her life, in such a manner that the surviving spouse had no power of disposition over the capital, then while estate duty was payable normally on the death of the first spouse to die, the settled property was entirely free of duty on the death of the second spouse. The principle applied also where the surviving spouse's interest arose under the intestacy rules, or under the Family Provision legislation, and also where no duty was in fact paid on the death of the first spouse because the size of the estate was sufficiently small. Where the first spouse died before 13 November 1974, then if under the estate duty rules the surviving spouse exemption would have applied to the settled property on the death of the surviving spouse, the property will be exempt from capital transfer tax on the death of the surviving spouse (s. 22 (4)).

Q GIFTS BEFORE 27 MARCH 1974

1 Charge to tax

The two main categories of property on which capital transfer tax is payable by virtue of the death of the deceased, namely property which he owned outright, and settled property in which the deceased had an interest in possession, have already been considered. As a result of the transition from estate duty to capital transfer tax, it is also necessary to consider certain gifts made by the deceased before 27 March 1974, and certain interests in settled property which the deceased had, and which came to an end before that date (p. 126, *post*).

2 Amount to be brought into account

Where the deceased made a gift before 27 March 1974 but within seven years from the date of his death, it is necessary to bring into account that gift for capital transfer tax purposes when he dies. This does not apply if the gift would have been exempt from estate duty (FA 1975, s. 22 (5); Sch. 6, para. 14). The rules are:

a if the gift was made in cash, the amount to be brought into account is the amount of that cash (FA 1957, s. 38; FA 1975, s. 22 (5));

  b if the gift was of an asset, which the donee retains until the
       death of the donor, the amount to be brought into account is
       the value of that asset as at the date of death of the deceased. If
       the gift was of shares or debentures, the value of any bonus
       shares or debentures is also to be brought into account, subject
       to a deduction for any subscription price paid by the donee
       (FA 1957, s. 38 (4), (5), (6));

  c if the gift was of an asset, but the donee does not retain it
       until the death of the deceased:

    i if the donee sold it for full value, the proceeds of sale are to
       be brought into account (FA 1957, s. 38 (1) (2));

    ii if the donee exchanged it for full value, the value of the
       property which he received in exchange, ascertained as at
       the death of the deceased, is to be brought into account
       (*ibid*);

   iii if the donee disposed of the asset by way of gift, the amount
       to be brought into account is the value of the asset ascer-
       tained as at the date when the donee disposed of it (FA
       1957, s. 38 (2), (3));

  d where the gift was made more than four years before the death
       of the deceased, a taper relief would have applied for estate
       duty, and this relief is applied also for capital transfer tax
       purposes (FA 1975, s. 22 (5)). This relief is obtained by
       bringing into account only a percentage of the value ascer-
       tained by rules *a, b* or *c* according to the following table (FA
       1968, s. 35):

Deceased dying	*Percentage of value to be brought into account*
more than 4 but less than 5 years from gift	85
more than 5 but less than 6 years from gift	70
more than 6 but less than 7 years from gift	40

3 *Agricultural and industrial property*

Where the gift was of, or included, agricultural property, or
industrial plant or property, then if certain conditions were satisfied
a reduction would have been allowed in the rate of estate duty
payable in respect of that property (FA 1926, s. 23; FA 1954, s. 28).
A corresponding reduction is given in the rate of capital transfer tax,
by charging tax on the agricultural or industrial property at a rate
calculated according to the following formula (FA 1975, s. 22 (6)):

$$55 \times \frac{\text{Amount of tax which would be chargeable on the whole value of the deceased's estate if no relief were given}}{\text{the whole value of the deceased's estate}}$$

Both the numerator and denominator of the fraction include the full value of the agricultural or industrial property.

4 Gifts made more than 7 years before death

For estate duty purposes, a gift which was made more than seven years before the death of the deceased was nevertheless dutiable if the deceased was not excluded from all benefit and enjoyment from the gifted property during the last seven years of his lifetime (FA, 1894, s. 2 (1) (c)). There is no corresponding provision for capital transfer tax purposes, so that if the gift was made more than seven years before his death, there will be no tax liability in respect of that property even if he continued to enjoy it up to the moment of his death.

5 Gifts to spouses

Estate duty as such continued to be chargeable in respect of the estates of persons dying before 13 March 1975, but in respect of deaths after 12 November 1974 and before 13 March 1975 according to rules which for the most part approximated to the capital transfer tax rules. Under these transitional rules a gift between one spouse and another was exempt to the same extent as for capital transfer tax. This has one unexpected result. If a person made a substantial gift in the last seven years of his lifetime to his spouse, estate duty in its final form would not have been payable in respect of it because of this exemption. Accordingly, gifts made between spouses even before 12 November 1974 will not have to be brought into account provided that they satisfy the ordinary capital transfer tax rules relating to gifts between spouses (FA 1975, Sch. 6, para. 1).

6 Non-aggregable life assurance policies

For estate duty purposes, a special rule was adopted where a life policy was effected by the deceased, but the deceased did not at any time have an interest in the policy. Under this rule if the value of all such policies did not exceed £25,000, the policies were treated as an estate by themselves and were exempt from aggregation with the remainder of the deceased's estate. If the value did exceed £25,000, a fraction of the value was exempt from aggregation, namely £25,000 divided by the total value of the policies. This special rule only applied to policies effected before 20 March 1968 (FA 1894, s. 4; FA 1968, s. 38; FA 1969, s. 40 (2) (c)).

Corresponding provisions are included for capital transfer tax purposes in respect of policies effected before 20 March 1968 which are given away prior to 27 March 1974. Accordingly, if the total value does not exceed £25,000, tax is chargeable as if a separate deceased had died leaving assets with an estate equal to the value of the policies, and had made no previous chargeable transfers (FA 1975, s. 22 (7)). If the aggregate value does exceed £25,000, a proportion is included in the value of the deceased's actual estate (*ibid*).

R INTERESTS IN SETTLED PROPERTY PRIOR TO 27 MARCH 1974

The last category of property which may have to be brought into account consists of certain settled property in which the deceased had an interest in possession before, but not after, 27 March 1974.

1 Entitlement within 7 years from death

Where at any time during the last seven years of his lifetime the deceased had a beneficial interest in possession in settled property, estate duty would have been payable on the value of the property in which that interest subsisted (FA 1894, s. 2 (1) (b)). Where estate duty would have been payable as a result of the deceased having had such an interest before, but at no time after, 27 March 1974, capital transfer tax will be payable according to special rules (FA 1975, s. 22 (5) (b)).

2 Amount to be brought into account

The value to be brought into is, generally:

a   if the settlement continues until the death of the deceased, the value of the property comprised in the settlement ascertained at the date of death of the deceased, or of that part of it in which the interest subsisted (FA 1957, s. 38 (12)). There is excluded any further property added to the settlement after the deceased's interest determined; and there is included the value of bonus shares or debentures;

b   if the settlement came to an end before the death of the deceased, the value is to be taken as at the date of determination of the settlement. There is, however, excluded any of the settled property to which the deceased became absolutely entitled on the determination of the settlement (FA 1957, s. 38 (12), proviso).

3 Earlier entitlement

Estate duty was also chargeable where the deceased ceased to have an interest in possession more than seven years before his death, but was not entirely excluded from possession and enjoyment of the settled property during the last seven years of his lifetime (FA 1894, s. 2 (1) (b) (ii)). There is no corresponding charge to capital transfer tax.

4   Interest under discretionary trusts

Where the deceased did not have an interest in possession in settled property, but was a beneficiary under a discretionary trust, then estate duty was chargeable, broadly, if he derived any benefit from the settled property during the last seven years of his lifetime (FA 1894, s. 2 (1) (b) (ii)). There is no similar provision for capital transfer tax, so that there will be no liability to tax even if the deceased did receive benefits from a discretionary trust during the last seven years of his lifetime, before 27 March 1974.

S   THE TAX PAYABLE

1   The principle of aggregation

In order to determine the amount of capital transfer tax payable by virtue of the death, there is aggregated:

a   the value of assets owned by the deceased outright, after deducting from that value:

   i   the value of assets which by their nature are exempt, (p. 96, *ante*);

   ii   the value attributable to other exemptions (p. 104, *ante*);

   iii   liabilities (p. 113, *ante*); and

   iv   to the extent allowable, the reduction in value attributable to restrictions on the right of disposition (p. 119, *ante*);

b   the value of settled property in which the deceased had an interest in possession at the date of his death (p. 121, *ante*);

c   the value of taxable gifts made by the deceased before 27 March 1974 (p. 123, *ante*); and

d   the value of certain settled property in which the deceased had an interest in possession before, but not after, 27 March 1974 (p. 126, *ante*).

The aggregate of these items is then applied to the death-time scale of rates.

2   The death-time scale of rates

The death-time scale of rates of tax is (FA 1980, Sch. 14):

Part II: Capital Transfer Tax Liability on Death

	"Slice" of value	Total at top of slice	Rate on slice	Tax on slice	Total tax at top of slice
First	£50,000	£50,000	nil	nil	nil
Next	£10,000	£60,000	30%	£3,000	£3,000
Next	£10,000	£70,000	35%	£3,500	£6,500
Next	£10,000	£80,000	40%	£4,000	£10,500
Next	£10,000	£90,000	40%	£4,000	£14,500
Next	£10,000	£100,000	45%	£4,500	£19,000
Next	£10,000	£110,000	45%	£4,500	£23,500
Next	£10,000	£120,000	50%	£5,000	£28,500
Next	£10,000	£130,000	50%	£5,000	£33,500
Next	£10,000	£140,000	55%	£5,500	£39,000
Next	£10,000	£150,000	55%	£5,500	£44,500
Next	£10,000	£160,000	55%	£5,500	£50,000
Next	£10,000	£170,000	60%	£6,000	£56,000
Next	£10,000	£180,000	60%	£6,000	£62,000
Next	£10,000	£190,000	60%	£6,000	£68,000
Next	£10,000	£200,000	60%	£6,000	£74,000
Next	£25,000	£225,000	60%	£15,000	£89,000
Next	£25,000	£250,000	60%	£15,000	£104,000
Next	£25,000	£275,000	60%	£15,000	£119,000
Next	£25,000	£300,000	60%	£15,000	£134,000
Next	£25,000	£325,000	60%	£15,000	£149,000
Next	£25,000	£350,000	60%	£15,000	£164,000
Next	£25,000	£375,000	60%	£15,000	£179,000
Next	£25,000	£400,000	60%	£15,000	£194,000
Next	£25,000	£425,000	60%	£15,000	£209,000
Next	£25,000	£450,000	60%	£15,000	£224,000
Next	£25,000	£475,000	60%	£15,000	£239,000
Next	£25,000	£500,000	60%	£15,000	£254,000
Next	£10,000	£510,000	60%	£6,000	£260,000
Next	£40,000	£550,000	65%	£26,000	£286,000
Next	£50,000	£600,000	65%	£32,500	£318,500
Next	£50,000	£650,000	65%	£32,500	£351,000
Next	£50,000	£700,000	65%	£32,500	£383,500
Next	£50,000	£750,000	65%	£32,500	£416,000
Next	£50,000	£800,000	65%	£32,500	£448,500
Next	£50,000	£850,000	65%	£32,500	£481,000
Next	£50,000	£900,000	65%	£32,500	£513,500
Next	£50,000	£950,000	65%	£32,500	£546,000
Next	£50,000	£1,000,000	65%	£32,500	£578,500
Next	£10,000	£1,010,000	65%	£6,500	£585,000
Next	£240,000	£1,250,000	70%	£168,000	£753,000
Next	£250,000	£1,500,000	70%	£175,000	£928,000
Next	£250,000	£1,750,000	70%	£175,000	£1,103,000
Next	£250,000	£2,000,000	70%	£175,000	£1,278,000
Next	£10,000	£2,010,000	70%	£7,000	£1,285,000
In excess of		£2,010,000	75%		

128

3 *Applying the table*

The table is used by:

a taking the aggregate value of all taxable gifts made by the deceased in his lifetime the 10 years prior to his death (FA 1981, s. 93);

b adding the aggregate value of the property taxable on his death (p. 127, *ante*);

c determining from the table the amount of tax which would be payable on the combined total of *a* and *b*;

d subtracting the amount of tax which would be payable according to the death-time table on the amount at *a*. It is important that the amount of tax which would be payable according to this table is deducted, even although the gifts were lifetime gifts, and even although they may in fact have been taxable at the lifetime rates.

These principles can be illustrated by a simple example. During his lifetime, Howard made taxable gifts of £30,000 and £50,000 (after taking into account available exemptions) and the recipients paid the tax on them. When Howard dies, he owns assets which, after deducting liabilities, are to be brought into account at a total of £220,000. The amount of tax payable on Howard's death is:

Taxable gifts made in his lifetime	£80,000
Net value brought into account on death	£220,000
	£300,000
Amount of tax payable on death-time scale applicable to £300,000	£134,000
Less: amount of tax payable on death-time scale applicable to £80,000	£10,500
Tax actually payable	£123,500

This procedure can be followed even if the lifetime transfers were made prior to 10 March 1981 when different rates applied. For any case the deduction of the amount payable on the death–time scale in respect of lifetime transfers will not be equal to the amount of tax actually paid.

T APPORTIONING THE TAX

In certain circumstances, it is necessary to apportion the actual amount of tax payable. These circumstances are where the responsibility for payment or the ultimate burden falls upon different persons. In these cases, the tax is apportioned according to the respective values brought into account to tax. Suppose that John was at the date of his death entitled to an interest in possession in settled property, worth £100,000. Suppose also that at the date of his death, John's assets consisted of his freehold house, worth £75,000, subject to a mortgage of £35,000, which he left to his nephew; and other assets, worth, after the deduction of other liabilities, £150,000, which he left to his niece. It has been seen that if there is no provision to the contrary in the will, the freehold property will bear its own tax.

The computation is:

a	Taxable gifts made by John in his lifetime			nil
b	Values to be brought into account on John's death:			
	i Own assets			
	(a) House	£75,000		
	less: mortgage	£35,000	£40,000	
	(b) Other assets		£150,000	
	ii Settled property		£100,000	£290,000
				£290,000
c	Tax payable according to death-time scale on aggregate of £290,000			£128,000
d	Tax payable according to death-time scale on lifetime taxable gifts			nil
	Tax actually payable			£128,000

This is now apportioned as follows:

i John's own assets:

(a) House, net:

$$\frac{£40,000}{£290,000} \times £128,000 = £17,655$$

(b) Other assets, net:

$$\frac{£150,000}{£290,000} \times £128,000 = £66,207$$

ii Settled property:

$$\frac{£100,000}{£290,000} \times £128,000 = £44,138$$

£128,000

U QUICK SUCCESSION RELIEF

If the deceased's estate was increased by a chargeable transfer made to him in the five years before his death, quick succession relief is available (FA 1981, s. 101). The previous chargeable transfer may have been in lifetime or on death.

In order to calculate the relief it is necessary first to ascertain:

a   the net benefit to the deceased from the previous transfer to the extent that it was chargeable. There is only taken into account the amount of the previous transfer which was chargeable. If, therefore, a transfer of £10,000, was made to the deceased, but £3,000 was exempt under the annual allowance, the net benefit would be £7,000. If the deceased paid the tax on that transfer, the amount of tax is deducted from the net benefit.

b   the value transferred by the previous transfer. This is the net benefit to the deceased, together with the amount of tax paid by the transferor in respect of that transfer.

c   the tax paid in respect of the previous transfer.

A reduction is then made from the tax payable on the death of the deceased. This reduction is of a percentage of the tax paid in respect of the previous transfer. The relevant percentage is:

Time of previous transfer	*Percentage*
Not more than 1 year before death	100
More than 1 year but not more than 2 years before death	80
More than 2 years but not more than 3 years before death	60
More than 3 years but not more than 4 years before death	40
More than 4 years but not more than 5 years before death	20

The actual reduction is found by applying the following formula, in which the symbols *a, b* and *c* refer to the paragraphs so lettered above:

$$\text{Relevant percentage} \times \frac{a}{b} \times c$$

Suppose, therefore, that after 9 March 1981 a person who had not made any previous chargeable transfers gave to the deceased £60,000 and paid the tax on that transfer. Suppose also that the deceased died 18 months later. The net benefit to the deceased from that transfer to the extent that it was chargeable was:

Transfer	£60,000
less: annual allowance	£3,000
	£57,000
Tax paid by deceased	nil
Net benefit	£57,000

The value transferred by the previous transfer and the tax paid on it was:

net chargeable transfer	£57,000
tax paid on £58,235	
(the grossed up equivalent	
of £57,000) at life-	
time rates	£1,235
	£58,235

The amount of the relief on the death of the deceased is, therefore:

$$\frac{80}{100} \times \frac{£57,000}{£58,000} \times £1,235 = £967$$

Accordingly, the amount of tax which would otherwise be payable on the death of the deceased is reduced by £967.

The principle applies to successive charges in respect of settled property (see p. 307, *post*). Where that relief has been claimed, it may reduce the relief available on death (FA 1981, s. 101).

Where the deceased died before 10 March 1981, a similar relief was available (see FA 1975, s. 30).

V PAYMENT OF TAX

1 Due date of payment

Capital transfer tax payable as a result of death is payable at the end of six months after the end of the month in which the death occurred (FA 1975, Sch. 4, para. 12 (1)). Unless the tax can be paid by instalments (*infra*) the whole amount of the tax is payable in one lump sum.

2 Payment of instalments

The tax which is payable in respect of certain classes of property can be paid by eight yearly, or sixteen half-yearly instalments (Sch. 4, para. 13). The first instalment, whether the tax is to be paid by yearly or half-yearly instalments, is due at the end of six months after the end of the month on which the death occurred (para. 13 (1)).

The classes of property in respect of which tax can be paid by instalments are:

a   Land, whether freehold or leasehold, and whether situated in the United Kingdom or abroad (para. 13 (1) (a));

b   Shares or securities of a company which gave the deceased control of the company immediately before his death (para. 13 (1) (b)). The deceased is regarded as having had control if the rights attaching to the shares or securities which he owned would have given him voting control in respect of all matters (para. 13 (7)). If the deceased's own holding was not sufficient to give him control, he will nevertheless be treated as having had control if his spouse's holding, when added to his own holding, would have given control (para. 13 (7) (a)). Further, if he had an interest in possession in settled property, he may add the rights attaching to shares or securities subject to that settlement to determine control (para. 13 (7) (b)).

Special rules apply where there are special classes of shares, and shares carry the right to vote on matters affecting that class, or an winding up (para. 13 (7) (c)).

The instalment option under this heading is available whether the shares or securities are unquoted or quoted;

c   Other unquoted shares or securities, if:

    i the tax on such shares or securities, together with the tax payable on all other property in respect of which the instalment option can be claimed (except under *e* below) is not less than 20% of the total tax for which the person paying the tax is liable in the same capacity (para. 13 (1) (c), (2)); or

    ii the Revenue is satisfied that the tax on such shares or securities cannot be paid in one lump sum without undue hardship (para. 13 (1) (c));

d   Unquoted shares in other circumstances.

    The instalment option is also available in respect of:

    i (a) unquoted shares, irrespective of dividend rights, which have a nominal value of at least 10% of all the shares in the company at the time of death (para. 13 (1) (d); (3) (a)); and

      (b) unquoted ordinary shares, or other shares which carry rights to dividends which are not restricted to dividends at a flat rate, and which have a nominal value of at least 10% of all the shares in the company at the time of death (para. 13 (1) (d); (3) (b); (8) (a)); and

    ii the market value of the shares at the time of death exceeded £5,000 (para. 13 (3)).

For the purposes of i (b), shares which are not ordinary shares, but which can be converted into ordinary shares, as so defined, are treated as ordinary shares (para. 13 (8) (b)), but loan stock and debentures can never come within this heading;

133

e   The net value of a business, or an interest in a business.

The business must be carried on with a view to the realisation of a gain, but the expression includes a profession or vocation (para. 14 (6)). The instalment option under this head is available if the business was that of the deceased alone, or, where he was in partnership, to his interest in the partnership (para. 14 (1)).

3   Balance of tax becoming payable

Where the instalment option has been claimed, the outstanding balance of tax may be paid at any time. If the asset in respect of which the option has been claimed is sold before the expiration of the 8 year period, the outstanding balance must be paid (para. 13 (4); 14 (3)). If the asset is sold within 6 months from the date of death, the date upon which the tax is due is the end of the period of six months following the end of the month in which the death occurred. In other cases, the date upon which the tax is due is the date of sale.

4   Interest

a   Generally   Interest is payable at the rate of 9% p.a. on any tax which is not paid by the due date, from the due date until the date of actual payment (para. 19 (1); Capital Transfer Tax (Interest on Unpaid Tax) Order 1979, S.I. 1979 No. 1688).

No income tax relief is available for payment of interest on overdue tax (para. 19 (4)).

b   Tax payable by instalments   Where the instalment option is exercised, in some cases interest is chargeable on the total amount of tax payable from the due date upon which the tax would have been payable if the instalment had not been exercised. In other cases, interest is only payable on each instalment from the due date for payment of that instalment.

i Interest payable on total tax outstanding.

In the following situations, interest is payable on the full amount of tax outstanding:

(a)   land, except (i) land which is an asset of a business (para. 16 (1) (a)) (other then a business included within (b)); or (ii) agricultural land to which either the 20% or 50% relief applies (FA 1981, s. 96 (2)).

(b)   shares or securities in companies which are share or land dealing companies or investment or holding companies (para.

16 (2); (3) (a)). This provision does not, however, include shares or securities in companies which are holding companies of shares in other companies which are not share or land dealing companies (para. 16 (3) (b)); nor to shares or securities in stock-jobbing companies or to companies carrying on the business of a discount house (para. 16 (3) (c));

(c) where the death occurred before 10 March 1981 any assets in respect of which the instalment option has been claimed in excess of an aggregate value of £250,000 (para. 16 (5)). There is no limit in the case of a death after 9 March 1981 (FA 1981, s. 95).

ii. Interest payable only on instalments.

The converse to these rules is that interest is only payable on instalments from the due date of the instalment in respect of:

(a) agricultural land to which the 20% or 50% relief applies;

(b) shares or securities in operating companies other than, generally, share or land dealing companies, or investment companies;

(c) shares or securities in holding companies, other than companies which hold shares in share or land dealing companies, or investment companies;

(d) shares or securities in stock-jobbing or discount house companies;

(e) businesses, or interests in businesses, including land which is used in the business.

W ACCOUNTABILITY

The persons who are accountable to the Revenue for tax payable on death are:

Property	Accountable person(s)	Remarks	Authority
a Assets owned outright by the deceased	i Personal representatives		s. 25 (5) (a)
		Liability limited to assets which they received, or would have received, as personal representative	s. 27 (1) (a)

135

	ii Executors de son tort	Liability limited to assets in their hands	s. 25 (6) (a)
	iii Beneficiary under the will or person entitled on intestacy in whom the property becomes vested at any time after the death	Liability limited to the property so vested	s. 25 (5) (c)
	iv A purchaser of the property, if an Inland Revenue charge is registered	Liability limited to the property	s. 26 (1)
	v Any person who becomes entitled to an interest in possession in the property at any time after the death	Liability limited to the property. Liability excluded if entitlement conferred by purchase, and no Inland Revenue charge registered	s. 25 (5) (c) s. 26 (1)
b land subject to a settlement until the death of the deceased, and which devolves upon the personal representatives	i As in the case of assets owned by the deceased outright		s. 25 (5) (a)
c Settled property generally in which the deceased had an interest in possession at the date of his death	i The Trustees of the Settlement		s. 25 (5) (b)
		Liability limited to assets which they received or could have received as trustees of the settlement	s. 27 (2)
	ii as *a* iii above		
	iii as *a* iv above		
	iv as *a* v above		

d Property given by the deceased prior to 27 March 1974	i The donee	s. 25 (7)
e Settled property in which deceased had an interest in possession before but not after 27 March 1974	as *c* above	

A nominee will not be liable as executor de son tort merely by receiving money or other assets. In *I. R. Comrs.* v. *Stype Investments (Jersey) Ltd.*, [1981] Simon's Tax Intelligence 151, Sir Charles Clore had transferred a landed estate to a Jersey company as nominee for him. The company sold the estate, and received the proceeds of sale in Jersey. It was held that merely by so doing, it had not made itself accountable to the Revenue as an executor de son tort.

X CERTIFICATES OF DISCHARGE

Two types of certificate of discharge are issued.

1 *Certificates of discharge of specific property*

Any person who is liable for the tax in respect of a specific item of property as a result of death may obtain a certificate from the Board of Inland Revenue that that tax has been, or will be, paid (FA 1975), Sch. 4, para. 25 (1)). Unless the certificate has been obtained by fraud, or non-disclosure of material facts, the certificate discharges the property from an Inland Revenue charge on its acquisition by a purchaser (para. 25 (3) (a)).

Application for such a certificate is made by letter sent to the Capital Taxes Office.

2 *Certificates of discharge of accountable persons*

Personal representatives, or other persons who are liable for the tax may obtain a certificate which, subject to their having been no fraud or non-disclosure, discharges both themselves and all other persons from liability to tax in respect of the death (para. 25 (3) (b)). It also extinguishes any outstanding Inland Revenue charge.

Application for this type of certificate is made on Form No. 30, which is submitted in duplicate to the Capital Taxes Office.

137

Y DEATH CAUSING LIABILITY TO ADDITIONAL TAX

In two circumstances the death of the deceased may cause additional tax to be payable in respect of lifetime gifts made by the deceased. First, if the deceased made a taxable gift within the last 3 years of his lifetime, the tax payable on that gift is payable on the death-time and not the life-time scale (s. 37 (2)). The difference between tax on the life-time scale and tax on the death-time scale in respect of that gift is payable by the transferee, and not by the personal representatives (s. 25 (2) (a); (4)). The tax is due six months after the end of the month in which the death occurred (Sch. 4, para. 12 (3)). This provision has been discussed earlier (p. 79, *ante*).

The second circumstance relates to gifts to charities and political parties. In general, such lifetime gifts are exempt from tax, but if the gifts were made within one year from the date of death, only the first £100,000 or £200,000 of gifts in each category is exempt (Sch. 6, para. 10 (1) (b); 11 (1) (b)). Where these limits are exceeded the recipient body alone is liable to pay the tax (s. 26 (3)), which becomes due at the date stated above (Sch. 4, para. 12 (3) (b)).

In neither of these circumstances, therefore, are the personal representatives liable for the tax or additional tax payable, although in the latter case, the amount of the gift which is not exempt will have to be brought into account in determining the total amount of lifetime gifts (p. 74, *ante*).

PART III

The Administration of the Estate

Chapter 7

Income Tax during the Administration of the Estate

A   THE "ADMINISTRATION PERIOD"

The same general provisions of the Income Tax Acts apply during the administration of an estate as at any other time, so that the same types of income and the same types of capital gain received by the personal representatives are taxable as they would have been had they been received by the deceased. Nevertheless, certain special provisions apply during the "administration period", which is the period from the date of death until the completion of the administration of the estate (TA 1970, s. 426). There is no satisfactory legislative rule to determine when the administration of an estate is complete (although some guidance can be obtained from s. 433 which deals with Scotland and Northern Ireland), but it seems that the administration is complete when the residue is ascertained, and is ready for distribution by the transfer, assent or appropriation to the residuary beneficiary or beneficiaries. Special formalities are necessary before some types of property, such as land, or shares in a company, can be transferred to the residuary beneficiary, but in many cases an informal assent is sufficient.

This chapter is concerned with income which arises during the administration period.

B THE GENERAL PRINCIPLES

The general principle has already been indicated, namely that if receipts would be taxable in the hands of an individual, they will likewise be taxable in the hands of his personal representatives.

Where receipts of an estate are taxable, an assessment is made upon the personal representatives. The personal representatives taken together are considered as one separate taxpayer, and therefore an assessment on personal representatives will not affect in any way the liability to tax of each personal representative for his personal income.

The assessment of the personal representatives will also usually be independent of the tax position of the deceased. It has been explained (p. 34) that for the period since the previous 6 April to the date of death, the deceased was entitled to full reliefs for a whole year. As the personal representatives are treated separately from the deceased, if the whole of the reliefs appropriate to the deceased were not used up in calculating his tax liability for the period to the date of death, the personal representatives cannot themselves claim the unused balance.

C SPECIAL PROVISIONS

There are, however, certain exceptions to the general principle that the personal representatives taken together are considered as any other separate taxpayer.

1 Reliefs

Personal representatives are not entitled to *personal* reliefs (p. 34, *ante*). Thus a personal representative is not entitled to claim the married or single man's personal allowance.

Personal representatives may, however, claim non-personal reliefs. Thus if personal representatives are carrying on a business they may claim loss relief, and they may also claim relief for interest paid if it would qualify for relief under the rules mentioned at p. 30.

2 Higher rates

Personal representatives are not liable to income tax at rates in excess of the basic rate, however high the income of the estate (*I.R. Comrs.* v. *Countess of Longford* (1928), 13 T.C. 573).

3 Additional rate

It will be seen (p. 230, *post*) that income which arises to trustees of most discretionary or accumulation settlements is liable to the additional rate of 15% as well as to the basic rate of 30% on the income which they receive. This does not apply, however, to income arising to personal representatives as such, although where personal representatives pay income to trustees, then the trustees themselves may be liable to the additional rate on that income (FA 1973, s. 16 (6)).

By taking the last three sections together, it will be appreciated that, with few exceptions, personal representatives are liable to tax at the basic rate on the whole of the income which they receive.

D PARTICULAR CASES

1 Businesses

If a personal representative carries on a business owned by the deceased, so that he may, for example, sell it, or transfer it to one of the beneficiaries, he will be liable to tax on the profits which he makes.

Profits from a business, however, are not taxable at all if the personal representatives have, for example, merely sold off the deceased's stock, and there has been no "trading". The expression "trading" implies that normal commercial methods are used. In each case it is a question of fact whether or not the personal representatives' activity amounts to trading, and it is difficult to lay down any precise test. Thus in the case *J. and R. O'Kane & Co.* v. *I.R. Comrs.* (1920), 12 T.C. 303, where the business of a wine merchant was brought to an end by selling off stock over a period of eighteen months, it was held that this amounted to trading, even though no new stock was bought. And in *Pattulo's Trustees* v. *I.R. Comrs.* (1955), 36 T.C. 87, profits made in fulfilling contracts entered into before the death of a trustee were held to be assessable. By contrast in *I.R. Comrs.* v. *Nelson* (1939), 22 T.C. 716, where the stock, goodwill and fixtures and fittings of a former wine merchant were sold off within fourteen days, it was held that there was no trading but only a realization of assets. Further, in *I.R. Comrs.* v. *Donaldson's Trustees* (1963), 41 T.C. 161, where personal representatives carried on the farming operations of a deceased farmer until they could arrange the sale of his cattle and farm, their operations were held to be carried on not for the *purpose* of farming, but for the purpose of terminating the business. The motive, the period during which the operations are carried on, and the surrounding circumstances generally are all taken into account in deciding whether the operations have been trading, or have been only to realize assets. If the latter, no tax is payable.

2 Expenses of estate

Where there is trading, expenses incurred wholly and exclusively in carrying on the business may of course be deducted from the receipts before the profit is calculated.

The expenses of the administration of the estate — as opposed to the expenses of the management of a business — are, however, not deductible from the general income of the estate.

3 Interest

Where a loan is taken out in order to discharge the capital transfer tax payable before a grant of representation is issued, the interest paid on that loan is deductible in computing the taxable income of the estate (FA 1974, Sch. 1, para. 17; FA 1975, Sch. 12, para. 19).

Capital transfer tax generally becomes due at the end of six months from the end of the month in which the death occurs, although in some cases the tax is payable by instalments, (FA 1975, Sch. 4, para. 15; p. 132, *ante*). Where payment is delayed, interest is payable at the rate of 9% from the due date to the date of actual payment (para. 19 (1)). No income tax relief can be obtained in respect of that interest (para. 19 (4)).

4 Dividends

It has been explained at p. 20, *ante* that where a dividend is received after the date of death, even though it is in respect of the period wholly or partly prior to the date of death, there is no apportionment for tax purposes, and the whole of the income should be included by the personal representatives in their estate's returns of income.

E POST CESSATION RECEIPTS

Where the deceased carried on a business before his death, the question will arise whether receipts of that business received after his death are taxable. To understand the rules which apply it is necessary to distinguish between the case where the profits of that business were assessed on a cash basis, and where they were assessed on an earnings basis. If a business is assessed on a cash basis, the assessable profit is calculated on the difference between the cash which was actually received, and the payments which were actually made in the year of assessment. On the other hand, where the profit is assessed upon the earnings basis, the profit figure includes all amounts which have been earned, even if they have not been received. Thus, where the earnings basis applies, the profit will include all bills or invoices delivered, even if the sums due have not been paid, and it will also include all work in progress at the last day of the accounting period.

1 Pre-cessation profits assessed on earnings basis

Where the profits of the business of the deceased were assessed on the earnings basis, it follows that all sums received after death ought already to have been brought into charge to tax. For example, if a bill rendered before death is paid afterwards, the accounts of the business to the date of death will normally have included that bill. If so, when the amount is actually received, the personal representatives will not be liable to tax on this sum again.

Tax is, however, payable by the personal representatives on all sums not included in the accounts before the discontinuance of the business (TA 1970, s. 143). If, therefore, a bad debt previously written off as irrecoverable is received after death this will be taxable.

2 Pre-cessation profits assessed on cash basis

The position is more complicated where the deceased's business was assessed on a cash basis. In this case, it is necessary to consider whether the post-cessation receipts would have been brought into charge to tax if the business had been assessed on an earnings basis. If the receipts would not have been brought into charge to tax because:

a they were not due until after the death (or other discontinuance); or

b the amount due was not ascertained until after that date,

then those receipts are taxable in the hands of the personal representatives (TA 1970, s. 144). If therefore the deceased was an author and his royalties were assessed on a cash basis, royalties received after death would be taxable in the hands of the personal representatives, for they would be within one or both of the categories just mentioned.

In other cases, the receipts are taxable in the year of assessment in which they are received. If the deceased was over 51 when the business was discontinued, the personal representatives are entitled to relief on a tapering scale (TA 1970, s. 150).

3 Reliefs for post-cessation receipts

Where the deceased was entitled to an unused balance of loss relief at the date of death, or an unabsorbed balance of capital allowances, these can be brought forward and offset against post-cessation receipts (TA 1970, s. 145).

4 Basis of assessment

The personal representatives will normally be assessed to tax on the post-cessation receipts in the year of assessment in which they are received. They cannot elect to have any sum charged for the year in which the death occurred.

F APPORTIONMENTS

Over the last two centuries, the courts have evolved a series of rules, known as the rules for equitable apportionments, which are designed to achieve fairness between two or more beneficiaries under a will or a trust, who are entitled to an interest in the trust property in succession. A simple example of the type of case where this may apply would be of property left on trust for Elizabeth for life, and after her death for Evelyn. It is beyond the scope of this book to explain the rules, but one in particular may be mentioned. The rule laid down in the case *Re Earl of Chesterfield's Trusts* (1883), 24 Ch.D. 643, deals with property which produces no income and which is left on trust for persons in succession. Suppose, then, that Geoffrey by his will leaves his property on trust for Elizabeth for life, and after her death for Evelyn. And suppose that one of his assets is an interest free loan of £300 which is not repayable until two years after his death. When the £300 is actually received, two years will have elapsed since the date of Geoffrey's death, during which time Elizabeth will have received no income from this asset. The rule laid down in *Re Earl of Chesterfield's Trusts (supra)* directs the personal representatives to ascertain what sum would, if invested at the date of death at £4 per cent compound interest with yearly rests, less income tax for the time being in force, have produced £300 at the time when it was in fact received. If the basic rate of tax were 50 per cent for each of the two years, the amount would be £288.35. This sum would be added to capital, and the remaining £11,65 paid to Elizabeth as compensation for the loss of income over the previous two years. The object is to compensate Elizabeth for loss of income: income tax is deducted when making the calculations because if the £288.35 had in fact been invested at the date of death, Elizabeth would have suffered income tax on the income from it.

It is, however, important to note that where the rules of equitable apportionment direct such calculations, they require apportionments to be made of sums which are in fact capital. Therefore, there is no liability actually to pay the tax which is notionally deducted in making the calculations to the Revenue; and the life tenant should not include the amount he or she receives in his personal tax returns.

This type of apportionment operates in favour of the life tenant. Other types of apportionment, for example by virtue of the rule in *Allhusen* v. *Whittell* (1867), L.R. 4 Eq. 295, operate against the life tenant. Whichever is the case, these apportionments should be ignored in calculating the personal representatives' liability to tax.

G DISTRIBUTIONS OF INCOME BY PERSONAL REPRESENTATIVES

We have so far considered the receipts in the hands of the personal representatives. All taxable income is either received by them subject to deduction of tax, or is assessable in their hands.

The expenses of the personal representatives in so far as they relate to income are deductible from this income, and the net income is available for distribution among the beneficiaries. A beneficiary may be entitled

a as a general legatee;

b as a specific legatee;

c as an annuitant; or

d as a residuary beneficiary.

1 General and specific legatees

A general legatee, that is a person entitled to a sum of money, is not usually entitled to any income at all. He is only entitled to the capital sum. The exceptions are:

a where the will directs payment of interest;

b in some circumstances where the legacy is given by a parent or some person standing *in loco parentis* to the beneficiary;

c where the legacy is not paid within one year from the date of death.

By contrast, a specific legatee, that is, a person entitled to a specified item of property, is, in the absence of any contrary provision in the will, entitled to the actual income from that property from the date of death, less expenses referable to that property.

Where a beneficiary is entitled to income other than interest, this must be paid by the personal representatives after deduction of tax, and a certificate of deduction of tax must be issued. The procedure is discussed at p. 235.

2 Statutory sum on intestacy

Where the deceased is survived by a spouse, the surviving spouse will in certain circumstances be entitled to a "statutory legacy" of £40,000 or £85,000, depending on whether there are any children. (Family Provision (Intestate Succession) Order 1981, S.I. 1981 No. 255. The amounts of the statutory legacies were less where the deceased died before 1 March 1981). Where these sums are payable, they carry interest at £7 per cent from the date of death to the date of payment. The interest payments should not be made subject to deduction of tax.

If the income of the estate is insufficient to meet the interest due to the surviving spouse, capital will have to be used for this purpose. In this case the gross sum is paid to the beneficiary, and the beneficiary is liable to pay the tax on it. Where, however, personal representatives use capital to make up deficiences in income for the payment of annuities, they must deduct income tax at the basic rate and account to the Revenue for it (p. 240).

The residuary beneficiaries will be entitled to all income after payment of such interest as is appropriate to general legacies, specific legacies, and after making annuity payments, but from it will be taken the general administration expenses of the estate which relate to income.

H ANNUITIES

1 Generally

An annuitant is entitled to receive payment from the date of death unless there is a provision in the will to the contrary. The whole of the payments made to the annuitant are of an income nature, and tax should be deducted when the payments are made.

The annuitant is entitled to insist that a capital sum is set aside so that there shall be security for his income. Where there is insufficient capital for this to be done, the annuitant is entitled to demand payment of a sum equal to the actuarial value of the annuity, subject to abatement with the legacies. When such a sum is paid the whole sum which is paid is treated as capital: the personal representatives do not make payment subject to deduction of tax, and the beneficiary is not assessable to tax on the amount received (*I.R. Comrs.* v. *Lady Castlemaine* (1943), 25 T.C. 408).

2 Directions to purchase annuities

A will sometimes directs the personal representatives to purchase an annuity. TA 1970, s. 230, provides that in general where an annuity is purchased from an insurance or similar company, the greater part of each payment is treated as a return of capital to the recipient leaving only the balance as income taxable in his hands. Annuities purchased under a direction in a will are, however, expressly excluded from this provision.

There are, therefore, serious tax objections to personal representatives purchasing an annuity. They will expend a capital sum in buying it: the recipient will be assessed to tax on the whole of the amount which he receives.

Where, however, the direction in the will to purchase an annuity is absolute, the beneficiary has the right to demand that the capital sum should be paid to him, rather than be applied in the purchase of the annuity. He has this right by virtue of a general provision of trust law known as the rule in *Saunders* v. *Vautier* ((1841), Cr. & Ph. 240). In all cases where he is able to do so, the beneficiary should exercise his right to have the capital paid to him, and the personal representatives may well remind him of his right. The capital sum will not be taxable. Then, if he needs an annuity, he himself may purchase one, and he will then be entitled to relief under TA 1970, s. 230.

3   Taxed income insufficient

It will be seen that because a residuary beneficiary is entitled only to what income remains, there will usually not be a "shortage" of income. In some cases, however, personal representatives may be under an obligation to make income payments in excess of the amount of income which they have received. There might, for example, be an obligation to pay interest to pecuniary legatees and there may be an insufficiency of income for this purpose. There may also be a direction in the will to make up an annuity or other similar payment from the capital of the estate. Where this is done, the personal representatives will have to take money from capital, deduct from it tax at the basic rate, and account to the Revenue for the tax so deducted (*Brodie's Will Trustees* v. *I.R. Comrs.* (1933), 17 T.C. 432).

In some cases, particularly where the will is not professionally drawn, or was prepared many years ago, the personal representatives may have no discretion as to what to do. But in all cases they should consider whether the will gives them a discretion as to the manner in which they may make payments, and if possible make advancements of capital, which are not subject to income tax, rather than taking capital to make payments of an income nature, which are subject to income tax. Advancements, and the capital gains tax which may be payable in respect of them, are discussed at p. 260, *post*.

4 Annuities directed to be paid "free of tax"

The special rules which govern a direction to make annuity payments free of income tax are considered at p. 243, *post*.

I ALLOCATION OF INCOME TO BENEFICIARIES

1 General and specific beneficiaries: annuitants

This book is concerned with the tax position of executors and trustees and not primarily with that of the beneficiaries under a will or settlement. There are, however, certain provisions which attribute to a beneficiary income of the estate, which although not of direct concern to personal representatives, they may wish to bear in mind.

In so far as interest or income payments are made to pecuniary or specific legatees, or annuitants, the actual amounts which they receive are treated as their income. For general tax purposes, the taxpayer is often assessable on all amounts to which he is entitled, whether or not he actually receives them, but as an exception to this general principle, where a person is entitled under a will to interest, and he refuses to accept it, he is sometimes not taxable on that amount. Thus, in the case of *Dewar* v. *I.R. Comrs.* (1935), 19 T.C. 561, a legatee was entitled to interest on a legacy of £1 million, which was not paid within one year from the date of death. He decided to refuse to accept the income, and it was held that he was not assessable on the amount of that interest. In this case money had not been set aside to meet the beneficiary's legacy. If, however, funds are set aside for a beneficiary, but he refuses to draw the interest, he is nevertheless liable to tax on it. So, in the more recent case of *Spens* v. *I.R. Comrs.*, [1970] 3 All E.R. 295, a beneficiary was entitled to the whole of the income from a fund, and was held to be assessable on it even though it had not been drawn.

2 Residuary beneficiaries

With regard to residuary beneficiaries, the rules depend on whether the beneficiary has a "limited" interest or an "absolute" interest in the residue. A person has a limited interest if he has a right to income only from the residuary property, whereas a person who has a right to capital upon the residue being ascertained has an absolute interest (TA 1970, s. 432).

The rules governing a residuary beneficiary with a "limited" interest are:

a all sums paid to the beneficiary during the administration period are treated as part of his total income for the year of assessment in which they are paid.

b on completion of the administration, the sums actually paid are added to those due to him. The total is then deemed to have accrued from day to day.

c final computations, and revised assessments, if necessary, to cover each of the years of assessment during the administration period are then made.

The total income paid to the residuary beneficiary will therefore be the total income of the estate, less income paid to others, and less management expenses, but spread out equally over the whole period of the administration.

Different rules govern the position of the beneficiary with an "absolute" interest. During the administration of the estate, various sums might be paid to the residuary beneficiary generally on account of the amount due to him and without distinguishing between capital and income elements. In order to distinguish between capital and income, the following process is adopted:

a the "residuary income" of the estate is calculated for each year of assessment or part of a year of assessment during the administration period. "Residuary income" for a period is the total income received by the personal representatives during that period, less interest paid on legacies, annuity payments, and management expenses relating to income.

b the payments actually made to the residuary beneficiary in each of the years of assessment are then regarded as having been of income up to the total of the residuary income for that year, the balance being treated as capital.

c revised assessments may then be necessary.

3 Treatment of income

The amount of trust income paid to a beneficiary will be received by him after tax is deducted by the trustees. For income tax purposes, however, his income is "grossed up" at the basic rate. Thus, while the basic rate of income tax is 30 per cent, each £70 received by the beneficiary is treated as £100 gross. In most cases this will not have any adverse effect upon the beneficiary, because tax of 30 per cent will have been deducted from each £1. But if the beneficiary is liable to income tax at the higher rates, the liability will be calculated according to the grossed up amount. (The grossing up may mean that the beneficiary's income for income tax purposes is increased, so that an additional repayment claim be made (see p. 227, *post*).)

4 Building Society interest

In general, because ·of the special arrangements which apply to building society interest, an income tax repayment cannot be made in respect of tax notionally deducted from building society interest. Where, however, personal representatives receive building society interest, and that is included in the income payable to a beneficiary with an absolute interest, a special rule applies. The beneficiary is treated as receiving his income from the estate itself, and not from the underlying source. Accordingly, the beneficiary receives all the income subject to deduction of income tax at the basic rate, and may, where appropriate, make a repayment claim in respect of the whole of that tax (SP 7/1980).

A special rule applies where the beneficiary is non-resident (*ibid*).

5 Income deficiencies

If in a year of assessment during the administration period the deductions which are made in determining the amount of the residuary income are greater than the gross income of the estate, the excess is allowable as a deduction in computing the net income of the preceding or succeeding years for higher rate purposes (Concession A15).

6 Relief for capital transfer tax

In certain circumstances, income which has accrued before the death of a person is paid afterwards. The most usual instance is of a company dividend which may relate to an accounting year wholly or partly before death, but which is actually paid after the death. Where this is so, that income will form part both of the deceased's estate for capital transfer tax purposes, being included in the value of those shares, and will also form part of the income of the residuary beneficiary. It is, therefore, provided that the residuary income is treated as reduced, for the purposes of income tax liability in excess of the basic rate only, by an amount equal to the capital transfer tax liability on that income, grossed up at the basic rate (TA 1970, s. 430; FA 1975, Sch. 12, para. 16).

J EXPENSES: CAPITAL OR INCOME

Where personal representatives incur management expenses during the administration of an estate, and they have a discretion whether the expenses should be taken from the income or from the capital, they may wonder which will have the more advantageous tax results. The answer will depend on the personal financial position of the person entitled to the income. If that beneficiary has a large income from other sources, it is better to weight the expenses against estate income: this will reduce the income deemed to be that of the beneficiary, and will reduce his total tax bill. If, however, the beneficiary has no or little other income, then the expenses might be weighted against capital. This will increase the total income deemed to be that of the beneficiary, and will probably increase the amount of the income tax repayment claim which he might make.

K RETURNS AND PAYMENT OF TAX

The making of returns by the personal representatives, and the methods of issue of certificates of deduction of tax to the beneficiaries is the same as in the case of a continuing trust, and is considered under that head at p. 227, *post*.

Personal representatives are personally liable for tax on income which has passed through their hands, and they should not distribute the estate until all tax has been paid.

Chapter 8

Capital Gains Tax during the Administration of the Estate

A   ASSETS HELD BY PERSONAL REPRESENTATIVES

1   Personal representatives not trustees

Although, for the purposes of the general law, the position of personal representatives is in most, but not all, respects equated with that of trustees, and although both personal representatives and trustees hold assets in a fiduciary and not a beneficial capacity, for capital gains tax purposes personal representatives are treated quite separately from trustees. The legislation prescribes two separate "codes":

   a "the personal representatives' code", which is found in CGTA 1979, ss. 47 to 49; and

   b "the trustees' code", which is found in CGTA 1979, ss. 52 to 56.

2   Individual assets to be considered

When considering a person who is a personal representative, it is necessary to distinguish his office as personal representative on the one hand, and his capacity in respect of a particular asset on the other hand. The general rule is that when a person takes a grant of probate of a will, or letters of administration to the estate of a deceased person, he will hold the office of executor or administrator for life. Exceptionally, the grant itself may be limited in time, or it may be revoked by the court, but apart from these circumstances, the office will continue after the end of the administration period. By contrast, a person will only hold an asset in the capacity of a personal representative for so long as his function in respect of that asset is that of a personal representative.

A person will cease to have the function of a personal representative in respect of an asset where:

   a he transfers the asset to a beneficiary, or to persons who are appointed by the will as trustees;

b   he appropriates, or sets aside, the asset for the beneficiary, or for other persons who are trustees;

c   he declares, whether or not by means of an assent, that thenceforth he holds the asset either beneficially or in the capacity as a trustee; or

d   he completes the estate account, so that the administration period (see p. 139, *ante*) comes to an end. By completing the estate account, the exact amount of the residue is ascertained, and the personal representative will thereupon automatically hold all the remaining assets under his control as a trustee for the persons entitled.

In the case of land, where a person acquires the legal estate as personal representative, and is due to hold it as trustee, he will continue to hold the legal estate itself as personal representative until he executes a formal assent in favour of himself as trustee (Administration of Estates Act, 1925, s. 36 (4); *Re King's Will Trusts*, [1964] Ch. 542). However, it seems that for capital gains tax purposes, the capacity in which the legal estate is held is irrelevant, and that if the function in respect of that asset is that of trustee, then the holder will be regarded as a trustee even if there has been no formal assent.

It follows from the description of the circumstances given above in which a person will cease to have the capacity of personal representative that during the course of the administration of an estate he will cease to have that capacity in respect of different assets at different times. Accordingly, the question whether a person holds an asset in his capacity as a personal representative can only be answered in the light of the circumstances at a particular point in time.

Although it seems reasonably clear that the intention of the legislature is that for capital gains tax purposes regard is to be had to the capacity which a person has at a particular time, rather than to his office as such, the legislation is unhappily worded. CGTA 1979, s. 155 (1) ascribes to the expression "personal representatives" the same meaning as it bears for the Taxes Act 1970. TA 1970, s. 432 (4) initially defines "personal representatives" by reference to the Administration of Estates Act 1925, which is more concerned with office than capacity, but the emphasis to be placed on capacity is seen in the latter part of TA 1970, s. 432 (4).

The other respect in which the legislation is unhappily worded is that there is no clear statement that the expression "personal representatives" excludes trustees, but that the expression excludes trustees must be so follows from the inconsistency between CGTA 1979, ss. 47 to 49 on the one hand and ss. 52 to 56 on the other.

153

B PROVISIONS AFFECTING PERSONAL REPRESENTATIVES

The basic features of CGTA 1979, ss. 47 to 49 are:

a the personal representatives are deemed to acquire the deceased's assets at their market value at the date of his death (s. 49 (1) (a));

b where an asset is sold in the course of the administration of the estate, the ordinary capital gains tax consequences will ensue from that disposal;

c where the asset is transferred to a beneficiary under the terms of the will or the intestacy provisions, the beneficiary is treated as if he had acquired the asset at the same time, and at the same deemed cost, as the personal representatives (s. 49 (4) (b));

d there is no liability upon the disposal of an asset to trustees, where those trustees acquire as legatee (s. 47 (2)); and

e there is no liability upon the change of capacity of the same persons from personal representatives to trustees (*ibid*).

It is now necessary to consider these principles in greater detail.

C ACQUISITION BY PERSONAL REPRESENTATIVES

1 The general rule

The personal representatives are deemed to acquire all the deceased's assets of which he was competent to dispose at the time of his death at their market value at the date of his death (s. 49 (1) (a)). The deceased is treated as being competent to dispose of certain types of property even if that property does not, or does not necessarily, pass to the personal representatives for the purposes of the administration of the estate. Thus, the deceased is regarded as being competent to dispose of his share in jointly owned property, even if, on death, that share passes automatically to the other joint owner (s. 49 (10)). Further, in determining whether the deceased was competent to dispose, it must be assumed that all his assets were situated in England, so that restrictions on disposition imposed by foreign law are for this purpose ignored; and if the deceased died whilst domiciled outside the United Kingdom he is, again for this purpose, treated as if he died whilst domiciled in England and Wales (*ibid*). The deceased is not treated as being competent to dispose of assets over which he had a power of appointment.

Where the deceased was not competent to dispose of assets, or is not treated as having been competent to dispose, the person who actually acquires them is treated as acquiring them at the date of death of the deceased, and at their market value at that date (s. 49 (1) (*a*)).

It is not possible for the personal representatives to claim that they have incurred notional expenditure on the acquisition (s. 32 (4)) although actual expenditure can be brought into account (see p. 159, *post*).

In theory the notional disposal and re-acquisition occurs at the moment after death for capital gains tax purposes (*Larter* v. *Skone James*, [1976] 2 All E.R. 615) and not at the moment before death, which is the rule adopted for capital transfer tax (FA 1975, s. 22).

2 *Value determined for capital transfer tax*

a   Generally   In general, the personal representatives are deemed to acquire the deceased's assets at their market value at the date of death. If the value of an asset which forms part of the deceased's estate has been ascertained for the purposes of capital transfer tax, that value will be adopted also for capital gains tax purposes (CGTA 1979, s. 153).

b   Valuation reliefs   The general rule only applies where the value which has been determined for capital transfer tax purposes is that of the asset itself. Where agricultural property relief, or business asset relief, is given for capital transfer tax purposes, those reliefs apply to reduce the value which is treated as being transferred and not the value of the assets concerned (FA 1976, Sch. 10, para. 2; FA 1981, Sch. 12, para. 2 (1)). Thus, where these reliefs are given, the value of the assets for capital gains tax is the value before the relief.

c   Related property   Where the related property provisions apply (see p. 85, *ante*), they operate to determine the value of the asset itself, and will, therefore, affect the capital gains tax value.

d   Assets sold during administration   It will be seen (p. 000 *ante*) that where stock exchange securities are sold within twelve months from the date of death, then, broadly, the gross sale value can be substituted for the market value at the date of death for capital transfer tax purposes. In such a case, subject to certain adjustments, the sale value is adopted as the market value at the date of death for capital gains tax purposes also (FA 1975, Sch. 10, para. 29 (1)). However, where a claim is made for capital transfer tax purposes to substitute the sale value of land sold within three years from death for the market value on death (see p. 169, *post*) no alteration is made to the market value on death for capital gains tax.

3   Gifts prior to 27 March 1974; deaths prior to 27 March 1981

Where a person made a gift *inter vivos* before 27 March 1974, but within seven years from the date of his death, a liability to capital transfer tax will arise on his death (see p. 123, *ante*). In this case, provided the donee retains the asset at the date of death of the deceased:

a   the donee is treated as disposing of the asset at the date of death of the deceased, and as re-acquiring it at that date at the value at which that asset is brought into account for capital transfer tax purposes; but

b   no chargeable gain is treated as accruing on that disposal (CGTA 1979, Sch. 6, para. 15).

D   DISPOSAL BY PERSONAL REPRESENTATIVES IN COURSE OF ADMINISTRATION

1   Generally

Where personal representatives dispose of an asset by way of sale in the course of the administration of the estate, they are assessable on any gain which they realise. The position will be the same where the personal representatives make an actual disposal of an asset in any circumstances other than to a beneficiary (see p. 157, *post*). Accordingly, there will be a liability if the personal representatives dispose of an asset to a creditor in satisfaction of this debt.

The general rule applies irrespective of the tax position of the beneficiaries. In *Prest* v. *Bettinson,* [1980] S.T.C. 607 a testatrix, had left her residuary estate, subject to the payment of annuities, to be divided between four charities and one non-charitable body. It was held that the personal representatives were assessable on the whole of the gains which accrued. However, the position would have been different if, before the sale of the chargeable assets, the personal representatives had appropriated the assets to the residuary beneficiaries freed from the burden of paying the annuities, or if they had appropriated other assets exclusively for the payment of the annuities. In either case, from the date of the appropriation (see p. 158, *post*) CGTA, s. 46 would have applied, and four-fifths of its gain would have been exempt.

2   Disposals to beneficiaries by agreement

Where an asset is sold to a beneficiary, that will be treated as a sale in the course of administration at the market value of the asset, and a gain or a loss may arise. It is the view of the Revenue that where an asset is transferred to a beneficiary as part of his entitlement to the estate, but the personal representatives have no unilateral power of appropriation, the beneficiary is to be treated as acquiring the asset by purchase, and not as legatee. The Revenue are, however, prepared to regard the beneficiary as acquiring as legatee if both the personal representatives and he agree that he should be treated as acquiring as legatee.

3   Relief for small gains

In each of the year of assessment in which the death occurs, and the two subsequent years of assessment, the personal representatives are treated as an individual for the purposes of the relief for small gains (p. 42, *ante*). Accordingly, the first £3,000 of gains is exempt, and where losses are brought forward, they are utilized only where necessary to reduce the gain to £3,000 (CGTA 1979, s. 5; FA 1980, s. 78). This is an exception to the general rule that personal representatives are not treated as an individual (CGTA 1979, s. 48 (2)).

There is no relief for small gains in the third and subsequent years of assessment after that in which the death occurs.

4   Deceased's main residence

There is no special statutory rule relating to the disposal of the house which was the deceased's main residence. Accordingly, the personal representatives will, in principle, be liable if there is an increase in value between the date of death and the date of sale.

By concession, however, the gain is treated as exempt if both before and after the death of the deceased, the house has been used as their only or main residence by individuals who, under the will or intestacy, are entitled to the whole or substantially the whole of the proceeds of sale of the house either absolutely or for life (Extra-Statutory Concession D5).

E   DISPOSALS TO LEGATEE

1   Actual transfers

Where an asset is transferred to a beneficiary in accordance with the terms of the will, or under the intestacy rules, or some combination of the two, the beneficiary is treated, retrospectively, as having acquired the asset at the date of the deceased's death, and at its market value at that date (CGTA 1979, ss. 47, 49). Accordingly, there can be no liability on the personal representatives in respect of any increase in the value of that asset between the date of death and the date of transfer.

The same rule applies where the beneficiary takes the asset not as a result of a specific bequest, but by way of appropriation towards satisfaction of a pecuniary legacy, or a share in residue (s. 47 (3)). The Revenue's attitude with regard to assets transferred to a beneficiary where the personal representatives do not have a unilateral power of appropriation was mentioned at p. 157.

It seems that the general rule will apply to a person taking an asset by virtue of an order made under the Inheritance (Provision for Family and Dependants) Act 1975, even although s. 19 of that Act refers specifically only to capital transfer tax and not to capital gains tax.

2 Appropriation before transfer

The expression "appropriation" is used in two senses. The first, which has just been considered, is where the personal representatives transfer an asset *in specie* to a beneficiary in or towards satisfaction of a pecuniary legacy of share in residue. The other sense is where, without transferring the asset, the personal representatives set it apart from the remainder of the deceased's estate and hold it for the beneficiary. Where there is an appropriation in this sense, the beneficiary is treated as having acquired the asset at the date of death, and the subsequent transfer to him is ignored (s. 46 (1)).

Prest v. *Bettinson* [1980] S.T.C. 607 (see p. 156, *ante*) shows the desirability of appropriating an asset to an exempt body, such as a charity, before disposal.

3 Beneficiary becoming absolutely entitled

Where, while an asset is held by personal representatives in their capacity as such, a beneficiary becomes absolutely entitled as against the personal representatives, there is no deemed disposal at that time by the personal representatives. The beneficiary will take as legatee at the value at the date of the deceased's death (s. 47 (3)). This contrasts with the rule which applies where a beneficiary becomes absolutely entitled as against a trustee, in which case there is a liability (s. 54; see p. 254, *post*). If a beneficiary is likely to become absolutely entitled, such as by attaining a specified age in the fairly near future, it may well be desirable for the personal representatives to continue to hold the asset as personal representatives until after that time.

F   DISPOSALS TO TRUSTEES

Where there is an actual disposal of an asset to trustees, the trustees are treated as legatees (CGTA 1979, s. 47 (2)). Accordingly, the trustees are deemed to acquire the asset at the date of death of the deceased, at its market value at that date.

G PERSONAL REPRESENTATIVES BECOMING TRUSTEES

There is no deemed disposal if the persons who hold an asset as personal representatives come to hold it as trustees. If they hold as bare trustees for a beneficiary who is absolutely entitled, the beneficiary will be treated as having acquired as legatee. If the trustees hold as any other type of trustee, they will themselves be deemed to have acquired as a legatees.

H EXPENSES OF SALE OF TRANSFER

1 *Expenses of sale*

Where an asset is sold, the personal representatives may deduct two types of expenditure. First, they may deduct that proportion of the cost of the administration of the estate that is necessary in order to put themselves into a position of being able to sell. This will include a proportion of the solicitor's costs of obtaining probate, and of making a valuation for estate duty purposes (*I.R. Comrs.* v. *Executors of Dr. Robert Richards,* [1971] 1 All E.R. 785, H.L.).

The Board of Inland Revenue have agreed with the various professional bodies the following scale for determining which part of the total cost of obtaining a grant of representation and administering the estate is to be attributable to the allowable costs within this decision:

Gross value of estate	*Allowable expenditure*
a Up to £13,000	1.5% of the probate value of the assets sold by the personal representatives.
b Between £13,001 and £20,000	A fixed amount of £200, to be divided between all the assets in the estate in proportion to their probate values and allowed in those proportions on assets sold by the personal representatives.
c Between £20,001 and £100,000	1% of the probate value of the assets sold.
d Between £100,001 and £135,000	A fixed amount of £1,000, to be divided as at *b* above.
e Between £135,001 and £250,000	0.75% of the probate value of the assets sold.

In the case of gross estates exceeding £250,000 the allowable amount is determined by individual negotiation. In all cases, a flat rate reduction is made in respect of quoted securities, not exceeding £5 per transaction unless there are exceptional circumstances.

The Revenue view is that these deductions are allowable only where the personal representatives themselves dispose of the assets by way of sale, and not where there is a subsequent disposal by trustees or beneficiaries under the rule now to be considered.

The second type of expenditure which the trustees can deduct is the actual expenses of sale or transfer (CGTA 1979, s. 32). If the personal representatives have incurred "enhancement expenditure" on the asset, that expenditure may also be taken into account in the usual way (p. 46, *ante*). Where the asset is leasehold property, however, rent paid under the lease from the date of death cannot be taken into account (*Emmerson* v. *Computer Time International, Ltd.,* [1977] 2 All E.R. 545, C.A.).

2 *Expenses of transfer to beneficiary*

Where an asset is transferred to a beneficiary under the terms of the will, or in accordance with the rules for intestacy, the personal representatives have a choice. They may deduct the cost of the transfer from the gains accruing to them on the sale of other assets, thereby reducing their own liability. Alternatively, they may decide not to claim this deduction, and in this case the *beneficiary* is entitled to add the cost of the transfer to the market value at which *he* is deemed to acquire the asset, even though he does not pay the cost of the transfer (CGTA 1979, s. 47 (1)). By adding this cost to the acquisition value, he thereby reduces the ultimate chargeable gain.

In addition to the actual expenses of the transfer, the costs reasonably incurred in making any valuation or apportionment for capital gains tax purposes, including particularly the expenses of ascertaining the market value may be deducted from the chargeable gain (CGTA 1979, s. 32 (2) (*b*)).

As stated above, the view of the Inland Revenue is that the cost of obtaining a grant of representation is not allowable where the asset is transferred to a beneficiary.

I LOSSES

The personal representatives are treated as being entirely separate from the deceased. Accordingly, unused losses sustained by the deceased cannot be used by the personal representatives, and unused losses sustained by the personal representatives cannot be carried back and offset against gains realised by the deceased.

Where, during the course of the administration of the estate, the personal representatives sustain a net loss, the benefit of that loss cannot be passed to the beneficiaries. It seems, however, that where the personal representatives are also trustees, they can carry forward losses which they sustain as personal representatives, and offset them against gains which accrue to them as trustees.

Chapter 9

Development Land Tax during the Administration of the Estate

A ACQUISITION BY PERSONAL REPRESENTATIVES

1 Personal representatives

As for the purposes of capital gains tax, personal representatives are treated for the purposes of development land tax as a single and continuing body of persons, distinct from the individuals who are the personal representatives for the time being (DLTA 1976, s. 9 (2)). Accordingly, if there is any change in the persons who are the personal representatives, that change will not constitute a disposal.

2 Acquisition

The personal representatives are not treated as acquiring the deceased's interest in land at its market value at the date of his death, but they are, in effect, treated as one person with the deceased. In the case of an intestacy, where, on death, for the purposes of the general law, the assets devolve first on the President of the Family Division, and onwards to the administrators when a grant of representation is issued, the deceased, the President, and the administrators are treated as being together one person (DLTA 1976, s. 9 (1), (3)).

The personal representatives are treated as having acquired the deceased's interest in land at the time when the deceased acquired it, and at the cost to the deceased. Anything done by the deceased is treated as having been done by the personal representatives at the time when it was actually done.

B DISPOSALS BY PERSONAL REPRESENTATIVES

1 Sales in course of administration ˙

Where the personal representatives sell an interest in land in the course of the administration of the estate, a liability can arise in the same way as on the occasion of a disposal by an individual. Because of the principles just discussed, in calculating Base A and Base C values, the personal representatives will have to take the acquisition cost to the deceased as their acquisition cost. The other factors are determined in the same way as in the case of a transfer of an interest, as noted below.

Personal representatives can claim the annual £50,000 exemption (DLTA 1976, s. 12, F (No. 2) A 1979, s. 24 (2)).

2   Transfers to beneficiaries

Where the personal representatives transfer an interest in land to a beneficiary, the transfer is treated as a disposal by way of gift. There will not, therefore, be any liability on the personal representatives.

The beneficiary is generally in the same position as if he had acquired the interest by gift *inter vivos* from the deceased. The detailed rules are as follows:

a   Acquisition cost   The cost of acquisition is:

   i   the acquisition cost to the deceased; and

   ii   any cost incurred by the beneficiary on the transfer of the interest to him (DLTA 1976, s. 10 (2) (*a*)).

b   Expenditure on improvements   Where Base C is used, the amount of the expenditure on improvements is:

   i   the expenditure on improvements incurred by the deceased up to the date of death; and

   ii   the expenditure on improvements incurred by the beneficiary following the death (s. 10 (2) (*b*)).

c   Expenditure on relevant improvements   Where Bases A or B are used, the expenditure on relevant improvements is:

   i   the expenditure on relevant improvements by the deceased up to the date of death; and

   ii   the expenditure on relevant improvements by the beneficiary following the death (s. 10 (2) (*b*)).

d   Current use value at acquisition   The current use value at acquisition is the current use value of the interest at the date of its acquisition by the deceased (s. 10 (2) (*c*)). If the deceased acquired the interest prior to 6 April, 1965, the current use value at acquisition is the current use value on 6 April 1965 (*ibid*).

e   Special addition and further addition   The general principle that the deceased and the beneficiary are treated as one person is broken in the case of the special addition and the further addition.

The amount of the special addition is the amount of the special addition which the deceased could have claimed at the date of his death. No special addition is available in respect of the period between the date of death and the date of disposal by the beneficiary.

C PRESERVATION OF RELIEFS

Care needs to be taken where, had the deceased disposed of an interest in land immediately before his death, he would have been entitled to the benefit of an exemption. The legislation preserves the benefit of the exemptions, within limits, for the personal representatives, but not for the beneficiaries. Thus, where the interest in land was in respect of a house which was the deceased's principal residence, the exemption will apply to a disposal by the personal representatives within two years from the date of death (DLTA 1976, s. 14 (7)). Further, where the deceased could have claimed the benefit of the exemption for land held by way of trading stock on 12 September 1974, the personal representatives will be entitled to the benefit of that exemption (DLTA 1976, s. 16 (4)). Accordingly, where a beneficiary is entitled to an interest in land, and the beneficiary himself intends to sell, it will be advantageous for the personal representatives themselves to effect the sale without transferring the interest to him. The personal representatives would then be obliged to account to the beneficiary for the proceeds of sale. If the personal representatives transfer the land to the beneficiary first, the benefit of the exemption will be lost.

Chapter 10

Capital Transfer Tax during the Administration of the Estate

A INTRODUCTION

The general position relating to capital transfer tax payable as a result of the death of a person has been dealt with in Chapter 6. During the course of the administration of the estate further assets or liabilities may come to light, and adjustments are made to the liability in accordance with the ordinary principles described in Chapter 6.

Five further points which might arise after the death, but during the course of the administration of the estate warrant separate mention here. These are:

a   rules relating to the position where stock exchange securities are sold at a loss during the course of the administration (*infra*);

b   rules relating to land and buildings sold at a loss during the course of the administration (p. 169, *post*);

c   rules relating to the sale of related property during the course of the administration (p. 171, *post*);

d   the effect of deeds of family arrangement, disclaimers, and similar instruments (p. 173, *post*); and

e   the position where a beneficiary deals with his beneficial interest during the course of the administration of the estate (p. 172, *post*).

B SALES OF SECURITIES DURING COURSE OF ADMINISTRATION OF ESTATE

1   Loss on realisation of securities

The normal basis for the valuation of securities which the deceased owned at the date of his death has already been noted (p. 88, *ante*). A special relief can be claimed by personal representatives, or by trustees, where certain securities are realised within twelve months from the date of death at a price lower than the value at which the securities were brought into account (Sch. 10, paras 14 – 30). The broad effect of the provisions is to enable the price actually obtained for the securities to be substituted for the valuation figure as at the date of death.

2   Securities to which provision applies

The provision applies to "qualifying investments", namely:

a   i   shares or securities which are quoted on a stock exchange at the date of the deceased's death or which are suspended at that date and subsequently quoted (FA 1976, s. 104);

    ii   holdings in an authorised unit trust (within TA 1970, s. 358); and

    iii   shares in a common investment fund established under s. 1 of the Administration of Justice Act 1965 (Sch. 10, para. 14 (1));

b   which were held by the deceased immediately before his death; and

c   which are sold within the period of twelve months immediately following his death (para. 15).

No relief is given where shares or units fall in value, but are not sold within the twelve month period.

3   Basic calculation

Subject to the adjustments referred to later, the relief is calculated in the following way:

a   the value of all qualifying investments which are sold within the 12 month period is ascertained in accordance with the normal basis of valuation (p. 88, *ante*) as at the date of death of the deceased (para. 15 (a));

b   the sale price of these investments as at the date of sale is ascertained (para. 15 (b)). This will normally be the actual sale price, but if the sale was at an undervalue, the price which could have been obtained is substituted (*ibid*). Only the actual sale price itself is considered, and selling expenses are not taken into account (para. 21);

c   the difference between the figure at *a* and the figure at *b* is known as "the loss on sale" (para. 14 (1));

d the value of the investments at *a* is reduced by the loss on sale (para. 16).

4 Restriction on relief

The relief will be restricted or entirely lost if

a the person making the claim for relief (*infra*);

b in the same capacity as that in which he claimed the relief;

c purchases any qualifying investments (subject to the exception noted below (*infra*));

d within the period commencing on the· date of death of the deceased and ending two months after the date of the sale of the last of the qualifying investments in respect of which the claim is made (para. 17).

The purchase of the new qualifying investments within *c* can be before or after the sale of the qualifying investments in respect of which the claim is made. Where this occurs, it is necessary to apply the formula (para. 17):

$$\text{loss on sale} - \text{loss on sale} \times \frac{\text{aggregate of purchase prices of new qualifying investments}}{\text{aggregate of proceeds of sale of original qualifying investments.}}$$

If the numerator of the fraction equals or exceeds the denominator, the loss on sale is extinguished.

5 Person making the claim

The claim will normally be made by the personal representatives in respect of qualifying investments which the deceased owned outright, and by the trustees of a settlement which is taxable as a result of the death of the deceased. If, however, someone else, such as a beneficiary, pays the tax, he may make the claim (para. 14 (1), 15).

Where the claim is made by personal representatives or trustees, they are treated as a single and continuing body of persons in that capacity (para. 19). Accordingly, the relief is not lost if a personal representative, in his capacity as such, sells qualifying investments and purchases other investments in his personal capacity.

If the claim is made by someone who is not a personal representative or trustee there are two modifications to the general position. First, the relief will be restricted or lost if, within the specified period, he purchases qualifying investments in any capacity other than that of personal representative or trustee (para. 18 (1)). However, the relief is only restricted or lost if the new qualifying investments are of the same description as the ones sold (para. 18 (a)).

6 Value and Identification of investments

There are a number of detailed rules relating to the value and identification of investments. The most important of these may be summarized as follows:

a if between the date of death and the date of sale a capital payment is received in respect of the investments, that payment is added to the sale price (para. 25 (1));

b if a bonus or rights issue is made, and the shares provisionally allotted are disposed of, the proceeds of sale are also added to the sale price (para. 25 (a));

c if a call is paid, the amount paid is added to the value of the investments at death (para. 26);

d where investments owned by the deceased are exchanged as part of a take-over or reconstruction, the new shares or securities are equated with the old, with appropriate adjustments made in respect of any cash received (para. 27);

e if investments are exchanged in any other circumstances, and their market value is greater when exchanged than at the date of death, they are treated as being sold at the date of exchange for a price equal to their market value at that time (para. 24);

f if the deceased did not own outright a holding of qualifying investments, but only had an interest in such a holding, relief related to the extent of his holding can be obtained (para. 23).

7 Adjustments in value for capital transfer tax and capital gains tax purposes

It has been seen that the relief is, subject to adjustments, given by reference to a block "loss on sale", without distinguishing one investment from another. It may, however, be necessary to determine the value of individual investments for the purposes of capital transfer tax, and also capital gains tax (see CGTA 1979, s. 153). The following rules are prescribed to enable this to be done (FA 1975, Sch. 10, para. 29):

a the general rule is that the value of a specific investment is its actual sale value (para. 29 (1)). It will be recalled that this is the gross selling price, and that selling expenses are not taken into account (p. 166, *ante*);

b if the relief is restricted or lost as a result of the purchase of other qualifying investments (p. 167, *ante*), it is necessary to ascertain:

    i the value of the investment at the date of the deceased's death; and

    ii the gross sale price of the investment:

        (*a*) if i is greater than ii, the value of the investment is ii together with a proportion of the difference between ii and i;

        (*b*) if ii is greater than i, the value of the investment is ii less a proportion of the difference between i and ii (para. 29 (3)).

C SALES OF LAND AND BUILDINGS DURING COURSE OF ADMINISTRATION OF ESTATE

1 Introduction

In certain circumstances, where an interest in land is sold within three years of the death of the deceased, the value at the date of sale can be substituted for the value at the date of death (FA 1975, Sch. 10, paras. 31 to 38, added by FA 1976, s. 101 and Sch. 13).

2 Sale value

In general, the gross selling price is taken, and no account is taken of the expenses of sale (para. 39). If an interest in land is not sold for the best consideration that could reasonably be obtained at the time of sale, the amount of that consideration is substituted for the actual selling price (para. 31 (1)). It is not necessary, however, for the interest to be sold at the time at which the best consideration is likely to be obtained.

3 Restrictions on relief

The sale value can only be substituted for the value on death where the deceased died after 6 April 1976 (FA 1976, s. 101 (3)).

Further, it cannot be substituted if the sale value differs from the value on death by less than £1,000 or 5% of its value on death, whichever is lower (para. 32 (2)).

The relief is not available if the sale is to a beneficiary or to a person connected with a beneficiary (para. 32 (3)).

4 Adjustments to sale value

Rules provide for adjustments to be made to the sale value in certain circumstances. These are:

    a if the land was not in the same state at the date of sale as at the date of death, the sale value is determined as if it had been in the same state (para. 33 (1));

b   if the interest in the land was not the same, or if there was any change in its incidents, the sale value is determined as if it had been in the same state (*ibid*);

c   where the value of the interest is reduced for any reason other than normal market forces, such as by the imposition of a restriction on the use or development of the land, and compensation is payable as a result before the sale, the amount of the compensation is added to the sale price (para. 33 (3));

d   where the interest is leasehold, and at the date of death the lease has 50 years or less to run, the sale price is increased by reference to the statutory table prescribed for use in connexion with capital gains tax (set out at p. 54, *ante*). The increase in the sale price is of an amount found by applying the following formula (para. 34):

$$\frac{\text{value of interest at death} \times \left(\text{statutory percentage attributable to lease at date of death} - \text{statutory percentage attributable to lease at date of sale}\right)}{\text{statutory percentage attributable to lease at date of death}}$$

e   the value at the date of death of the interest sold may have depended partly on other interests, either in the same or other land. This will often be so where the deceased owned separate freehold and leasehold interests in the same land, and only the leasehold interest is sold; or where the deceased owned two adjoining plots and only one is sold. In such cases an addition is made to the sale value. This addition is of the amount by which the actual value at the date of death of the interest sold exceeded the value which it would have had at that date if no other interests had been taken into account (para. 35).

f   adjustments are made in the case of exchanges of land, particularly where equality money is paid (para. 36).

g   adjustments are also made where the person who makes the claim purchases any interest in land in the same capacity as that in which the land was sold, and the purchase is within the period commencing with the date of death and ending four months after the last of the sales (para. 37). The provisions in this respect generally correspond to those where stock exchange securities are bought and sold (p. 167, *ante*).

5   *Date of sale*

The relief is only available where the interest is sold within three years from the date of death. For this purpose, the date of sale is usually the date of the contract to sell (para. 40 (1)). If the sale is effected in pursuance of an option, and the option was granted not more than six months earlier, the interest is treated as being sold at the date of the grant of the option (para. 40 (2)). Special rules apply in the case of compulsory acquisition (para. 40 (3), (4)).

6   All interests sold taken into account

Where a claim is made for relief, it must apply to all interests in land owned by the deceased and sold within the period of three years after the death which are sold by the same person in the same capacity (para. 32).

7   Person to make claim

The claim is made by the person who is liable to pay the tax attributable to the value of the interest sold (para. 32 (1)). Where more than one person is liable, the claim is made by the person actually paying the tax (*ibid*).

D   SALES OF RELATED AND OTHER PROPERTY DURING COURSE OF ADMINISTRATION OF ESTATE

1   Introduction

Where property which was comprised in the deceased's estate was "related" to other property, it will have been valued on the special basis noted earlier (p. 85, *ante*). In this case, if the property which was owned by the deceased is sold within three years from the date of death, relief can be claimed whereunder the value of that property, ascertained without taking into account the related property provisions, is substituted (FA 1975, Sch. 10, para. 9A, added by FA 1976, s. 102).

A similar rule applies where the property sold was valued at the date of death in conjunction with property which was also comprised in the deceased's estate, but which has not at any time since the death been vested in the vendors (para. 9A (1) (b)).

2   "Qualifying sales"

The relief can only be claimed where the property is sold by means of a qualifying sale. The sale is a qualifying sale if (para. 9A (3)):

  a   (i) the vendors are the deceased's personal representatives; or

   (ii) the vendors are the persons in whom the property became vested immediately after the death of the deceased;

  b   the sale is at arm's length for a price freely negotiated at the time of sale;

> c the sale is not made in conjunction with a sale of any of the related property;
>
> d the vendors and purchasers are unconnected; and
>
> e neither the vendors nor a beneficiary obtain in connexion with the sale the right to acquire or re-acquire the property sold, or any interest in or created out of it.

3 *Restrictions on relief*

There are certain restrictions on the availability of the relief. These are:

> a the deceased must have died after 6 April 1976 (FA 1976, s. 102 (2));
>
> b if the property consists of securities in a close company, the value must not have been reduced by any alteration in the company's share or loan capital, or rights attaching to it (para. 9A (5));
>
> c the value of the property sold must be less than its value at the date of death after making any adjustment necessary to take account of any difference in circumstances between the date of death and the date of sale (para. 9A (4)).

E BENEFICIARY ENTITLED TO INTEREST IN POSSESSION IN RESIDUE

The rules by which the residuary income of an estate is attributed to one or more residuary beneficiaries have already been described (p. 148, *ante*). It will be appreciated that there will always be an interval of time between the date of death, and the date when the residue is ascertained.

If a person would have been entitled to an interest in possession in the residue, but dies, or deals with his interest, before the residue is ascertained, a capital transfer tax liability will arise in the same way as if the residue had been ascertained immediately after the death of the deceased (FA 1975, Sch. 5, para. 22; see. p. 288, *post*, for the general rules).

Chapter 11

Alterations to Dispositions after Death

A INTRODUCTION

The provisions of the deceased's will, or of the intestacy rules applying to his estate, may be modified by:

1 a variation of the beneficial interest by agreement between all beneficiaries affected;
2 a disclaimer by a beneficiary of his interest; or
3 an order of the court under the Inheritance (Provision for Family and Dependants) Act 1975.

This chapter is concerned with the taxation effects of such modifications, together with the effects of:

4 the execution within two years from the death of the deceased of a discretionary trust created by his will;
5 the commutation by a surviving spouse of her entitlement to a life interest under the intestacy rules; and
6 the giving effect to precatory words.

B VARIATIONS: CAPITAL TRANSFER TAX

1 *Requirements*

The present rules were introduced by FA 1978, replacing previous provisions which applied to deeds of family arrangement. FA 1978, s. 68 deals with any variation made within two years from the date of death of any of the dispositions effected by the will or the intestacy rules. The variation must be made in writing, but need not be by deed. Any persons may be introduced to take a benefit under the variation, even if they were not beneficiaries under the will itself, and even if they are not members of the family. It is not necessary for the instrument of variation to be a deed of family arrangement.

In order to be effective, the variation must be made by all persons who are, or might be, affected by it. Further, it seems that where there have been two deaths, there cannot be an effective alteration of the dispositions made by the second person to die if that would have the effect of increasing the estate of the first person to die (*Re Corbishley's Trusts*, (1880) 14 Ch.D. 846; *Re Tilt*, (1896) 74 L.T. 163).

2   Capital transfer tax effects

Where a variation is made within two years from the date of death, and the conditions noted below are satisfied, the capital transfer tax effects are:

- *a*   the variation does not constitute a transfer of value by any of the parties to it (s. 68 (1) (*a*)); and
- *b*   the capital transfer tax liability in respect of the death of the deceased is determined as if he had made the variation himself (s. 68 (1) (*b*)).

If the effect of the variation is to increase the amount of tax payable in respect of the deceased's estate, the liability to interest on the tax will be calculated from six months from the death, and not by reference to the date of the instrument.

3   Conditions

The provision applies only if the persons who are the parties to the instrument and the personal representatives give notice of election to that effect within six months from the date of the instrument, or within such longer period as the Revenue allow (s. 68 (2)). The personal representatives must join in unless the effect of the instrument will be that additional tax is payable and they have insufficient assets with which to discharge that liability (*ibid*).

The relief is not available where the variation is made for a consideration in money or money's worth, other than a benefit arising under the same or a similar variation (s. 68 (3)).

The relief can be claimed even if the assets which are subject to the instrument have been distributed, and even if the administration of the estate is complete (s. 68 (5)).

4   Interests in possession

Where the deceased was entitled to an interest in possession in settled property, the provision does not apply to that property (s. 68 (5)). Accordingly, if settled property was held upon trust for the deceased for life, with remainder to Andrew, Andrew cannot make a tax free disposition of his right to that property after the death of the deceased.

C VARIATIONS: CAPITAL GAINS TAX

There are capital gains tax rules which correspond with the capital transfer tax rules previously considered. Accordingly, where the variation is made within two years from the date of death, the parties to the instrument of variation may claim that the variation shall be treated as if it had been made by the deceased himself (CGTA 1979, s. 49 (6)). Where the claim is made, the variation does not constitute a disposal for capital gains tax purposes (s. 49 (6) (*a*)).

D VARIATIONS: INCOME TAX

1 *Effective date*

There is no corresponding provision for income tax purposes, with the result that, under the general law, the instrument only takes effect from the date on which it was executed (*Waddington* v. *O'Callaghan* (1931), 16 T.C. 187). Accordingly, where under the variation a party gives up an interest, he will nevertheless be subject to income tax on the income derived between the date of death and the date of the variation. It will, therefore, usually be appropriate in such circumstances to include in the variation a provision to ensure that the party giving up the interest receives at least the amount required to discharge that liability.

2 *The "settlement" provisions*

The instrument of variation will be a disposition, agreement or arrangement, and so, if there is any element of bounty, there will be a "settlement" for the purposes of TA 1970, ss. 444 and 454 (see p. 195, *post*). Accordingly, it will be necessary to consider whether any of the provisions referred to in Chapter 15 will apply. This is particularly important where the variation is for the benefit of an infant unmarried child of any of the parties to the variation.

E VARIATIONS: STAMP DUTY

There is no stamp duty exemption on instruments of variation. Accordingly, if the instrument effects a transfer of property or of an interest in property, *ad valorem* duty will be payable, either because there is a conveyance or transfer on sale (see *Oughtred* v. *I.R. Comrs.*, [1960] A.C. 206, H.L.) or a voluntary disposition (see *Thorn* v. *I.R. Comrs.*, [1976] 2 All E.R. 622).

F DISCLAIMERS

1 Generally

Where a person is entitled to any interest under the deceased's will, or in his estate by virtue of the intestacy rules, he may, under the general law, disclaim that interest (*Townson* v. *Tickell*, (1819) 3 B & Ald. 31). The disclaimer may be made at any time before the asset is vested in or transferred to the beneficiary.

Where the beneficiary is entitled to more than one asset, then he cannot disclaim one and keep the other if, on a true construction of the will, it appears that they are intended to be taken together (*Guthrie* v. *Walrond,* (1883) 22 Ch.D. 573). If, however, separate gifts are made in the will, the subject matter of one gift may be disclaimed and the subject matter of the other retained (*ibid*).

A gift cannot be disclaimed when the beneficiary has unequivo- cally accepted it (*Re Hodge,* [1940] Ch. 260). If a beneficiary knowingly and willingly receives income from property, that will constitute acceptance of the gift of that property (*Re Wimperis,* [1914] 1 Ch. 502).

2 Capital transfer tax

The capital transfer tax rules which apply in the case of an effec- tive disclaimer are generally the same as those which apply in the case of a variation. However, the disclaimer applies automatically from the date of death, so that there is no scope for election.

3 Capital gains tax

The position is the same as in the case of a variation.

4 Income tax

Because a disclaimer operates under the general law from the date of death, and there can only be an effective disclaimer before any benefit has been knowingly and willingly received, there will be no income tax liability on the person disclaiming.

However, a disclaimer will constitute a disposition for the settle- ment provisions.

5 Stamp duty

If the disclaimer is effected by deed, the stamp duty liability is restricted to 50p (*Re Stratton's Deed of Disclaimer,* [1958] Ch. 42).

G ORDERS UNDER THE INHERITANCE (PROVISION FOR FAMILY AND DEPENDANTS) ACT 1975

Where an order is made under the Inheritance (Provision for Family and Dependants) Act 1975, the capital transfer tax effects are broadly the same as if the terms of the order had been effected by the deceased (FA 1976, s. 122). The position is the same where proceedings under the Act are stayed or dismissed on agreed terms (FA 1980, s. 92).

There are no special capital gains tax or income tax provisions.

H EXECUTION OF DISCRETIONARY TRUSTS WITHIN TWO YEARS FROM DATE OF DEATH

1 Capital transfer tax

A special rule applies where the deceased settled property by will on discretionary trusts and the trusts are executed within two years from the date of death. This is that an actual distribution, the creation of an interest in possession, or the satisfaction of the conditions for an accumulation and maintenance settlement are not treated as capital distributions (FA 1975, s. 47 (IA)); they are, however, treated as distribution payments. Further, the liability in respect of the deceased's death is determined as if his will had provided that the property should be applied or held on his death in the manner in which it is held following the exercise by the trustees of their discretions.

2 Capital gains tax

There is no corresponding rule for capital gains tax purposes. Accordingly, when the discretion is exercised, if assets are distributed *in specie,* the trustees will be deemed to dispose of them at their market value at that time, and to re-acquire them at that value as bare trustees for the beneficiary (p. 254, *ante*). The beneficiary is treated as acquiring the assets at that value, and not at the value at the date of death.

I COMMUTATION OF LIFE INTEREST BY SURVIVING SPOUSE

Where a person dies intestate, leaving both a surviving spouse and children, the surviving spouse receives, subject to minor exceptions, a statutory legacy, at present, £40,000, and a life interest in one half of the remainder of the estate (Administration of Estates Act 1925, s. 46 (1); Family Provision (Intestate Succession) Order 1981, S.I. 1981 No. 255). However, the surviving spouse can elect to take a further capital sum in lieu of her life interest (AEA, 1925, s. 47A). If a surviving spouse, by making this election, gives up her life interest and receives a capital sum, she is not treated as making a transfer of value for capital transfer tax purposes, and she is treated as if she had been entitled to that capital sum (FA 1975, s. 47 (3)).

J   PRECATORY WORDS

It is not unusual for a person when making his will to leave money or property to a beneficiary, and at the same time to express a wish that that beneficiary should apply the whole or part of that money or property to some other person. It is of the essence of this arrangement that the testator's wish does not impose a legally binding obligation on the beneficiary.

Strictly, if the beneficiary carries out the testator's wishes, he will be making a gift. However, where the beneficiary carries out the testator's wishes within a period of two years from the date of death, those wishes are treated for capital transfer tax purposes as if they were terms of the will itself (FA 1975, s. 47 (IB)). Accordingly, no liability will fall upon the beneficiary named in the will in consequence of his giving effect to the testator's wishes.

PART IV

General Considerations Affecting the Taxation of Trusts

Chapter 12

Effective and Ineffective Acts of Trustees

A INTRODUCTION

The question sometimes arises: to what extent is the Revenue bound by acts of the trustees if those acts are unauthorised, or of a nature of which a court would disapprove? The answer appears to be as follows:

    a if an act is void, neither the Revenue nor any other person need take account of it. It is as if that act had never been done;

    b if an act is voidable, it remains an effective act until it is avoided, so that, until it is avoided it will bind the Revenue. This will be so even if the act was done with the sole motive of mitigating a liability to tax; and

    c the Revenue has no power to apply for the act to be avoided.

It is, therefore, necessary first to distinguish between acts which are void and those which are voidable.

B ACTS IN RELATION TO BENEFICIAL INTERESTS

1 Generally

If trustees purport to interfere in any way with the beneficial interest of a beneficiary, without authority either from the trust instrument or the Trustee Act 1925, that act will be void unless each

179

beneficiary, whose interest is affected, agrees. For example, in *Re Alfred Herbert Pension and Life Assurance Scheme*, [1960] 1 All E.R. 618 where there was a purported amendment to the trusts affecting a pension fund, and that amendment was outside the terms of the trust deed, it was held that the amendment was not valid because it could have had the effect of changing the beneficial interests of employees participating in the scheme.

2 *Appropriation*

The exercise of a power of appropriation affects beneficial entitlement, because, if the power is validly exercised, it has the effect of depriving a beneficiary of the right of recourse to other trust property to satisfy his interest. The circumstances in which trustees can appropriate are considered elsewhere (p. 264, *post*), but if trustees purport to appropriate when they have no power to do so, that act will be void. However, because beneficiaries can agree to action taken by a trustee in so far as it relates to their own interest, if all the beneficiaries who could in any circumstances be affected by an appropriation agree, the appropriation will be effective even where there is no power in the trust instrument or under the general law.

3 *Accumulation*

The exercise of a power of accumulation also affects beneficial entitlement, because, where it is exercised, it has the effect of reducing the amount of income to which a beneficiary would otherwise be entitled, or of reducing the amount of income available for distribution among discretionary objects. The circumstances in which income can be effectively accumulated are also mentioned elsewhere (p. 000, *post*), but if trustees purport to accumulate income when they have no power to do so, the income will retain its character as income, and will be subject to the obligation of the trustees to distribute it. Thus, in *Re Gourju's Will Trusts*, [1943] Ch. 24 trustees held a fund upon protective trusts for the benefit of the settlor's widow for life, with remainders over. By virtue of the protective trusts, the widow's fixed interest would come to an end if any event occurred which would deprive her of the right to receive the income. The widow was resident in France before the outbreak of the 1939 – 1945 War, and by virtue of the Trading with the Enemy Act, 1939, the widow ceased to be entitled to the income, and the discretionary phase of the protective trust arose. The trustees credited the income to a suspense account, intending to keep it until the end of the war, and then to pay it to the widow. It was held that the discretionary trust having arisen, the trustees had no power to retain the income, but were bound to distribute it as and when they received it.

Where the trustees purport to accumulate, in pursuance of a power in the trust instrument, they can only effectively do so if that power is itself valid (see *Re Rochford's Settlement Trusts,* [1965] Ch. 111; *Baird* v. *Lord Advocate,* [1979] A.C. 666, H.L.). If a trust for accumulation infringes the perpetuity rule, it is wholly void (*Curtis* v. *Lukin* (1842), 5 Beav. 147). If the trust does not infringe the perpetuity rule, but within the perpetuity period directs accumulation for a period longer than that authorised by the Law of Property Act 1925, and the Perpetuities and Accumulations Act 1964 (see p. 237, *post*) the accumulation is void only to the extent of the excess over the nearest authorised period (*Re Ransome's Will Trust,* [1957] Ch. 348 at 361).

C ACTS IN RELATION TO TRUSTEESHIP

There can only be an effective change in the trusteeship in exercise of an authority conferred by the Trustee Act or the trust instrument, and any purported change made without such authority is void. For example, Trustee Act 1925, s. 36 (6) provides that the person who has the power to appoint new trustees may, within certain limits, appoint *another* person to be an additional trustee. In *Re Power's Settlement Trusts,* [1951] Ch. 1074 the person having the power of appointment purported to appoint himself to be an additional trustee, but it was held that this was void.

If, however, an appointment is made in pursuance of a power conferred by statute or the trust instrument, but it is made in circumstances in which the court would not itself have made it, the appointment will be effective unless and until a beneficiary takes action to set it aside. In *Re Whitehead's Will Trusts,* [1971] 2 All ER 1334 where non-resident trustees had been appointed, Pennycuick, V. – C., said (at p, 837):

"... the law has been quite well established for upwards of a century that there is no absolute bar to the appointment of persons resident abroad as trustees of an English trust. I say 'no absolute bar', in the sense that such an appointment would be prohibited by law and would consequently be invalid. On the other hand, apart from exceptional circumstances, it is not proper to make such an appointment, that is to say, the court would not, apart from exceptional circumstances, make such an appointment; nor would it be right for the donees of the power to make such an appointment out of court. If they did, presumably the court would be likely to interfere at the instance of the beneficiaries".

D   ACTS IN RELATION TO THE TRUST PROPERTY

1   Generally

Where trustees do an unauthorised act in relation to trust property, that act is in principle voidable only. The position is best illustrated where trustees sell trust property to themselves without there being a power to do so in the trust instrument, or without the sanction of the court or the consent of the beneficiaries. The sale is effective, in order to pass title to the purchasing trustee, and, if he re-sells, from him to an ultimate purchaser (*Cookson* v. *Lee* (1853), 23 L.J. Ch. 473; *Aberdeen Town County Council* v. *Aberdeen University* (1877), 2 App. Cas. 544). If requested to do so, the court will usually, but not always (*Holder* v. *Holder,* [1968] Ch. 353), upset the sale against the trustee, and against a third party who purchased with knowledge of the circumstances (*Wright* v. *Morgan,* [1926] A.C. 788). Until, however, the transaction is upset, the sale will be effective. Accordingly, if the property had risen in value before it was sold, a capital gains tax liability would arise on the sale.

There are many circumstances in which an act (unless and until avoided) will be effective to cause the legal title to pass. If, however, the person who acquires the property holds it on a constructive trust for the original beneficiaries, then for so long as the constructive trust continues, the act will have few taxation consequences.

2   Acts void by statute

In certain circumstances, acts in respect of trust property are not merely voidable, but are declared to be void by statute (see, e.g. the Settled Land Act 1925, s. 18). In this case there will be no effective act.

3   Acts for which consent is required

If by statute consent is required for an act in relation to the trust property, and that consent is not obtained, the act is void. (see, e.g. the Law of Property Act 1925, s. 30).

4   Acts also affecting beneficial entitlement

Certain acts both relate to the trust property and also directly affect beneficial entitlement. The rule as to beneficial interests prevails, so that if the act is on that account void, it will be void, even if otherwise it would only be voidable.

E   REVENUE HAS NO *LOCUS STANDI*

Where an act is voidable, it is voidable at the instance only of a beneficiary. The dictum of Pennycuick, V. – C., quoted above (see p. 181) refers to the court interfering at the instance of the beneficiaries. As a further illustration, in the context of a trustee selling trust property to himself, in *Tito* v. *Waddell (No. 2),* [1977] 3 All E.R. 129 Megarry V. – C., said (at p. 241) that "if a beneficiary sells the trust property to himself the sale is voidable by any beneficiary". There appears to be no reported decision in which the Revenue has itself attempted to have an act avoided, but as, despite the view of the cynic, the Revenue is not a beneficiary under a trust, it seems clear that it has no *locus standi* to make such application.

Chapter 13

Settlements and Settlors

A ·TYPES OF SETTLEMENT

1 Meaning of "Settlement"

Before considering the taxation provisions affecting settled property and the income from settled property, it may be helpful to consider certain concepts of the general law on which they are based. There is often difficulty over terminology.

For the purposes of the general law there are at least three meanings of the word "settlement":

a the act of transferring property to trustees to be held on certain trusts;

b the deed of settlement, which specifies the trusts powers and provisions on which the property is held; and

c the state of affairs which exists when property has been transferred to trustees and is held by them upon the trusts of a deed of settlement.

For taxation purposes, "settlement" is primarily used in the third sense of a state of affairs. It follows that if different property is held on different trusts for different beneficiaries, there can be more than one settlement, although there is only one deed of settlement (see, eg. *Roome* v. *Edwards,* [1981] 1 All E.R. 736, H.L.; p. 264, *post*).

2. Trusts and settlements

Fundamentally, there is a trust whenever one person, the trustee, holds property for one or more others, the beneficiaries. All settlements therefore create trusts but the expression "trust" is also sometimes used to denote the state of affairs in which property is held on trust. It has not been necessary for the general law to draw a careful distinction between a trust in this sense and settlement, but traditionally there is said to be a trust:

a   if it is created by will; or
b   if it is created by a person declaring himself to be a trustee of certain property for others; or
c   if it is created *inter vivos*, and is not complicated, as where a parent receives property to hold on behalf of his infant child; or
d   where the general law imposes on a person the duties of a trustee irrespective of the intention or wishes of that person.

Where the expression is contrasted with a trust, a "settlement" is conventionally used to described an elaborate *inter vivos* disposition on trust.

For taxation purposes, there is no distinction between a trust and a settlement. Although in certain instances the legislation refers to a trust (see, e.g. FA 1972, s. 86 (5)), in general the references are to settlements. Thus, even if a trust is created by will, it will come within the expression "settlement".

3   Estates in course of administration

Although there are many similarities, where an estate is in the course of administration, there is no settlement or settled property. This is so for the general law, because no beneficiary under a will or intestacy has any individual beneficial interest in any asset which is being administered, but only the right to ensure proper administration of the estate (*Stamp Duties Commissioner for Queensland* v. *Livingston,* [1965] A.C. 694, P.C.). This distinction is followed for taxation purposes, so that provisions affecting settled property do not apply to property which forms part of a deceased's estate in the course of administration.

B   CLASSIFICATION FOR TAXATION

It is possible to distinguish the following different types of settlement for taxation purposes

a   "ordinary" settlements, namely settlements which are not within any of the other categories;
b   bare trusts, and nomineeships. In both cases there are one or more persons concurrently and beneficially entitled to the property, but under a bare trust the trustee has administrative powers and discretions vested in him, whereas in the case of a nomineeship those powers and discretions are usually wholly or mainly excluded by contract;
c   bare trusts for infants, where, although the infant is the bene-

ficial owner of the property, because he is an infant, he cannot give an effective direction to the trustee how to deal with it;

d part XVI settlements, which are various structures and devices which may or may not be settlements under the general law. These are considered separately later (*infra*);

e deemed settlements, namely devices which are not settlements for the general law, but which are treated as settlements for taxation purposes. These apply for capital transfer tax purposes only, the main example being a lease for life.

The following summarises the taxation treatment of property subject to, and income derived from, these settlements and quasi-settlements.

Whether treated as a settlement for the purposes of:

Type of settlement	Income tax	Capital gains tax	Capital gains tax (Foreign trust)	Development land tax	Capital transfer tax
Bare trust for adult	Yes	No	No	No	No
Bare trust for infant	Yes	No	No	No	No
Ordinary voluntary settlement	Yes	Yes	Yes	Yes	Yes
Ordinary settlement for full consideration	Yes	Yes	No	Yes	Yes (except annuities)
Part XVI settlement	Yes (but liability usually that of settlor)	No, unless an ordinary settlement	Yes	No, unless an ordinary settlement	No
Deemed settlement	No	No	No	No	Yes

C PART XVI SETTLEMENTS

1 Generally

These settlements are so called because they are defined by TA 1970, s. 444 and 454, which are both within Part XVI, of that Act. They are important primarily for income tax purposes, but the concept is used also for some capital gains tax purposes. Although often what is a settlement for the purposes of the general law will be a

Part XVI settlement, however, Part XVI is in one respect narrower, and in many respects wider, than the definition for the purposes of the general law.

2 Requirement for bounty

For the purposes of the general law, and for taxation purposes generally, there can be a settlement even though it was created for full consideration. However, there can only be a Part XVI settlement where it was created with at least some element of bounty (*Bulmer* v. *I.R. Comrs.*, [1967] Ch. 145; *I.R. Comrs.* v. *Plummer*, [1979] 3 All E.R. 775, H.L.; *Chinn* v. *Collins* [1981] 1 All E.R. 189, H.L.; see p. 377, *post*).

3 Width of definition

Provided that there is some element of bounty, there will be a Part XVI settlement if there is any disposition, trust, covenant, agreement or arrangement (ss. 444 (2) and 454 (3)). For the purposes of s. 444, an outright transfer of assets is also a settlement (*infra*).

There will often be more than one element in a Part XVI settlement. The definitions in ss. 444 and 454 attempt to achieve for income tax very broadly what the associated operations provision sets out to achieve for capital transfer tax. If, therefore there are two or more elements it seems that all those elements can together be regarded as constituting an "arrangement" and thus a settlement if they all came into being as a result of a plan carried out by, or at the instance of, the same orchestrator. A person might, for example, transfer money to trustees to hold upon certain trusts, on the basis that they will use some of that money to promote an investment company and subscribe for the shares in that company. Both the trust and the company can together constitute an arrangement, and so be a Part XVI settlement. An ordinary settlement can, therefore, either be, or be part of, a Part XVI settlement.

4 Examples

It is impossible to give a comprehensive list of Part XVI settlements, but the following are examples:

a Outright gift (for s. 444) (*Hood-Barrs* v. *I.R. Comrs.* (1946), 27 T.C. 385; *Thomas* v. *Marshall* (1953), 34 T.C. 178).

b Surrender of a life interest (*I.R. Comrs.* v. *Buchanan* (1957), 37 T.C. 365). In this case a fund was held upon protective trust for B for life, with remainder to her children. The trust deed provided that if B disclaimed her interest, it was to be assumed that she were dead. B disclaimed her interest, and it was held that she had created a Part XVI settlement.

c   Consent order of court directing property to be held in trust for a child (*Yates* v. *Starkey* (1951), 32 T.C. 38). There is, however, no settlement if a court order is made for the payment of income directly to a child (p. 220, *post*).

d   Increase in capital of company otherwise than to benefit the company (*Copeman* v. *Coleman,* [1939] 2 K.B. 484). The taxpayer and his wife owned the share capital in a company of which they were the directors. They procured the company to increase its share capital by the creation of preference shares, which were made available on advantageous terms to their children and other relations. This was an arrangement and so a settlement.

e   Loans (*I.R. Comrs.* v. *Leiner* (1964) 41 T.C. 589). The taxpayer's mother had lent, without interest, £34,000 to a company in which the taxpayer was interested. The mother created a discretionary settlement for the benefit of the taxpayer and his children, whereupon the company repaid the loan to the mother; the mother settled that sum; the trustees lent it to the taxpayer at interest; and the taxpayer lent the proceeds of the loan to the company without interest. The company was left in the same net position, but the taxpayer was not subject to a liability to pay interest to the trustees. This was held to be an arrangement and so a settlement.

f   Guarantee deposits (*I.R. Comrs.* v. *Wachtel* [1971] Ch. 573). The settlor guaranteed a loan to trustees of an ordinary settlement, and deposited a sum with the bank in support of the guarantee. As the trustees repaid the loan, the deposit was progressively released. This was an arrangement and so a settlement.

g   Formation of company and ancillary agreements (*Crossland* v. *Hawkins* (1961), 39 T.C. 493 and *I.R. Comrs.* v. *Mills,* [1975] A.C. 38). The essence of both cases was that an ordinary settlement was created for the benefit of children, and the trustees applied part of the settled fund in subscribing for the share capital in a new company with which the parent entered into a service agreement to provide services on terms advantageous to the company. This was also an arrangement and so a settlement.

It is stressed that these are examples only, which are intended to illustrate the very wide scope of the provisions governing Part XVI settlements.

D UNWITTING SETTLEMENTS

Even where a Part XVI is not in point, a settlement can come into being as a result of a different transaction, even though this was not the intention of the parties. The problem arises particularly with transactions affecting landed property. In the ordinary conveyancing transaction for the sale of a house, there is an exchange of contracts followed after, say, a month by completion of the conveyance. When contracts are exchanged the general principle is that the vendor becomes a type of trustee for the purchaser, but the vendor is entitled to retain possession of the property until the date specified in the contract for completion. It can be said, therefore, that between exchange of contracts and completion the vendor holds the property on trust for himself until the date specified for completion, with remainder to the purchaser. The point is not taken in the ordinary case, but the Revenue view is that where the date for completion is postponed for much longer than the normal period, the property is settled property at least for the purposes of capital gains tax and capital transfer tax.

E SETTLORS

The definitions of settlor follow the definitions of settlement (TA 1970, ss. 444 (2), 454 (3); FA 1975, Sch. 5, para. 1 (6)). In general, a person is a settlor if:

a he himself creates the settlement and provides the initial trust property; or

b he is not a party to the settlement, but directly or indirectly provides funds for it; or

c he makes with another person a reciprocal arrangement for that other person to make the settlement.

With regard to the last case, the notion of reciprocity implies an approximate balance of consideration moving between the persons concerned. If, therefore, the person who makes the settlement does so at the request of another, but without consideration provided by that other, that other would not appear to be a settlor. It may well be that if there is consideration, but disproportionate to the amount settled, there will also not be a *reciprocal* arrangement.

More than one person can be a settlor.

PART V

The Creation of a Trust in Lifetime

Chapter 14

Tax Consequences of the Creation of a Trust

A CREATION OF A TRUST

A trust may be created by a person *inter vivos,* in which case it is usually called a settlement, or by will, to take effect on his death. The creator of a trust is called a settlor. However the trust is created, trustees may be constituted in more than one way.

A trust may be created by the settlor in his lifetime by either:

1   declaring himself to be the sole trustee; or
2   transferring property to one or more other persons, of whom he may be one, to be held on trust.

It may be convenient to note here that where a trust is created by will the persons appointed executors of the will are usually appointed as trustees. The distinction between their office as personal representatives, which will usually last for life, and the capacity in which an asset is held, has already been noted in the context of capital gains tax (see, p. 153, *ante*). For the purposes of income tax, their capacity will terminate on the completion of the administration of the estate (p. 139, *ante*) but they may have acquired the capacity of trustees in respect of particular assets or funds at an earlier date.

B INCOME TAX: THE GENERAL RULE

The general rule is that when a trust is created, income which arises from the assets put into trust is treated for all purposes as the income of the trustees and not of the settlor. The only general exception to this rule is where the whole or part of the income is payable to the settlor in his capacity as a beneficiary. In that event, from the creation of the trust the settlor is taxable on the income to the same extent as any other beneficiary, in accordance with the principles described in Chapter 2.

The general rule that where the settlor is not himself a beneficiary then he is not subject to income tax in his personal capacity applies even where the trust is created by a method under which the settlor declares himself to be the sole trustee.

Where the trust is a Part XVI settlement (p. 186, *ante*) the whole or part of the income may continue to be regarded as that of the settlor. The circumstances in which this is so are considered in Chapter 15.

C CAPITAL GAINS TAX

1 *Where settlor retains an interest*

Where a settlement is created by the settlor in his lifetime with the transfer of specific assets into the settlement, there is a disposal for capital gains tax purposes of the entire property which becomes settled (CGTA 1979, s. 53). This general rule applies even if the settlor retains a beneficial interest under the settlement, and even if the settlement is revocable (*ibid*). This is so irrespective of the type of transfer by which the property becomes settled (FA 1981, s. 86).

2 *Cash settlement*

There is no capital gains tax liability where a settlement is created with cash, although if the settlor had to dispose of assets in order to obtain cash, a liability to capital gains tax may have arisen as a result of that disposal in the usual way (pp. 39, *ante, et seq*).

3 *Asset settlement*

Where an asset is transferred into a settlement, in principle there is a disposal of that asset at its market value, and an acquisition of it by the trustees at that value (CGTA 1979, s. 29A(1); FA 1981, s. 90). However, the settlor can elect that the gain shall be rolled over into the settlement (FA 1981, s. 78). Where this election is made, the acquisition value to the trustees is correspondingly reduced (see FA 1980, s. 79).

The settlor and his trustees are treated as "connected persons" for capital gains tax purposes (CGTA 1979, s. 63 (3)). As a result, in general, if an asset is transferred to a settlement and a loss arises on that disposal, that loss can only be used to offset gains on other disposals to the trustees of the same settlement (s. 62 (3)). There is, however, no such restriction on the use of losses where the settlement is created for charitable, cultural, or recreational purposes (s. 62 (3), *proviso*).

D   DEVELOPMENT LAND TAX

Where a person makes a voluntary disposition of an interest in land to a settlement, the position is the same as if he made a gift. Accordingly, no liability will arise on the settlor, and, in general, the settlor and the trustees will, thereafter, be regarded as being one person.

If there is a sale of an interest in land to a settlement, the liability will be computed in the same way as in the case of a sale to a third party. The liability will not be reduced because the settlor has a beneficial interest under the settlement.

E   CAPITAL TRANSFER TAX

There is no special capital transfer tax provision which applies on the creation of a settlement, so that the general capital transfer tax principles apply. As a result:

1   Where the settlor retains no beneficial interest under the settlement, the creation of the settlement will usually involve a transfer of value of an amount equal to value of the settled property (FA 1975, s. 20 (2)). If the settlor pays the capital transfer tax, the value of the property transferred will have to be grossed up p. 69, *ante*).

2   As exceptions to this general principle, there will be no liability to capital transfer tax, or only a limited liability where:

a   the settlor's spouse takes the first "interest in possession" under the settlement (FA 1975, Sch. 6, para. 1; Sch. 5, para. 3 (1)). The expression "interest in possession" is defined later (p. 288, *post*);

b   one or more of the general exemptions from capital transfer tax apply (pp. 76, *ante, et seq*); or

c   where the creation of the settlement comes within the specific exemption for dispositions for family maintenance (p. 78, *ante*).

3   Where the settlor takes the first interest in possession under the settlement, there will be no liability to capital transfer tax when the settlement is created (FA 1975, s. 20 (2); Sch. 5, para. 3 (1)). There will usually be a charge to tax when that interest comes to an end (Sch. 5, para 10).

4   Where the settlor does not take an immediate interest in possession under the settlement, but takes some future interest, it is necessary to value his interest immediately after the settlement is made. There will be a liability to capital transfer tax on the difference between the value of the property put into settlement, and the value of the settlor's interest retained. Although account is not usually taken of future or reversionary interests which are given away (but see FA 1976, s. 120), account is taken of such interests which are retained by the settlor (FA 1975, s. 20 (3)).

5   Care should be taken to ensure that there is no binding agreement on the part of the trustees to pay the capital transfer tax due on the transfer of assets into the settlement. The implications are discussed later (see p. 221, *post*).

Income Treated as that of the Settlor

Chapter 15

I Income Treated as that of
the Settlor
II Settlements Where Settlor May
Derive Some Benefit
III Settlements for Settlor's
Children

I INCOME TREATED AS THAT OF THE SETTLOR

A SETTLEMENTS

The wide definitions of "settlement" given by TA 1970, s. 444 and 454 have already been noted (p. 187, *ante*). Where there is a settlement within these definitions there may be a liability on the settlor in respect of the whole or part of the income which arises to the trustees.

Where the provisions might apply, there are four important questions:

a which of the provisions, if any, does apply?

b is the settlor liable on the whole of the income of the settlement, or only part?

c is the settlor liable to income tax for all purposes, or only for the purposes of income tax in excess of the basic rate?

d does the settlor have a right to recover from the trustees the amount of tax which he has suffered on the trust income?

Particular care is needed over question *a*, because two or more provisions may apply concurrently.

The provisions may be considered in the following groups:

1 provisions affecting covenants;
2 provisions applying where the settlor or his spouse do or might derive some benefit from the settled property; and
3 provisions for the benefit of the settlor's infant unmarried children.

B POSITION OF SETTLOR

1 Income unearned

Where income is deemed to be that of the settlor, it is always treated as a separate source of income. This is so even if the income originated from the settlor. If, therefore, a person pays income under a covenant to trustees, and, had he not entered into that covenant, the income would have been taxable in his hands as earned income, the effect of it being deemed to be his income will be to treat it as unearned income in his hands (*Ang* v. *Parrish,* [1980] 2 All E.R. 790).

2 Right of recovery

In certain circumstances, the settlor has the right to require the Revenue to furnish a certificate of the amount of tax which he pays on the income of the settlement, and the right to require the trustees to pay to him from the trust fund the amount of tax so certified. Where this right exists, it is noted in the context of each provision discussed in this Chapter.

3 Repayment to the trustees

The effect of deeming income to be that of the settlor can be to give the settlor a right to the repayment of income tax if his marginal rate is less than the rate at which the income has been taxed in the hands of the trustees. In all cases where the settlor has a right to recover from the trustees tax which he pays on trust income, a settlor is liable to account to the trustees for any tax repayment which he receives in respect of the trust income (ss. 435 (2), 441 (2), 449 (4)).

4 Highest part of income

Any income which is deemed to be that of the settlor under these provisions is treated generally as being the highest part of his income (ss. 435 (3), 441 (3), 449 (5)). The settlor's income is, however, calculated without taking into account certain special forms of income (s. 529).

5 Exempt British government securities

Where the provisions apply the income will still be deemed to be the income of the settlor even if the settled property consists of exempt British Government securities (see p. 405, *post*), and the person whose actual income it is could satisfy the conditions for the exemption (TA 1970, s. 99 (3)).

C COVENANTS

1 Covenants as settlements

Both ss. 444 and 454 expressly define settlement as including "covenant", and any deed of covenant is, therefore, to be treated as a settlement, even although the covenantor has not disposed of any capital.

The effect of the legislation is that it is necessary to consider separately:

a voluntary non-charitable covenants;
b covenants for valuable consideration; and
c voluntary charitable covenants.

It is proposed to consider first the effect of various statutory provisions before seeing their combined effect on these three types of covenant.

2 The period of a covenant

Section 434 (1), which applies particularly to non-charitable covenants, operates where income is payable "for a period which cannot exceed six years". Section 434 (1A), which applies to charitable covenants, applies where the income is payable for a period which cannot exceed three years. For the purposes of both provisions, the period is measured:

a *from* the *later* of:

　(i) the date of the deed; and
　(ii) the date of the first payment due under the deed
b *to* the date of the last payment due under the deed.

In *I.R. Comrs.* v. *St. Luke's Hostel Trustees* (1930), 15 T.C. 682 the deed was dated 3 February 1927, and provided for payments to be made for a term of seven years from 31 December 1926. The last payment would fall due on 31 December 1932. Although seven payments were to be made, the period between 3 February 1927 and 31 December 1932 was one which could not exceed six years.

It is not necessary to show that the period must in any event exceed a stated period, merely that it can do so. Thus, a covenant for seven years or until the earlier death of the covenantor will not be caught by s. 434. Further, the fact that, when a covenant is in force, there is a subsequent agreement between the covenantor and the covenantee that the covenant should be terminated will not in itself bring the covenant within s. 434. It is otherwise if at the time when the covenant was made there was an agreement that the covenant would be prematurely determined.

3   The main statutory provisions

If a covenant is to be effective for tax purposes, it is necessary to show that it does not come within three main provisions:

a   s. 434 which applies for all purposes, but is often of primary importance in determining basic rate relief;

b   s. 457 which is concerned with relief at rates of income tax in excess of the basic rate; and

c   FA 1977, s. 48, which is concerned with both basic and excess rates.

The other provisions to be taken into account are noted below (p. 201, *et seq, post*).

4   TA 1970, s. 434

a   The general rule   Section 434 provides that any income which is payable to or applicable for the benefit of any other person for a period which cannot exceed six years is deemed to be the income of the covenantor for all the purposes of the Income Tax Acts (s. 434 (1)). It therefore applies to income tax both at the basic rate and at the higher rates.

b   Covenants for valuable and sufficient consideration   Section 434 has no application where the covenant is made for valuable and sufficient consideration. In *I.R. Comrs.* v. *Plummer,* [1979] 3 All E.R. 775 H.L. it was held that a covenant for five years to pay the sum of £500 after deduction of income tax at the basic rate granted in exchange for a capital sum of £2,480 was entered into for valuable and sufficient consideration. In this case, it was said that the taxation position of the covenantor was relevant to be taken into account in deciding whether the consideration was sufficient.

c   Death   The section ceases to apply to a covenant on the death of the covenantor. Accordingly, if the burden of the covenant passes to the covenantor's estate, and through the estate to one of the beneficiaries, payments by that beneficiary will not fall within the section.

5   TA 1970, s. 457

a   The general rule   Section 457 provides that, generally, where income is payable under covenant, the income is to be treated as that of the covenantor for the purposes of rates of income tax in excess of the basic rate (s. 457 (1)). The section does not apply, however, where, under some other provision, such as s. 434, the income is treated as the income of the settlor for all income tax purposes (s. 457 (1) (*e*)).

b   Partnership agreements   The section does not apply to annual payments made under a partnership agreement to or for the benefit of a former member of the partnership, or his widow or dependants, provided the liability was incurred for full consideration (s. 457 (1) (*a*)).

c   Payments for the acquisition of a business   The section also does not apply to annual payments made in connection with the payer's acquisition of the whole or part of a business, if the payments are made to the vendor or, if he is dead, to his widow or dependants (s. 457 (1) (*b*), (2) (*a*)). A similar provision applies where the business or interest in the business was acquired from a partnership (s. 457 (2) (*b*)). In both cases, the liability must have been incurred for full consideration.

d   Maintenance payments   Further, the section does not apply where payments are made by one party to a marriage for the benefit of the other party to that marriage (s. 457 (1) (*c*)). This provision applies where the parties are permanently separated, or where the marriage is ended by a decree of divorce or nullity. This exception is confined to payments for the benefit only of the other party to the marriage: provision for children is not excluded under this heading (in respect of the Revenue's concessionary treatment of income payable under court orders for the maintenance of children, see, p. 220, *post*).

e   Death   As in the case of s. 434, the section ceases to apply to a covenant on the death of the covenantor. The same effects ensue as in the case of s. 434 (*supra*).

f   Basis rate   Section 457 applies only in respect of rates of tax in excess of the basic rate. Accordingly, if a covenant is caught only by s. 457, the covenantor will be able to obtain basic rate relief.

6 FA 1977, s. 48

a The general rule FA 1977, s. 48 applies where the payment of an annuity or other annual payment is made under a liability incurred for a consideration in money or money's worth, and that consideration is not required to be brought into account in computing for the purposes of income tax the income of the covenantor (s. 48 (2)). It seems that the only circumstances in which such consideration is to be brought into account in computing the income of the covenantor is where he conducts a trade of granting annuities, or where a liability arises under Schedule D, Case VI.

Where the general rule applies, the amount of the covenanted payment is not deductible in computing his income or total income either for basic rate or higher rate purposes (s. 48 (1)). Further the payments must be made gross.

b Partnership agreements The section does not apply where the payment is made under a partnership agreement, and the payment is outside the scope of s. 457 (s. 48 (3) (*a*): see p. 199, *ante*).

c Payments for the acquisition of a business The same exception applies as in the case of s. 457 (*ibid*).

d Maintenance payments Again the same exception applies as in the case of s. 457 (*ibid*).

e Payments in respect of beneficial interests Section 48 does not apply where the payment is made to an individual under a liability incurred in consideration of his surrendering, assigning or releasing an interest in settled property to or in favour of a person having a subsequent interest in that property (s. 48 (3) (*b*)).

f Income from foreign source Section 48 applies only where the payment is charged with tax under Schedule D, Case III. If, therefore, the income is paid from a source outside the United Kingdom, such as from interest earned on a deposit account with an overseas bank, the interest will be charged to tax under Schedule D, Case V, so that section 48 will not apply.

7 Charitable covenants

a Covenanted payments to charity FA 1980, s. 55 introduced special provisions in respect of covenanted payments to charity. These are payments made under a covenant in favour of a body of

persons or trust established for charitable purposes only. The covenant must be for a period which may exceed three years, and is not
capable of earlier termination under any power exercisable without
the consent of the charity (s. 434 (2); FA 1980, s. 55 (1) (c)). A payment is not a covenanted payment to charity if the covenant was
entered into for a consideration in money or money's worth (*ibid*).

b   Four year covenants   Where the covenant is within the terms
just described, s. 434 will have no application in relation to payments
made after 5 April 1980 (FA 1980, s. 55 (4)).

c   Charitable covenants not exceeding £3,000 p.a.   It has been
seen (p. 199, *ante*) that even where s. 434 does not apply, s. 457 will
usually make the settlor liable to income tax on covenanted income
at the rates of tax in excess of the basic rate. This does not apply,
however, to the first £3,000 of gross covenanted payments to charity
(s. 457 (1A); FA 1980, s. 56 (2)). This provision operates only in
respect of payments made after 5 April 1981 (FA 1980, s. 56 (6)).

d   Charitable covenants exceeding £3,000 p.a.   Where the
amount of covenanted payments to charity exceeds £3,000 in a year,
the covenant, being outside s. 434 (1), will entitle the covenantor to
basic rate relief, but, being within s. 457, will not entitle the covenantor to excess rate relief on the excess over £3,000.

8   Covenants for infants

Covenanted income payable to or for the benefit of an infant
unmarried child of the settlor is treated as that of the settlor in all
circumstances (s. 437; see p. 218, *post*).

9.   Revocable covenants

If the covenantor or any other person has the power to revoke or
terminate a covenant, then income is treated as that of the covenantor (s. 445, see p. 210, *post*). The power to revoke or determine
must be contained in the deed of covenant itself. The fact that any
covenant can be determined by agreement between covenantor and
covenantee does not cause this provision to apply.

The section does not apply where the power to revoke or determine
does not arise for at least six years from the making of the covenant.
In the case of covenanted payments to charity, the corresponding
period is three years (s. 445 (1A); FA 1980, s. 55 (2)).

10 Undistributed income

There are two separate provisions dealing with the position where income paid under a covenant during a year of assessment is not distributed in that year.

a   Where settlor retains an interest   If the covenanted payments are made to trustees, and they do not distribute the whole of the income so paid, that undistributed income is treated as the income of the settlor for all purposes if he retained an interest in the settlement (s. 447; see p. 206, *post*).

b   Where covenantor does not retain an interest   A further provision applies where the covenantor does not retain any interest in the settlement (s. 450). In this case, the covenantor's liability is only to the rates of income tax in excess of the basic rate.

11 Exceptions from the settlement provisions

Where a covenant is *prima facie* within one of the provisions considered, there are three possible grounds on which the particular covenant may be outside them. These are where:

a   the covenant is of a type which is expressly excluded, as in the case of maintenance payments which are expressly excluded from s. 457 and s. 48 of the Finance Act, 1977; or

b   the covenant was made for valuable and "sufficient" consideration (s. 434); or, where it was made for one of the purposes excepted from s. 457, it was made for "full" consideration; or

c   the covenant is not a "settlement" because it was not made with any element of bounty (see p. 187, *ante*). This applies to all the provisions considered except FA 1977, s. 48. This section has effect whether or not there was an element of bounty, provided that there was some non-taxable consideration for the grant of the covenant.

12 Recovery by covenantor

The provisions so far considered in this Chapter apply only for income tax purposes. They do not in any way affect the liability of the covenantor under the general law to make the covenanted payments. However, in some, but not all, cases the covenantor may obtain from the Revenue a certificate of the amount of income tax which he has paid on the covenanted income, and recover that tax from the covenantee.

The covenantor's right of recovery is shown by the following table:

Vitiating provision	Whether right of recovery	Authority
s. 434	Yes	s. 435 (1)
s. 457	No	
FA 1977, s. 48	No	
s. 437	Yes	s. 441
s. 445	Yes	s. 449 (3)
s. 447	Yes	s. 449 (3)
s. 450	No	

13   Obtaining relief

Where the covenanted payment is treated as the income of the covenantee, and not as the income of the covenantor, the covenantor should deduct income tax at the basic rate under s. 52, and furnish the covenantee with a certificate of deduction of tax. By retaining the sum so deducted, the covenantor obtains basic rate relief.

Where the covenanted payment carries relief also for higher rate purposes, the gross amount of the payment is deducted from the covenantor's total income in determining his liability to income tax at the higher rates (FA 1971, s. 32)

14   Summary

The following table summarizes the position in respect of covenanted payments in ordinary circumstances. Reference should be made to the pages indicated where:

a   the covenant is for the benefit of the covenantor's infant unmarried child (p. 218, *post*);

b   the covenant is revocable (p. 210, *post*);

c   the covenant is to the trustees of a settlement in which the settlor retains an interest (p. 206, *post*); or

d   the income is paid to trustees but not fully distributed by them (p. 202, *ante*).

Part VI: Income Treated as that of Settlor

Period of covenant	Amount of covenant	Extent of relief	Authority
A. *Voluntary non-charitable covenants*			
1. Less than 7 years	Any	None	s. 434 applies
2. More than 6 years	Any	Basic rate only	s. 434 does not apply, so relief available at basic rate. s. 457 applies
B. *Voluntary charitable covenants*			
3. Less than 4 years	Any	None	s. 434 applies
4. More than 3 years	Up to £3,000 p.a.	Basic rate and higher rates	s. 434 (1A) and s. 457 (1A) apply
5. More than 3 years	In excess of £3,000 p.a.	Basic rate only	s. 434 (1A) does not apply, so relief available at basic rate. s. 457 (1A) applies
C. *Covenants for full/sufficient consideration*			
6. Partnership agreements	Any	Basic and higher rates	s. 434 does not apply, irrespective of period, if covenant for sufficient consideration. s. 457 does not apply if covenant for full consideration. FA 1977, s. 48 does not apply.
7. Transfers of businesses	Any	Basic and higher rates	As for partnership agreements
8. Maintenance	Any	Basic and higher rates	As for partnership agreements
9. Interests in settled property	Any	Basic and higher rates	s. 434 does not apply if either: (i) consideration is sufficient or (ii) there is no element of bounty, so the covenant is not a settlement. s. 457 does not apply if the covenant is not a settlement. FA 1977, s. 48 does not apply.
10. Other	Any	None	FA 1977, s. 48 applies

204

II SETTLEMENTS WHERE SETTLOR MAY DERIVE SOME BENEFIT

D GENERAL CONSIDERATIONS

1 The provisions

There are a number of provisions, which often over-lap, which are designed broadly to attack the same target, namely a settlement in which income might be accumulated subject to income tax at only the basic rate and the additional rate of 15% in circumstances in which the settlor or his spouse might derive some benefit from it.

The circumstances are:

a   where the settlor retains an interest under the settlement;

b   where the settlor transfers property into trust, but does not absolutely divest himself of it;

c   where the settlement is revocable;

d   where the amount of the trust fund can be reduced to the benefit of the settlor; and

e   where the settlor receives a capital sum which can be regarded as representing undistributed income.

2 Inoffensive benefits

In general, the possibility of the settlor or his spouse deriving any type of benefit will cause the whole or part of the income to be deemed to be his. However, if the only circumstances in which the benefit can be derived are those listed below, the provisions will not apply. The circumstances are:

a   the bankruptcy of a beneficiary;

b   the assignment of, or charge of, his equitable interest by a beneficiary;

c   in the case of a marriage settlement, the death of both parties to the marriage and of all or any of the children of the marriage; and

d   the death under the age of twenty-five, or some lower specified age, of a beneficiary who would be entitled to the income or property on attaining that age.

3 The spouse of the settlor

The provisions treat a benefit to the spouse of the settlor in the same way as a benefit to the settlor himself. If, however, the benefit can accrue to a person only at a time when he or she is the widow or widower of the settlor, that benefit is not within the scope of the provisions (*Vestey* v. *I.R. Comrs.* (1949), 31 T.C. 1).

E INTEREST RETAINED BY SETTLOR TA 1970, S. 447

1 The general rule

If the settlor has an interest in any income arising from property comprised in a settlement, or in the settled property itself, the income of the settlement which is not distributed is treated as if it were the income of the settlor (s. 447 (1)). The settlor is treated as having an interest in any income which may at any time arise from property comprised in the settlement, or if any settled property may at any time become payable to or for the benefit of the settlor, or of his spouse (s. 448 (1)).

2 When the rule applies

a Interest under the trust The rule applies where the settlor has any equitable interest in the property, whether this is expressly conferred or arises by virtue of a resulting trust (*Hannay's Executors* v. *I.R. Comrs.* (1956), 37 T.C. 217). The interest must, however, arise under the settlement itself, or under some concurrent arrangement which is enforceable (*Muir* v. *I.R. Comrs.,* [1966] 1 All E.R. 295 at 305). *I.R. Comrs.* v. *Wachtel,* [1971] Ch. 573 (see p. 188, *ante*) is an example of a benefit arising under a concurrent arrangement.

b Deemed interest The settlor is deemed to have an interest in a settlement if any income which may at any time arise under the settlement, or any property which may at any time be comprised in the settlement, may become payable to or applicable for the benefit of the settlor or his spouse in any circumstances whatsoever (s. 447 (2)). In *I.R. Comrs.* v. *Wachtel* (*supra*), the trustees used the trust income to discharge the debt, and a corresponding amount of the settlor's deposit was released. Although the settlor did not have an actual interest in the settlement, as the income could be said to be applied for his benefit, he was deemed to have an interest in it.

c Power of appointment If the settlor has a power of appointment which he can exercise in favour of himself, he is treated as having an interest under the settlement. If there is a power of appointment exercisable by the settlor and a third party jointly, and the circumstances in which that power was conferred are themselves to be taken into account in deciding what constitutes the settlement (see p. 187, *ante*) the section does apply (*Glyn* v. *I.R. Comrs.,* [1948] 2 All E.R. 419).

3 When the rule does not apply

a Arm's length transactions It seems that a transaction will only confer a "benefit" where there is some gratuitous element, and not where the transaction is one on full commercial terms. Thus, if trust money is lent to the settlor on the same terms as to security, length of term, and interest, as would apply to a loan to a third party it seems that that will not be a "benefit" (*Vestey* v. *I.R. Comrs.,* (1949) 31 T.C. 1).

b Act of third party In one sense, it can be said of any settlement that the property comprised in it, or the income to arise from it, may be paid to the settlor. This is that where the trustees make an income or capital payment to a beneficiary, that beneficiary can make a separate gift to the settlor. The possibility that this might occur is ignored, and, likewise, if it actually happens, it will not cause the section to operate (see *Muir* v. *I.R. Comrs.* [1966] 1 All E.R. 295). If, however, one of the terms of the overall arrangement which constitutes the settlement is that the beneficiary will or might pass on such a benefit to the settlor, the settlor will be treated as having an interest.

c Inoffensive circumstances Section 447 will not apply if the settlor or his spouse can benefit only in the specified inoffensive circumstances (p. 205, *ante*).

There is, however, a fifth inoffensive circumstance which applies in this case. This is if a beneficiary is alive and under the age of twenty-five, and during the lifetime of that beneficiary the income or property can only be applied to or for the benefit of the settlor if the beneficiary becomes bankrupt, or assigns or charges his interest (s. 448 (2) (*b*)).

4 Duration

a Lifetime of the settlor The section applies only during the lifetime of the settlor (s. 447 (1)). A settlement which was caught during the settlor's lifetime will automatically be free after his death.

b For so long as the interest subsists The section applies only for so long as the settlor or his spouse has any interest (s. 447 (1)). If the settlor transferred property to trustees on terms that the trustees would discharge the capital transfer tax out of the settled property, that will give the settlor a benefit only until the tax has been paid. See, however, the discussion on p. 221 of the other provisions which may operate.

5. Quantum

The section applies to all the income of the settlement, other than that which is distributed, and other than that which is already caught by s. 445 and 446, which apply to revocable settlements (see p. 210, *post*).

If the settlor's interest is in only part of the income, or part of the capital, the section applies only to that part (s. 447 (1), *proviso (a)*).

In general, the undistributed income for a year is the income which arises, less payments which are of an income nature in the hands of the recipient, and expenses which are by their nature properly chargeable to income (s. 455).

In determining the amount of income in the hands of a recipient, there is left out of account:

a   payments made to a body corporate connected with the settlement;

b   payments to the trustees of another settlement made by the trustees of the settlement under consideration;

c   payments to the trustees of another settlement made by the same settlor; and

d   payments to the settlor or his spouse on which an income tax liability arises by virtue of s. 451 (p. 212, *post*).

Payments of interest are in general treated as expenses properly chargeable to income (s. 456 (1)). If a distribution of income were made to the settlor or his spouse, a fraction of the interest cannot be treated as an expense. This fraction is:

$$\text{Interest} \times \frac{A - B}{A}$$

where: A is the whole of the income arising under the settlement, less expenses other than interest; and

B is the income paid to persons other than the settlor or his spouse (s. 456 (3)).

6   All tax purposes

Where the section applies, it operates for both basic rate and higher rate purposes (s. 447 (1)).

7   Settlor's right of recovery

The settlor has a right to recover from the trustees the tax paid by him (s. 449 (3) (*a*)).

F   PROPERTY OF WHICH SETTLOR NOT ABSOLUTELY DIVESTED: TA 1970, S. 457

1   The general rule

If the settlor has not absolutely divested himself of property which has become settled, then, irrespective of whether the income has been accumulated, or paid to other persons, the income is treated as that of the settlor for the purposes of excess rate liability (s. 457 (1) (*d*)).

2   When the rule applies

It seems that the section can only apply where the settlor had the property before it became settled, for a person must have property vested in him before he can divest it.

The settlor is not deemed to have divested himself of any property if that property, or any property directly or indirectly representing its proceeds, will or may become payable to or for the benefit of the settlor or his spouse (s. 457 (6)). Likewise, the settlor is not deemed to have divested himself of any property if any income from that property, or from property which represents it, will or may become payable to for the benefit of the settlor or his spouse (*ibid*).

Other rules apply if the settlement was made before 7 April 1965 (see s. 458).

3   When the rule does not apply

Section 457 does not apply if the settlor has divested himself of the settled property except for the right to benefit in one or more of the inoffensive circumstances (p. 205, *ante*).

4   Duration

The section applies only during the lifetime of the settlor (s. 457 (1)), and it will cease to apply if, after the settlement has been created, the settlor does absolutely divest himself of the property.

5   Quantum

The section applies to all the income of the settlement, even if that income has been paid to other persons, but it does not apply where under some other provision, such as s. 447, the income is treated as that of the settlor for all tax purposes (s. 457 (1) (*e*)).

6   Higher and additional rates only

The section applies only for the purpose of rates of tax in excess of the basic rate, but it also applies for the purposes of the additional rate payable in respect of investment income (s. 457 (1)).

7   No right of recovery

There is no provision giving the settlor the right to recover from the trustees the tax which he has suffered.

G REVOCABLE SETTLEMENTS AND SETTLEMENTS WHERE TRUST PROPERTY CAN BE DIMINISHED: TA 1970, S. 446

1 The general rule

If any person has the power to revoke a settlement, or to diminish the property comprised in the settlement, and on the exercise of that power the settlor or his wife will or may become beneficially entitled to the whole or part of the settled property, the income is treated as that of the settlor (s. 446 (1), (2) (*a*).

2 When the rule applies

a Power of any person It is not necessary that the power to revoke the settlement should be that of the settlor; it is sufficient if any person has that power. Further it is not necessary for the power to be presently exercisable. If, however, it cannot be exercised for at least six years, a special provision applies (see, *infra*).

b Power to diminish trust property The provision is disturbingly wide, in that it applies not only to the revocation of a settlement, but also where there is any power to diminish the property comprised in the settlement (s. 446 (2)). Thus, the existence of a power of advancement is a power to "revoke" in this sense (*Countess of Kenmare* v. *I.R. Comrs.,* [1958] A.C 267). However, for the section to apply it is still necessary to show that on the exercise of that power the settlor or his spouse will benefit.

If the trustees have power to apply trust money in the discharge of a liability of the settlor, that will be a power to diminish the property comprised in the settlement. So, it is the view of the Revenue that if a person transfers property to trustees on the basis that the trustees will be obliged to discharge the capital transfer tax in respect of it, that power will be treated as a power to revoke.

3 When the rule does not apply

a Power not in settlement Section 446 applies only if the power to revoke the settlement is contained in the trust instrument, or in some collateral agreement which forms part of the totality of the arrangements which constitute the "settlement" (see p. 187, *ante*). In *I.R. Comrs.* v. *Wolfson,* [1949] 1 All E.R. 865 the settled property consisted of a holding of shares in a company which was controlled by the settlor. The settlor could, therefore, by controlling the company's dividend policy, control whether the trust would receive any income, but it was held that he did not have a power to revoke the settlement. In that case the company had been incorporated in 1931, and the settlor had been in control since 1933. The settlement was made in 1940. The "settlement" did not, therefore, include the company. It seems, however, that if the settlement, in the narrow sense, and the company had come into existence at about the same time, and as part of an overall arrangement, then the settlor would have had a power to revoke (*I.R. Comrs.* v. *Payne* (1940), 23 T.C. 610).

b   The six year rule   If the power to revoke the settlement, or to diminish the property comprised in the settlement, cannot be exercised within six years from the time when the property first becomes comprised in the settlement, the rule does not apply until the power becomes exercisable (s. 446 (1), *proviso*).

c   Future spouses   Strictly, the section applies if, on the exercise of the power, the person who is then the spouse of the settlor can benefit, even if such person is not the spouse of the settlor when the settlement is created (see *I.R. Comrs.* v. *Tennant* (1942), 24 T.C. 215). Where the settlor is unmarried when the settlement is made it is the Revenue practice to regard the section as applying if under the terms of the settlement a benefit may be conferred on any person who may become the spouse of the settlor ((1959) 56 Law Soc. Gaz. 53). Whether or not the settlor is unmarried when the settlement is made, the section is also treated as applying if the terms of the settlement show a specific intention that a future spouse shall benefit.

4   Duration

The six year rule has been noted (*supra*). Where the section applies, it does so only for so long as under the terms of the settlement the power to revoke or diminish subsists (s. 446 (1)).

The section only applies during the lifetime of the settlor.

5   Quantum

The section applies to the whole of the income of the settlement whether or not it has been distributed to any other person (s. 446 (1)). If the settlor or his spouse can only benefit from part of the property, the section catches only the income from that part.

6   All tax purposes

Where the section applies, it operates for both basic rate and higher rate purposes.

7   Settlor's right of recovery

The settlor has a right to recover from the trustees the tax paid by him (s. 449 (3) (*a*)).

H   DISCRETIONARY POWER TO BENEFIT SETTLOR

1   The general rule

If any person has a discretionary power to pay or apply income or capital to or for the benefit of the settlor or his spouse, the income of the settlement is treated as that of the settlor (s. 448 (1)).

2   When the rule applies

The section applies also where a person has the power to secure the payment or application of the income or property to or for the benefit of the settlor or his spouse (s. 448 (1) (*b*)).

3   When the rule does not apply

a   The six year rule   If the power cannot be exercised within a period of six years from when the property first became comprised in the settlement, then until the power first becomes exercisable the section does not apply (s. 448 (2)).

b   Inoffensive circumstances   The section does not apply if the settlor or his spouse can benefit, but only in the inoffensive circumstances (p. 205, *ante*).

4   Duration

Subject to the six year rule, the section applies for so long as under the terms of the settlement the power can be exercised (s. 448 (1)).

5   Quantum

The section applies to all the income of the settlement, whether or not it is distributed to any other person (s. 448 (1)). If the discretion can be exercised in respect of only part of the income or capital of the settlement, the section applies only to the income from that part.

6   All tax purposes

Where the section applies, it operates for both basic rate and higher rate purposes (s. 448 (1)).

7   Settlor's right of recovery

The settlor has a right to recover from the trustees the tax paid by him (s. 449 (3) (*a*)).

I   CAPITAL PAYMENTS TO THE SETTLOR: TA 1970, S. 451

1   The general rule

Where the trustees of a settlement make any capital payment to the settlor or his spouse, the undistributed income of the settlement is treated as that of the settlor so far as he is concerned (s. 451 (1), (8)). This is so whatever the type of payment, provided it is of a capital nature. Thus, in principle a sum paid by way of loan or repayment of a loan comes within the scope of the provision.

2 When the rule applies

The section applies where there is a payment of a "capital sum" to the settlor, his spouse or to either or both of them jointly with a third party. A capital sum is:

a   a sum paid by way of loan (s. 451 (8) (i));

b   a sum paid by way of repayment of a loan (*ibid*);

c   any other sum which is not paid as income, and which is not paid for full consideration in money or money's worth (s. 451 (8) (ii)); or

d   a sum paid or applied by the trustees for the benefit of the settlor (s. 451 (9) (*b*); FA 1981, s. 42).

Although the section applies to any capital sum as so defined, it is particularly important in the case of loans and repayments of loans.

3 Loans to the settlor

a   *Making the loan*   The section applies if a loan is made to the settlor or his spouse, even although that loan is made on full commercial terms, and even although, for the purposes of s. 447, the settlor would not be treated as deriving any benefit from it (see p. 207 *ante*).

b   *Effect of repayment*   If, after a loan has been made to the settlor, and the whole or part of the income of the settlement has been treated as his income, he repays the loan, he is not entitled to any credit in respect of, or repayment of, the tax which he has paid on that income.

Repayment of the loan will, however, affect liability in subsequent years. It will be seen (see p. 216, *post*) that, in general, where the amount of the "available income" in the year of assessment in which the capital sum is paid is less than the amount of that capital sum, the balance of the capital sum will be treated as the income of the settlor in subsequent years as income arises. Where, however, the settlor repays the loan in full, no liability will attach to him in respect of the original loan in the years of assessment after that in which the loan is repaid (s. 451 (3A) (*a*)).

c   *Loans after repayment*   A special rule applies where (i) there has been a loan to the settlor (ii) that loan has been repaid in full, and (iii) a further loan is made to him. In this case, the amount of the further loan is treated as being only of so much as exceeds the amount which was treated as his income by virtue of the first loan (s. 451 (3A) (*b*)).

4   *Loans by the settlor*

a   Making the loan   No liability will arise under this section if the settlor makes a loan to the trustees. It has been seen, however, (p. 188, *ante*) that particularly if the loan is made otherwise than on commercial terms, the making of the loan may itself cause the lender to be treated as a settlor of a settlement even if, apart from the loan, he would not be.

b   Effect of repayment   The repayment by the trustees of a loan made by the settlor is treated as the payment of a capital sum to the settlor. So, in *De Vigier* v. *I.R. Comrs.*, [1964] 2 All E.R. 907, the settlor's wife lent money to the trustees to enable them to take up a rights issue. The settlor was held to be taxable on the money applied in the repayment of that loan. But the decision appears to have even wider scope. The settlor's wife was one of the trustees, and, strictly, the sum which she received was not by way of repayment of loan, but by way of the discharge of the right which she had to be indemnified from the trust fund. The decision does however, show that the mere repayment of a loan is clearly within the statute.

c   Subsequent loan by settlor   As the repayment of a loan is treated as the payment of a capital sum, the income of the settlement will be treated as that of the settlor to the extent that it is "available". If there was insufficient available income for the year in which the loan was repaid, the income of subsequent years will be treated as that of the settlor up to the amount of the repayment. If, however, (i) the settlor has made a loan to the trustees (ii) the trustees have repaid that loan and (iii) the settlor makes a new loan of at least equivalent amount, the making of the further loan will prevent any part of the income of the settlement from being treated as the income of the settlor for any year of assessment after that in which the subsequent loan is made (s. 451 (3B)).

5   *Payments from connected companies*

a   Generally   A further provision deals with the position where the trustees hold shares in a close company, and the close company makes a capital payment to the settlor. The general principle is that if the trustees make a payment to the company, and the company makes a payment to the settlor, then s. 451 should apply as if the trustees had made the payment directly to the settlor.

This provision applies where

    i a capital sum is paid to the settlor by a body corporate which is "connected with the settlement" in the year of assessment in which the sum is paid; and

    ii an "associated payment" is made directly or indirectly to that body corporate by the trustees of the settlement (s. 451A).

b   *Companies "connected with" the settlement*   A body corporate is treated as connected with a settlement for the whole of a year of assessment if it is a close company and the participators at any time in that year include the trustees of the settlement (s. 454 (4); FA 1981, s. 44 (2)).

A body corporate will also be treated as connected with the settlement if

    i it is not a close company only by virtue of the fact that it is not resident in the United Kingdom (s. 454 (4) (*a*)); or

    ii it is controlled by a close company, or a company which would be a close company were it resident in the United Kingdom (s. 454 (4) (*b*)).

c   *"Associated payments"*   An associated payment is

    i any capital sum paid by the trustees to the company within five years of the payment by the company to the settlor (s. 451A (3) (*a*)); and

    ii any other sum which is paid, or asset which is transferred, by the trustees to that company within the five year period, where it is not paid or transferred for full consideration in money or money's worth (s. 451A (3) (*b*)).

If the trustees make a payment to a company which is associated with the company which makes the payment to the settlor, the trustees' payment is treated as having been made to the company which makes the payment to the settlor (s. 451A (4)).

d   *Short-term transactions*   The rule does not apply where the company makes a payment to the settlor by way of loan or repayment of a loan if the whole of the loan is repaid within 12 months of the date on which it was made (s. 451A (6) (*a*)). In the case of loans made to the settlor, it is also necessary to show that the loans were not outstanding for more than 12 months in any period of five years (s. 451A (6) (*b*)).

6   When the rule does not apply

a   Commercial transactions other than loans   The section does not apply if the capital payment is otherwise than by way of loan or repayment of a loan, and is for full consideration in money or money's worth (s. 451 (8) (ii)). Thus, a purchase by the trustees from the settlor of an asset at full value will not be caught by the section.

b   Loan by company to participator   Where a close company makes a loan to a participator, the company is liable to pay an amount equivalent to the rate of advance corporation tax on the loan (s. 286). If thereafter the debt is released, the participator is treated as if he had received income equivalent to the grossed up amount of the debt (s. 287 (1)). In order to prevent a double charge to tax, if the loan has been caught by s. 451, then to the extent that the income is treated as that of the settlor, section 287 is not to apply. If, however, the settlor has been first assessed under s. 287, the amount of the loan is excluded from the charge under s. 451 (s. 451 (3)).

c   Inoffensive circumstances   The section does not apply if the capital sum could only have become payable in the inoffensive circumstances (p. 205, *ante*).

7   Duration

The section applies only during the lifetime of the settlor. Accordingly, a payment to his widow or widower will not be caught (*Vestey v. I.R. Comrs.,* (1949) 31 T.C. 1), nor will the repayment of a loan to his estate.

8   Quantum generally

The section requires there to be calculated the "available income" which is, broadly, the income which has arisen since the creation of the settlement, but which has not been distributed. If that exceeds the capital sum paid to the settlor or his spouse, the liability is by reference to the whole of the capital sum. If, however, the available income is less than the capital sum, the balance is carried forward until there is available income. A further charge then arises on the settlor in respect of that balance. The "available income" is the total income which has arisen since the creation of the settlement, less:

a   income which has been distributed (as to which see p. 000, *post*);

b   previous capital sums paid to the settlor;

c   any undistributed income treated as that of the settlor under s. 445 (revocable settlements allowing release of obligation); s. 446 (revocable settlements generally; p. 210), and s. 448

(settlements where discretionary power to benefit settlor) and s. 457 (excess rate liability);

d any income, whether or not distributed, treated as that of the settlor under s. 447 (settlements where settlor retains an interest);

e any income paid by the settlor to the settlement which is disallowed as a deduction from his total income under s. 450;

f any amount treated as the income of the settlor under s. 438 (settlements for children of settlor);

g any income of a company apportionable to a beneficiary (see s. 454 (1) (*b*)); and

h generally, the basic rate and additional rate liability suffered by the trustees on undistributed income (s. 451 (2)).

The rules for determining what income is to be regarded as distributed have been stated above (p. 208, *ante*).

9 Quantum: payments by companies

The income of the settlement will be treated as that of the settlor to the extent that the capital sum which a company pays to the settlor is covered by the total of associated payments made to the company up to the end of the year of assessment in which the capital sum is paid (s. 451A (2) (*a*)). Where the total of associated payments is less than the capital sum, further income will be treated as that of the settlor if the trustees subsequently make additional associated payments (s. 451A (2) (*b*)).

10 Tax position of trustees and settlor

Unlike most of the provisions considered in this chapter, the section does not deem income arising from the settled property to be the income of the settlor. Without disturbing the taxation position of the trustees, the section treats the settlor as if he had received certain income. This is the amount of the capital sum, up to the amount of the available income, grossed up at the basic and additional rates (s. 451 (5)).

11 Tax credit for settlor

The settlor is entitled to a credit against the tax chargeable under this section of an amount equal to tax at the basic rate and the additional rate on the amount treated as his income (s. 451 (6); FA 1981, s. 42 (5)). This credit is restricted to so much of basic and additional rate tax as is equal to the tax charged on the settlor (*ibid*).

12   No right of recovery

The settlor has no right to recover from the trustees the amount of tax paid by him. Further, as has been seen, if the liability arises by way of loan, the settlor cannot obtain any credit or repayment of tax if he repays the loan.

III   SETTLEMENTS FOR SETTLOR'S CHILDREN

J   SETTLEMENTS AND GIFTS FOR SETTLOR'S CHILDREN

1   The general rule

If the settlor creates an irrevocable capital settlement for the benefit of his infant unmarried child or children, and the income is accumulated during their infancy, there is no special rule which applies because the settlement is for the benefit of the settlor's children. In any other circumstances, if income is paid to or applied for the benefit of infant unmarried children of the settlor that income is treated as that of the settlor (ss. 437, 438).

2   When the rule applies

a   Actual payment of income   The rule applies whenever any income is paid to or for the benefit of an infant unmarried child of the settlor if the settlor is alive at the date of payment.

b   Deemed payment of income   Unless the settlement is an irrevocable capital settlement (*infra*), income is deemed to be paid to or for the benefit of a child if it will or may in any circumstances become payable to or applicable for the benefit of a child of the settlor (s. 438 (1) (*a*)). The position is the same where assets representing the income will or may become payable to or applicable for the benefit of the child (*ibid*). This is so even if the child may be an adult at the time when he receives it.

c   Capital payments   A further provision applies if a capital payment is made to an infant unmarried child of the settlor, and that payment, together with any previous similar payments exceed the aggregate amount of the income which has been paid to or for the benefit of a child of the settlor. In this case, to the extent of that excess, the capital payment is treated as income (s. 438 (2) (*b*)).

d   Payments of interest by trustees   If interest is paid by trustees, the general rule is that the whole or part of that interest is treated as

218

income paid to or for the benefit of an infant unmarried child of the settlor (s. 440 (1)). The amount of interest so treated is determined by the formula:

$$\text{Interest paid in year} \times \frac{\text{net income arising in year paid to infant unmarried child of settlor}}{\text{whole of net income arising in year}}$$

This rule does not apply if either the interest is eligible for tax relief, or the interest is paid to the settlor or his spouse (s. 440 (2)).

e   Gifts   The definition of "settlement" is widened specially to include a transfer of assets (s. 444 (2)). If, therefore, a person makes an absolute gift to his infant unmarried child, income derived from that gift will be treated as income of the settlor (*Thomas* v. *Marshall*, [1953] A.C. 543).

f   Assignments and surrenders   If a parent assigns an interest under a settlement to his infant unmarried child, or if he surrenders an interest in order to accelerate the interest of an infant unmarried child, the income arising to or for the benefit of the child by virtue of the assignment or surrender will be treated as that of the parent (*I.R. Comrs.* v. *Buchanan* (1957), 37 T.C. 365).

3   When rule does not apply

a   Irrevocable capital accumulation settlements   The rule does not apply where the income arises from an irrevocable settlement of capital, and the income is not paid to or for the benefit of a child of the settlor while that child is an infant or unmarried (s. 438 (2)).

For this purpose, a settlement will be irrevocable if:

i   it is irrevocable for the purposes of the general law;
ii   either:
    (*a*) there is no provision for determination; or
    (*b*) there is a provision for determination; but such determination would not benefit the settlor or the spouse of the settlor during the lifetime of any child of the settlor who is a beneficiary under the settlement (s. 439 (1) (*b*) and *proviso* (ii));
iii either:
    (*a*) the terms of the settlement do not provide for the payment of any income or property to or for the benefit of the settlor or his spouse during the lifetime of any child of the settlor who is a beneficiary (s. 439 (1) (*a*)); or
    (*b*) the terms of the settlement do provide for the payment of income or property to or for the benefit of the settlor or

his spouse during the lifetime of a child of the settlor who is beneficiary, but only in the event of the bankruptcy of that child, or in the event of any absolute assignment or assignment by way of charge by such a child of his equitable interest (*proviso* (i));

iv   the terms of the settlement do not provide for the payment by the settlor of a penalty in the event of his failing to comply with the provisions of the settlement;

v   if the settlement is on protective trusts, the trust period (see the Trustee Act 1925, s. 33 (1)) is the lifetime of the child, and the discretionary phase can only come into operation in the circumstances specified in the Trustee Act 1925, s. 33 (1) (i) (TA 1970, s. 439 (1) (*b*) (iii)).

b   *Income not exceeding £5*   Where the income paid to an infant unmarried child of the settlor does not exceed £5 in any year of assessment, that income is not treated as the income of the settlor (s. 437 (3)).

c   *Court orders*   Because for the purpose of s. 437 the definition of settlement includes a transfer of assets (s. 444 (2)), it may be thought that payment by a parent to a child under a court order would give rise to liability under s. 437. It is clear that where a parent makes a payment or transfer of assets, the provision can apply, even although the payment is made under compulsion (*Yates* v. *Starkey*, (1951) 32 T.C. 38). If, however, there is no element of bounty, there can be no "settlement" (see p. 187, *ante*), so that the provision cannot apply. The Revenue, therefore, do not regard payments under a court order directly to a child as coming within the section.

4   Duration

a   *Lifetime of the settlor*   The section applies only during the lifetime of the settlor (s. 437 (1)).

b   *Infancy of the child*   If the income from an irrevocable accumulation settlement has been accumulated, or retained by the trustees without being accumulated, that income will not be treated as being the income of the settlor if it is paid to or applied for the benefit of the child after he has married or attained the age of eighteen.

5   Quantum

The section applies to all income which is actually paid to, or is deemed to be paid to or applied for the benefit of a child of the settlor if at the time of actual or deemed payment or application the child is unmarried and under the age of eighteen.

220

6 All tax purposes

Where the section applies, it operates for both basic rate and higher rate purposes (s. 437 (1)).

7 Settlor's right of recovery

The settlor has a right to recover from the trustees the tax paid by him (s. 441 (1)).

K EFFECT OF UNDERTAKINGS BY TRUSTEES TO PAY CAPITAL TRANSFER TAX

Where there is a transfer into settlement, and capital transfer tax is payable in respect of that transfer, there is a liability both on the settlor and on the trustees to pay the tax (FA 1975, s. 25 (2) (*a*)). If the trustees pay the tax, they thereby relieve the settlor from his liability, and in certain circumstances the settlor could become liable to income tax on the income of the settlement under s. 439 (application of settled property for benefit of settlor: p. 219, *ante*), s. 447 (settlement in which settlor retains an interest: p. 206, *ante*), s. 451 (capital payments for benefit of settlor: p. 212, *ante*) and s. 457 (income from property of which settlor has not absolutely divested himself: p. 208, *ante*).

Under ss. 447 and 457 the income is treated as that of the settlor until the capital transfer tax is paid. There is, strictly, no limit in time on the operation of ss. 439 and 451.

The Revenue view is that:

1   If there is a power in the trust instrument authorising the trustees to pay the tax, or a duty either arising under the trust instrument or under a collateral agreement or understanding, then such of the sections as are relevant in the particular case do apply; but

2   If the trustees do pay the tax without any such power or obligation, then the sections do not apply.

It is also the Revenue practice to regard the sections as operative only until the tax has been paid.

L   THE OVERLAP OF THE SECTIONS

As has just been seen there is no principle that only one of the sections considered in this chapter can apply in any one circumstance. Thus, as a further example of the overlap of the sections, suppose that a person creates a settlement for his infant child and transfers to the trustees a block of shares which he owns. Suppose also that under the settlement if the child does not obtain five 'O' level passes in the GCE examination the trustees are to hold upon discretionary trusts for the settlor and the child. The settlement is, or may be, caught simultaneously by ss. 437, 447, 448 and 457.

If more than one section appears to apply in the same circumstances, the structure of the legislation is:

a   sections which deem the whole income to be that of the settlor are applied first;
b   sections which deem undistributed income to be that of the settlor are applied second; and
c   sections which deem income to be that of the settlor only for the purposes of excess rates are applied third.

This is shown by the following table:

Vitiating Circumstance	Section TA 1970	Extent of income caught	Whether section applies for all purposes, or excess rates only	Remarks
Covenants for less than 7 years	434	All	All	
Infant unmarried child	437	All	All	
Revocable covenants	445	All	All	
Revocable settlement/ power to diminish	446	All	All	
Discretionary benefit for settlor	448	All	All	
Interest retained	447	Undistributed income	All	Does not apply where ss. 445 or 446 apply
Undistributed income	450	Undistributed income	All	Does not apply where ss. 445, 446, 447 or 448 apply.

Vitiating Circumstance	*Section TA 1970*	*Extent of income caught*	*Whether section applies for all purposes, or excess rates only*	*Remarks*
Capital sum to settlor	451	"Available" income	All	ss. 438, 445, 446, 447, 448 and 450 taken into account in determining available income
Settlor not entirely divested	457	All	Excess rate only	Does not apply to extent where any other provisions apply.

The Administration of a Trust

Chapter 16

Administration of a Trust: Income Tax

SCOPE OF THE CHAPTER

This chapter is concerned only with income which is *not* deemed to be the income of the settlor under any of provisions discussed in Chapter 15.

A GENERAL PRINCIPLES

1 Trustees as a separate body

The law relating to the liability of trustees to income tax in respect of trust income has developed haphazardly, and with little direct statutory authority. One of the principles which has emerged is that trustees are for the purposes of income tax to be regarded as a single, continuing and separate body of persons. This proposition denotes that the body of trustees are in general to be regarded as separate from the individuals who are for the time being the trustees, and that changes in the persons who are the trustees have no effect on the position of the trustees as such. There is no statutory authority for the proposition for income tax, but there is for capital gains tax (CGTA 1979, s. 52 (1)) and development land tax (DLTA 1976, s. 30 (1)). The effect is that the body of trustees can be considered for most taxation purposes as having a separate legal personality.

2 Basis of liability of trustees

One result of the haphazard development of this part of the law is that there is no universal principle which determines the basis of the trustees' liability. However, the position appears to be as follows:

a   the fundamental principle is that any person, whatever his capacity, is liable to United Kingdom income tax if he receives income which arises here, or in some cases, if he is entitled to receive it (TA 1970, ss. 68 (1), 94 (1), 114; FA 1972, s. 86). This applies to bodies of trustees (TMA 1970, s. 71 (1));

b   the trustees as such are in general liable to income tax on income in their hands in the same circumstances as an individual would be liable if it was his income, and in no other circumstances. Accordingly, in most respects the principles discussed earlier with regard to each type of income will apply to trustees in the same way as they apply to individuals.

3 Trustees as agents

Income tax law is uncertain whether it wishes to regard trustees as liable by virtue of their receiving or being entitled to receive income in their own right, or whether they are to be considered as agents for the beneficiary. The position is that:

a   they are treated, in effect, as agents in respect of income to which an infant or a person under mental incapacity is absolutely entitled (TMA 1970, s. 72);

b   where the beneficiary has a vested interest in income which is not liable to be divested, it is necessary to "look-through" the trustees to the underlying source of income (*Baker* v. *Archer-Shee*, [1927] A.C. 844; p. 374, *post*);

c   in other cases, trustees are liable because they receive or are entitled to receive income in their own right.

4 Principles

The basic principles which govern the taxation of trust income are as follows:

a   all trust income is taxable in the hands of the trustees if it would be taxable in the hands of an individual. The trustees are personally liable for ensuring payment;

b   trustees are not entitled to personal allowances, but they are entitled to non-personal reliefs (p. 140, *ante*);

c   trustees are not assessable to the higher rates of income tax. This is so irrespective of the size of the income, and even if one beneficiary is entitled to the whole of the income;

d where the settlement confers a fixed beneficial entitlement to income on a beneficiary, the trustees are assessable only at the basic rate which for 1981/82 is 30%. Where the trustees have a discretion as to income, or it is to be accumulated, they are also liable to the additional rate which, for 1981/82 is 15% (p. 230, *post*).

e management expenses are payable out of income which has been taxed at the basic rate, but at the basic rate only. This is so even if the trustees are liable to tax at the additional rate. No relief is available from income tax at the basic rate for management expenses (*Aikin (Surveyor of Taxes)* v. *Macdonald's Trustees,* (1894), 3 T.C. 306);

f all income payments made to the beneficiaries represent income from which income tax has been deducted, either at the basic rate, or at the basic rate and at the additional rate. The trustees must issue to the beneficiaries the appropriate certificate of deduction of tax;

g if a beneficiary is not liable to pay income tax on his own income when augmented by the trust income at the rate deducted by the trustees, he can use the certificate of deduction of tax supplied to him by the trustees to obtain a repayment of the whole or part of the tax deducted. Conversely, if the beneficiary is liable to pay income tax at a higher rate, an additional assessment may be raised on him.

B BASIC RATE LIABILITY OF TRUSTEES

1 *Income taxable*

All income of a nature which in the hands of an individual is taxable is taxable in the hands of trustees. This stems from the fact that trustees are liable not because of a special charging code, but because of the general principle of liability arising from the receipt of income.

Income is to be calculated for the purpose of each Schedule and Case according to the ordinary rules.

2 *Income not taxable*

The following categories of income are those which do not, or may not, form part of the income of the trustees:

a *Not received* Where trustees do not receive income, they are not liable in respect of it. So, in *Williams* v. *Singer,* [1921] 1 A.C. 65 trustees were held not to be liable on income arising abroad and paid directly to a beneficiary who was domiciled and resident abroad.

b Mandated income Where trustees authorise a beneficiary to receive income direct, and the beneficiary does so, the only action which the trustees need take is notify the Revenue of the name and address of the beneficiary, and the income in question (TMA 1970, s. 76).

c Income in which beneficiary has vested interest It will be seen (p. 247, *post*) that where a beneficiary has an interest in income which is vested and not liable to divesting, the Revenue "look-through" the trustees to the ultimate source of income. There are dicta to the effect that this income is assessable only on the beneficiary and not on the trustees, even if the beneficiary does not receive it direct (*Baker* v. *Archer-Shee,* [1927] A.C. 844, H.L.). This dicta has not been followed, and it seems unsafe to rely on it (*Reid's Trustees* v. *I.R. Comrs.,* (1929) 14 T.C. 513).

d Income on which beneficiary not liable It has also been said that where income is that of a beneficiary, and the beneficiary is not liable to income tax on it, then neither are the trustees (*Reid's Trustees* v. *I.R. Comrs.,* (1929) 14 T.C. 512 at 525; *Kelly* v. *Rogers,* [1935] 2 K.B. 446 at 463). There is no direct decision to that effect, and if the principle is correct, presumably it applies only to those cases in which, under the rule in *Baker* v. *Archer-Shee* (p. 374, *post*), the income is regarded as that of the beneficiary.

3 Trust management expenses

Trust management expenses are payable out of trust income which has been taxed at the basic rate. Accordingly, no relief from liability at the basic rate is available in respect of such expenses *(Aikin (Surveyor of Taxes)* v. *Macdonald's Trustees,* (1894) 3 T.C. 306).

However, trust management expenses are relevant:

a in determining the liability of the trustees to income tax at the additional rate (p. 231, *post*); and

b in determining the income of the beneficiary (p. 246, *post*).

Where, for these purposes, trust management expenses are taken into account, they are calculated on the basis of when they are due, not when they are paid.

4 Interest

Where the trustees pay interest, it will either constitute a charge on the trust income, or will be treated as a trust management expense. It will be a charge on the trust income if, were it paid by an individual, it would be eligible for relief.

Where the interest does not constitute a charge on income, it will rank as a trust management expense. The effect is that while it is not deductible for basic rate purposes, it will be deductible for additional rate purposes (p. 231, *post*).

There have been noted previously the effects of the payment of interest where an infant unmarried child of the settlor is a beneficiary (TA 1970, s. 440; p. 218, *ante*) or where the settlor has a liability in respect of undistributed income (s. 456; p. 208, *ante*).

The main circumstances in which interest paid by trustees will be a charge on the trust income are where the loan in respect of which the interest is paid:

a   was made before 26 March 1974 and the interest is payable before 6 April 1982 (FA 1974, s. 19 (4); F(No. 2)A 1979, s. 10); or

b   was made before 6 April 1975 to replace a previous liability on overdraft, and the interest is payable before 6 April 1982 *(ibid);* or

c   was applied in the purchase or improvement of landed property which is let (FA 1974, Sch. 1, para. 4 (1) (*b*)).

If trustees borrow in order to purchase a house which is used by a beneficiary as his main residence, interest paid by the trustees is not eligible for relief, because such interest is not paid by the person who occupies the property as his residence (para. 4 (1) (*a*)). There is a limited exception in the case of interest paid by the trustees of a will trust (para. 8 (1); FA 1977, Sch. 8, para. 10).

Trustees cannot obtain relief in respect of interest paid on a loan to acquire a shareholding in a close company, or to acquire an interest in a partnership, because they are not an "individual" (FA 1974, Sch. 1, paras. 9, 11).

5 Capital Allowances

Trustees may claim capital allowances in the same manner as individuals.

6 Losses and income deficiencies

If trustees carry on a trade, and incur losses in so doing, they may carry forward these losses (TA 1970, s. 171). Likewise, if there is an excess of expenditure over income in respect of landed property owned by the trustees, that excess can sometimes be carried forward and offset against future rental income (TA 1970, s. 72).

If, however, taking the trust as a whole, there is an excess of expenditure over income, that excess cannot be carried forward and set against income of the trust in future years.

Although individuals may, in certain circumstances, obtain income tax relief for losses which they sustain from investing in trading companies, trustees are not entitled to this relief (FA 1980, s. 37).

7 Personal reliefs

Trustees cannot claim personal reliefs and allowances, which are available only to individuals.

8 Rate of tax

Trustees are liable for the payment of income tax at the basic rate on income received, less interest eligible for relief, subject to adjustment in respect of capital allowances and such losses as are available and are brought forward.

In general, where income is accumulated, or is subject to discretionary trusts, trustees are also liable to the additional rate of tax. This is considered later (*infra*).

9 Higher rates

Trustees are never liable to higher rates of income tax, irrespective of the size of the trust income.

C ADDITIONAL RATE LIABILITY

1 Provisions imposing additional rate liability

There are two separate provisions which impose on trustees a liability to income tax at the additional rate. These are:

a   FA 1973, s. 16 which imposes a liability in respect of the income which *arises* in a year, by virtue of the manner in which that income is to be dealt with; and

b   FA 1973, s. 17 which imposes a liability in respect of income which is *distributed* in a year.

2 Income giving rise to the liability

In general, where trustees receive income which is to be accumulated or which is payable at the discretion of the trustees or of any other person that income is taxable at the additional rate of 15% as well as at the basic rate of 30% (FA 1973, s. 16 (1), (2) (*a*)). As exceptions to the general rule, the following types of income are not subject to the additional rate liability:

a   income which belongs to a beneficiary under a fixed entitlement before it is distributed (FA 1973, s. 16 (2) (*b*)). An example is where trustees hold a fund upon trust to pay £100 p.a. to one beneficiary, with a discretion as to the remainder of the income;

b   income which is treated as the income of the settlor under the special provisions already described (s. 16 (2) (*b*); p. 195, *ante*);

c   income arising under a trust which is established for charitable purposes only (s. 16 (2) (*c*)). In this case there is no liability to the additional rate even if the income is not applied for charitable purposes in the year in which it arises;

d   income arising under certain trusts for the provision of retirement benefits (*ibid*);

e   income which is applied in defraying the expenses of the trustees in that year which are:

    i expenses which would be properly chargeable to income under the general law even if there is some express provision of the trust instrument which prevents them from being charged to income; and

    ii expenses which would be properly chargeable to capital under the general law, but which are authorised to be charged to income by some express provision of the trust instrument (s. 16 (2) (*d*)).

3   *Amount on which additional rate payable*

The liability is calculated by reference to the gross income of the trust which does not come within one of the excepted categories. In certain cases special rules are prescribed to determine the amount of the gross income:

a   building society interest which is paid or credited to the trustees is grossed up at the basic rate, and is treated as having been received by the trustees subject to deduction of income tax at the basic rate (s. 16 (5));

b   in certain circumstances, the income of a close company may be apportioned among the participators (FA 1972, Sch. 16, para. 1). Where income is apportioned to trustees they are treated as having received, at the end of the company's accounting period, the amount of that income together with the advance corporation tax attributable to it (FA 1973, s. 16 (3), (4));

c   where on or before the completion of the administration of the estate personal representatives pay to trustees a sum representing income, that sum is treated as having been paid to the trustees as income, and to have borne income tax at the basic rate (s. 16 (6));

d   where the trustees receive a scrip dividend (p. 235, *post*) they are treated as having received an amount equal to the grossed up equivalent of the value of that scrip (F(No. 2)A 1975, s. 34 (6)).

4 Calculating the liability

The additional rate liability is calculated on Form 31, of which the following is an example:

Sources of income

Bank interest (preceding year basis)		£200
UK Dividends	£300	
Tax credit thereon	£129	£429
Building Society interest: £100 received grossed up to		£143
Income of close company apportioned to trustees	£250	
Advance corporation tax applicable thereto	£107	£357
Income payment from personal representatives: £350 received, grossed up to		£500
	TOTAL (A)	£1,629

Deductions

Gross interest paid by trustees	£300	
Gross income allocated to specific purposes	nil	
Expenses chargeable to income: £150, grossed up to	£214	
Income treated as that of settlor	nil	
Income of annuitant: £100, grossed up to	£143	
Charitable income: exempt		
	TOTAL (B)	£657
Trust income chargeable at additional rate (A)−(B)		£972
Total additional rate tax: 15% × £972		£149

D ADDITIONAL LIABILITY ON DISTRIBUTION

1 Distribution of income

Where there is a distribution of income which is made in the exercise of a discretion by the trustees or of some other person, the general rule is that the payment made to the beneficiary is treated as a net payment of a gross amount from which income tax has been deducted at a rate equivalent to the basic rate and the additional rate (FA 1975, s. 17 (1), (2)). Where the basic rate is 30% and the additional rate is 15%, the payment to the beneficiary therefore has to be grossed up at 45%. Thus, if an income payment of £250 is made to a beneficiary, he is treated as having received £455, subject to deducted of tax of £205 and he is entitled to a certificate of deduction of tax of £205 (s. 17 (4)).

The general rule applies only where the sum is income in the hands of the recipient. Thus, it applies where the distribution is made out of income which has been retained, but not out of income which has been accumulated (see p. 237, *post*) unless the payment from the accumulation is to be treated as income (p. 239, *post*). The general rule does not apply where the income would be treated as income of the recipient apart from the payment, as where it is treated as income of the settlor. In the view of the Revenue, trustees are treated as making a payment to a beneficiary for the purposes of this provision at the time when he is entitled to call for it. If, therefore, the trustees decide on 25 March 1985 to make the payment, but do not actually make it until 10 April 1985, the liability arises in respect of 1984/85.

2   Trustees' liability for tax deducted

The trustees are liable to account for the tax which is treated as having been deducted from the payment to the beneficiary (s. 17 (2) (*b*)). They account for this tax by certain offsets, and an assessment is raised to the extent that these offsets are not sufficient.

The offsets are:

a   the amount of tax on income charged at the basic rate and the additional rate under FA 1973, s. 16, (FA 1973, s. 17 (3) (*a*)). The amount of this tax is tax at the basic rate, and tax at the additional rate;

b   the amount of credit to which the trustees are entitled in respect of overseas tax, by virtue of double tax relief (s. 18). The trustees must certify that:

  i   the income out of which the payment was made included overseas tax income; and

  ii the income arose to them not earlier than six years before the end of the year of assessment in which the payment is made (s. 18 (2)).

c   the amount of additional rate tax charged to the trustees on the income of a close company apportioned to the trustees (s. 17 (3) (*b*)). It has been seen that this income, which includes the advance corporation tax attributable to it, is included in the trustees' liability under s. 16. A special provision applies where income is apportioned to the trustees in one year, and is

233

  actually paid out by them by way of dividend in a following
  year (FA 1972, Sch. 16, para. 5 (6); FA 1973, s. 17 (3) (c));

d   where the trustees receive a scrip dividend (p. 235, *post*) the
  amount of additional rate tax charged on the grossed up
  equivalent of the value of that dividend (F(No. 2)A 1975,
  s. 34 (6));

e   where income was available to the trustees for distribution at
  5 April 1973, an amount of tax which is taken to be two thirds
  of the net amount of that income (FA 1973, s. 17 (3) (*d*)). The
  Revenue accept that income which arose prior to 6 April 1973
  but which had not been distributed was available for distribution on that date provided it had not been accumulated.

Where within offset *a* above there is building society interest, it is
necessary to produce a certificate from the building society that it
will account for income tax on the amount specified.

The effect of these provisions is that there will be no liability under
s. 17 where income which is received and charged at the additional
rate in one year of assessment is distributed in that year. If, however,
it is distributed in a later year, when the combined basic and additional rate is higher, there will be a liability. In the converse case,
there will be an amount of tax available to be carried forward.

E   TRUSTEES' LIABILITY FOR EXCESS RATE

Under TA 1970, s. 36, the Revenue may serve a notice on the
trustees of a discretionary trust where a beneficiary under that trust is
liable to pay income tax at rates in excess of the basic rate, but has
not done so. The effect of such a notice is that the trustees must
thereafter pay to the Revenue in or towards satisfaction of the liability any income or capital to which the beneficiary becomes entitled
as a result of the exercise of their discretion. The notice does not
impose any duty on the trustees to exercise their discretion in favour
of the miscreant beneficiary. If the trustees do not exercise their
discretion in favour of the beneficiary and if they hold no funds for
him when the notice is served, they will not be under any obligation
to make any payment to the Revenue.

F   PAYMENT TO BENEFICIARY

1   *Trustees liable at basic rate*

Although difficulties can arise with regard to the assessment of
income tax on income in which the beneficiary has a vested interest

(p. 245, *post*), it may be said at this stage that payments of trust income are a form of annual payment, and are therefore chargeable under Schedule D, Case III. Accordingly, trustees must deduct income tax from each payment of trust income under TA 1970, ss. 52 or 53.

2 Trustees liable at additional rate

Where there is a liability under FA 1973, s. 17 (p. 232, *ante*), that section applies in lieu of TA 1970, ss. 52 and 53. The trustees therefore deduct tax at the aggregate of the basic and additional rates.

3 Certificates of deduction of tax

The beneficiary is entitled to a certificate on form R185E of the amount of tax deducted.

G BONUS ISSUES AND SCRIP DIVIDENDS

There are no income tax consequences when a bonus issue is made, but special rules apply to scrip dividends. These provisions apply both where the trustees have an option to take scrip or cash, and exercise their option to take cash, and also where the trustees hold shares which carry with them the right to receive bonus shares (F(No. 2)A 1975, s. 34 (1)).

1 Entitlement

It is first necessary for the trustees to determine for the purposes of ordinary trust law the entitlement to the scrip dividend. The principles are as follows:

a   if the trustees have an option whether to accept shares or cash, they must exercise the option so that they receive the greatest benefit (*Re Evans, Jones* v. *Evans,* [1913] 1 Ch. 23; *Re Malam, Malam* v. *Hitchins,* [1894] 3 Ch. 578);

b   if the trustees take cash, that will be treated as an ordinary dividend;

c   if the trustees take shares, the position depends on whether a beneficiary has a life or similar interest, and on the respective values of the shares and the cash alternative;

d   a beneficiary with a life or similar interest will be entitled to the shares, if the shares and the cash alternative are of the same value (*Re Despard, Hancock* v. *Despard* (1901), 17 T.L.R. 478).

e   if the shares are of greater value than the cash, the beneficiary
    with the life or similar interest is entitled to so much of the
    value of the shares as is equivalent to the dividend. The excess
    value forms an accretion to the capital of the trust (*Re North-
    age, Ellis* v. *Barfield* (1891), 64 L.T. 625; *Re Malam, supra;
    Re Hume Nisbet's Settlement* (1911), 27 T.L.R. 461).

f   these rules are subject to a contrary intention expressed in the
    trust instrument;

g   the rules are also subject to the rule in *Bouch* v. *Sproule*
    (1887), 12 App. Cas. 385, H.L., that if the company intends to
    capitalise profits, and does so, the shares will be capital.

2   Life tenant entitled to scrip

Where the life tenant is entitled to the scrip, there are no income
tax consequences so far as the trustees themselves are concerned. So
far as the life tenant himself is concerned, however, he is treated as
having received a net dividend equivalent to the amount of the dividend which could have been received in cash; or, in the case of bonus
shares to which the provisions apply, a net dividend equivalent to the
market value of those shares at the date of issue (s. 34 (4); Sch. 8,
para. 1). The dividend is treated as being of an amount equal to the
dividend grossed up at the basic rate of tax, from which tax at the
basic rate has been deducted. If the beneficiary's highest personal
rate of income tax is less than the basic rate, he cannot make a repayment claim in respect of the tax notionally deducted, but if his
highest personal rate of tax is above the basic rate, an additional
assessment can be raised on him in respect of the grossed up
equivalent of the amount treated as a dividend (s. 34 (4)).

3   Scrip forming part of capital

Where the trust confers fixed beneficial entitlements, and the
trustees are obliged to retain the shares as an accretion to capital,
there is no income tax charge on the trustees. Their capital gains tax
position is described later (p. 272, *post*).

4   Discretionary and accumulation settlements

Where the trust is one in which, had the trustees received a cash
dividend, it would have been liable to the additional rate under FA
1973, s. 16 (p. 230, *ante*), the trustees are treated as having received
a dividend of the grossed up equivalent of the value of the shares,
and are liable to account for the additional rate on that grossed up
equivalent (F(No. 2)A 1975, s. 34 (6)). This is so whether for the purposes of the administration of the trust the shares are to be treated as
income or capital.

H   ACCUMULATED AND RETAINED INCOME

1   *Accumulations*

If the whole of the trust income, after payment of income tax and trust management expenses, is not distributed in the year in which it arises, the part which remains will either be accumulated, or will be retained without being accumulated. Whether or not income is accumulated depends entirely on matters of the general law and not on specific provisions of the tax legislation. For most purposes, the income tax legislation imposes the same liability at the time when the income arises whether the income is accumulated or is merely retained, but the distinction is important at the time of distribution as well as underlying certain provisions. It is, therefore, considered at this stage.

Accumulation is the conversion of income into capital. In order to be effectively accumulated:

a   there must be power to accumulate conferred either by the trust instrument or by the Trustee Act 1925. While there is statutory authority to accumulate income from funds held for an infant beneficiary to the extent that it is not applied for his maintenance (Trustee Act 1925, s. 31), there is no statutory authority conferred on trustees generally to accumulate (*Re Gourju's Will Trusts, Starling* v. *Custodian of Enemy Property* [1943] Ch. 24 at 34);

b   the power must not be void, as being for a period beyond the maximum of one of six prescribed periods. These are:

  i   the life of the settlor;

  ii   a term of twenty-one years from the death of the settlor;

  iii   the duration of the minority or respective minorities of any person or persons living or *en ventre sa mere* at the death of the settlor;

  iv   the duration of the minority or respective minorities of the infant beneficiaries who, if of full age, would be entitled to the income;

  v   a term of twenty-one years from the credition of the settlement; and

  vi   the duration of the minority or respective minorities of any person or persons in being when the settlement is created, whether or not they are beneficiaries or have any other connection with the settlement (Law of Property Act 1925, s. 164; Perpetuities and Accumulations Act 1964, s. 13).

237

If a provision of the trust instrument prescribes accumulation for a period longer than that permitted by statute, that provision is void only as to the excess (*Re Joel's Will Trusts, Rogerson* v. *Brudenall-Bruce,* [1967] Ch. 14).

c   the trustees must decide to accumulate. Strictly, the accumulation is effected by the trustees reaching the decision itself, and no formality is required. In the case of well-ordered trusts, the decision of the trustees will be recorded in a minute, but it will also be adequately evidenced by their signing or approving accounts or returns showing that income has been accumulated.

The trustees have a reasonable time within which to decide whether to accumulate (*Re Gulbenkian's Settlement Trusts (No. 2), Stephens* v. *Maun,* [1970] Ch. 408). If they do not reach a decision within a reasonable time, the position depends on whether the trust instrument requires them to reach a decision, or merely requires them to consider whether to reach a decision. In the former case, their discretion is not lost by the passage of time (*Re Locker's Settlement Trusts, Meachem* v. *Sachs,* [1978] 1 All E.R. 216) whereas in the latter case it is (*Re Allen-Meyrick's Will Trusts, Mangnall* v. *Allen Meyrick,* [1966] 1 All E.R. 740).

Where no positive decision is reached, the position will also depend on whether the trust instrument imposes a trust to accumulate, subject to a power to apply the income for other purposes, or a trust to apply the income for other purposes subject to a power to accumulate. With the passage of time, a presumption will arise that the trustees have followed their primary obligation, that is, that they have given effect to the trust and not to power.

2   Use of accumulated income for infants

A further complication arises from the Trustee Act 1925. When income has been accumulated, it is generally treated as capital, although either the trust instrument or the Trustee Act (see s. 31 (2) (i)) may direct that the accumulated fund is to be dealt with in a manner different from the other capital. However, where in one year during the infancy of a beneficiary income is accumulated, the trustees may in a subsequent year apply that accumulation as if it were income of that subsequent year (s. 31 (2), *proviso*).

3   Nature of accumulated income in hands of trustees

For the purposes of general trust law, when income has been accumulated it is treated as capital, subject to the provision just noted under which accumulated income may be applied as income for infant beneficiaries. The nature of accumulated income for tax purposes is less clear.

In *Postlethwaite* v. *I.R. Comrs.* (1963), 41 T.C. 224 the trustees were directed by the trust instrument to accumulate net income, and to make payments out of capital. It was held that the payments were of an income nature; and also that, notwithstanding the accumulation, it represented, for the purposes of what is now TA 1970, s. 52, profits or gains brought into charge to tax. Wilberforce, J., said (at p. 232):

"It may be true that the settlor has, for trust purposes as between the beneficiaries, placed the character of capital upon this income; but that does not mean for tax purposes it loses the character of income which has already borne tax. It seems to me that it must inevitably remain income which has borne tax, and that nothing in the settlement can take away that character from it or turn it into something which is not of that nature".

By virtue of this decision, in deciding whether s. 52 applies, trustees can take into account income of the year in question which has been taxed, even if that income has been accumulated.

4   Nature of payment received from accumulated income

Although accumulated income may in the hands of the trustees have to be treated as retaining the character of income which has borne tax, where a payment is made from accumulated income, it will generally be treated as capital in the hands of the beneficiary. So, in *Stanley* v. *I.R. Comrs.*, [1944] K.B. 255 an infant had an interest in income which, by virtue of the Trustee Act 1925 fell to be treated as a contingent interest (see p. 242, *post*). When he attained his majority he became entitled to the accumulated income which was paid to him. It was held that he received the accumulated sum as a capital receipt, and was not liable to income tax on it.

It seems, therefore, that where a payment is made to a beneficiary out of accumulated income, FA 1973, s. 17 will not apply.

I   PAYMENTS FROM CAPITAL

1   Income or capital?

Where trustees make a payment from capital, although that payment is made from capital, it may be treated as income in the hands of the beneficiary. This is so whether the payment is made from pure capital, or from income which has been accumulated. The taxation position of the trustees as well as that of the beneficiary will depend on how the payment is treated in the hands of the beneficiary, and that will be governed by the nature of the payment in his hands, and not the source from which the payment is made (*Brodie's Will Trustees* v. *I.R. Comrs.* (1933), 17 T.C. 432 at 439).

It is proposed to consider first the taxation effects of a payment being treated as income, and then such principles as can be discerned to determine whether a payment is of an income or capital nature.

2 Taxation effects

  a Beneficiary with fixed entitlement Where the beneficiary has a life or similar interest, the trustees must deduct out of a "payment" made to him income tax at the basic rate, and account to the Revenue for that tax deducted (TA 1970, ss. 52, 53). Although the authorities are not entirely clear, it seems that the amount of the "payment" is the sum which the trustees intend to withdraw from capital. This in turn will depend on whether the trustees intend the sum paid to the beneficiary to be net or gross.

If the trustees intend the payment to be net of basic rate tax, they will have intended, or will be presumed to have intended, to have withdrawn from capital the amount actually paid, grossed up at the basic rate (see, for example, the assessments on the grossed up equivalents which were confirmed in *Cunard's Trustees* v. *I.R. Comrs.*, [1946] 1 All E.R. 159, (CA)).

Where, however, the trustees intend the payment to be gross, their liability will be restricted to that on the payment actually made, and not to that on the grossed up equivalent of the payment. Thus, in *Morant's Settlement Trustees* v. *I.R. Comrs.*, [1948] 1 All E.R. 732, the trustees raised from capital and paid to the beneficiary £3,895, and were assessed only on that sum and not on the grossed up equivalent. (For a further example of assessments being restricted to those on the payments actually made, see *Milne's Executors* v. *I.R. Comrs.* (1956), 37 T.C. 10).

  b Beneficiary with discretionary entitlement Where the trustees make a payment in the exercise of a discretion, and the payment is of an income nature in the hands of the beneficiary, FA 1973, s. 17 applies. In this case, irrespective of how much the trustees intended to withdraw from capital, the sum paid is treated as a net payment, and the liability of the trustees is on the amount of the net payment grossed up at the aggregate of the basic and the additional rate (s. 17 (2)).

3 Nature of payment

There is no single criterion to determine whether a payment is of a capital or income nature in the hands of a beneficiary, but the following principles can be discerned:

a Beneficiary absolutely entitled to capital Where a beneficiary is absolutely entitled to capital, a payment made from that capital to the beneficiary will be treated as a capital payment. It is as if the beneficiary transferred his own capital from one pocket to another. This principle also applies where the payment is made to a third party for the benefit of the beneficiary, and it applies whether the beneficiary is an adult or an infant. Accordingly, (see *Brodie's Will Trustees* v. *I.R. Comrs.* (1933), 17 T.C. 432 at 439) if an infant beneficiary is absolutely entitled to a fund, and a payment is made to a school by way of composition of school fees, that payment will be treated as a capital payment.

b Beneficiary with only fixed income entitlement Where the beneficiary has no entitlement to capital, but a fixed entitlement to income, such as an annuity, or the right to receive income of a specified annual amount, the payment will be treated as wholly income in his hands, even if the payment is made from capital (*Brodie's Will Trustees* v. *I.R. Comrs., supra*).

c. Beneficiary with discretionary entitlement Where the beneficiary has no entitlement to capital, and an entitlement to income which depends on the discretion of the trustees, it is necessary to consider:

   i the purpose for which the payment is made; and

  ii whether the beneficiary is a direct or indirect object.

If the beneficiary is a direct object, and the purpose is of an income or recurrent nature, the payment will be treated as income. This will be so, for example, if the trustees resort to capital expressly to augment the beneficiary's income, or to enable the beneficiary to maintain his standard of living (*Drummond* v. *Collins,* [1915] A.C. 1011; *Lord Tollemache* v. *I.R. Comrs.* (1926), 11. T.C. 277; *Lindus and Hortin* v. *I.R. Comrs.* (1933), 17 T.C. 442; *Cunard's Trustees* v. *I.R. Comrs.* (1945), 27 T.C. 122).

If the beneficiary is not a direct object of the trust, but indirectly obtains a benefit, it seems that the beneficiary is treated, in principle, as if he received capital. This is illustrated by the exceptional case of *Stedeford* v. *Beloe,* [1932] A.C. 388. In that case, the trustees held a fund for the benefit of a school. They exercised their discretion by giving a voluntary pension to a former headmaster of the school. It was held that he was in no way "entitled" to the pension, and that it was not of an income nature in his hands.

Although this decision shows that, in principle, a person who benefits indirectly can receive his benefit in the form of capital, whereas in the hands of a direct beneficiary it would be income, were the particular facts to be repeated now, the headmaster would be subject to income tax on the pension under TA 1970, s. 182.

d   Beneficiary with contingent or discretionary interest in capital
The circumstances which usually present the greatest difficulty are those where the beneficiary can receive benefits of a capital or of an income nature. Examples are where the trust is discretionary, and the trustees can apply both income and capital to the same beneficiary; or where a beneficiary is entitled to income, but the trustees have a power of advancement. In these cases it is necessary to consider:

i   recurrence; and
ii purpose.

To be of an income nature in the hands of the beneficiary the payment must be one of a number which do in fact recur, or which in itself has the quality of recurrence (see Lord Maugham in *Moss Empires Ltd.* v. *I.R. Comrs.*, [1937] A.C. 785 at 795). The fact of recurrence is present in most of the reported decisions (e.g. *Brodie's Will Trustees* v. *I.R. Comrs.*, *supra;* *Cunard's Trustees* v. *I.R. Comrs.*, *supra*).

However, by itself the fact of recurrence or the quality of recurrence, is not conclusive (see *Lawson* v. *Rolfe*, [1970] 1 Ch. 612).

In addition to the fact or quality of recurrence, it seems that the payment will only be treated as an income payment if it is made for an income purpose. Difficulty can arise when payments are made in respect of school fees. If capital is used for the payment of school fees, these payments will be of an income nature. If, however, capital is used to make a payment by way of composition of school fees, it seems that that payment can be regarded as the purchase of an education, and so as capital. The Revenue sometimes take the contrary view, particularly where the payment does not cover the whole of the remainder of the child's education, so that such payment may recur.

e   Payments from accumulated income   It has been seen (p. 238, *ante*) that where income is accumulated during the infancy of a beneficiary, the accumulations may be applied as income of a subsequent year. It has also been seen (p. 239, *ante*) that at least for some purposes income which is accumulated never loses its character as income which has borne tax. Although, strictly, so far as the

242

beneficiary is concerned payments from accumulated income should have the same results as payments from other capital, where there is doubt as to the nature of a payment in the hands of a beneficiary, it seems that it will more likely be treated as income where it has been paid from accumulated income.

J "TAX FREE" PAYMENTS

1 Payments of fixed amounts after deduction of tax

Where it is desired to give a beneficiary an annuity or other periodic payment which is of a fixed amount in his hands, that is, where the sum after tax will remain constant, it is usual to provide that the beneficiary will receive "such a sum as after the deduction of income tax at the basic rate for the time being in force will leave £X". Where this formula is used the trustees are not under an obligation to make the payments free of tax in excess of the basic rate, so that the beneficiary cannot claim from the trustees repayment of his tax in excess of the basic rate on that sum (*Re Bates, Selmes* v. *Bates*, [1925] Ch. 157).

As far as the trustees are concerned, the provision takes effect as one to pay an amount equal to the stated sum grossed up at the current basic rate. They must, therefore, issue a certificate of deduction of tax in the usual way. If the beneficiary is able to obtain a repayment of tax, he is under no obligation to pay this amount to the trustees.

Where the document under which the obligation arose came into force when there was a standard rate of income tax and not a basic rate, a direction to pay an amount which after the deduction of income tax at the standard rate is equal to £X will take effect as a direction to pay an amount which after the deduction of income tax at the basic rate is equal to £X (FA 1971, Sch. 7, para. 2).

2 Directions to pay "tax free"

It is not permissible to make an agreement to make payments without deducting tax (TMA 1970, s. 106). However, there is no objection to agreeing to make payments "free of income tax" provide that the parties intend that the agreement shall be to pay such a sum as after the deduction of tax will leave £X (*Ferguson* v. *I.R. Comrs.*, [1969] 1 All E.R. 1025). Likewise, there is no objection to providing in a will or trust deed that payments shall be made free of income tax in this sense. The result is not the same as where the express formula mentioned in paragraph 1 (*ante*) is used, because in the case of "tax free" payments:

a "tax free" means free of income tax at both the basic and higher rates. Thus if the beneficiary pays income tax at the higher rates, he is entitled to recover from the trustees the amount of excess tax which he pays on the trust income;

b the beneficiary is accountable to the trustees for any tax repayments which he receives (*Re Pettit, Le Fevre* v. *Pettit,* [1922] 2 Ch. 765) unless there is an indication to the contrary in the trust instrument; and

c to obtain any repayment, the trustees may compel the beneficiary to make a repayment claim (*Re Kingcome's Will Trusts, Hickley* v. *Kingcome,* [1936] 1 All E.R. 173; [1936] Ch. 566).

3 Pre-war tax-free annuities

Provisions for "tax-free" annuities in wills or settlements coming into force before 3 September 1939, when the standard rate of tax was 5s. 6d. in the pound, equivalent to 27.5%, require special mention. Under TA 1970, s. 422, (and FA 1971, Sch. 6, para. 48) any provision made before 3 September 1939 and not varied after that date takes effect as if the stated amount were reduced in accordance with the fraction:

$$\text{stated amount} \times \frac{\text{difference between 100 and the current basic rate}}{72.50\%}$$

Thus, a provision for tax free payments of £100 p.a. in a settlement before 1939 would, where the basic rate of tax is 30% be reduced as follows:

$$£100 \times \frac{(100 - 30 = 70)}{72.5} = £96.55 \text{ net}$$

£96.55 grossed at 30% = £137.92

(This is equivalent to £100 grossed at 27.5%)

There are further provisions for calculating reliefs on 1938/39 rates.

K APPORTIONMENTS

It will frequently be necessary to apportion dividends received between two or more beneficiaries. Suppose, for example, that trustees hold money upon trust to pay the income to Isabel during her life, and then to Evelyn during her life, and then to Colin. Suppose also that a company in which the trust has an investment pays dividends for the year ended 31 December. If Isabel dies on 27

February (the 58th day of the year) her estate will be entitled to 58/365ths of the dividends declared for that year on each of the shares held by the trust. The remainder will belong to Evelyn. These dividends will in general be received by the trustees after deduction of tax, and the apportioned part of the income will be payable likewise. Thus the need to apportion dividends in accordance with the Apportionment Act 1870 should not cause any tax difficulty.

The other type of apportionment, between capital and income, which was discussed at p. 20, again will cause no taxation problems, because although the apportionment is made by taking tax into account, it is never necessary to account to the Revenue for that tax (*I.R. Comrs.* v. *Henderson's Executors,* (1931) 16 T.C. 282).

L   INCOME OF BENEFICIARY: GENERALLY

1   Nature and sources of income

In the course of trust administration, it is customary to think of the trustees, in their capacity as such, being entitled to the income from the various sources which are due to the trust; for that income to lose the earmark of its origin when in the hands of the trustees; and for the beneficiaries to be entitled to income from a new source, namely the trust.

The strict position, however, has been made more complicated by the decision in *Baker* v. *Archer-Shee,* [1927] AC 844. In that case, Lady Archer-Shee was the sole life tenant under an American will trust. The trustees were resident in America, and the trust fund consisted entirely of investments made outside the United Kingdom. There was no doubt that the income was assessable under Schedule D, Case V, but at that time the Case V rules were that income from foreign stocks, shares or rents was assessable on an arising basis, but income from other foreign possessions was assessable on a remittance basis. The House of Lords held that Lady Archer-Shee was entitled to the income from the foreign stocks themselves, and so was taxable on the arising basis. Although the case itself was concerned with foreign income, its principle applies whenever a beneficiary has an indefeasible vested interest in income. Where the rule applies, it is necessary to "look through" the trustees to the underlying sources of income.

2   Application of Rule in Baker v. Archer-Shee

a.   *Vested interest in income*   The rule in *Baker* v. *Archer-Shee* applies where the beneficiary has a vested interest in the income, and

245

that interest is not liable to be divested. Accordingly, it will apply where:

i the beneficiary is an adult, and is absolutely entitled both to income and capital, as in the case of a bare trusteeship or nomineeship;

ii the beneficiary is an adult, and has a life or similar interest (except an annuity) whereby he is entitled to the income as it arises; and

iii the beneficiary is an infant and is absolutely entitled to capital and income, but not where he is only entitled to income (see p. 249, *post*).

The rule does not apply where:

i the beneficiary is contingently entitled (*Stanley* v. *I.R. Comrs.*, (1944) 26 T.C. 12; *Dewar* v. *I.R. Comrs.*, [1931] A.C. 566);

ii the beneficiary is only a discretionary beneficiary;

iii the beneficiary is an infant, and has, according to the trust instrument a vested interest in income, but that interest is treated as a contingent interest by virtue of the Trustee Act 1925, s. 31 (see p. 249, *post*);

iv the trustees have a power to accumulate, or a power to divest income, so that the beneficiary does not have the right to income as it arises; or

v the interest of the beneficiary is liable to be divested (*Cornwell* v. *Barry* (1955), 36 T.C. 268).

b Income derived from trust Where the rule in *Baker* v. *Archer-Shee* applies, the income is treated as being derived from its underlying source. Where, however, a receipt which is income is the hands of the beneficiary was derived from capital in the hands of the trustees, the income is treated as being derived from the trustees.

c. Annuitants Annuitants are treated separately. Their income is regarded as being derived directly from the trust, and not from the underlying source.

3 *Effects where rule in* Baker v. Archer-Shee *applies*

Where the rule in *Baker* v. *Archer-Shee* applies, the effects are as follows:

a the beneficiary is assessable on the income under the Schedule and Case appropriate to the underlying source;

b the rules applicable to the appropriate Schedule and Case are to be followed. This might lead, for example, to the preceding year basis being adopted;

c except where income from the underlying source is chargeable under Schedule D, Case III, the trustees have no authority to deduct income tax at the basic rate, because TA 1970, ss. 52 and 53 apply only to Case III income;

d   it has been said in *Baker* v. *Archer-Shee,* but not finally decided, that the trustees are not assessable on the income, even if it passes through their hands; and

e   more specifically, it has been said in *Reid's Trustees* v. *I.R. Comrs.* (1929), 14 T.C. 512 at 525 but not finally decided, that if the beneficiary is not liable, because, for example, he is non-resident, the trustees are not assessable on the income even if it passes through their hands.

4   *Trust income differing from taxable income*

In certain circumstances the amount of income actually paid to the beneficiaries will differ from the amount of taxable income paid to them. For the purposes of the general trust law, the trustees will pay out the actual income received (irrespective of the amount of taxable income) but less the amount of income tax payable in respect of the taxable income. The differences between the actual income and the taxable income will arise mainly where one or more sources of income are assessable on a preceding year basis, and where the trustees obtain the benefit of non-personal allowances, such as the agricultural buildings allowance. Where there are these differences, the amounts paid to the beneficiaries will not be the same as the net payments of taxable income.

M   TOTAL INCOME OF ADULT BENEFICIARY

1   *Trust income*

Income which forms part of the total income of an adult beneficiary is as follows:

a   income which is paid to the beneficiary or to which the beneficiary is entitled;

b   income in which the beneficiary has an interest which is vested and is not liable to be divested, even if that income is accumulated. For this purpose, an interest is vested if it can be said that the beneficiary will in any event receive the income or the accumulations (*I.R. Comrs.* v. *Hamilton-Russell's Executors,* [1943] 1 All E.R. 474);

c   income to which the beneficiary is entitled, even though his interest under the trust is contingent. Under the Trustee Act 1925, where an adult beneficiary has a contingent interest in settled property, then provided that the gift is not subject to any contrary intention, and provided the gift carries the inter-mediate income he is entitled to the income until he dies, attains a vested interest, or his interest fails (s. 31 (1) (ii));

d   annual sums which are applied for the benefit of a beneficiary. This includes the case where income is applied in the payment of rates or other outgoings of the property in which the bene-ficiary resides (*I.R. Comrs.* v. *Miller,* [1930] A.C. 222, H.L.);

e   where the trust property is woodlands, which are occupied by the beneficiary under the terms of the trust, and are assessed under Schedule B, the annual value for the purposes of that Schedule (*Lord Tollemache* v. *I.R. Comrs.* (1926), 11 T.C. 277; *Lady De Robeck* v. *I.R. Comrs.* (1928), 13 T.C. 345, H.L.); and

f   payments of capital which are treated as income (p. 239, *ante*).

The following income does not form part of a beneficiary's total income:

a   income in which the beneficiary does not have an indefeasible vested interest, where that income is accumulated;

b   the annual value of any property which the beneficiary is allowed to occupy (*I.R. Comrs.* v. *Miller,* [1930] A.C. 222, H.L.), other than woodlands assessable under Schedule B;

c   charges on the income to which the beneficiary is entitled, such as an annuity payable to another beneficiary and interest which is eligible for relief (see p. 228, *ante*); and

d   trust management expenses (see p. 228, *ante*) (*Murray* v. *I.R. Comrs.* (1926), 11 T.C. 133; *Macfarlane* v. *I.R. Comrs.* (1929), 14 T.C. 532).

N TOTAL INCOME OF INFANT BENEFICIARY

1 Effect of the Trustee Act 1925, s. 31

In determining the total income of an infant beneficiary, it is necessary first to take account of the Trustee Act, 1925, s. 31 which in some cases converts what appear to be vested interests in income into contingent interests. The effects of the section are as follows:

a   where trustees hold any property on trust for an infant, the trustees have a power to apply income for the maintenance of the infant, and are under an obligation to accumulate the remainder (s. 31 (1)). This is so whether the interest appears to be vested or contingent;

b   if the infant is entitled absolutely both to capital and income, so that the incapacity of an infant to give a good receipt is the sole reason why he cannot call for the capital to be transferred to him, he will be entitled to the accumulated income, as well as to the capital, when he attains the age of 18. If he dies before attaining that age, his estate will be entitled. In this case the infant is treated as having a vested interest in income, even though the whole or part of that income may be accumulated (*Roberts* v. *Hanks* (1926), 10 T.C. 351; *Edwardes Jones* v. *Down* (1936), 20 T.C. 279);

c   if the infant had what appears from the trust instrument to be a vested interest in income during his infancy, the destination of the accumulated income will depend on whether he attains the age of eighteen. If he does so, (or marries under the age of eighteen), he will then become entitled to the accumulated sum (s. 31 (2) (i) (*a*)). If, however, he dies before reaching the age of eighteen, the accumulated sum will be added to capital (s. 31 (2) (ii)). Accordingly, although it could appear from the trust instrument that the infant has a vested interest in income, the Act converts this interest into one contingent on his attaining the age of eighteen or marrying under that age;

d   if the infant had *ex facie* an interest contingent on his attaining the age of eighteen, or marrying under that age, the position is the same as that stated in *c* (*ante*);

e   if the infant had an interest subject to any other contingency, on attaining the age of eighteen the accumulation is added to capital;

f   all the provisions of the Trustee Act 1925, s. 31 yield to a contrary intention in the trust instrument (s. 69 (2)).

During the minority of the infant, interests within *c*, *d* and *e* are all treated as contingent interests (*Stanley* v. *I.R. Comrs.*, [1944] KB 255).

2   *Interests liable to be divested*

An interest which falls within *b* above will be vested, but it may be liable to be divested. This will be so where at the point of time being considered there is only one child, but if another is born, that other will be entitled to benefit (see *Cornwell* v. *Barry* (1955), 36 T.C. 268).

3   *Total income of infant beneficiary*

The rules are generally the same as in the case of an adult beneficiary (p. 247, *ante*) and it may particularly be noted that where sums are applied for the maintenance of an infant, these sums, grossed up, are treated as forming part of his income (*Drummond* v. *Collins,* [1915] A.C. 1011). To the extent that income is accumulated during the infancy of the beneficiary, it will only be treated as part of his total income where his interest is vested and is not liable to be divested (*ibid*).

4 Use of personal allowances

Unless the Trustee Act 1925, s. 31 is excluded by the trust instrument, all income paid to, or applied for the benefit of, an infant must have been paid or applied in the exercise by the trustees of their discretion. It will, therefore, be income on which income tax has been paid at the aggregate of the basic rate and the additional rate (p. 230, *ante*).

While this income will form part of the infant beneficiary's total income, he is entitled to a single person's personal allowance of the same amount as a single adult person. For 1981/82 this is £1,375.

5 Repayment claims on behalf of infant beneficiaries

a By parent Usually trust income which forms part of an infant's total income will have suffered income tax by deduction at the aggregate of the basic and additional rates. If, after taking into account the infant's other income, if any, and his personal allowance, his marginal rate is lower than that at which tax has been suffered, a repayment claim can be made. This claim is made by the parent or guardian (TMA 1970, s. 72).

b By infant On attaining majority, the beneficiary can himself make a repayment claim in respect of the previous six years if the parent or guardian has not done so (TMA 1970, s. 43 (1)).

c Pre-1969 income Before 1969, where a beneficiary had a contingent interest (or an apparent vested life interest which is treated as a contingent interest (*supra*)), although a repayment claim could not be made each year, it could have been made within six years of the end of the year of assessment in which the contingency is fulfilled (TA 1970, Sch. 14, para. 1). In this case the accumulated income was treated as part of the beneficiary's total income for that year, and the appropriate reliefs were then given by way of repayment. However, a claim could not be made in respect of the tax paid for the year 1969/70 or for any subsequent year, although a claim can still be made in respect of the tax paid during such part of his minority as fell before 6 April 1969. Such a claim can only be made if:

i   the contingency was:
   (*a*) the attainment of a specified age; or
   (*b*) marriage; and
ii the accumulation was for the benefit of the person who fulfilled the contingency.

d   Accumulated income paid out: treated as a capital sum
Where income is accumulated for an infant beneficiary, those accumulations, when paid to the beneficiary, are received by him as a capital sum, and so do not give rise to a claim for income tax at either the basic or the higher rates (*Stanley* v. *I.R. Comrs.* (1944), 26 T.C. 12). Payments of accumulated income are, however, treated as payments of capital, and may be liable to capital transfer tax as a result.

Chapter 17

Administration of a Trust: Capital Gains Tax

A GENERAL PRINCIPLES

1 Trustees a separate body of persons

The trustees of a trust are treated for capital gains tax purposes as a single, distinct, and continuing body (CGTA 1979, s. 52 (1)). The significance of this concept has been considered earlier (p. 225, *ante*) but the effect is that in general the taxation affairs of the trust will be entirely separate from the taxation affairs of the individuals who are for the time being the trustees.

2 Sole trustee not "an individual"

The principle that the trustees are a separate body for capital gains tax purposes applies also where there is only one trustee. Where there is at any time only one trustee, he is not "an individual", so that no provisions of the legislation which are expressed to apply to "individuals" apply to trustees (s. 48 (2)).

3 Relevance of general law of trusts

Although in the broadest sense the capital gains tax legislation on settled property is based on general trust law, in many respects the tax legislation departs from the general law. Thus, some property which the general law will treat as trust property is not, for capital gains tax purposes, treated as settled property. Conversely, some property which the general law does not treat as trust property is treated as settled property for capital gains tax.

More dangerously, the capital gains tax legislation uses concepts which are near to those used by the general law, but which are nevertheless distinct from it. Accordingly the greatest care is necessary when endeavouring to deduce from the general law the significance of an event for capital gains tax. This is shown most clearly from the attempts to ascertain the meaning of "absolute entitlement" from the concept in general trust law of beneficial entitlement (see p. 254, *post*).

4 Assets and settled property

The Capital Gains Tax Act 1979 uses the expressions "assets" and "settled property". Fundamentally, capital gains tax is concerned with the gain or loss which arises on the disposal of an "asset" (s. 1), and this principle is applied to assets which are held by trustees. Thus, where a beneficiary becomes absolutely entitled as against the trustee, there is a deemed disposal and re-acquisition of the assets themselves (s. 54 (1); see p. 254, *post*).

The expression "settled property" is used to denote the property which is, according to the general law, the property which is comprised in a settlement. The interest which a beneficiary has under a settlement is an interest in settled property. If, therefore, to take the same example as in the previous paragraph, a beneficiary becomes absolutely entitled as against the trustee, he becomes absolutely entitled to settled property, and it is that which causes a deemed disposal and re-acquisition of the underlying assets. Likewise, if a beneficiary has a life interest in possession, and that interest comes to an end, there is a termination of an interest in possession in settled property, which gives rise to a deemed disposal and re-acquisition of the underlying assets (s. 55 (1)).

For most purposes, the primary concern is with the assets themselves, but if it is necessary to consider what property is settled property, that question is to be answered in the context of ordinary trust law. For example, in *Crowe* v. *Appleby,* [1976] 2 All E.R. 914 freehold land was held in trust for various beneficiaries in different shares. It was held at first instance ([1975] 3 All E.R. 529 at 536), and supported in the Court of Appeal, that the settled property was the land itself and not the share of any beneficiary in it.

5 Types of settled property

The legislation distinguishes five types of trust or similar property:

a   what might conveniently be called "ordinary" settled property, that, is, property which the general law would recognise as trust property, and which for capital gains tax purposes does not fall into any of the other categories noted below;

b   assets which are held on bare trusts, or by a nominee;

c   property which is jointly owned;

d   property which the general law does not regard as settled property, but which is treated as settled for some taxation

purposes. This includes in some circumstances property subject
to an agreement or arrangement; and

e   property which is held by personal representatives in the course
of the administration of an estate. This has previously been
considered (Chapter 8).

B WHEN THE CHARGE ARISES

In the case of an asset which is treated as settled property for
capital gains tax purposes, a charge for tax may arise:

a   on the disposal of the asset in the course of the administration
of the trust;

b   on a beneficiary becoming entitled absolutely to the settled
property;

c   on trustees of another trust becoming entitled to the settled
property; and

d   on the termination of an interest in possession in settled property, otherwise than on death.

C DISPOSAL IN COURSE OF ADMINISTRATION

Where trustees dispose of an asset in the course of the administration of the trust, and the asset has appreciated in value, the amount
of the chargeable gain or allowable loss is computed according to the
ordinary capital gains tax principles. These have been discussed in
Chapter 3.

D BENEFICIARY BECOMING ABSOLUTELY ENTITLED

1 *The rule*

At the time when a beneficiary becomes absolutely entitled as
against the trustees to any settled property, the trustees are deemed
to dispose of the assets which comprise that settled property at their
market value at that time, and to re-acquire them at that value
(CGTA 1979, s. 54 (1)). This notional disposal is deemed to take
place whether or not there is any actual transfer to the beneficiary.
After the deemed disposal, the trustees are treated as holding the
assets as bare trustees for the beneficiary, so that no further liability
will arise on the actual transfer of the assets to the beneficiary (s. 46;
p. 267, *post*).

2 *Absolute entitlement*

The concept of absolute entitlement is one peculiar to capital
gains tax, and has no direct equivalent in the general law of trusts.

The concept is that the person in question has the exclusive right to direct how the asset is to be dealt with (CGTA 1979, s. 46 (2)). This is extended to include the case where a person would have the right to direct how the asset is to be dealt with were it not subject only to a charge or lien in favour of the trustees for taxes, costs, or other outgoings (*ibid*). In *Prest* v. *Bettinson* [1980] S.T.C. 607 (see p. 156, *ante*) property was hold by personal representatives for five bodies, of whom four were charities, subject to the payment of annuities. It was held that because of the obligation to pay the annuities, the residuary beneficiaries were not absolutely entitled as against the personal representatives, and that the position would have been the same of the personal representatives were trustees.

There is a further extension of the concept, under which a person who is under the legal disability of infancy or mental illness is treated as if he were absolutely entitled if that disability is the only reason for him not actually being so (s. 46 (1)). The special problems which affect infants are considered later (p. 269, *post*).

Where an individual becomes absolutely entitled, his absolute entitlement to the settled property will usually be accompanied by absolute beneficial entitlement of the underlying assets. This entitlement may be either directly under the terms of the trust instrument or by act of the trustees. If, therefore, an asset is held in trust for Adrian when he reaches the age of thirty, on attaining that age he will be absolutely and beneficially entitled. Or if the trustees of a discretionary trust resolve to transfer an asset to a beneficiary, when they make that resolution the beneficiary will become absolutely and beneficially entitled to the asset. Further, if trustees decide to transfer a house to a beneficiary by way of advancement, upon their making that decision he becomes absolutely and beneficially entitled to it.

While, therefore, in the case of an individual, absolute entitlement will usually be accompanied by beneficial entitlement, for the purposes of the charge to capital gains tax, the fact of beneficial entitlement is irrelevant. This is because the absolute entitlement need only be as against the trustees, and not as against everyone else.

3 *Absolute entitlement otherwise than on death of life tenant*

It will be seen (p. 259, *post*) that under CGTA 1979, s. 55, where a life interest in possession in settled property comes to an end, and the property does not on that occasion cease to be settled, the trustees are deemed to dispose of the assets in which that interest subsisted at their value at that time, and to re-acquire them. If when the life interest terminates the property ceases to be settled property, and a beneficiary becomes absolutely entitled, there will be a deemed disposal and re-acquisition under this provision.

4   *Absolute entitlement following death of life tenant*

Where property ceases to be settled property on the death of a life tenant, and another beneficiary then becomes absolutely entitled, the property is uplifted to its market value at the date of death of that beneficiary, but no chargeable gain accrues (CGTA 1979, s. 56 (1)). If, however, on the death of the life tenant, the settled property reverts to the settlor, the deemed disposal and re-acquisition is not at market value, but at the value which will show neither a gain nor a loss (CGTA 1979, s. 56 (1) (*b*)).

E   TRUSTEES BECOMING ABSOLUTELY ENTITLED

1   *Generally*

Because the concept of absolute entitlement does not involve any connotation of beneficial entitlement, a person can become absolutely entitled in a fiduciary capacity as against trustees. Suppose, for example, that there are two entirely separate settlements, created by different settlors. Suppose also that the trustees of the first settlement are directed to hold an asset upon the trusts of the first settlement for a period of ten years, and then to transfer it to the trustees of the second settlement to be held on the trusts of that settlement. At the expiration of the period of ten years, the trustees of the second settlement have become absolutely entitled as against the trustees of the first settlement. It is clear law that:

a   one body of trustees can become absolutely entitled as against another body of trustees (*Hart* v. *Briscoe,* [1978] 1 All E.R. 791; *Hoare Trustees* v. *Gardner* (*ibid*)); and

b   this is so even if the individuals who comprise these bodies of trustees are the same (*ibid*).

2   *Absolute entitlement and separate settlements*

There are two concepts which often overlap, but which are nevertheless distinct, namely those of absolute entitlement and separate settlements. The legislation uses the concepts for different purposes, and the law has been developed according to the separate provisions. There are many aspects which have not been worked out, but the position appears to be as follows:

a   one body of trustees will be absolutely entitled in their capacity as the trustees of one settlement as against themselves or others in their capacity as the trustees of another settlement if they are to be treated as being able to give for all purposes an effective direction as to how the trust property is to be dealt with;

b   they will only be able to do so if, after the event in question, the terms on which the property is held are exhaustive; in essence, it must never be necessary to look back to the original trust instrument; and

c   trustees will only become absolutely entitled as against themselves or others if after the event in question a new settlement has come into being, in accordance with the rules noted later (see p. 262, *post*).

3   *Powers of appointment and advancement*

a   *The intermediate category*   There will usually be no difficulty where property subject to one settlement comes to be held on the trusts of a separate settlement, where that separate settlement has an entirely different origin. Difficult questions do however arise when an asset comes to be held on different trusts, but a link remains with the original settlement. This is so where there is the exercise of a power of appointment or a power of advancement. It may be helpful to re-state the nature of these powers before proceeding.

b   *Powers of advancement*   There are two ideas in the notion of advancement. One is that of time. In this sense, a power of advancement is seen as a power to advance, or bring forward, the time at which a beneficiary will receive his benefit (*Re Morris' Settlement Trusts, Adams* v. *Napier*, [1951] 2 All E.R. 528). The other is that of preferment. In this sense, a power of advancement is seen as a power whereby trust assets can be used to secure the advancement, or preferment, in life, of the beneficiary (*Roper-Curzon* v. *Roper-Curzon* (1871), L.R. 11 Eq. 452) The element of purpose has been considerably widened, so that it now includes benefit in a general sense (TA 1925, s. 32). Often when the power is exercised, the beneficiary becomes absolutely entitled to the asset, but the power can also be used so that the assets become subject to further trust provisions for the general benefit of the beneficiary (*Pilkington* v. *I.R. Comrs.*, [1964] A.C. 612). In this case the assets are said to become held on sub-trusts.

c   *Powers of appointment*   A power of appointment is a power to direct how trust property shall devolve or shall be dealt with. The general law classifies powers of appointment in different ways for different purposes, but perhaps the most helpful general classification is into:

257

i   general powers of appointment, where no restriction is placed on the donee's choice;

ii   hybrid powers, where the donee can appoint in favour of anyone except a named person or group of persons; and

iii special powers, where a class of persons is prescribed, and the donee can only appoint in favour of a member of that class.

On the one hand, a general power is tantamount to ownership, because the donee of the power can make the appointment in favour of himself (*Re Penrose, Penrose* v. *Penrose,* [1933] Ch. 793). On the other hand, when exercising a special power, the donee is merely, as it were, filling in a gap which the settlor left when creating the settlement.

The exercise of any type of power can cause a beneficiary to become absolutely entitled. On the other hand, on the exercise of the power the property can remain settled property. In this case, if a general power is exercised, the result may be very similar to the donee of the power having created a new settlement with his own property. However, if a special power is exercised, the property may seem to continue to be subject to the original settlement, but with the beneficial interests refined.

4   Are the new trusts exhaustive?

Where there is the exercise of a power of advancement or a power of appointment, and upon the exercise of that power the property ceases to be settled property, the beneficiary will become absolutely and beneficially entitled. If, however, the property remains settled property, the question is whether the provisions of the instrument exercising the power are exhaustive.

In *Hart* v. *Briscoe*, [1978] 1 All E.R. 791, the original settlement was created in 1955 for the benefit of the settlor's issue, the spouses of his issue, and certain other persons. In 1962 an *ad hoc* settlement was created for the benefit of some of the beneficiaries named in the original settlement. The persons who were the trustees of the original settlement were also the trustees of the *ad hoc* settlement. The terms of the *ad hoc* settlement dealt exhaustively with the trusts affecting the property subject to it, and contained comprehensive administrative provisions. The trustees, in their capacity as the trustees of the original settlement then declared that they would hold assets upon the trusts of the *ad hoc* settlement. It was held that in their capacity as the trustees of the *ad hoc* settlement, they had become absolutely entitled as against themselves in their capacity as the original settlement.

In *Hoare Trustees* v. *Gardner*, [1978] 1 All E.R. 791 under the original settlement, the trustees held the trust fund for the benefit of the issue of a named person, and were given power to advance certain assets, and make them subject to new trusts. This power was exercised, and the instrument by which it was exercised was exhaustive both as to beneficial interests and administrative provisions. It was held that the trustees in their capacity as the trustees of the advanced fund had become absolutely entitled as against themselves in their capacity as trustees of the original settlement.

The test is whether, on the exercise of a power, in respect of the assets over which the power has been exercised, "all the trusts, powers and provisions of the original settlement are irrevocably gone, completely new trusts, powers and provisions being created to take their place, so that no one will even again need to refer to the original settlement except to confirm that it has ceased to exist", (per Brightman, J., [1978] 1 All E.R. at 807).

The decisions of *Hart* v. *Briscoe and Hoare Trustees* v. *Gardner*, do not themselves draw distinctions between beneficial interests on the one hand and administrative provisions on the other, but it is the Revenue practice to do so. In the view of the Revenue, trustees of an appointed fund can become absolutely entitled as against themselves in their capacity as trustees of the original settlement if the instrument effecting the appointment is exhaustive with regard to beneficial interests, even if it is not entirely exhaustive with regard to administrative provisions.

F TERMINATION OF LIFE INTEREST

1 The general rule

Where a life interest in possession terminates otherwise than on the death of the beneficiary and the property remains settled property, the trustees are deemed to dispose of the assets at their then market value, and to re-acquire them at that value (CGTA 1979, s. 55 (1)). This general rule applies whether some other beneficiary then has a new life interest in possession, or whether the property is then held on discretionary or other trusts.

2 *"Life interest in possession"*

a Same meaning as for capital transfer tax The expression "life interest in possession" has the same meaning as "interest in possession" for capital transfer tax purposes, and the meaning is considered in that context (p. 288, *post*).

b "In possession" The general rule applies only where the life interest is "in possession". If, therefore, a fund is held upon trust to pay the income to Arnold for his life, and after his death to Bernard until Bernard reaches the age of thirty, and subject thereto for Colin, during the lifetime of Arnold, and while Bernard is under the age of thirty, Arnold has a life interest in possession and Bernard has a future life interest. The termination of Bernard's interest upon his attaining the age of thirty during the lifetime of Arnold will not give rise to any liability.

3 Advancement

Where there is a life interest in settled property, and the whole or part of the settled property is taken out of settlement by way of advancement, there may be a liability in respect of the assets actually taken out of settlement under the rule governing the position where a beneficiary becomes absolutely entitled (p. 254, *ante*) but there is no liability under the rule relating to the termination of life interests (CGTA 1979, s. 55 (2)). The position is the same where a life interest is surrendered for the purpose of advancement (*ibid*).

4 Annuities

Where an annuity is payable out of settled property, the position depends on whether some or all of the settled property is appropriated by the trustees as a fund out of which the annuity is payable, and there is no right of recourse to other settled property. Where there is such appropriation, the annuity is treated as a life interest, so that on the termination of the annuity, otherwise than on death, the general rule applies.

In any other case, the annuity is not treated as a life interest, so that no liability can arise under this head (CGTA 1979, s. 55 (4) (*c*)).

5 Property ceasing to be settled

Where on the termination of an interest in possession the property ceases to be settled, CGTA 1979, s. 55 does not apply, but if a beneficiary becomes absolutely entitled, CGTA 1979, s. 54 does apply (see p. 254, *ante*).

6 Death

Where a life interest in possession terminates on the death of the life tenant, so far as the trustees are concerned, they are deemed to dispose of the assets at their market value at the date of death, and to re-acquire them at that value (CGTA 1979, s. 55 (1)). However, no chargeable gain accrues (CGTA 1979, s. 56 (2)). The effect is to uplift the base value of the assets for capital gains tax purposes without any capital gains tax liability arising.

The position is the same where a person who was entitled to an interest *pur autre vie* dies (CGTA 1979, s. 55 (3)), and where an annuitant dies, even if the annuity was not treated as a life interest (CGTA 1979, s. 57).

The rules which apply when, on the death of a life tenant, the property ceases to be settled property have been noted (p. 256, *ante*).

7 Identification of assets

Where a life interest in part of a fund comes to an end in any circumstances, the trustees may, within three months of the termination of that interest, appropriate specific assets to the part in respect of which the termination occurred. The Revenue will then accept that the deemed disposal and re-acquisition applies only to these specific assets and not to any of the other assets comprised in the fund (Press Notice, 1 November 1973). Where this is done, the Revenue and the trustees give mutual undertakings to the effect that this basis will be binding on any subsequent disposal. Under this procedure the trustees can agree a list of specific assets where the gain is lowest, and so, in effect, defer liability.

8 Release to remainderman

Where a life tenant releases his life interest in part of the settled property to the remainderman, there is no deemed disposal and re-acquisition at that time of the remainder of the settled property (Press Notice, 1 November 1973).

9 Surrender

Where an interest in possession is surrendered, then, depending on the terms of the trust instrument, the interest of the next beneficiary may not be accelerated. Where this is so, following the surrender, the income will be paid to another beneficiary, or it will be accumulated. On the occasion of the surrender there will be a deemed disposal and re-acquisition. Further, if the settlement comes to an end on the death of the beneficiary who has surrendered, there will be a further deemed disposal and re-acquisition at that time, when the next beneficiary becomes absolutely entitled (p. 254, *ante*). There will be no exemption on the death because the beneficiary who effected the surrender would not at that time have had an interest in possession.

G PROTECTIVE TRUSTS

Protective trusts are harshly treated for capital gains tax purposes. If the fixed interest phase comes to an end during the lifetime of the principal beneficiary, there will be a deemed disposal and re-acquisition of the assets which comprise the settled property at that time. This is by virtue of the general rule which governs the termination of an interest in possession in lifetime (p. 259, *ante*).

Further, as the principal beneficiary will not have had an interest in possession on his death if the fixed interest phase has terminated, there will not be an uplift in the value of the assets at his death. If the property ceases to be settled on his death, there will be a deemed disposal and re-acquisition at that time (CGTA 1979, s. 54 (1)) but no exemption in respect of any gains which are thereby realised (s. 56 (1)).

There are no capital gains tax provisions which correspond with these for capital transfer tax (p. 344, *post*).

H SEPARATE SETTLEMENTS

1 *When settlements are separate*

a Generally Although the capital gains tax legislation is generally concerned with assets which are settled property, for some purposes (see p. 265, *post*) it is necessary to determine whether there is one settlement, or more than one. Particularly where the settled property was derived from a separate disposition from a separate settlor, there will often be no difficulty. If, however, the point is not clear, it seems that regard should be had to the following factors:

i whether there is separate and defined settled property;

ii whether there are separate "trusts", in the sense of the provisions governing beneficial entitlement;

iii whether there are separate trustees;

iv whether there were separate dispositions into settlement;

v whether there were separate settlors; and

vi whether there has been separate administration.

b Separate settlements and separate trusts In this context, the word "trusts" is sometimes used in the sense just noted, namely of the provisions of the trust instrument which govern beneficial entitlement, as modified by any impact of the general law. In this sense, there can be separate property held on separate trusts, but within the same settlement (see Lord Wilberforce in *Roome* v. *Edwards* [1981] 1 All E.R. 736 at 741). Suppose, for example, that a block of 10,000 BP shares is held upon trust:

  i during the lifetime of Andrew to pay the income therefrom to him for life; and

 ii on the death of Andrew to appropriate 4,000 shares and to pay the income therefrom to Brian for life, and to appropriate 6,000 shares and to pay the income therefrom to Charles for life; with different

iii remainders over.

At least following the death of Andrew, it would be said that 4,000 shares are held on one set of trusts, and 6,000 shares are held on another set of trusts, but that all 10,000 shares are subject to the same settlement.

c Property formerly subject to one settlement The problem arises most acutely where property has been subject to one settlement, and becomes subject to a new regime which may or may not constitute a separate settlement. The position appears from *Roome* v. *Edwards, supra,* at 740 to be as follows:

  i if the original trust instrument continues to apply to the settled property, that property cannot be subject to a separate settlement; this will be so even if the original trust instrument will only apply in certain circumstances;

 ii accordingly, the property will only become subject to a new settlement if an entirely new set of trusts is declared in respect of it;

iii where there is a special power of appointment, the exercise of that power will be read back into the instrument by which the power was created (see p. 258, *ante*);

    It is highly unlikely that the exercise of a special power will cause the property to become subject to a separate settlement, even if there are separate trustees of the appointed fund (*Roome* v. *Edwards,* at p. 740).

iv where property is appropriated from the other trust property, and exhaustive new trusts are created in respect of it, it may then become subject to a new settlement.

More generally, Lord Wilberforce enunciated (at p. 739) the test as follows:

"Since 'settlement' and 'trusts' are legal terms, which are also used by business men or laymen in a business or practical sense, I think that the question whether a particular set of facts amounts to a settlement should be approached by asking what a person, with knowledge of the legal context of the word under established doctrine and applying this knowledge in a practical and common-sense manner to the facts under examination, would conclude."

2 *Appropriation*

The principle applies not only where the original settlement creates different trusts in respect of different properties, or where a power of appointment is exercised in respect of part of the property comprised in the original settlement, but also where, as an administrative act the trustees effectively appropriate separate property to specific trusts.

In *Roome* v. *Edwards* ([1981] 1 All E.R. 736 at 740) the example given of the creation of a separate settlement was where the trustees effectively appropriate part of the trust property to beneficiaries and declare new trusts of it for their benefit.

The question then arises as to the circumstances in which an effective appropriation can be made. The position is as follows:

a   trustees do not have any general power to appropriate. Accordingly, if there is to be an effective appropriation, it must be made in one of the following circumstances;

b   the trust instrument may expressly direct appropriation;

c   if the trust instrument directs different property to be held on different trusts, that will be treated as an implied direction to appropriate (*Fraser* v. *Murdoch* (1881), 6 App. Cas. 855; *Re Walker, Walker* v. *Walker* (1890), 62 L.T. 449; *Re Nicholson's Will Trusts, Ortmans* v. *Burke*, [1936] 3 All E.R. 832). Thus, if the trust instrument directs £50,000 to be held on trust for Edward with remainder to Frank; £25,000 to be held on trust for George with remainder to Harry; and the remainder of the settled property to be held on trust for Ian with remainder to Keith effective appropriations can, and should, be made of £50,000 and £25,000;

d   the trust instrument may confer an express power to appropriate;

e   if all beneficiaries affected by a proposed appropriation are adult, they can effectively consent to it, even if there is no power or direction to appropriate in the trust instrument;

f   it seems that if property is held on trust for sale, the trustees can appropriate unless there is a direction to the contrary in the trust instrument (*Re Nickels, Nickels* v. *Nickels*, [1898] 1 Ch. 630; *Re Brooks, Coles* v. *Davis* (1897), 76 L.T. 771). While the law is not entirely clear, it seems that unless there is a power to appropriate in the trust instrument, adult beneficiaries affected by it need to consent, although no consent need be obtained on behalf of infant beneficiaries;

g personal representatives are given a statutory power of appropriation by the Administration of Estates Act 1925, s. 41, but this power does not apply to trustees.

The result of an effective appropriation is that beneficiaries who have an interest in the appropriated fund have no right of recourse against the remainder on the settled property.

3 Additions to settled property

If, after a settlement has been created, the trustees accept further property to be held as an accretion to the existing settled property, it may be that the original property and the additional property are subject to one settlement.

The Revenue practice is to allow the trustees to treat the additional property either as being comprised in a separate settlement, or as being comprised in the original settlement.

4 Effects of separate settlements

Where there are two or more settlements, the following effects should also be considered:

a a loss sustained within one settlement cannot be offset against a gain in another settlement;

b each settlement is entitled to its own small gains relief. It seems that if a separate settlement comes into being after 6 June 1978, the settlor of the original settlement will be treated as the settlor of the new settlement, in that he will directly or indirectly have provided funds for the new settlement (TA 1970, s. 454 (3); FA 1980, s. 78 (7)). Accordingly, the small gains relief will be apportioned.

c where there is a termination of a life interest, only the property in that settlement can be affected;

d trustees will only be liable for the tax payable in respect of the property comprised in the settlement of which they are trustees (*Roome* v. *Edwards,* [1980] 1 All E.R. 850).

5 Whether deemed disposal on creation of separate settlement

There will not be a deemed disposal of property merely because it passes from one settlement to another (*Roome* v. *Edwards, supra*). For there to be a deemed disposal, it must be shown that the trustees of the new settlement have become absolutely entitled to that property (see further p. 256, *ante*).

I PARTS, SHARES AND FRACTIONS

It has been seen (p. 262, *ante*) that different property can be held on separate trusts within the same settlement. If, there is a termination of a life interest in only part of the property comprised in the settlement, there will be a deemed disposal and re-acquisition of only a corresponding part of the underlying assets (CGTA 1979, s. 55 (1); *Stephenson* v. *Barclays Bank Trust Co Ltd.*, [1975] 1 All E.R. 625; *Pexton* v. *Bell*, [1976] 2 All E.R. 914).

J BARE TRUSTEESHIPS AND NOMINEESHIPS

1 Bare trustees and nominees

A person is a bare trustee if he holds property on trust for another, but has administrative powers and discretions with regard to that property. A person is a nominee if he holds property for another, but is obliged to act in accordance with that other's directions. Bare trustees and nominees are treated alike for capital gains tax purposes.

A person is treated as a bare trustee in the following circumstances:

a   where the beneficiary is absolutely entitled to the property as against the trustee (CGTA 1979, s. 46 (1)). The concept of "absolute entitlement" has been considered at p. 254, *ante*;

b   where there are two or more beneficiaries together absolutely entitled to the property as against the trustee (see p. 267, post);

c   where there are one or more beneficiaries who are infants, and infancy is the sole reason which prevents him or them from being absolutely entitled (p. 269, *post*); and

d   where there are one or more beneficiaries who are mentally ill, and that illness is the sole reason which prevents him or them from being absolutely entitled (CGTA 1979, s. 46 (1)).

2 Effect

Where an asset is held by a nominee or bare trustee, for capital gains tax purposes, the asset is treated as being vested in the beneficiary; and the acts of the trustee are treated as acts of the beneficiary (CGTA 1979, s. 46 (1)).

Disposals between a bare trustee and the beneficiary are disregarded for capital gains tax purposes (*ibid*).

3 Ordinary trustee becoming bare trustee

When a beneficiary becomes absolutely entitled to any property which is settled property, the trustee is deemed to dispose of the assets at their market value at that time, and to re-acquire them as a bare trustee at that value (CGTA 1979, s. 54 (1)). When, thereafter, the trustee, then in his capacity as a bare trustee, transfers the asset to the beneficiary, that transfer is disregarded (CGTA 1979, s. 46 (1); *supra*).

The same result ensues where the beneficiary does not become absolutely entitled, but would have become so were it not for infancy or mental incapacity (CGTA 1979, s. 54 (3); FA 1981; s. 87).

K   JOINTLY OWNED PROPERTY

1   When property not settled property

Where an asset is jointly owned by two or more persons, it may or may not be settled property. The position is as follows:

a   where two or more persons are concurrently entitled to the asset, in principle they are each treated as owning directly a share in that asset. The asset is not settled property, and if the legal title is vested in trustees, those trustees will be treated as holding as bare trustees for the beneficial owners (CGTA 1979, s. 46 (1));

b   this principle will apply even if any individual beneficiary does not have a power of disposition, provided that the interests of all beneficiaries are concurrent, and they can continue together to bring the trust to an end. So, in *Booth* v. *Ellard*, [1980] 3 All E.R. 569, CA twelve individuals who wished to ensure that control of a company remained effectively in the hands of the family transferred their shares to trustees, to be held by the trustees for a period of fifteen years. In certain respects the trustees were to act in accordance with directions given to them by the beneficial owners of three quarters of the shares. It was held that the shares were not settled property for the purposes of capital gains tax;

c   provided that the interests of the beneficiaries are all concurrent, the principle will apply whether, for the purposes of general trust law, the beneficiaries are equitable joint tenants or equitable tenants in common (*Kidson* v. *Macdonald*, [1974] Ch. 339; *Harthan* v. *Mason*, [1980] S.T.C. 94).

2   Beneficiary becoming absolutely entitled

a   *Generally*   Where property is held for more than one beneficiary, and the beneficiaries are not concurrently and together

267

absolutely entitled, the property is settled property. In principle, one beneficiary can, in respect of his share, become absolutely entitled even if others in respect of their shares do not (*Stephenson* v. *Barclays Bank Trust Co Ltd*, [1975] 1 All E.R. 625; *Pexton* v. *Bell*, [1976] 2 All E.R. 914). Suppose, therefore, that trustees hold a block of ICI shares in trust for Andrew, Basil and Charles, if and when they attain the age of twenty-five in equal shares. When Andrew reaches the age of twenty-five, he is able to direct how his one third of the holding of the shares is to be dealt with. He has become absolutely entitled.

   b   Where land is the settled property   Where the settled property is land, it might be thought that to be consistent with the general scheme of the legislation that the land should be regarded as being capable of being divided into shares, so that when one of several beneficiaries becomes absolutely and beneficially entitled to his interest in the land, he should, as regards that share, be regarded as having become absolutely entitled. The position would appear to be the same if the land is held on trust for sale, so that, for some purposes of the general law, it is regarded notionally as having been sold and converted into money. However, it seems that this is not the case. In *Crowe* v. *Appleby*, [1976] 2 All E.R. 914 the settled property consisted solely of land, and a beneficiary became absolutely entitled to a 5/30ths share of that land. It was held that the settled property was the land itself, and that as the beneficiary could not give an effective direction in respect of the land, he had not become absolutely entitled as against the trustee (see in particular the report of the case at first instance: [1975] 3 All E.R. 529 at 536, 537).

   c   Shares in private companies   In general, when a person becomes beneficially entitled to shares in a company, he is entitled to demand that those shares are transferred to him (*Re Marshall*, [1914] 1 Ch. 192). If, however, special circumstances exist, the trustees may be justified in refusing to transfer them (*Re Marshall*, at 200). The mere fact that control will be lost is not a "special circumstance". If, therefore, trustees hold sixty out of one hundred issued shares upon trust for Andrew, Bernard and Charles when they attain the age of twenty-five in equal shares, when Andrew reaches that age, he will be entitled to call for a transfer of twenty shares, even though the trustees will be left with a 40% holding (see *Re Weiner's Will Trusts, Wyner* v. *Braithwaite*, [1956] 2 All E.R. 482). If, however, the trustees knew that within a year or so they would be able, if they had a 60% holding, to give effect to an advantageous scheme, but would not be able to do so if their holding was reduced to 40%, it seems that they could be justified in refusing to transfer the twenty shares to Andrew until the scheme had been carried through (*Re Weiner's Will Trusts, supra,* at 485).

If such special circumstances exist, it seems that for so long as they exist the beneficiary is not to be regarded as absolutely entitled (*Crowe* v. *Appleby,* [1975] 3 All E.R. 529 at p. 537).

d   Mortgages   Where the trust property is a mortgage over land, the position is the same as where the trust property is land itself (*Re Marshall,* [1914] 1 Ch. 192 at 199; see also *Crowe* v. *Appleby* [1975] 3 All E.R. 529 at 537).

L   SETTLED PROPERTY HELD FOR INFANTS

1   Where deemed absolute entitlement

Where property is held for an infant, the infant is deemed to be absolutely entitled if infancy is the sole reason which prevents him from being able to give an effective direction as to how the property is to be dealt with. If, however, the interest of the infant is contingent, or is defeasible, then infancy is not the sole reason which prevents him from being actually absolutely entitled, and the property will be settled property. This is so even if the contingency must be satisfied, if at all, or the interest become indefeasible, when the beneficiary attains his majority. In *Tomlinson* v. *Glyn's Executor and Trustee Co.,* [1970] Ch. 112 the trust property was held for such of certain named beneficiaries as should attain the age of majority or marry under that age. It was held that during the infancy of one of the beneficiaries, the property was settled property, because the infant had to satisfy the condition of attaining the age of majority or marrying under it before he became absolutely entitled.

The result is that:

a   if a person holds property on trust for an infant absolutely, the property is treated as being vested in the infant; but

b   if a person holds property on trust for an infant subject to his attaining a future age or satisfying a future condition, the property is treated as settled property.

2   Infant becoming absolutely entitled

Where property is held for an infant contingently on his attaining a specified age, such as eighteen, upon his attaining that age he will become absolutely entitled, and there will accordingly be a deemed disposal and re-acquisition (CGTA 1979, s. 54; p. 254, *ante*).

M "SETTLEMENTS" IN THE EXTENDED SENSE

It was shown in Chapter 15 that for some income tax purposes, Part XVI of the Taxes Act gives an extended meaning of the expression "settlement" to include disposition, trust, covenant, agreement or arrangement (TA 1970, ss. 444 (2), 454 (3)) and in certain respects also to include an outright transfer of assets (TA 1970, s. 444 (2)). This extended meaning is not generally adopted for capital gains tax purposes, but it is with regard to the definition of connected persons, where a trustee is connected with the settlor of any "settlement" (CGTA 1979, s. 63 (3)).

The extended meaning of "settlor" is used in the definition of a "group of settlements" for the purposes of the small gains relief available to settlements made after 6 June 1978 (see p. 273, *post*).

N COMPUTATION OF THE LIABILITY

1 Ordinary principles apply

Whether there is an actual disposal of asset in the ordinary course of the administration of a trust, or a deemed disposal on the occasion of a beneficiary or other trustees becoming absolutely entitled, or on the termination in lifetime of an interest in possession, the computation of the liability is made in the same way as in the case of a disposal by an individual. The first question will be to determine the acquisition and disposal values of the asset in question.

2 Acquisition values

Trustees are treated as acquiring assets at the following actual or notional values:

  a Assets originally settled

     i *Generally* Assets transferred into trust by *inter vivos* disposition either on the creation of the settlement or as an addition to the settled fund, will be treated as having been acquired by the trustees from a connected person, the settlor, and so at their market value at the time (CGTA 1979, s. 63 (3), 62 (2), 19 (1)).

    ii *Held-over gain* A reduced value will apply where "business assets" were transferred into trust after 11 April 1978, and both the settlor and the trustees claimed relief under s. 126; or where any type of asset was transferred into trust after 5 April 1981 and the settlor alone claimed relief (FA 1980, s. 79; FA 1981, s. 78).

b   Assets settled by will   Where the trust was created by will, the trustees are treated as having acquired the assets, as legatees, at the date of death of the deceased, and at their market value at that date (s. 49 (4); p. 159, *ante*).

c   Assets owned on 6 April 1965   Where the trust was in being on 6 April 1965, special rules apply to the valuation of assets owned on that date. These rules vary according to the type of asset held by the trust, and are discussed at pp. 48, *ante*.

d   Assets subject to estate duty charge   Where a settlement was created before 13 March 1975 by *inter vivos* disposition, but within seven years from the death of the settlor, a liability to estate duty will usually have arisen in respect of the settled property on the death of the settlor (FA 1894, s. 2 (1) (*b*)). Where this was so, and the settlor died between 30 March 1971 and 12 March 1975, the trustees were deemed to have disposed of a portion of the assets which comprised the settled property for a consideration equal to the corresponding portion of the market value of the assets at that time; and to have reacquired that portion at that value (FA 1965, s. 25 (4A); FA 1971, Sch. 12, para. 12; FA 1975, Sch. 13). No chargeable gain arose.

The appropriate portion was the value on which estate duty was chargeable divided by the market value of the whole of the settled property at the time of death.

e   Assets subsequently acquired   Where assets are acquired in the ordinary course of administration, the cost price will be the acquisition cost. Special rules apply to scrip dividends (p. 272, *post*).

3   Disposal values

a   In course of administration   Where the trustees dispose of an asset by way of bargain at arm's length to a non-connected purchaser, the disposal value will be the actual value of the consideration which they receive.

b   Actual disposal to beneficiary   Trustees are not treated as persons connected with beneficiaries (see CGTA 1979, s. 63 (3)), so that if there is an actual disposal by way of sale to a beneficiary, in principle the disposal value is the amount of the consideration which the trustees receive. The market value will be substituted, however, if the transaction is not at arm's length (CGTA 1979, s. 29A; FA 1981, s. 90) or if the beneficiary is connected with the settlor, and so, in that way, is connected with the trustees (CGTA 1979, ss. 62 (2), 63 (3)).

c   Absolute entitlement; termination of interest in possession   Where the trustees are deemed to dispose of an asset when a

271

beneficiary becomes absolutely entitled, or when the trustees of another trust become absolutely entitled, or when an interest in possession terminates, the deemed disposal will be at the market value of the asset at the time of the deemed disposal (CGTA 1979, ss. 54 (1), 55 (1)). If, however, the deemed disposal occurs on the death of a life tenant, and the property reverts to the settlor, the disposal value is that which gives rise neither to a gain nor a loss (CGTA 1979, s. 56 (1) (*b*)).

O SCRIP DIVIDENDS

1 Generally

It has been seen that in certain cases liability to income tax arises in respect of scrip dividends (p. 235, *ante*). In these cases it is necessary to ascertain "the appropriate amount in cash" which is, in general, either the amount of the cash dividend which could have been received or the market value of the new shares or stock (F(No. 2)A 1975, Sch. 8, para. 1). The tax credit which would have been available if a cash dividend had been taken is left out of account. The acquisition cost of the scrip for capital gains tax purposes is the appropriate amount in cash (para. 5). This rule applies whether the scrip is transferred to the tenant for life, or is retained by the trustees as an accretion to the trust fund.

2 Scrip accruing to tenant for life

Where the tenant for life is entitled to the scrip, he will be treated as having paid for the scrip the appropriate amount in cash. No allowance is available for notional expenses of transfer, but where expenses are actually incurred in transferring the scrip to the life tenant, those expenses can be dealt with according to the general rules explained earlier (p. 276, *post*).

3 Scrip retained by trustees

If the scrip is retained by the trustees as an accretion to the trust fund, it will be added to the original holding and the appropriate amount in cash will be added to the acquisition of the original holding. If part of the combined holding is subsequently sold, the total acquisition cost is then apportioned according to the rules described previously (p. 49, *ante*).

4 Beneficiary absolutely entitled as against trustee

It was shown at the beginning of this chapter that in certain circumstances property which is held in trust is not treated as settled property for the purposes of capital gains tax. Mainly this is where a person is absolutely entitled as against the trustee, or would be so entitled were he not under a disability. In these cases the person who is or would be entitled beneficially to the scrip is treated as having acquired the scrip for a consideration equal to the appropriate amount in cash (F(No. 2)A 1975, s. 62).

P EXEMPTIONS AND RELIEFS

1 Small gains

Where trustees realise a gain which is in principle chargeable, the position is as follows:

a Settlement for disabled beneficiary Trustees can claim the same relief as an individual (see p. 42, *ante*) if during the whole or part of a year of assessment not less than one half of the income and of the capital which is taken out of trust is applied, wholly or mainly for a disabled beneficiary (CGTA 1979, Sch. 1, para. 5; FA 1981, s. 89).

A beneficiary is treated as being disabled if by reason of mental disorder he is incapable of administering his property or managing his affairs, or if he is physically disabled and receiving an attendance allowance (para. 5 (2)).

This relief applies whether the trust was created before or after 7 June 1978. Where, however, two or more settlements were created after 10 March, 1981, the exemption is restricted, but will never be less than £300.

b Other settlements created prior to 7 June 1978 In the case of other trusts, provided they were created before 7 June 1978, the first £1,500 of net gains are exempt (CGTA 1979, Sch. 1, para. 6; FA 1980, s. 78).

If the trustees have unused brought forward losses the position is as follows:

i where there are allowable losses to be brought forward, but the net gain does not exceed £1,500, the taxable amount remains the amount of the net gain for that year, and the losses from the previous year can be carried forward in full to the subsequent year; and

ii where there are allowable losses to be brought forward, and the net gain exceeds £1,500, the brought forward losses are used only to the extent necessary to reduce the net gain to £1,500 and any balance of losses are then carried forward to the subsequent year (CGTA 1979, s. 5 and Sch. 1, para. 6).

c   Other settlements created after 6 June 1978   Where a settlement is created after 6 June 1978, it is necessary to consider all the settlements which are treated as constituting a "group". A group of settlements is all the settlements which are made by the same settlor after 6 June 1978 other than:

i   charitable settlements;

ii   settlements in respect of certain superannuation funds; and

iii settlements of which the trustees are not treated as resident and ordinarily resident in the United Kingdom (FA 1980, s. 78 (7)).

The £1,500 annual allowance is divided equally between all the settlements in the group, but if there are more than five settlements, each has a minimum annual allowance of £300 (FA 1980, s. 78 (3)).

2   Main residence exemption

If trustees dispose of an asset which, by its nature, does not give rise to a chargeable gain, no liability can arise. In particular, it may be noted that where a dwelling-house was owned by trustees, and used by a beneficiary in accordance with the terms of the trust deed, the main residence exemption is available (CGTA 1979, s. 104). The exemption is also available where it is occupied by a beneficiary as a result of a decision made by the trustees in the exercise of their discretion (*Sansom* v. *Peay,* [1976] 3 All E.R. 375).

3   Business asset relief

In certain circumstances, a deemed disposal and re-acquisition can be treated as taking place at a value different from the market value at the time. Where relief is claimed a deduction of the "held-over gain" (see p. 192, *ante*) is made both from the disposal consideration deemed to be received by the trustees and the deemed re-acquisition cost. The effect is to give roll-over relief to the trustees, but to increase the beneficiary's potential liability.

The relief can only be claimed where:

a   the asset is:

    i (*a*) used for the purposes of a trade profession or vocation, or is an interest, such as a partnership share, used in a trade, profession or vocation; and

        (*b*) the trade profession or vocation is carried on prior to the deemed disposal by:

           (i) the trustees; or

           (ii) the beneficiary who immediately prior to the disposal had an interest in possession (CGTA 1979, Sch. 4, para. 2 (1) (*a*), (3) (*a*));

    ii (*a*) a holding of shares or securities of a trading company; and

        (*b*) the trustees had not less than 25% of the voting rights in the company at the time of the deemed disposal (para. 2 (1) (*b*));

  or

    iii (*a*) woodlands which are managed on a commercial basis with a view to the realisation of a profit; and

        (*b*) the management is by
            (i) the trustees; or
            (ii) the beneficiary who immediately prior to the disposal had an interest in possession (para. 2 (1) (*a*), (3) (*a*));

  or

    iv agricultural property which is not as such a business asset, but in respect of which a claim could be made for agricultural property relief for capital transfer tax purposes (para. 1);

and

  b the trustees are resident or ordinarily resident in the United Kingdom (CGTA 1979, s. 126 (1)).

    The roll-over relief is only partial where the asset has not satisfied the tests throughout the period of ownership by the trustees (s. 126 (5); Sch. 4, paras. 4 – 7).

Q LOSSES

1 *Ordinary dealings*

Where trustees actually dispose of trust assets, and sustain a loss in so doing, they may offset that loss against gains arising in that year of assessment, and carry forward any balance of that loss to offset against future gains.

2 *Effect on small gains relief*

Brought forward losses are used only to the extent necessary to reduce what would otherwise be the amount of the chargeable gain to £1,500 (see p. 273, *ante*).

3 *Transfer of benefit to beneficiary*

Where a person becomes absolutely entitled to any settled property as against the trustee, and there is, therefore, a deemed disposal by the trustee under CGTA 1979, s. 54, that deemed disposal might give rise to a loss. If it does, and if the trustee cannot deduct that loss from chargeable gains which accrue to him in the same year of assessment as that in which the deemed disposal occurs, he can transfer the benefit of that loss to the beneficiary (s. 54 (2)). Likewise, if the trustee has brought forward losses which he cannot use, he can transfer the benefit of those to the beneficiary (*ibid*). The beneficiary is able to use these losses even though he did not himself incur them. The losses are treated as immediately allowable losses in the hands of the beneficiary, and he is, therefore, able to offset them against gains accruing on the disposal of assets which have never had any connection with the trust.

The same rule applies where there are two settlements and the trustees of one settlement become absolutely entitled as against the trustees of the other.

To assist the beneficiary in claiming the benefit of the losses, it is helpful if the trustees supply him with a certificate. No statutory or official form is prescribed, but the following is an example of the type of certificate which might be individually prepared:

I certify that _____
of _____
is a beneficiary of the trust known as _____
and the particulars given below are correct. Information regarding the trust has been sent to H.M. Inspector of Taxes _____
District, Reference No. _____ I further certify that, in accordance with the Capital Gains Tax Act 1979, section 54 (2) the beneficiary became entitled on 5th April (*b*) to losses of £ _____
which may be used by him to offset his own chargeable gains realised after 5th April (*a*).

.... Trustee   Date....................

(*a*) Note: this will be one calendar year before the date stated at (*b*).

R EXPENSES

1 Transfer to beneficiary

Where a trustee incurs expenditure in transferring trust property to a beneficiary, those expenses will usually be incurred after the trustee has become a bare trustee for the beneficiary (see p. 254, *ante*), and so, strictly, they cannot be offset against gains which accrued to him in his capacity as trustee of the settlement. Accordingly, when the beneficiary himself comes to dispose of the asset, he may in the computation of his gain or loss include the cost of the transfer of the asset to him, even although he did not incur that expenditure himself (s. 47 (1) (b)).

The Revenue practice, however is to allow the trustee to deduct these costs in the computation of his gain or loss on the deemed disposal if the transferee foregoes his entitlement.

Where the transferee is to be able to claim the costs, it is helpful to supply the beneficiary with a certificate of the amount of the expenses in the form suggested where the benefit of losses is transferred.

In each case, it is a question of fact how much expenditure was incurred. The Revenue have agreed with the Association of Corporate Trustees and the Trustee Departments' Committee of the Committee of London Clearing Bankers, a scale of expenses which will be allowable in respect of the transfer of assets to beneficiaries by corporate trustees which are members of these bodies. In the case of expenditure incurred by other trustees, the scale may well provide a useful guide. The scale is as follows:

Quoted stocks and shares:

a	where there is one beneficiary	£7 per holding
b	where there are two beneficiaries	£8 per holding
c	where there are more than two beneficiaries	£8 plus £1 for each beneficiary beyond the first two, per holding.

Other assets

As for quoted stock and shares, together with any exceptional expenditure.

2 Deemed disposals

Where there is a deemed disposal and re-acquisition there are not brought into account the costs which would be incurred on an actual disposal (CGTA 1979, s. 32 (4)). However, actual costs which are incurred can be brought into account. These will include professional fees and stamp duty on any instrument, such as a surrender or partition, which causes the deemed disposal to occur. (*I.R. Comrs.* v. *Chubb's Trustee* (1971), 47 TC 353). Valuation fees are also allowable. In the case of a deemed disposal of quoted stocks and shares, the Revenue allow a valuation fee of £2 a holding. In respect of all other assets, the amount allowable is the actual cost of valuation.

277

3   Deemed disposal followed by transfer

If there is a deemed disposal and re-acquisition on the occasion of a beneficiary becoming absolutely entitled, followed by a transfer of the asset to the beneficiary, both the valuation fee on the deemed disposal and the actual costs of the transfer are allowable as expenses.

S   LIABILITY

Where the property is settled property, the trustees are primarily responsible for the tax, but if it is not paid within six months, and the asset or proceeds of sale are transferred to a beneficiary who is absolutely entitled, the Revenue may recover the tax from him (CGTA 1979, s. 52 (4)).

T   PAYMENT BY INSTALMENTS

1   Deemed disposals

Where certain types of assets are deemed to be disposed of by trustees, and re-acquired, either on the occasion when a beneficiary or the trustees of another trust become absolutely entitled, or when there is the termination of an interest in possession, the capital gains tax may be paid by instalments (CGTA 1979, s. 8 (1)).

The assets in question are:

a   land, or an interest in land;

b   shares or securities of a company which, immediately before the deemed disposal, gave control of the company to the trustees, whether or not the company is a quoted company;

c   shares or securities of any non-quoted company, whether or not they gave the trustees control of the company; and

d   assets used exclusively for the purposes of a trade carried on by the trustees (s. 8 (3)).

The tax may be paid by either eight yearly or sixteen half yearly instalments. The whole of the balance of the tax outstanding becomes payable when there is a subsequent disposal for valuable consideration (s. 8 (4)).

2   Interest

Where the instalment option is claimed in respect of:

a   shares or securities in companies (except shares or securities in investment companies and share or property dealing companies); or *b*   trade assets;

each instalment only carries interest from the date at which the instalment is payable, subject to a cumulative maximum of £250,000 (CGTA 1979, s. 9).

Where the instalment option is claimed in respect of:

   a   shares or securities in investment companies, or share or property dealing companies; or

   b   land;

interest is payable on the total amount of tax for the time being outstanding (s. 8 (4)).

U BENEFICIAL INTERESTS

1 *Equitable interests as assets*

All equitable interests in settled property are assets for capital gains tax purposes (CGTA 1979, s. 19 (1) (*a*)). Accordingly, in principle, when any such interest is disposed of, a chargeable gain or an allowable loss would usually result. However, in view of the rules noted below, it is only necessary to take this into account where the interest is directly acquired for a consideration in money or money's worth, or is derived through a person who acquired it for such a consideration.

If the interest is that of a life tenant, and the predictable expectation of life of the life tenant is fifty years or less, the interest is treated as a wasting asset (s. 37 (1) (*d*)).

2 *Disposal by original beneficiary*

Where there is a disposal of an equitable interest by the person for whose benefit it was created by the settlement, no chargeable gain can arise on that disposal (CGTA 1979, s. 58 (1)), and accordingly, there can be no allowable loss (s. 29). This rule applies whether the beneficiary was a voluntary beneficiary, or whether he provided value for the making of the settlement.

3 *Disposal by voluntary assignee*

Where an equitable interest is disposed of by an assignee from an original beneficiary, or by a person on whom the interest has devolved on death, the general rule is again that the disposal cannot give rise to a chargeable gain or an allowable loss (s. 58 (1)). The rule noted below applies where the disponor acquired title through a person who furnished consideration.

4   Non-resident settlements

Special rules apply where the interest is in a non-resident settlement. These are considered later (see p. 387, *post*).

5   Disposal by assignee for value

If an equitable interest has been acquired for a consideration in money or money's worth, that interest becomes a chargeable asset. Accordingly, it will be treated as an ordinary asset when it is disposed of by the person who acquires it. Further, if the person who acquires the interest for value makes a voluntary disposition of it, the interest will continue to be treated as a chargeable asset.

The interest is not regarded as being acquired for a consideration in money or money's worth if the only consideration given for it is another interest under the settlement (CGTA 1979, s. 58 (1)).

Where the interest is a chargeable asset, the beneficiary is deemed to dispose of it at the time when he becomes absolutely entitled to the settled property (s. 58 (2)). There will also be a deemed disposal of the assets themselves by the trustees (p. 254, *ante*). The amount of capital gains tax, if any, payable by the trustees on their deemed disposal is deducted from the value of the settled property. The beneficiary is deemed to dispose of his equitable interest for a consideration equal to the net value which he will receive from the trustees.

Chapter 18

The Administration of a Trust: Development Land Tax

A BARE TRUSTS AND SETTLED PROPERTY

The Development Land Tax Act 1976 distinguishes property which is held on a bare trust from settled property.

1 Bare Trusts

In general, where property would not be regarded as settled property for the purposes of capital gains tax (see p. 253, *ante*) it will not be treated as settled property for the purposes of development land tax. Accordingly, an interest in land which is held on trust is treated as being held on a bare trust where:

a one person is absolutely entitled to that interest as against the trustees (DLTA 1976, s. 28 (1) (a));

b one person would be absolutely entitled to that interest as against the trustees but for being an infant or other person under a disability (s. 28 (1) (b));

c two or more persons are jointly entitled to that interest as against the trustees (s. 28 (4));

d two or more persons would be jointly entitled to that interest as against the trustees but for being an infant or infants, or otherwise under a disability (*ibid*);

e one or more persons is, are, or would be entitled to the interest under rules *a* to *d*, subject only to satisfying any outstanding charge, lien or other right of the trustees to resort to the interest for the payment of duty, taxes, costs or other outgoings (s. 28 (3)).

2 Settled Property

An interest in land is treated as settled property if it is held on trust except:

> *a*   where it is held on a bare trust (s. 30 (1)); or
>
> *b*   where it is held by a person as an assignee or trustee in bankruptcy, or under a deed of arrangement (s. 30 (8)).

B   INTERESTS HELD ON BARE TRUSTS

1   *The General Principle*

The general principle is that where an interest in land is held on a bare trust, the existence of the trust is ignored, and the position is determined as if the interest were directly vested in the beneficiary (s. 28 (1), (5)). Accordingly, no liability can arise on the transfer between a bare trustee and the beneficiary.

2   *Disposal by sole beneficiary*

If there is only one beneficiary under the bare trust, the disposal by him of his beneficial interest is treated as a disposal of the interest in land itself (s. 29 (4)). By virtue of the general principle noted immediately above, the disposal by the trustee of an interest in land is treated as a disposal by the beneficiary. Accordingly, there is no difference in result if the trustee disposes of the interest in land itself, or if the beneficiary disposes of his beneficial interest.

3   *Disposal where more than one beneficiary*

a   *Generally*

If there is more than one beneficiary under the bare trust, an apportionment is made of the cost of acquisition of the interest in land itself, and of market values, current use values, and expenditure on improvements (s. 29 (5)). The apportionment is made by applying to each relevant item the fraction (s. 29 (6)):

$$\frac{\text{Market value of beneficial interest at time of disposal}}{\text{aggregate of that and all other beneficial interests at that time}}$$

If the transaction affecting the interest in land consists of the part disposal of that interest, this apportionment is made before the other apportionments which are prescribed in the case of any part disposal (s. 29 (5); the rules as to part disposals generally, contained in DLTA 1976, s. 3 and Sch. 2, are not described in this book).

b   *Acquisition from other beneficiary*

Where a beneficiary acquired his interest from a person who was a beneficiary at the time, the general rule stated above does not apply to determine the cost of acquisition of the interest (s. 29 (7)). Instead, the actual acquisition cost is taken.

A further rule deals with the position where a beneficiary acquired his interest from a person who was a beneficiary at the time. When there is a disposal of the interest in the land itself, the beneficiary may claim to have the disposal treated as a disposal at the same time of all the separate beneficial interests (s. 29 (8)). The effect of doing so is that his cost of the acquisition of his beneficial interest will be taken into account.

4 Land and other assets subject to the same trust

Where the bare trustees hold on the same trusts an interest in land and other assets the rules so far described apply as if the interest in land was the only asset of the trust (s. 27 (2) (a)). However, where the beneficial interest is disposed of, the consideration for the disposal is reduced to an appropriate amount having regard to the value of that portion of the trust property which does not consist of an interest in land (s. 29 (2) (b)).

5 Commencement of project of material development

Where a project of material development is commenced in respect of land an interest in which is held on a bare trust, that interest itself is treated as being disposed of and re-acquired at that time (s. 2 (1)). In this case, the market value and the current use value are ascertained upon the assumption that the interest could be sold at that time in the open market free from the interests of the beneficiaries (Sch. 1, para. 8 (3)). This will be so even if the interest in land could not in fact be sold free from the interests of the beneficiaries.

Each beneficial interest is then treated as being disposed of and re-acquired, and apportionments are made in accordance with the rules already described. Apart from this the beneficial interests are not treated as being separately disposed of and re-acquired (s. 28 (6)).

6 Distinction between actual and deemed disposals

In the case of an actual disposal, the chargeable person is the beneficiary. However, if there is a deemed disposal on the commencement of a project of material development, the interests of the beneficiaries, not being major interests, are not deemed to be disposed of. The interest of the trustees is the interest, and the chargeable persons are therefore the trustees.

C SETTLED PROPERTY

1 Separate "persons"

a Trustees of the settlement

Where an interest in land is settled property, the trustees of the settlement are treated as a single and continuing body of persons, which is distinct from the persons who may from time to time be the trustees (s. 30 (1)). This will be the position where the land is held on trust for sale.

b Settled land

Where the land in which the interest subsists is settled land within the terms of the Settled Land Act 1925, the tenant for life, or other statutory owner, and the trustees for the purposes of the Settled Land Act, together constitute a single and continuing body of persons, which is distinct from the persons of whom that body is for the time being composed (s. 30 (2)).

2 Trustees treated as individual

The effect of these provisions is that the single and continuing body of persons so constituted is treated as an individual. The first £50,000 of development value realised by them in a financial year will therefore not be subject to development land tax (p. 62, *ante*).

3 Calculation of development value realised: Interest purchased by trustees

Where the trustees purchased the interest in land which is disposed of, or is treated as being disposed of, the calculation is made in exactly the same way as if the interest had been acquired by an individual.

4 Calculation of development value realised: other cases

In most circumstances the trustees will not have purchased the interest in land, but will have acquired it for no consideration. This will be so where the interest in land is settled *inter vivos,* or becomes settled following the death of a person under the provisions of his will. In these cases the following special rules apply:

a *Acquisition cost* The acquisition cost is the aggregate of the settlor's or the testator's acquisition cost, together with any incidental costs incurred by the trustees at the time when they themselves acquired the interest (s. 10 (2) (a)).

b *Improvements* The amount of enhancement or similar expenditure which can be taken into account is the aggregate of that incurred by the settlor or testator prior to the creation of the settlement and that incurred by the trustees subsequently (s. 10 (2) (b)).

c *Current use value at acquisition* The current use value at acquisition, for the calculation of Base A, is generally the current use value at the time when the settlor or testator acquired the interest (s. 10 (2) (c)). It seems, however, that where the interest in land had been settled before 6 April 1965, the current use value at acquisition is to be taken as the current use value at that date.

d *Special addition* The amount of special addition which had accrued while the interest in land was owned by the settlor or testator can be claimed, but no special addition runs thereafter (s. 10 (2) (d)).

e *Leases* Where the interest in land is leasehold, it is treated as being acquired for a consideration, even if the settlement was voluntary (s. 10 (6)). The cost of acquisition in this case is treated as being a sum equal to the value to the landlord at the time when the trustees acquired the lease of the right to receive rent during the unexpired term of the lease and of the right to the performance of the other obligations of the tenant, apart from that to give up possession at the end of the term (Sch. 2, paras. 13 (2), 16 (2) (b)).

In all cases where the interest is leasehold, therefore, the rule stated in section 3 above applies.

Chapter 19

The Administration of a Trust: Capital Transfer Tax

A   TRUSTS SUBJECT TO CAPITAL TRANSFER TAX

1   Definition of "Settlement"

This chapter is concerned with the special provisions which the capital transfer tax legislation applies to most trusts. However, these provisions apply only to those trusts which are to be taken as "settlements" (FA 1975, Sch. 5, para. 1 (1)). There is a settlement in any of the following circumstances:

1   where property is held in trust for persons in succession, as in the case of a fund held upon trust to pay the income to Angus during his lifetime, with the capital to be paid to Brian on the death of Angus (Sch. 5, para. 1 (2) (a));

2   where property is held in trust for any person subject to a contingency, as in the case of a fund held upon trust for Colin if and when he shall attain the age of 21 (*ibid*);

3   where property is held upon trust that the whole or part of the income is to be accumulated (para. 1 (2) (b));

4   where property is held upon trust, and the trustees have a power, but not, it seems, a duty, to pay out the whole or part of the income, whether or not there is a power to accumulate surplus income (*ibid*);

5   generally, where property is charged with the payment of an annuity or other periodical payment which is payable for the life of any person, or during any other limited or terminable period (para. 1 (2) (c)). There is, however, excluded from this heading property which is charged with the payment of an annuity or other periodical payment in return for full consideration in money or money's worth paid to the person charging the property for his own use or benefit;

6   where property is governed by the law of any other country and the provisions of that law are equivalent in effect to any of *1* to *5* above (para. 1 (2));

7   generally where a lease of property is granted for the life or lives of one or more persons, or for a period which is terminable on or at a date ascertainable only by reference to a death (para. 1 (3)). In this case, the property out of which the lease is granted is treated as settled property. The provision does not apply where the lease was granted for full consideration in money or money's worth. If a lease which would not otherwise fall within this category is not granted as a lease at a rack rent, but the rent can be increased at a time by reference to the death of any person, then that lease also is brought within this category (*ibid*).

The provisions do not apply:

1   where property is held by one person upon trust for another person who is entitled outright; or by one person as nominee for another;

2   where property is held upon trust for two or more persons who between them are immediately entitled to the whole of the property in accordance with their beneficial interests;

3   possibly, where the property appears to come within categories *1* to *5* above, but the settlement was created in a *bona fide* commercial transaction for full consideration in which there was no intention to confer a gratuitous benefit upon any person (*cf. I.R. Comrs.* v. *Plummer,* [1979] 3 All E.R. 775, H.L., on provisions of the income tax legislation; p. 187, *ante*).

2   A separate code

It has been seen (p. 64, *ante*) that capital transfer tax is payable by virtue of the provisions of FA 1975, when an individual makes a gift, or enters into certain other transactions during his lifetime, or dies. Capital transfer tax is also payable in a number of circumstances where settled property is concerned, and most of these are governed by a separate code contained in Sch. 5 to the 1975 Act. Accordingly, in this chapter, unless otherwise stated the references are to the paragraphs of Sch. 5. In one important respect, however, the code is not comprehensive. Where a beneficiary had an "interest in possession" (p. 288, *post*) at the date of his death, liability to tax in respect of the settled property arises by a combination of the Sch. 5 code, and the general charging provision contained in s. 22 relating to the tax payable on death (p. 84, *ante*).

The Sch. 5 code applies only when the trust has been set up, and the general principles apply to the creation of a trust (p. 193, *ante*).

3   Deemed transfers of value

The basis of the code is to treat certain transactions and events as if they were transfers of value, and, having identified the events which are to be treated as chargeable transfers, and the extent of the value transferred, to apply many of the general provisions of the tax to the value treated as transferred (s. 51 (2)).

The Sch. 5, code divides trusts into three categories:

a   those where there is an "interest in possession";

b   those where there is no "interest in possession"; and

c   those which are given privileged status.

It is, however, only appropriate to consider a trust as coming within one of these categories according to the circumstances prevailing at a particular time, and it by no means follows that because a trust is placed in one category at one time, it will remain in that category during the whole period of its existence. The expression "interest in possession" is considered below but broadly it denotes that a beneficiary has a right to enjoy the whole or part of the income of settled property. Accordingly, if a fund is held in trust to pay the income to Andrew for his life, and after his death the trustees have a discretion to distribute the income from the trust fund among such of Bernard, Charles and Douglas as they select, during the lifetime of Andrew there is an interest in possession, and after his death there is not.

B   INTEREST IN POSSESSION

1   The principle

A beneficiary has an interest in possession in settled property if he has:

a   a present right of present enjoyment;

b   of the net income of the settled property;

c   without any further decision of the trustees being required (*Pearson* v. *I.R. Comrs.*, [1980] 2 All E.R. 479, H.L.).

a   Present right   The beneficiary must, at the point of time being considered, have a right to enjoy the income as it arises. If trustees hold a fund upon trust to pay the income to Malcolm for life, with remainder to Norman for life, with remainder to Oswald, during the lifetimes of all three, all of them have a present right, in the sense of a right of which they can dispose. However, during the lifetime of Malcolm, Norman's right is a present right to future enjoyment. Malcolm has an interest in possession, but Norman does not.

   b   Right to the net income   It is not necessary for the beneficiary to be entitled to the gross income from the settled property. Thus, where, as will usually be the case, the trustees incur administrative expenses which are payable out of income, they will, in general, be entitled to deduct these expenses from the gross income. The beneficiary has an interest in possession if he is entitled to the gross income after the payment thereout of the administrative expenses. It follows that the beneficiary need not be entitled to the income immediately it arises. He may have to wait until, for example, the end of the year of assessment in order to determine the quantum of the net income.

   It is necessary to draw a distinction between powers which are dispositive and powers which are administrative (*Pearson* v. *I.R. Comrs., supra*). Where trustees exercise, or are entitled to exercise, an administrative power to apply income for a certain purpose, the income which remains is the net income for this purpose. If, however, the trustees have a dispositive power, that is treated as affecting the net income after payment of administration expenses. If a dispositive power can be exercised in favour of any person other than the beneficiary in question, that beneficiary cannot have an interest in possession.

   In many respects there is no clear authority as to what powers are to be regarded as administrative and what dispositive. In the absence of authority, the following classification is suggested:

Administrative powers

   i   power to charge for services;
   ii   power to retain commission, brokerage, directors' fees;
   iii   power to engage and pay agents and professional advisers;
   iv   power to hold investments in nominee name, or by a custodian, and to pay the nominee or custodian;
   v   power to insure trust assets, and to pay the premiums.
   vi   power to insure the life of the settlor, and to pay the premiums; the premiums;
   vii   power to pay taxes and duties (as to which see *Pearson* v *I.R. Comrs.* itself); and
   viii power to use income to improve land.

Dispositive powers

   i   power to accumulate income;

ii   power to pay or apply income to or for the maintenance, education, or benefit of another beneficiary;

iii   power to allow another beneficiary to use trust assets (even if on the exercise of that power an interest in possession in the assets is not created: see p. 292, *post*);

iv   power to pay the premiums on a policy of assurance which is effected for the benefit of another beneficiary; and

v   power to pay or apply income in securing the discharge of an obligation owing by another beneficiary, or in guaranteeing the performance of an obligation by another beneficiary.

c Existence, not exercise, of right If there is a dispositive power, there will not be an interest in possession in the property over which the power can be exercised. This will be so because the power exists, and this is irrespective of whether it is exercised.

d Trustees' decisions For there to be an interest in posession, the beneficiary must be entitled without any decisions of the trustees being necessary to confer that entitlement. If, therefore, trustees hold property upon trust to pay so much of the income as they think fit to Peter, and the remainder to Roger, Peter does not have an interest in possession because his entitlement to income will only arise when the trustees reach a decision in his favour. Roger also does not have an interest in possession.

2 Income from part of a fund

It is possible to have an interest in possession in part only of a fund. Thus, trustees may be directed to pay a given proportion of the income of a fund to Edward, and to distribute the remaining income at their discretion among George, Gordon and Gwendoline. In this case there is an interest in possession in the part of the fund providing the income for Edward, but no interest in possession in the remainder (para. 3 (2)). The position is the same if the trustees are to pay not a proportion of the income to Edward, but a specified sum, such as £1,000 p.a. There is a special provision, considered later (p. 301, *post*) which prescribes the part of the fund in which the interest in possession subsists.

3 Appointments of income

Under the terms of some trust instruments, trustees can make an appointment in respect of income. An appointment in this sense is a decision that all, or some specified part, of the future income of the fund shall be payable to a beneficiary, without any further decision being required. The appointment may be irrevocable, in which case the beneficiary receives the income so long as it continues to arise, or the appointment may be revocable. There is an important distinction between a trust where there is a power to appoint income, and a discretionary trust. In the former case the decision is taken before the income arises, and the single decision to make the appointment governs all future income until the decision is altered. In the case of a discretionary trust, the decision is made after the income has arisen, and a separate decision has to be made in respect of each tranche of income. If there is a discretionary trust, there is no interest in possession: if an appointment of income is made, if only for a short period of time, there is an interest in possession. So if trustees make a revocable appointment of income in favour of Harry on 1 January 1976; then on 1 January 1977 revoke that appointment and make a new appointment in favour of Ian; and on 1 January 1978, revoke that appointment and make a new appointment in favour of Jack, Harry, Ian and Jack have successive interests in possession.

The existence of a power of appointment will not prevent a beneficiary having an interest in possession (*Pearson* v. *I.R. Comrs.*, [1980] 2 All E.R. 479, H.L). Likewise, if a power of appointment is exercised so as to confer an interest in possession on a beneficiary, he will take such an interest notwithstanding the existence of a power to revoke the appointment (*Lord Inglewood* v. *I.R. Comrs.* [1981] Simon's Tax Intelligence 131).

4 Trusts and powers to accumulate

If there is a trust or power to accumulate, the existence of that power will generally prevent a beneficiary having an interest in possession (*Pearson* v. *I.R. Comrs., supra*). If, however, there is a power to accumulate, but the accumulations must be held solely for the beneficiary or his personal representatives, the beneficiary is treated as having an interest in possession (Inland Revenue Press Notice, 25 February 1976). The circumstances in which accumulations must be held for the beneficiary or his personal representatives were described earlier (p. 237, *ante*).

5 Non-income producing assets

A beneficiary can have an interest in possession even if no income is being produced. Here the test is: if the asset were income producing, would the beneficiary be entitled to the income from that asset? So, if a trust fund is held upon trust for Leonard during his life, and after his death for Mark, Leonard has an interest in possession even if the whole fund is invested in, say, works of arts, from which no income is derived.

6 Rights of use and enjoyment

a Existence of power Where the trust instrument gives the trustee a power to allow a beneficiary to use a trust asset, such as to reside in a home which is trust property, in the view of the Revenue the existence of this power does not take away an interest in possession which already exists (Inland Revenue Statement of Practice 10/79).

b Exercise of power It seems that where the power is exercised in order to give the beneficiary a temporary right, that right will not be of sufficient substance to be an "interest", and so it cannot be an interest in possession. If, however, the trustees exercise the power in respect of a dwelling-house, in order to give the beneficiary a sole or joint right of residence, and so to give him a permanent home, in the view of the Revenue, an interest in possession is created (Inland Revenue Statement of Practice 10/79). As to a suggested method of preventing the exercise of the power creating an interest in possession, see ((1980) 77 Law Society's Gazette, p. 450).

An interest in possession will be created, if none existed before, if the trustees go beyond granting a permission to reside, and create a lease for life. If the trustees create a lease in favour of the beneficiary at less than the rack rent, and as a result the value of the property as an asset of the trust is reduced accordingly, liability may arise under the provisions relating to depreciatory transactions (p. 300, *post*).

7 Leases for lives

It has been seen (p. 287, *ante*) that in some circumstances the grant of a lease for less than full consideration is treated as the creation of a settlement. Where this is so, it is first necessary to value the lessor's interest in the property. To do this it is necessary to establish the value of any consideration which the lessee gave when the lease was granted; and the amount of what would then have been the value of a full consideration in money's worth. The value of the lessor's interest in the property is determined by reference to the proportion which the value of the consideration furnished for the grant of the lease bore to the value of what would have been full consideration at that time (Sch. 10, para. 8).

The lessee is then treated as having an interest in possession in the whole property let, less such part of it as corresponds to the proportion which the value of the lessor's interest bears to the value of the property.

8   Interests in possession and life interests

For the purposes of the general law of trusts, the concept of a life interest is very well known. This is not, however, the same concept as an interest in possession, for it seems that in general an interest in possession has the connotation of being personal to a beneficiary, and not to be capable of existing separately from that particular beneficiary's entitlement to it. Thus it will be seen that if a life interest is given away, while the life interest itself will continue to exist, the interest in possession will be treated as coming to an end. As an exception to this, where a life interest is given away in a disposition which is exempt as coming within the provisions relating to dispositions for family maintenance, the interest in possession is not treated as coming to an end (s. 46 (5)).

C   TRUSTS WITH AN INTEREST IN POSSESSION

1   The principles

Where there is an interest in possession, the following general principles apply to govern the capital transfer tax position.

a   A liability to tax arises whenever a beneficiary who is entitled to an interest in possession ceases to be entitled to it. When a beneficiary ceases to be entitled to the interest, he is treated as making a transfer of value.

b   A beneficiary who has an interest in possession is treated as being the owner of the trust fund itself, or in that part of it in which the interest subsists (para. 3 (1)). Accordingly, where he is treated as making a transfer of value, the value transferred is not the value of the interest in possession, but the capital value of the fund, or part of the fund, itself.

c   As a corollary to *b*, in general there is no liability when a reversionary interest is dealt with. So, in the case of a fund held upon trust to pay the income to Norman for his life, with remainder to Oliver, Oliver can give away his interest during the lifetime of Norman without any capital transfer tax liability (s. 24 (3)).

d   The amount of tax payable as a result of a deemed transfer of value is exactly the same as *a* if an actual transfer of value had been made by the beneficiary entitled to the interest in possession. Thus, the amount of tax depends on the extent to which, if at all, that beneficiary has made previous actual or deemed transfers of value.

    e   The primary liability for the payment of the tax is that of the trustees, who pay it out of the trust fund.

These general principles, and the exceptions to them, are considered in the remaining part of this section of this chapter.

2   Deemed transfers of value

Where there is an interest in possession, a transfer of value is deemed to be effected in the following circumstances:

    a   an interest in possession comes to an end during the lifetime of the beneficiary entitled to it (para. 4 (2));

    b   an interest in possession comes to an end as a result of the death of the beneficiary entitled to it (s. 22 (1); para. 3 (1));

    c   the trustees enter into a "depreciatory transaction" (para. 4 (9));

    d   a company in which the trust has an investment itself makes a transfer of value (para. 24 (2) (a)).

3   Termination of interest in possession during lifetime of beneficiary

    a   *The general rule*   Where during the lifetime of a beneficiary entitled to an interest in possession that interest comes to an end, the general rule is that the beneficiary is charged to tax as if he had made a transfer of value (para. 4 (2)). This will be so whether the trust is wound up, and the capital paid to another beneficiary; or whether some other beneficiary becomes entitled to an interest in possession. So, if trustees hold a fund upon trust to pay the income to Peter until he reaches the age of 30, and then to pay the income to Queenie for her life, when reaches the age of 30 Peter is treated as making a transfer of value of the whole of the capital of the trust fund.

If the interest in possession was in the whole fund, the tax charge is calculated as if the whole of the capital of the fund had been transferred. The position where the interest in possession was in only part of the fund is considered later (p. 301, *post*).

If an interest in possession is held by a close company, the interest is treated as being held by the participators (para. 24 (5)). If the interest is held by any body other than an individual or a close company, there will be a charge under the discretionary trust code (para. 11 (10)), but not on the termination of an interest in possession. This is because on the termination of an interest in possession tax is charged as if the person beneficially entitled had made a transfer of value, and by virtue of s. 20 (5), only transfers of value made by individuals are chargeable.

To the general charging rule, there are a number of total or partial exceptions.

b Exception 1: beneficiary taking further interest   If on the termination of one interest in possession, the beneficiary becomes
entitled to another interest in possession in the same settled property,
no tax is generally chargeable when the first interest in possession
comes to an end (para. 4 (3)). The position is the same if on the termination of the interest in possession the beneficiary becomes
absolutely entitled to the settled property (*ibid*). If trustees hold a
fund of £50,000 upon trust to pay the income to Roger until he
reaches the age of 30, and upon his reaching that age to pay the
capital to him, there is no deemed transfer of value when he reaches
that age, and so no charge to tax.

It does not matter how the beneficiary becomes entitled to the
settled property or to the further interest in possession. If under the
trust instrument the trustees are to pay the income to Roger until the
age of 30, and then two thirds of the income to Queenie, but the trust
is varied, either with or without the intervention of the court, so that
Roger then becomes entitled to a further interest in possession in the
whole fund upon reaching the age of 30, there is no deemed transfer
of value when he reaches that age.

If one interest in possession comes to an end, and the beneficiary
becomes entitled to part only of the capital of the fund, or to a
further interest in possession in part only of the fund, there is a
deemed transfer of value, and the value deemed to be transferred is
the difference between the value of the whole fund, and the value of
that part of the fund to which the beneficiary becomes entitled, or in
which he becomes entitled to the further interest in possession (para.
4 (10) (b)). Thus, if trustees hold a fund of £50,000 upon trust to pay
the income to Roger until he reaches the age of 30, and upon his
attaining that age to divide the fund as to 2/5ths to Roger and 3/5ths
to Susan, when he reaches the age of 30 Roger is treated as making a
transfer of value of £50,000, less £20,000, = £30,000.

c Exception 2: beneficiary selling interest   If an interest in
possession comes to an end because the beneficiary entitled to it sells
it, or disposes of it by some other method, such as exchange, for
money or money's worth, he is treated as making a transfer of value,
and the value transferred is the difference between the value of the
fund in which the interest in possession subsisted, and the consideration received for it (para. 4 (4)). It will be appreciated that a charge
to tax will therefore arise even if the beneficiary entitled to the
interest in possession disposes of it at the full open market value of
that interest. Suppose that trustees hold a fund of £100,000 upon
trust to pay the income to Thomas for life, and on his death to pay
the income to Ursula. Suppose also that the actuarial value of

Thomas' interest in possession is £30,000, and he sells his interest to Veronica for that sum. Thomas is treated as making a transfer of value of £100,000 − £30,000 = £70,000.

Any value received by the beneficiary disposing of his interest in possession can be taken into account except the value of a reversionary interest in the same property (para. 4 (4)). So, in the example just considered, if Thomas and Ursula agree that the trust should be brought to an end and that the fund should be divided as to £30,000 to Thomas and as to £70,000 to Ursula, Thomas in effect is giving up his interest in possession in the £70,000 which Ursula will receive, and he is receiving instead Ursula's reversionary interest in the £30,000. He cannot, however, take the value of that interest into account, and will derive no benefit from this exemption. Under the first exception, however, the deemed transfer will be treated as being restricted to £70,000.

d *Exception 3: reverter to settlor or spouse or settlor's widow.* There is no liability to capital transfer tax on the termination of an interest in possession in either of the following circumstances:

i (a) an interest in possession comes to an end during the lifetime of the settlor; and

(b) upon the coming to an end of that interest the property reverts to the settlor; and

(c) the settlor did not acquire a reversionary interest in the property for a consideration in money or money's worth (para. 4 (5)); and

(d) the exemption does not depend on a reversionary interest having been transferred into a settlement after 9 March 1981 (FA 1981, s. 104).

ii (a) an interest in possession comes to an end (whether during the lifetime of the settlor or within two years after his death) and

(b) upon the coming to an end of that interest the settlor's spouse or, in certain circumstances, his widow becomes beneficially entitled to the property; and

(c) when the termination occurs the recipient spouse is domiciled in some part of the United Kingdom (FA 1976, Sch. 14, para. 13 (b)); and

(d) neither the settlor nor his spouse acquired a reversionary interest in the property for a consideration in money or money's worth (para. 4 (6); FA 1976, s. 110 (2)); and

(e) the exemption does not depend on a reversionary interest having been transferred into a settlement after 9 March 1981 (FA 1981, s. 104).

The Revenue take the view that these provisions also apply if the settlor, his spouse or widow do not take the property itself, but only take an interest in possession in the property (see para. 3 (1)).

It will be noted under i (c) and ii (d) the exemption will be lost if the settlor, or spouse, acquires any reversionary interest in the property for money or money's worth.

e Exception 4: Assignment where surviving spouse exemption applies When estate duty was payable in respect of property owned by a person at his death, there was a specific exemption known as the surviving spouse exemption (p. 122, *ante*). Under this, if a person left his property upon trust for his spouse to derive the income or enjoyment of it during his or her life but so that the spouse was not able to deal with the capital, no estate duty was payable on the death of the surviving spouse (FA 1894, s. 5 (2)). This provision has no effect where the death occurred on or after 13 November 1974, but if the death occurred before that date, and the conditions for the surviving spouse exemption were satisfied, then if the interest in possession of the surviving spouse comes to an end after that date, no capital transfer tax is payable on its termination (para. 4 (7)).

f Exception 5: "Excluded property" There is no liability to capital transfer tax when an interest in possession comes to an end if the settled property is "excluded property" (para. 4 (11)). Excluded property is certain property situated outside the United Kingdom (p. 387) and certain reversionary interests (p. 355, *post*).

g Exception 6: Protective trusts A protective trust is a trust under which a beneficiary, who is known as the principal beneficiary, is entitled to income from a fund as it arises, but where his entitlement will come to an end if he does anything, or anything happens, which would take away or reduce his right to that income. Protective trusts are usually established to protect the fund against bankruptcy: if the principal beneficiary becomes bankrupt, his trustee is bankruptcy and not the principal beneficiary himself would normally be entitled to the income, so that bankruptcy is one event which will cause the principal beneficiary's interest to determine. A protective trust may be established by incorporating the provisions of the Trustee Act 1925, s. 33, or by expressly declaring the trusts which need not be the same as those of the statute.

If the protective trust is statutory, and the interest of the beneficiary determines, a discretionary trust arises, the objects of which are the principal beneficiary, his spouse, his children and remoter issue, and in some circumstances, certain other persons.

Where the principal beneficiary's fixed interest comes to an end during his lifetime, or during such shorter period as the trust instrument prescribes, the coming to an end of the principal beneficiary's fixed interest is disregarded for capital transfer tax purposes. Accordingly, no liability arises at that time (FA 1975, Sch. 5, para. 18; FA 1978, s. 71).

h Exception 7: Dispositions for family maintenance There is a far reaching exemption from the general provisions of capital transfer tax where a disposition is made for the maintenance of a spouse, child, or dependent relative (s. 46). Where a person who has an interest in possession in settled property disposes of that interest, for the purposes of this provision his interest in possession is not treated as coming to an end, so that no tax is payable as a result (s. 46 (5)). The Revenue view is that the exemption applies only where there is an assignment. On this view, which may well not be legally correct, if a life tenant releases part of his interest to enable a payment to made to the beneficiary next entitled, or consents to an advancement being made to another beneficiary, the exemption is not available.

i Exception 8: Following death In some cases, a will provides that a beneficiary is entitled to a benefit if he survives the testator or some other person for a given period. If the gift carries the intermediate income from death, and the condition as to survivorship is not satisfied, in principle a charge to capital transfer tax would arise by virtue of the termination of that interest in possession. However, if the survivorship period does not exceed 6 months, the disposition which takes effect at the end of the survivorship period or on the earlier death of the person concerned is treated as taking effect at the beginning of the survivorship period (FA 1975, Sch. 5, para. 22A, added by FA 1976, s. 105 (1)). Accordingly, if a person leaves, say, £5,000 to his brother for life if the brother survives him for 28 days, but if he does not survive him for this period to his sister for life, then even if the gift carries the intermediate income, upon the death of the brother after, say, 21 days, there will be no termination of an interest in possession, and the sister will be treated as having acquired her interest in possession at the date of death of the deceased. This will be so even although for the purposes of the general law the deceased brother's estate is entitled to income for the 21 days for which he did in fact survive the deceased.

4 Termination of interest in possession on death

a The general rule It has just been seen that the general rule is that where an interest in possession comes to an end during the lifetime of the beneficiary entitled to it, he is treated as making a transfer of value. The corresponding rule is that where a person was entitled to an interest in possession when he died, he is treated as making a transfer of value of the settled property when he dies, as well as making a transfer of value of the property which he owned outright (s. 22 (1); s. 23 (1); para. 3 (1); p. 121, *ante*).

b Exceptions To the general rule, there are certain exceptions which correspond with those which have been considered in the context of the coming to an end of an interest in possession during the lifetime of a beneficiary. These exceptions are:

i where the beneficiary entitled to the interest in possession dies during the lifetime of the settlor, and upon the death of the beneficiary the property reverts to the settlor (s. 22 (2)). This exception does not apply where the settlor acquired a reversionary interest in the property for a consideration in money or money's worth. Nor does it apply where the exemption depends on a reversionary interest having been transferred into a settlement after 9 March 1981 (FA 1981, s. 104).

ii where the beneficiary who was entitled to an interest in possession dies during the lifetime of the settlor, or within two years after his death, and the settlor's spouse or widow becomes beneficially entitled to the settled property, provided

  (a) the recipient spouse was domiciled at the time of death in some part of the UK; and

  (b) neither the settlor nor the settlor's spouse had acquired a reversionary interest in the property for a consideration in money or money's worth (s. 22 (3); FA 1976, s. 110 (1); Sch. 14, para. 13 (a)); and

  (c) the exemption does not depend on a reversionary interest having been transferred into a settlement after 9 March 1981 (FA 1981, s. 104).

iii where one spouse died before 13 Novembe 1974, and the other spouse dies after 13 March 1975, and the conditions for the surviving spouse exemption (p. 125, *ante*) were satisfied, there is no liability to capital transfer tax upon the death of the surviving spouse in respect of the property complying with that condition (s. 22 (4)).

The exception for excluded property noted above (p. 97, *ante*) also applies on death.

5   Depreciatory transactions

a   The rule   Where capital transfer tax is payable as a result of the coming to an end of an interest in possession, it is payable by reference to the whole or some part of the value of the trust fund. At first sight, it might appear attractive to attempt to reduce the amount of tax payable by reducing the value of the trust fund. For example, if trustees hold a fund consisting of assets valued at £100,000 upon trust for William for life, with remainder to Xanthe, they might be tempted to sell the investments to Xanthe for, say, £20,000, so that on the death of William, although the whole fund would be taxable, the value transferred would be £20,000 and not £100,000. Such devices are not usually effective.

It is provided that, in general, if trustees enter into any transaction which causes a reduction in the value of the assets of the trust fund, or any of them, then that transaction is treated as if an interest in possession had come to an end in part of the fund (para. 4 (9)). For this purpose, it is necessary to value the fund before the transaction took place and the interest in possession is treated as coming to an end in that part of the value of the fund before the transaction took place which is represented by the reduction in value as a result of the transaction.

b   Applies where transaction with person connected with the settlement   The rule will only apply where the transaction is between the trustees and a person who comes within one of the following classes, or with a person who is connected with someone coming within one of the following classes:

  i the person beneficially entitled to an interest in the property which is the subject of the transaction;

 ii a person beneficially entitled to any other interest in the property which is the subject of the transaction, or to any interest in any other property which is comprised in the settlement;

iii a person for whose benefit any of the settled property may be applied.

The expression "connected person" is generally the same as that for the purposes of capital gains tax (CGTA 1979, s. 63) but is extended in certain respects (FA 1975, s. 51 (4)).

c   Exception   The rule does not apply where, if the transaction had been entered into by an individual who was beneficially entitled to the absolute ownership of the property, he would not be treated as making a transfer of value under the general provisions of the Act. Accordingly, if the trustees sell the trust assets to a beneficiary at an undervalue, not because they wish to confer a benefit on him, but because they make a bad bargain, there will be no liability (s. 20 (4)).

6 Transfer of value by close company

In some circumstances a company is treated as making a transfer of value (s. 39). Where this is so, in general terms, the value transferred by the company is apportioned to the shareholders and certain other persons proportionately according to their interest in the company. A calculation is then made of the amount of tax which each shareholder would pay if he made a transfer of value equivalent to the value apportioned to him. The amount of tax payable by the company is the aggregate of the amounts which each of the shareholders would be required to pay.

A special rule applies where an amount is apportioned to trustees by virtue of the trust shareholding in the company. Where an interest in possession exists, it is necessary to ascertain:

(a) the value of the settled property before the apportionment is made; and

(b) i the amount apportioned to the trustees less

　　 ii the amount (if any) by which the value of the settled property is more than it would be apart from the company's transfer, but not taking into account the value of any shares or other interest in the company.

An interest in possession is then treated as coming to an end on that part of the value in (a) which corresponds to the amount at (b) (para. 24 (1), (2), (3)).

7 Interest in possession in part of fund

a Generally Where a beneficiary is entitled to a fraction or a proportion of the income which a fund produces, he is treated as having an interest in possession in a corresponding fraction or proportion of the settled property (para. 3 (2) (a)). This applies whether the beneficiary is treated as making a transfer of value either during his lifetime, or on his death.

b By reference to specific amount The position is more complicated where the beneficiary is entitled to a specified amount of income, such as £1,000 p.a., or to the income of the fund less a specified amount. In this case the starting point is to calculate the part of the property which produces the specified amount (para. 3

301

(3)), and to treat the beneficiary as having an interest in possession in that part of the settled property. Suppose, then, that trustees hold a fund of £40,000 which is producing income of £4,000 p.a., and they are directed to pay £1,000 p.a. to Alan and the remainder of the income to Anthea. £10,000 will be treated as producing an income of £1,000 p.a., and Alan will be treated as having an interest in possession in £10,000.

The complication arises because the legislation does not prescribe any rules as to the period which is to be considered in calculating the proportion of the income. Consider further the example of Alan and Anthea. What is the position if the whole income of the fund during the previous 12 months is £4,000; but the income during the previous 6 months is only £1,000? If the period of 12 months is considered, Alan has an interest in possession in 25% of the fund, whereas if the period of 6 months is considered, Alan has an interest in possession in 50% of the fund. In the absence of statutory guidance, it seems that the notional income should be calculated at the date when the transfer of value is treated as being made, or, perhaps, the actual income from the beginning of the year of assessment in which the transfer is treated as being made to the actual date of the transfer. The Revenue practice is to take the period immediately before the relevant date; to disregard any variations which appeared to be temporary; but to take into account any apparently permanent charge during that period.

c Deemed rates of income   A further complication arises. In the absence of any other provision, it would be easy to reduce artificially the proportion of the fund which would be chargeable on a particular occasion. Consider again the example of Alan and Anthea. If the notional income produced by the fund was £4,000 p.a., and it was known that Alan was likely to die, the trustees might temporarily switch investments into very high yielding assets so that the income of the fund at the date of Alan's death was, say, £10,000 p.a. In this event, he would be treated as having an interest in possession in 10% of the fund instead of in 25% of the fund. In order to prevent such devices, the Treasury is given power from time to time to prescribe higher and lower rates of income (para. 3 (4)). The rates which have been in force since 15 August 1980 are fixed by reference to the yield on irredeemable British Government stocks in the Financial Times — Actuaries Share Index (in the case of the higher rate) and the Financial Times — Actuaries All Share Index (in the case of the lower rate) (Capital Transfer Tax (Settled Property Income Yield) Order 1980 S.I. 1980 No. 1000). The rates are determined for the day on which the value has to be ascertained, or, if there are no indices for that day, for the latest earlier date. The easiest way of ascertaining the rates is by telephoning the Capital Taxes Office (01-603 4622) between 9 a.m. and 5 p.m. on working days. Where the beneficiary who is treated as making a transfer of value was entitled to a specified sum the higher rate must be used; and where the beneficiary was entitled to the income from the fund other than a specified sum, the lower rate must be used.

i Beneficiary entitled to specified amount of income Where the beneficiary is entitled to a specified amount of income, he is treated as having had an interest in possession in the *higher* of:

(a) the proportion of the fund ascertained in accordance with para. *b* above; and

(b) the sum which if invested at the prescribed higher rate would produce the specified sum payable to the beneficiary.

If, however, the sum in (b) should exceed the total value of the fund, the beneficiary is treated as having an interest in possession in the total fund.

Take again, the example of Alan and Anthea. Suppose that the income of the fund is £4,000 p.a. calculated according to whatever is the appropriate method (p. 302, *supra*) and that the specified higher rate is 12%. The operation of the rules can be considered by taking different values for the capital of the fund.

a Capital value of fund: £45,000

   i the proportionate basis produces a figure of £11,250 (25% of the value of the fund);

   ii by applying the higher rate, there is produced a figure of £8,333 (£8,333, if invested at £12% would produce an income of £1,000 p.a.).

Alan is therefore treated as having an interest in possession in £11,250.

b Capital value of fund: £30,000

   i the proportionate basis produces a figure of £7,500 (25% of the value of the fund);

   ii application of the higher rate produces a figure of £8,333, as before.

c Capital value of fund: £7,000

It is unlikely that the capital value of the fund will be so low, but this is possible where the fund is invested in high income producing, but short life, assets, such as short leasehold investments:

   i the proportionate basis produces a figure of £1,750;

   ii the higher rate method produces a figure of £8,333.

As, however, the application of the higher rate method is restricted to the value of the whole fund, Alan is treated as having an interest in possession in £7,000.

ii Beneficiary entitled to income less a specified amount Where the beneficiary is entitled to an interest in possession in the income of the fund less a specified amount, his interest is treated as being in the *lower* of

(a) the proportion of the fund ascertained in accordance with the ordinary principle in para. *b* above; and

(b) the value of the whole fund, less the amount which if invested at the lower rate of interest prescribed by the Treasury would produce the specified sum.

These rules can again by illustrated by the example of Alan and Anthea, upon the assumption that the specified lower rate is 5%.

a Capital value of fund: 45,000

   i the proportionate basis produces a figure of £33,750;

   ii application of the lower rate produces a figure of £25,000 (the value of the fund, £45,000, less £20,000 being the amount which, if invested at 5% would produce £1,000 p.a.).

Anthea is treated as having an interest in possession in £25,000.

b Capital value of fund: £30,000

   i the proportionate basis produces a figure of £22,500;

   ii application of the lower rate produces a figure of £10,000.
Anthea is therefore treated as having an interest in possession in £10,000.

As *b* is less than *a* Anthea is therefore treated as having an interest in possession in £10,000.

d Exception It is not necessary to take account of the higher and lower rates where all the interests in possession are disposed of at the same time (para. 3 (4)). Accordingly, if Alan and Anthea both dispose of their respective interests at the same time, the proportionate method is adopted.

8 Enjoyment of assets

It has been seen (p. 292, *ante*) that where a person is entitled to enjoy the use of trust assets, he may be treated as having an interest in possession in those assets. Where he is entitled to share the use of the asset with one or more other persons, it is necessary to calculate the annual value of his interest, and the annual value of the interests of the other person or persons who can use the asset. The beneficiary treated as making a transfer of value is regarded as transferring such part of the value of the property as corresponds to the proportion which the annual value of his interest bears to the aggregate of the annual values of his interest and those of the other persons concerned (para. 3 (5)).

There is no statutory indication of how the annual value is to be calculated, but it is presumably the amount of rent or similar periodic payment which would be payable in an arm's length transaction for the use of the asset.

9 The tax payable

a   Lifetime transfers   The rules so far discussed indicate the occasions on which the tax is payable where there is an interest in possession, and the amount which is treated as being transferred. Where the interest comes to an end during the lifetime of the beneficiary, it is necessary to calculate the tax which would be payable if the beneficiary made a gift at that time equivalent to the value which is treated as being transferred. The tax is calculated, at least in the first instance, at the lifetime rates. Suppose that a fund of £100,000 is held upon trust for Basil for life, with remainder to Denzil, and that in his lifetime Basil gives his life interest to Ethel. If Basil had made chargeable gifts since 9 March 1981 of £60,000 on which tax of £1,500 had been paid, there would be a liability on the fund of the amount of tax attributable to the slices £60,000 to £160,000, namely £24,250. If Basil had made no previous chargeable transfers of value, the £50,000 nil rate band would be available on the transfer, and the total tax payable would be £9,500.

If the beneficiary who was entitled to the interest in possession dies within 3 years, tax is payable at the death-time rates (s. 37 (2)). It follows clearly from this that the trustees cannot calculate the tax for which they are primarily responsible (see p. 354, *post*) without full information as to the CTT "history" of the beneficiary.

b   Small exemptions   The exemptions which an individual can claim when making gifts not exceeding £250 in the case of any one beneficiary (Sch. 6, para. 4) and gifts forming part of the normal expenditure out of income (Sch. 6, para. 5) are not available in calculating the charge on the coming to an end of an interest in possession. This is because these exemptions apply only to actual transfers of value. Although when an interest in possession comes to an end it is treated as if a transfer of value had been made (s. 51 (2); Sch. 5, para. 4 (2)), it is not itself an actual transfer of value (para. 4 (1)).

The position is different with regard to the exemptions in respect of annual transfers up to £3,000 (FA 1981, s. 94) and in respect of gifts in consideration of marriage (FA 1975, Sch. 6, para. 6). Within six months from the termination of an interest in possession in the whole or part of the settled property, the beneficiary who was entitled to that interest can surrender to the trustees the whole or part of these two exemptions which he himself could have claimed on an outright transfer of value (FA 1981, s. 94). This is done by notice given by the beneficiary to the trustees (sub-s. 94 (5)).

In the case of the exemption in respect of gifts in consideration of marriage, the exemption is available, if certain conditions are satisfied, if an interest in possession terminates in consideration of marriage, whether the property subject to the settlement remains settled, or then ceases to be settled (FA 1981, s. 94 (4)).

If the beneficiary surrenders to the trustees his annual exemption or exemption in consideration of marriage, no liability will arise in respect of that amount of the settled property in which the interest in possession terminates. Further, that value will not form part of the beneficiary's cumulation.

c   Transfers on death   Where an interest in possession comes to an end on the death of a beneficiary, the value which is treated as being transferred is aggregated with the value of the deceased's own net estate, and also the value of any fund which is treated as being transferred at the same time (ss. 22 (1), 23 (1)). That aggregate when considered in conjunction with the deceased's CTT history shows the total amount of tax payable, and that amount is then apportioned according the respective aggregate values (p. 129, *ante*).

The method of calculating the liability can be illustrated by supposing that Isobel made chargeable transfers of value in her lifetime of £40,000. She dies worth £100,000 after payment of her debts. She had an interest in possession in the whole fund of Trust No. 1, valued at £50,000, and an interest in possession in the whole fund of Trust No. 2, valued at £200,000. Isobel is treated as making a transfer of value of £100,000, + £50,000, + £200,000 = £350,000. The total tax payable is £188,000, and this will be payable:

i   out of own assets: $\dfrac{£100,000}{£350,000} \times £188,000 = £53,714$

ii   out of Trust Fund No. 1: $\dfrac{£50,000}{£350,000} \times £188,000 = £26,857$

iii   out of Trust Fund No. 2: $\dfrac{£200,000}{£350,000} \times £188,000 = £107,429$

d   Transfers within 3 years of death   Where an interest in possession comes to an end during the lifetime of a beneficiary, it has been seen that tax is payable initially at the lifetime rates (p. 79, *ante*). If the beneficiary then dies, a further liability occurs, because the tax is payable at the death-time rates (s. 37 (2)). It is not, however, necessary to consider the other circumstances of the beneficiary at death. Tax is recalculated merely by reference to the value transferred at the date of the transfer, according to the death-time table, and the additional tax is then payable.

e No grossing up Where capital transfer tax is payable as a result of the coming to an end of an interest in possession, the tax is paid out of the trust fund. Accordingly, no grossing up is appropriate. If, however, an interest comes to an end in part of the property, but continues in the remainder, the amount paid out will be treated as the coming to an end of the grossed up equivalent. So, where there have been no previous chargeable transfers of value, and with the consent of the beneficiary entitled to an interest in possession, £70,000 is paid to the reversioner, that will be treated as the coming to an end of an interest in possession in £74,062, and tax of £4,062 will be payable out of the trust fund.

10 Relief for successive charges

a Generally A special provision applies where a charge to capital transfer tax arises in respect of settled property in which an interest in possession subsists, and there had been a charge to capital transfer tax in respect of the same property within the previous five years (FA 1981, s. 101). If certain conditions are satisfied, by virtue of this provision, although no adjustment is made to the tax payable on the first transfer, the tax payable on the second transfer is reduced.

b Conditions In order to claim the relief, it is necessary to show that:

i There was a transfer which increased the value of the estate of the beneficiary who has at the time of the second transfer the interest in possession. This condition is satisfied if at the time of creation of the settlement, the first interest in possession was conferred on the beneficiary, or if he became entitled following the termination of a previous interest in possession (FA 1975, Sch. 5, para. 3 (1)).

ii The first transfer was, or included, the making of the settlement, or the termination of a previous interest in possession, or was any other event after the creation of the settlement (FA 1981, s. 101 (2) (*c*)).

iii The second transfer is the actual or deemed termination of an interest in possession (s. 101 (2) (*a*)).

iv The second transfer takes place within five years from the first transfer (s. 101 (1)).

v The value transferred by the first transfer also fell to be determined by reference to the value of the settled property in which the interest in possession terminates (s. 101 (2) (*b*)). It is not necessary for the property to be in the same form at the time of the second transfer, so that a change in investment will not preclude the availability of the relief.

The relief is not available to the extent that the value by which the beneficiary's estate was increased by the first transfer consisted of a reversionary interest (s. 101 (6)).

c   Calculation of relief   In order to calculate the relief, it is necessary first to ascertain:

  i The amount by which the beneficiary's estate was increased by the first transfer, excluding any part of such amount as was transferred by an exempt transfer.

  If the first transfer was the creation of the settlement, and the trustees paid the tax out of the initial settled fund, the amount of that tax is deducted when calculating the increase in the beneficiary's estate. If the first transfer was the termination of an interest in possession, the increase in the beneficiary's estate will be the net value of the settled property in which the interest in possession arose, after deducting the tax payable out of it by virtue of the termination of the previous interest.

  ii The value transferred by the first transfer. This is the amount by which the beneficiary's estate was increased by the first transfer, together with the tax paid in respect of that transfer.

  iii The tax paid in respect of the first transfer.

A reduction is then made from the amount of tax which would normally be payable on the second transfer. This reduction is of a percentage of the tax paid in respect of the first transfer. The relevant percentage is:

Time of first transfer	*Percentage*
Not more than 1 year before second transfer	100%
More than 1 year but not more than 2 years before second transfer	80%
More than 2 years but not more than 3 years before second transfer	60%
More than 3 years but not more than 4 years before second transfer	40%
More than 4 years but not more than 5 years before second transfer	20%
More than 5 years before second transfer	nil

The actual credit against the tax which would otherwise by payable on the second transfer is found by applying the following formula:

$$\text{tax paid on first transfer} \times \text{relevant percentage} \times \frac{\text{increase in beneficiary's estate by first transfer}}{\text{value transferred by first transfer}}$$

d Subsequent transfers In general, the relief is available only against the tax payable on the transfer which follows the first transfer (s. 101 (4)). If, however, the relief on that transfer is less than the whole of the tax charged on the first transfer, the balance of relief can be claimed in respect of the next transfer (*ibid*).

e Terminations prior to 10 March 1981 These provisions apply only where the actual or deemed termination of an interest in possession which constitutes the second transfer occurred after 9 March 1981. A different form of relief applied in respect of terminations before that date. That relief is not considered in this book.

D TRUSTS WITH NO INTEREST IN POSSESSION

1 Interests in possession

It will be recalled that it is necessary to consider the classification of trusts for capital transfer tax purposes according to the circumstances prevailing at a particular time (p. 288, *ante*) and it is now proposed to consider the position where at a particular time there is no interest in possession. From the earlier discussion (p. 288, *ante*) it will be appreciated that the main types of trust where there is no interest in possession are those where there is a discretion as to income, and where there is a power or a duty to accumulate income. A discretion as to capital is irrelevant for this purpose (p. 289, *ante*). It has also been seen that if there is a primary duty to pay out or apply income, but a power to accumulate, there will only be an interest in possession if the beneficiary who would have received the income, or his personal representatives, will be entitled to the accumulations (p. 291, *ante*).

A special rule applies to companies. It is legally effective to create a trust under which the income is to be paid for, say, 20 years, to a named company, and on general principles that company would have an interest in possession. However, a company is only treated as having an interest in possession where it would do so under the general principles if two conditions are satisfied namely:

309

a that the business of the company consists wholly or mainly in the acquisition of interests in settled property; and

b that the company has acquired the interest for full consideration in money or money's worth from an individual who was beneficially entitled to it (para. 11 (10)).

This provision applies only for the purposes of that part of Sch. 5 to FA 1975 which deals with trusts which do not have an interest in possession. As a result, where a company has an interest which on general principles would be an interest in possession but those special conditions are not satisfied, liability to capital transfer tax will arise both in respect of the termination of that interest, under the rules previously considered in this chapter, and also in respect of those circumstances now to be considered in which trusts with no interest in possession are liable.

2 The principles

The principles governing trusts where there is no interest in possession are:

a A charge to tax will arise whenever income ceases to be subject to a discretion. For example, it will cease to be subject to such a discretion where capital is taken out of the trust and paid over to a beneficiary outright. It will also be subject to such a discretion where the trust is converted into one in which there is an interest in possession.

b In general, the trustees are treated as having their own CTT history. Accordingly, when tax is payable, the rate is determined by reference to the amount of value transferred by previous transfers of value which the trustees are treated as having made, so that the CTT history of the settlor and the beneficiaries is irrelevant. A different rule is adopted, however, where the settlement was created after 26 March 1974.

3 Events giving rise to charge to tax

Trustees of a trust where there is no interest in possession are treated as making a transfer of value, and so as becoming subject to tax, whenever any of the following circumstances occur:

a Money or assets are taken out of the settlement, and paid over to a beneficiary outright (p. 319, *post*);

b An interest in possession is created where none existed immediately beforehand (p. 325, *post*);

c The trustees enter into a depreciatory transaction which reduces the value of the trust fund (p. 328, *post*);

d   The terms of the trust are altered so that the conditions governing "accumulation and maintenance settlements" are satisfied when they were not satisfied immediately beforehand (p. 329, *post*);

e   A company in which the trustees have an investment makes a transfer of value, and the whole or part of that value is apportioned to the trustees (p. 330, *post*);

f   There is a tenth anniversary of the creation of the settlement (p. 330, *post*); and

g   If the trust is non-resident, there is an anniversary of the creation of the settlement (p. 332, *post*).

These circumstances are each considered in detail at the pages stated.

4   *Exceptions*

Some trusts are given privileged status for capital transfer tax purposes. The ones considered in this book are:

a   accumulation and maintenance settlements (p. 348, *post*);

b   protective trusts (p. 344, *post*);

c   trusts for the benefit of mentally disabled persons (p. 345, *post*); and

d   charitable trusts (p. 398, *post*).

Other trusts which are given privileged status, but which because of their specialized nature are not considered in this book are:

e   trusts governing superannuation schemes (para. 16);

f   trusts for the benefit of employees (para. 17; FA 1976, s. 107);

g   trusts governing compensation funds (para. 21); and

h   newspaper trusts (FA 1976, s. 108).

5   *The relevant questions*

When one of the events specified in section 3, *supra,* occurs it is necessary to ask three questions in order to determine whether there is any, and, if so, what liability. These are:

a   In the particular circumstances are the trustees treated as making a transfer of value?

b   If so, what is the amount of the value deemed to be transferred? and

c   What is the appropriate rate of tax?

Each of these three questions is considered in the context of each of the events giving rise to a charge to tax. It is, however, necessary to consider first the rate of tax which normally applies to a trust where there is no interest in possession.

E   NORMAL RATES OF TAX

1   *Trusts created after 26 March 1974*

The rates of tax normally payable by the trustees of a settlement created after 26 March 1974, in which there is no interest in possession, are governed by para. 7 of Sch. 5. This applies where:

a   There has been a transfer of value which

　　i   was a chargeable transfer of value; or

　　ii   would have been a chargeable transfer of value had it not been an exempt transfer because of the exceptions relating to:

　　　(a)   trusts for the benefit of mentally disabled persons (para. 19; p. 345, *post*);

　　　(b)   transfers not exceeding £1,000 in any year up to 1975/76 or £2,000 in any year between 1976/77 and 1980/81, or £3,000 in any year thereafter (Sch. 6, para. 2; p. 76, *ante*);

　　　(*c*)   transfers not exceeding £100 in any year up to 1979/80 or £250 in any year thereafter in favour of the same donee (Sch. 6, para. 4; p. 77, *ante*);

　　　(*d*)   transfers forming part of the normal expenditure out of income of the transferor (Sch. 6, para. 5; p. 77, *ante*);

　　　(*e*)   transfers made in consideration of marriage (Sch. 6, para. 6; p. 78, *ante*).

b   The transfer of value was made

　　i   on the creation of the settlement; or

　　ii   where the settlement arose on the death of a person, on his death; or

　　iii   at any time after i or ii.

c   The transfer of value at *a* was made before the deemed transfer of value now being considered; and

d   The value of the property comprised in the settlement in respect of which the charge to tax now arises was taken into account in determining the value transferred by the transfer of value in *a* (paras. 7 (1), 11 (2)).

In the simple situation, if Adrian created after 26 March 1974 a discretionary trust by transferring to trustees £100,000, and in the exercise of their discretion the trustees are now proposing to make a capital payment of £10,000 to Benjamin, the transfer to the trustees of £100,000 on the creation of the settlement would satisfy all these conditions.

Where these conditions are satisfied, it is then necessary to calculate the "initial value" which is a term used by the legislation; and it is also necessary to calculate what may be called the "initial rate", although this is not a term used by the legislation. The initial value is the value of the property comprised in the settlement immediately after it was created (para. 11 (2), (3), (9)).

In the ordinary case of the creation of a settlement by a chargeable transfer of value, and where no other settlement was created at the same time, the initial rate is the rate of tax which is found by using the following formula (para. 7 (2)):

$$\frac{\text{amount of tax which would normally be charged on the initial value} \times 100}{\text{the initial value}}$$

In calculating the amount of tax in the numerator, it is necessary to take into account the chargeable transfers of value made by the settlor *before* the creation of the settlement, but, it seems, *not* the actual amount of tax which was paid on the creation of the settlement. The amount of tax is that which would be payable by a person who has made chargeable transfers of value of an amount equivalent to the amount of the chargeable transfers of value made by the settlor before the creation of the settlement, and who then makes a net transfer of value of an amount equivalent to the initial value. A net transfer is one out of which the tax is paid by the transferor.

Suppose that after 26 March 1974 Adrian created a settlement with no interest in possession, and that the amount transferred to the trustees was £100,000. The initial value would be £100,000. If Adrian had made no previous chargeable transfers of value the amount of tax which would have been charged on a net transfer £100,000 at the time when the settlement was created would be, on the lifetime scale (p. 70, *ante*) £13,103. The initial rate is, therefore:

$$\frac{£13,103}{£100,000} \times 100 = 13.10\%$$

In the Revenue view, it makes no difference to the calculation whether Adrian transferred to the trustees a net sum of £100,000, on which he himself paid the tax; or whether he actually transferred, a larger sum on which the trustees paid the tax and were left with £100,000. This is because the initial value is the value of the fund immediately after the creation of the settlement, when liabilities involved in the creation of its settlement have been taken into account (para. 11 (9)).

A more complicated calculation is required where more than one settlement was created at the same time (para. 7 (2), 11 (6)).

The amount of tax payable on an occasion when a liability arises depends upon whether the amount of the transfer made by the trustees exceeds the initial value.

2 Transfer which does not exceed the initial value

Where the trustees are treated as making a transfer of value and the value treated as being transferred does not exceed the initial value, the normal rate of tax payable is the initial rate (para. 7 (2)). Where there is an actual payment out of the trust, this will often have to be grossed up (*infra*) and in this case the grossed up equivalent is used.

3 Transfer which does exceed the initial value

Where the trustees are treated as making a transfer of value, and the value treated as transferred exceeds the initial value, the initial rate is applied up to the amount of the initial value. The excess beyond the initial value is calculated by ascertaining (para. 7 (3)):

a   the aggregate amount of value, if any, transferred by any chargeable transfer of value which the settlor had actually made before the creation of the settlement. Where these had had to be grossed up, the gross value is taken;

b   the initial value; and

c   the amount of any value treated as having been transferred by the trustees out of the settlement to the extent that they exceed the initial value.

There is then calculated the rate of tax which an individual who had made chargeable transfers of value equivalent to the total of *a*, *b* and *c* would be required to pay if he were now to make a further chargeable transfer of value equivalent to the value of the amount now treated as being transferred.

Suppose that before creating a settlement Barbara made a chargeable transfer of value of £60,000 net (grossed up equivalent £61,818); that she created a settlement of £80,000 on which she paid the tax (grossed up equivalent £107,028); that the trustees of the settlement had paid out £80,000, and that a further gross sum of £10,000 is now being paid out of the settlement. This extra £10,000 is derived from capital growth of the trust investments rather than from the injection of further funds. The initial value of this settlement is £80,000, and the amounts to be brought into the computation are:

a	£61,818
b	£80,000
c	nil
	£141,818

By applying the lifetime rates (p. 70, *ante*) it will be seen that an individual who had made chargeable transfers of value of £141,818, and who was proposing to make a further chargeable transfer of value of £10,000 gross would have a tax liability of £3,000. This is their liability. It is important that this process is followed: it cannot be short-circuited by asking how much tax Barbara would have to pay if she made a gross gift of £10,000. In the first place, she herself is treated as having transferred previously £61,818 + £107,028 = £168,846, so that if she made a gross of £10,000 she would have a tax liability of £3,942. In the second place, she may herself have made further chargeable transfers of value after the creation of the settlement, but before the trustees are treated as making their transfer of value.

4 Related settlements

The calculation of the initial rate, and the rate payable where the initial value is exceeded is different where there is a related settlement. A settlement is related to another if both settlements were created by the same transfer; or by separate transfers made by the same person on the same day (para. 11 (6)).

5 Example

It may assist if a progressive example is given. Charles, who has not made any previous chargeable transfer of value, creates a settlement after 26 March 1974, with a capital of £100,000. There is no interest in possession.

a The initial value is £100,000

b The initial rate is $\dfrac{£9,500}{£100,000} \times 100 = 9.5\%$

Step 1a

The trustees make payment out of the trust to Dennis of £20,000. Dennis pays the tax on it.

The tax payable by Dennis is $9.5\% \times £20,000 = £1,900$
The balance of the initial value is $£100,000 - £20,000 = £80,000$.

315

Step 1b

The facts are the same as in Step 1a, but the trustees pay the tax. The payment of £20,000 is grossed up at 9.5% to £22,099.

> The tax payable by the trustees is £2,089.
> The balance of the initial value is £100,000 − £22,099 = £77,901.

Step 2a

Following the distribution in Step 1b, the trustees make a payment of £80,000 to Edwina. Edwina pays the tax.

The tax payable is

	Gross part of distribution	Rate %	Net	Tax payable on part
a On balance of initial value	£77,901	9.5	£70,501	£7,400
b On remainder of distribution	£2,099	22.5	£1,627	£ 472
	£80,000		£72,128	£7,872

The total of distributions now made is £22,099 (Step 1b) + £80,000 (Step 2) = £102,099, and the excess over the initial value is £2,099.

Step 2b

The facts are the same as in Step 2a, but the trustees pay the tax.

The tax payable is

	Gross part of distribution	Rate %	Net	Tax payable on part
a On balance of initial value	£77,901	9.5	£70,501	£7,400
b On remainder of distribution				
on first £10,000 gross	£10,000	22.5	£7,750	£2,250
on remainder	£2,332	22	£1,749	£583
	£90,233		£80,000	£10,233

The total of distributions now made amounts to £22,099 + £90,233 = £112,332; and the excess over the initial value is £12,332.

Step 3

Following the facts in Step 2b the trustees now make a payment of £10,000 to Fergus, and the trustees pay the tax.

The trustees make the calculation referred to on p. 315, *ante,* when it appears that:

a   the value transferred by chargeable transfers of value before the creation of the settlement is: nil

b   the initial value is: £100,000

c   the amount treated as having been transferred by the trustees out of settlement in excess of the initial value is: £12,332

£112,332

The rate payable, by reference to the lifetime scale is:

Gross distribution	Rate %	Net	Tax payable
£13,333	25	£10,000	£3,333

6   Settlements created before 27 March 1974: generally

Where the settlement was created before 27 March 1974, the position is in general very much more straightforward. The general rule is that the trustees have their own CTT history, and that the position of settlor and beneficiaries is irrelevant (para. 8). The trustees are treated as a separate person, so that, for example, the first £50,000 which the trustees are treated as transferring will be within the £50,000 nil rate band.

In all cases the lifetime scale of rates (set out at p. 70) applies (para. 6 (4)). There is no need for any adjustment to be made if the trust is wound up shortly afterwards, or if the beneficiary dies within a short time of receiving the benefit.

The same principle of cumulation applies as in the case of an individual, but the cumulation begins only with events after 12 March 1975 ((1980) B.T.R. 832).

7   Settlements created before 27 March 1974: exceptional circumstances

The legislation provides that where there has already been a transfer of value in certain circumstances, the rate of tax is to be determined in accordance with the rules governing a settlement created after 26 March 1974 (paras. 7 (1), 11 (2), (3)). The circumstances are that:

a the previous transfer of value satisfies the four conditions set out on p. 312, *ante,* namely:

  i the previous transfer of value was a chargeable transfer of value, or would have been had it not been exempt because of the specified exemptions;

  ii the previous transfer was made at any time after the creation of the settlement. (In the case of a pre-27 March 1974 settlement it cannot have been made on the creation of the settlement);

  iii the transfer was effected previously to the transfer now being considered; and

  iv the previous transfer took into account the value being transferred by the transfer now being considered; and

b the previous transfer was not a transfer treated as having been made

  i on the termination of an interest in possession (para. 11 (2) (c)); or

  ii on death (*ibid*); or

  iii as a result of either of the periodic charges (para. 12 (8); pp. 330, 332, *post*).

The making of a previous capital payment out of the settlement does not satisfy condition *a* iv, because the value taken into account on the previous transfer did not take into account the value being transferred by the transfer under consideration. It seems that the provision will only apply in highly exceptional circumstances. An example would be where a pre-27 March 1974 settlement was created with no interest in possession; an interest in possession was then created (when tax would have been payable under the ordinary pre-27 March 1974 settlement rules); that interest in possession terminated (when tax would have been payable under the rules relating to the termination of an interest in possession); and that a further interest in possession was then created. The creation of the first interest in possession would appear to qualify as the previous transfer for the purpose of the rules, so that the tax payable on the creation of the second interest in possession would be calculated in accordance with the rules for post-26 March 1974 settlements.

The Revenue, however, take the view that the paragraph 7 rules can in no circumstances govern a pre-27 March 1974 settlement in which no interest in possession exists. Accordingly, the taxpayer need not consider the possible application of paragraph 7 unless it is in his interest to do so.

8   Pre-27 March 1974 Settlement: previous distribution payments

The amount of tax payable in respect of a settlement created before 27 March 1974 in which no interest in possession exists is calculated generally having regard to the previous CTT history of the trust as such. If, therefore, a capital payment of £70,000, gross is made to a beneficiary the trustees will deduct from that sum tax of £3,250. If thereafter a capital payment of a further £20,000 gross is made, the tax is calculated by reference to the tax on the "slices" between £70,001 and £90,000, which amounts to £4,000.

For the purpose of determining the CTT history of the trust, it is necessary to take into account all distribution payments made on or after 27 March 1974 (para. 8 (2)). The definition of a distribution payment is considered shortly (*infra*), but it will be seen that not all distribution payments are capital distributions. Whether or not a distribution payment is also a capital distribution, it will have to be taken into account when the tax payable on a subsequent event is calculated.

F   CAPITAL DISTRIBUTIONS

1   Introduction

Now that the normal rates of tax have been described, it is possible to consider each of the events which can give rise to a charge to capital transfer tax where there is no interest in possession. These have been summarized earlier (p. 310, *ante*) and it is proposed to consider in respect of each of these events:

a   the circumstances in which the charge applies;

b   specific exceptions to the charge;

c   the amount of the value treated as being transferred;

d   the rate of tax payable.

2   Capital distributions and distribution payments

The first event which gives rise to the charge to tax is the making of a capital distribution. The legislation uses two similar expressions, namely capital distribution, and distribution payment. A capital distribution is an event which gives rise to the payment of tax, and a distribution payment is an event which forms part of the settlement's cumulation. The expressions are now defined:

a   Distribution payment   A distribution payment is any payment of money or transfer of assets made by the trustees of a trust, except (para. 11 (7)):

    i a payment of money or transfer of assets where the money paid or asset transferred is treated in the hands of the recipient as income for the purposes of United Kingdom income tax;

    ii a payment of money or transfer of assets which is made to a person who is not resident in the United Kingdom where the money paid or asset transferred would. be treated as income in the hands of the recipient if he were resident in the United Kingdom;

    iii a payment of money, or transfer of assets, which is made in respect of costs or expenses; and

    iv a payment of money or transfer of assets which is made in the ordinary course of the re-investment of the trust fund.

The first three of these categories is covered by para. 11 (7), and the fourth is the product of Revenue interpretation, as following from iii.

b Capital distribution There is an actual capital distribution where a distribution payment is made out of property comprised in a settlement at a time when no interest in possession subsists in the property, or in the part of the property out of which the payment is made (para. 6 (1)). The most obvious example is where the trustees of a discretionary trust make a capital payment to a beneficiary.

3 The charge to tax

Subject to the exceptions noted below, capital transfer tax is payable on every capital distribution (para. 6 (4)).

4 The exceptions

a Distribution payment to settlor A distribution payment which is made to the settlor is not a capital distribution, and so does not give rise to a charge to capital transfer tax, if the settlor is domiciled in some part of the United Kingdom at the time when the payment is made (para. 6 (6); FA 1976, Sch. 14, para. 13 (c)).

b Distribution payment to settlor's spouse A similar exception applies in the case of a distribution payment to the settlor's spouse, provided the spouse satisfies the condition as to domicile (*ibid*).

c Distribution payment to settlor's widow Another similar exception applies in the case of a distribution payment made to the settlor's widow or widower, provided the settlor himself died not earlier than two years before the distribution payment was made (FA 1976, s. 110 (3)) or where the distribution payment was made before 1 April 1977.

These exceptions appear to apply where the payment is actually made to the settlor or his spouse, even if they are not within the class of discretionary beneficiaries.

d   Distribution payment to charity   Where a payment is made to a charity, that payment is not a capital distribution (Sch. 6, para. 10 (2)). Accordingly, no tax will be payable, irrespective of the amount of the distribution. In the case of a distribution payment made to a charity after 6 April 1976, the payment will not be a distribution payment either (FA 1976, s. 111 (1)).

e   Political parties   Where a payment is made after 6 April 1976, that payment is not a distribution if the political party satisfies certain conditions (FA 1975, Sch. 6, para. 11) and the gift satisfies certain conditions (p. 108, *ante*; FA 1976, 111 (2)).

f   Accumulation and maintenance settlements   The position where a payment is made out of an accumulation and maintenance settlement is described later (p. 348, *post*).

g   Protective trusts   A distribution made out of settled property for the benefit of the principal beneficiary is not a capital distribution (para. 18 (2) (b); p. 344, *post*).

h   Exempt quality objects   It has been seen (p. 98, *ante*) that subject to certain conditions, works of art of national, scientific, historic or artistic interest; buildings of historic or architectural interest, and their associated objects; and land of outstanding scenic or historic or scientific interest are conditionally exempt from capital transfer tax. Where such objects are comprised in a settlement in which there is no interest in possession, a similar exemption is available if, at the time when the distribution of those objects is made, they have been comprised in the settlement for the previous six years (FA 1976, s. 81 (1)).

When such objects are taken out of settlement there is neither a capital distribution nor a distribution payment. Liability to tax will arise in the same circumstances as if an individual made a conditionally exempt transfer of the objects, namely in certain circumstances on sale, or upon a material breach of the undertakings. The tax is calculated by reference to the trust's cumulative history to the date upon which the tax becomes due (FA 1976, s. 81 (4)).

5   The amount of the value transferred

a   Generally   The value which is treated as being transferred by a capital distribution is the grossed up equivalent of the amount actually paid to the beneficiary (para. 6 (4) (a)). In the usual case, therefore, the trustees will wish to set aside the maximum sum which is to be taken from the trust fund; pay the tax out of it; and pay the balance to the beneficiary. If, however, they do not do so, they will be liable to pay capital transfer tax on the grossed up equivalent of the amount paid.

b   Recipient paying tax   Where the recipient pays the tax, the trustees are not obliged to gross up (para. 6 (5)). The legislation refers to the tax being "payable" by the beneficiary, but this probably means "paid" by the beneficiary.

c   Where previous deemed capital distributions   A capital distribution is deemed to be made where

  i an interest in possession is created where none subsisted immediately before (para. 6 (2); p. 325, *post*);

 ii there is a depreciatory transaction affecting property in which no interest in possession subsists (para. 6 (3); p. 328, *post*);

iii the conditions for an "accumulation or maintenance" settlement become satisfied where they were not satisfied immediately before (para. 15 (3); p. 329, *post*);

 iv where part of the value transferred by a close company is apportioned to the trustees of a settlement in which no interest in possession subsists (para. 24; p. 330, *post*).

Where there has been one or more of these deemed capital distributions, the amount of the actual capital distribution is reduced by the amount of the deemed capital distributions valued at the time when they were deemed to have been made (para. 11 (8)). Where the trustees are to pay the tax on the actual capital distribution, so that it is necessary to gross up, the grossing up is of the reduced amount.

d   Where previous periodic charge   It has just been seen that where there is a previous deemed capital distribution, the amount of the *value* treated as being transferred by the subsequent actual capital distribution is reduced. Where there has been a previous charge to capital transfer tax under the provisions relating to the periodic charge (p. 332, *post*) the amount of the subsequent capital distribution is not reduced, but there is a reduction in the *rate* of tax payable. This is dealt with later (p. 333, *post*).

6   The rate of tax

a   Generally   In general, the rate of tax payable where there is an actual capital distribution is the normal rate (p. 312, *ante*). It is calculated by reference to the lifetime scale of rates (para. 6 (4)).

b   Where previous periodic charge   It will be seen that, in general, a capital distribution is treated as being made out of property comprised in a settlement in which there is no interest in possession on each tenth anniversary of the creation of the settlement (p. 330, *post*). Generally, the tax is at 30% of the normal rate, but this is subject to adjustment where an interest in possession has subsisted for some part of the period of ten years ending on the tenth anniversary date, and where further property has been added to the settlement.

Where an actual capital distribution is made within 20 years following the anniversary date for the periodic charge, there is a reduction in the rate of tax payable in respect of the capital distribution. In order to calculate this, it is necessary to ascertain:

   i the amount of tax which was paid in respect of the periodic charge;

   ii the effective rate at which tax was paid on the occasion of the periodic charge;

   iii the amount of tax which would be payable in respect of the capital distribution if there were no reduction in rate;

   iv the effective rate at which tax would be payable in respect of the capital distribution if there were no reduction.

The actual rate payable in respect of the capital distribution is the rate at iv less the rate at ii. This, however, is subject to the limitation that the amount by which the tax at iii is reduced by the tax at i cannot exceed the amount of tax at i (para. 13 (1)).

c   Where previous distribution payments   In some cases, a distribution payment which is made out of settled property in which there is no interest in possession is not treated as a capital distribution. These cases are where the exemptions, mentioned at the pages stated, apply to distribution payments to:

   i the settlor (p. 320, *ante*);

   ii the settlor's spouse (p. 320, *ante*);

   iii the settlor's widow (p. 320, *ante*);

   iv the principal beneficiary under a protective trust (p. 344, *post*);

   v a person entitled under an accumulation and maintenance settlement (p. 348, *post*).

Although these distribution payments do not themselves give rise to a charge to tax, they do have to be taken into account in calculating the tax payable upon a subsequent capital distribution (para. 8 (2) (a)).

Suppose, therefore, that the trustees of a pre-27 March 1974 settlement make a distribution payment of £100,000 to the settlor and a distribution payment of £50,000 to beneficiary A, no tax is payable on the first distribution payment. The tax payable on the second distribution payment is calculated upon the basis that tax was payable on the first distribution, so the actual tax payable, if it is paid by the beneficiary, is that applicable to the slices between £100,000 and £150,000, namely £13,250.

Where a capital distribution is made and on the same day a distribution payment which is not also a capital distribution is made out of the same settlement, the capital distribution is treated as being made before the distribution payment which is not a capital distribution (FA 1975, Sch. 5, para. 10A, added by FA 1976, Sch. 14, para. 14).

d   Capital distribution made before 1 April 1983   Provided that certain conditions are satisfied, the rate at which tax is charged on a capital distribution is lower than the normal rate where the capital distribution is made after 31 March 1979 and before 1 April 1983 (FA 1981, s. 102). These conditions are:

  i the settlement must have been made before 27 March 1974;

 ii the capital distribution must not be made out of property added to the settlement after 26 March 1974;

iii the payment must be for the benefit of an individual person, and not for the benefit of a company or another settlement;

iv the recipient must be domiciled in some part of the United Kingdom at the time when the capital distribution is made (para. 14 (1), (2), (5) (c); FA 1976, Sch. 14, para. 13 (d)).

Where these conditions are satisfied, the rate payable on the capital distribution is 20% of the normal rate.

e   Capital distribution after termination of interest of settlor or settlor's spouse   Special rules apply where a capital distribution is made out of property comprised in a settlement and the following conditions are satisfied:

  i the settlement was made after 26 March 1974;

 ii immediately after the making of the settlement, either the settlor or his spouse was entitled to an interest in possession (para. 10 (a));

iii the settlor or his spouse was entitled either to the same or to another interest in possession in the property before the capital distribution was made (*ibid*);

324

iv the making of the settlement was either not a transfer of value, or was a totally or partially exempt transfer (para. 10 (b)).

Where a settlement is made, and the settlor is entitled to the first interest in possession, the settlor will be treated as remaining beneficially entitled to the property itself (para. 3 (1)), so that there will be no transfer of value (s. 20 (2)).

Where these conditions are satisfied, the tax payable on the capital distribution is calculated as if the property was comprised in a separate settlement, and as if that settlement was created by whichever of the settlor or his spouse had the interest in possession before the capital distribution was made. The separate settlement is treated as being made when that interest in possession came to an end (para. 10).

Further rules deal with the position where the conditions are satisfied with regard to part only of the property.

G   DEEMED CAPITAL DISTRIBUTION: I—CREATION OF AN INTEREST IN POSSESSION

1   Creation of an interest in possession

a   Generally   A capital distribution is treated as being made when a person becomes entitled to an interest in possession in property comprised in a settlement at a time when there was no interest in possession in that property immediately beforehand (para. 6 (2)). If an interest in possession is created in part only of the property comprised in a settlement, the capital distribution is treated as having been made only of that part. The most common example of the operation of this provision is where trustees hold property upon discretionary trusts, and appoint it so that they hold it upon trust to pay the income to William for life, and upon his death to pay the capital to Mary.

The reason for this provision is that where a person is entitled to an interest in possession in settled property, the capital in that property can be transferred to him without capital transfer tax being payable. This provision prevents trustees evading the charge to tax completely by first converting a discretionary trust into one of the William and Mary type just mentioned, and then paying out all the capital to William.

b   Exemption 1: settlor, settlor's spouse, or settlor's widow taking interest in possession   Where an interest in possession is created in favour of the settlor, a distribution payment is treated as being made to the settlor, but not a capital distribution (para. 6A, added by FA

1976, Sch. 14, para. 12). Accordingly, no tax will be payable at the time when the interest in possession is created, but it will affect the amount of tax payable on a subsequent occasion.

The provision also applies where the settlor's spouse takes an interest in possession in his lifetime, or where the settlor's widow takes an interest in possession within two years after his death.

c Exception 2: following death Some wills provide that a person will only become entitled to a benefit if he survives the deceased, or some other person, for a specified period, such as 28 days or 3 months. Where the will is worded in this way, there may be no interest in possession during that specified period, so that even if it is only a twenty eight day period, at the end of that time an interest in possession would arise, and on general principles a charge to tax would arise under the provision just considered.

However, where the survivorship period is for not more than six months, if the beneficiary survives for the specified period and thereby becomes entitled to an interest in possession, he will be treated as if he had been entitled to it from the death of the deceased (para. 22A, added by FA 1976, s. 105 (1)). In this case also, therefore, there will be neither a deemed capital distribution nor a deemed distribution payment at the end of the survirorship period. The position will be the same if the beneficiary does not live for the whole of the survivorship period, so that as a result of the death of that beneficiary another beneficiary becomes entitled to an interest in possession.

d Exception 3: increase in share A further specific provision applies where there is a "class gift". A class gift is a gift to a group of persons who are not individually named, but are identified by reference to their membership of a class, such as the children of Alice, the nephews of Bernice or the employees of Clarice. The provision has the effect that where a beneficiary has an interest in possession in part of the property comprised in the settlement by virtue of his membership of a class, then there is no deemed capital distribution where he acquired an interest in possession in another part of the property as a result of the death under full age of another member of the class (para. 6 (8)). Suppose that a fund is held in trust for the children of Donald, on the basis that they will become entitled to an interest in possession upon reaching the age of 21. Suppose also that Donald has three children, Edward, aged 27, Ernest, aged 17, and Ethel, aged 13. Edward has an interest in possession in one third of the fund. If Ethel dies before reaching the age of 21, the fund would be equally divisible between Edward and Ernest, so that Edward would acquire an interests in possession in one half of Ethel's share. In this case, the specific exemption applies, and there is no charge to tax as a result of the coming into existence of an interest in possession in respect of part of Ethel's share.

If, however, Ethel did not die until the age of 20, the provision would not operate, because it only applies where the member of the class dies under the age of 18.

e   Exception 4: accumulation and maintenance settlements   If the conditions relating to accumulation and maintenance settlements are satisfied (p. 348, *post*) there is no deemed capital distribution when the beneficiary becomes entitled to an interest in possession in the settled property or part of it (para. 15 (2) (a)).

2   *The amount of the value treated as being transferred*

Where an interest in possession arises in the whole of the settled property, the capital distribution is treated as being made of the whole value of the fund (para. 6 (2)). Where it arises in only part of the settled property, the capital distribution is treated as being made only of the part (*ibid*).

Where the interest in possession was created after 28 July 1976 there is grossing up, unless the tax is payable out of the property in which the interest in possession is created (para. 6 (5), as amended by FA 1976, Sch. 14, para. 11).

3   *The rate of tax*

a   Generally   The position as to the rate of tax in the usual circumstances, and also where there has been a previous periodic charge, are the same as in the case of an actual capital distribution (p. 322, *ante*).

b   Deemed capital distribution before 1 April 1983   The position where the deemed capital distribution is made before 1 April 1983 is also the same as in the case of an actual capital distribution. The condition as to domicile must be satisfied by the person who becomes entitled to the interest in possession (para. 14 (5) (a); FA 1976, Sch. 14, para. 13 (d)).

H   DEEMED CAPITAL DISTRIBUTION: II—APPOINTMENT TO NON-CLOSE COMPANY

1   *Scope of provision*

Although this is not entirely free from doubt, the Revenue view is that paragraph 6 (2), which has just been considered, is wide enough to include the case of the absolute appointment of settled property to an individual. If this is correct, there will also be a deemed capital distribution on the creation of an interest in possession if there is an absolute appointment in favour of a close company (para. 24 (5)). A separate provision deals with the position where there is an absolute appointment in favour of a non-close company, or any other entity, such that an individual does not as a result of that appointment become entitled to the settled property itself, or to an interest in possession in the settled property (para. 6 (2A); FA 1978, s. 70). In this case there is a deemed capital distribution.

2 The amount of the value treated as being transferred

The distribution is treated as being equivalent to the value of the property which is subject to the appointment (para. 6 (2A)). The value is grossed up unless the tax is paid out of the appointed property (para. 6 (5); FA 1978, s. 70 (1), (6)).

3 The rate of tax

The rate of tax payable is the same as in the case of an actual capital distribution (p. 322, *ante*). Transitional relief is available where the appointment is made before 1 April 1983. For that relief, there is no requirement as to domicile.

I DEEMED CAPITAL DISTRIBUTION: III—DEPRECIATORY TRANSACTIONS

1 Depreciatory transactions

The concept of a depreciatory transaction has been discussed in relation to settlements where there is an interest in possession (p. 300, *ante*). A corresponding provision has the effect that a capital distribution is deemed to be made where the trustees of a settlement enter into a depreciatory transaction at a time when no interest in possession subsists (para. 6 (3)). For this provision to apply, the transaction must be with

a any beneficiary under the settlement;

b any person for whose benefit any of the settled property may be applied; or

c any person who is connected with a person coming within *a* or *b*.

2 The amount of the value treated as being transferred

The amount which is treated as being transferred is the amount by which the value of the settled property is reduced by the transaction

328

(para. 6 (3)). There is no need to gross up (para. 6 (5); FA 1976 Sch. 14, para. 11).

3   The rate of tax

The position both with regard to the rate of tax generally, and also where the deemed capital distribution is made before 1 April 1983, is the same as for an actual capital distribution (p. 322, *ante*). In the latter case, the condition as to domicile must be satisfied by the person for whose benefit the transaction is effected (paras. 6 (3), 11 (8), 14 (5) (c)).

J   DEEMED CAPITAL DISTRIBUTION: IV—CONVERSION INTO ACCUMULATION AND MAINTENANCE SETTLEMENT

1   The charge to tax

Certain settlements under which income is to be applied for the maintenance education or benefit of a beneficiary, or is to be accumulated, are given privileged treatment for capital transfer tax purposes (p. 348, *post*). In order to prevent capital transfer tax being avoided by converting an ordinary settlement in which there is no interest in possession into one which satisfies these conditions, it is provided that if there is no interest in possession in a settlement which does not satisfy the conditions, and the settlement is converted into one which then does satisfy the conditions, a capital distribution is deemed to be made at the time when the conditions first become satisfied (para. 15 (3)).

2   The amount of the value treated as being transferred

The amount of the value which is treated as being transferred upon the conversion of a settlement into one which satisfies the conditions relating to accumulation and maintenance settlements is an amount equal to the value of the property in respect of which the conditions are satisfied (para. 15 (3)).

Where the tax is payable out of the property in respect of which the conditions become satisfied and the conditions become satisfied after 28 July 1976 there is no grossing up (para. 6 (5), as amended by FA 1976, Sch. 14, para. 11). In other cases it is necessary to gross up (para. 6 (4) (a)).

3   The rate of tax

The position both with regard to the rate of tax generally and also where the conversion takes place before 1 April 1983 is the same as for an actual distribution (p. 322, *ante*). Where the reduced rates are claimed as a result of conversion before 1 April 1983, the condition as to domicile must be satisfied by each of the beneficiaries (para. 14 (5) (b); FA 1976, Sch. 14 para. 13 (d)).

K DEEMED CAPITAL DISTRIBUTION: V—TRANS-ACTIONS AFFECTING CLOSE COMPANIES

1 The charge to tax

It has been shown that where a close company makes a transfer of value, and part of the value is apportioned to the trustees of a settlement where there is an interest in possession, a liability to capital transfer tax arises (p. 301, *ante*). A corresponding provision applies where there is no interest in possession, under which a capital distribution is deemed to be made at the time when the company effects a transfer of value (para. 24 (2) (b)).

2 The amount of the value treated as being transferred

The deemed capital distribution is of an amount equal to the value apportioned to the trustees, less the amount, if any, by which the value of the settled property is increased by virtue of the transfer of value made by the company (para. 24 (2), (b), (3)). However, in considering any increase in the value of the settled property, there is to be excluded any increase in the value of any shares or other rights in the company.

There is no need to gross up (para. 6 (5); FA 1976, Sch. 14, para. 11).

3 The rate of tax

The rate of tax is the same as in the case of an actual capital distribution (p. 322, *ante*). Where the company effects its transfer of value before 1 April 1983, the reduced rates of tax apply if the condition as to domicile is satisfied by the person for whose benefit the transaction was entered into (para. 14 (5) (c); FA 1976, Sch. 14, para. 13 (d)).

L THE 10 YEAR PERIODIC CHARGE

1 The charge to tax

The general rule is that every 10 years there is a charge in respect of every settlement in which there is no interest in possession. The basic rule is that the 10 year period is reckoned from the date on which the settlement was made (paras. 11 (2), 12 (6)). Where, however, the settlement was created before 27 March 1974, and further property was added to the settlement after its creation but before 27 March 1974, it seems that a separate calculation has to be made from the date on which the further property was added (para. 11 (2) (a)). The position where further property is added to the settlement after 26 March 1974 is described later (p. 333, *post*).

The end of each period of 10 years which is on or after 1 April 1983 is known as the relevant anniversary (para. 12 (6); FA 1981, s. 102).

A capital distribution is deemed to be made on every relevant anniversary at which no interest in possession subsists in the property comprised in the settlement (para. 12 (1)).

2 *The amount of the deemed capital distribution*

Where there is no interest in possession in any part of the property comprised in the settlement, the capital distribution is deemed to be made of an amount equivalent to the whole value of the settled property at the date of the relevant anniversary (para. 12 (1)). If there is an interest in possession in part only of the property, the capital distribution is deemed to be made of an amount equal to the value of the remainder.

The value of the property is not grossed up (para. 6 (5)).

3 *Non-cumulation*

The capital distribution which is deemed to be made by virtue of the ten year periodic charge is not taken into account in the cumulative history of the settlement (para. 12 (8)).

4 *Exempt quality objects*

Where objects in respect of which a conditionally exempt distribution could have been made (p. 321, *ante*) are comprised in the settlement, there are provisions for the periodic charge to be deferred (FA 1976, s. 82).

5 *The rate*

a Generally Where a capital distribution is deemed to be made, the rate of tax is normally 30% of the rate at which tax would have been payable on an actual capital distribution of that amount if made at the date of the relevant anniversary (para. 12 (1)).

b Transitional relief Where the settlement was created before 27 March 1974, the transitional relief noted previously (p. 324, *ante*) is not applicable because no date falling before 1 April 1983 can be a relevant anniversary (para. 12 (6); FA 1981, s. 102).

331

c   Reduction in rate   The normal rate of 30% of the rate applicable to an actual capital distribution is reduced in respect of any
property in either or both of the following circumstances:

  i property was added to the settlement after the end of the first of
     the 10 years ending with the relevant anniversary; and
  ii an interest in possession subsisted in the property throughout at
     least one of these 10 years.

In respect of the property coming within either of these categories,
the rate is reduced by one tenth of that which would otherwise be
payable for each year in the 10 year period throughout which either
the property comprised in the settlement did not include the property added by the settlor; or for which an interest in possession subsisted in that property (para. 12 (4)).

6   Tax credit for annual charge

It will be seen (*infra*) that in some cases there is an annual periodic
charge in addition to the 10 year periodic charge. The amount of tax
paid by virtue of this annual charge can be claimed as a credit
against the tax payable on the next actual or deemed capital
distribution made out of the property (except a capital distribution
which is deemed to be made by virtue of a subsequent annual charge)
(para. 12 (3), as amended by FA 1976, Sch. 14, para. 8 (1)).

Accordingly, if the next deemed capital distribution is under the
10 year periodic charge, the tax paid on the annual charge can be
offset against that payable on the 10 year charge.

M   THE ANNUAL PERIODIC CHARGE

1   When it applies

In addition to the 10 year periodic charge just described, in certain
circumstances a capital distribution is treated as being made at the
end of each of the first nine years in the period of 10 years calculated
from the relevant anniversary (*supra*). The conditions are that at the
end of each of those nine years:

  a   there is no interest in possession (para. 12 (3)); and
  b   the general administration of the trust is ordinarily carried on
      outside the United Kingdom or a majority of the trustees is
      resident outside the United Kingdom (para. 12 (5)).

2   The first anniversary date

Although obscurely stated, the first annual periodic charge will
apply at the later of

> *a*   the anniversary falling 10 years before the date at which the first 10 year periodic charge will apply, and
>
> *b*   the anniversary falling within 1976 (para. 12 (2)).

3   *The amount of the deemed capital distribution*

The amount which is treated as being distributed under the annual periodic charge is equivalent in value to the settled property comprised in the settlement, or, as the case may be, the value of that part of the property in which no interest in possession subsists (para. 12 (2)).

The amount is not grossed up.

4   *The rate*

The rate of tax is 3% of the rate at which tax would be charged on an actual capital distribution of the amount of the deemed capital distribution. The provisions under which a reduced rate applies in the case of an actual or deemed capital distribution made before 1 April 1983 does not apply to the annual charge (para. 14 (4)).

5   *Credit*

It has been noted above that where the annual periodic charge is paid, the amount paid is available as a credit against the tax payable on the next actual or deemed capital distribution. If the tax then payable is less than the amount paid under the periodic charge, the balance of the tax paid can be carried forward (FA 1980, s. 91).

6   *Position of settlor*

In general, a settlor of settled property where the trustees are resident abroad is liable to pay the tax due in respect of that property (FA 1975, s. 25 (3) (*d*)). This does not apply in relation to a settlement made before 11 December 1974 if the trustees were resident in the United Kingdom when the settlement was made and, in the case of distribution after 10 December 1974, if the trustees had not been resident between that date and the date of the distribution.

Where a settlor is liable, he is given a right to recover from the trustees the amount of tax which he pays. It is the Revenue view that if the settlor fails to exercise his right to recover, he will thereby make a transfer of value unless he can show that his omission was not deliberate (s. 20 (7)).

N   ADDITIONAL PROPERTY ADDED TO SETTLEMENT

1   *Treatment as separate settlement*

Where property is added to a settlement after 26 March 1974, that addition is treated as the creation of a separate settlement, and that property is treated as being comprised in that separate settlement (para. 9 (1)). This is so whether the original settlement itself was created before or after 26 March 1974.

2 Identification of property

Rules are prescribed to identify that property which is treated as being comprised in the original settlement and that property which is treated as being comprised in the separate settlement.

a Post-26 March 1974 settlement Where the original settlement was created after 26 March 1974, and there has been only one addition of property, a capital distribution is treated so far as possible as being made out of the original settlement, and only the excess as coming from the additional property (para. 9 (5) (a)). Where there has been more than one tranche of additional property, when the capital distribution is treated as being made first out of the original settlement, then out of the first additional property, and only thereafter out of the further additional property.

b Pre-27 March 1974 settlement Similar provisions determine the identity of property which is the subject of a capital distribution made out of a pre-27 March 1974 settlement and subsequent additions to it, but when the property comprised in the original settlement has been exhausted, the *rates* of tax applicable to a post-26 March 1974 settlement apply.

O RELATIONSHIP BETWEEN SETTLEMENTS

Where, by the same disposition, property ceases to be comprised in one settlement and becomes comprised in another settlement, the property shall be treated as remaining comprised in the first settlement (para. 11 (4)). The legislation itself is expressed in terms to cover events whenever they occurred, but the Revenue practice is to treat the provision as applying only to events on or after 27 March 1974 (Law Society's Gazette, 7 January 1976).

As a result of the provision, if property is held on discretionary trusts, and part or the whole of it is appointed on separate discretionary trusts, that appointment will not itself give rise to any liability. If, however, a capital distribution is made out of the separate settlement, the amount of tax payable will be exactly the same as if the distribution had been made at that time out of the original settlement. It follows that the trustees of the separate settlement will only be able to determine the liability on their fund in consultation with the trustees of the original settlement.

The provisions can have serious consequences where an interest in possession has come into existence in respect of part of the original fund. Suppose, for example, that in 1975 trustees held a fund of £200,000 upon discretionary trusts, and that in that year they appointed £100,000 to be held upon trust for Raymond for life, with a power to advance capital to him. Separate trustees might have been appointed of that fund. If in 1976 those separate trustees decide to bring the trusts of that fund to an end, and to transfer the assets to Raymond there will be no capital transfer tax liability as a result (para. 4 (3)), although there would have been on the original appointment. However, the separate fund will have been treated as subject to the original settlement, and the payment to Raymond will be a distribution payment (para. 11 (7)). If thereafter the original trustees make a capital distribution of £20,000 to a discretionary beneficiary, the tax payable will be calculated as if they themsleves had made a previous capital distribution of £100,000 when the original appointment was made (para. 8 (2) (a), 11 (8); p. 319, *ante*) although not, on these facts, when the payment was made to Raymond (para. 11 (8)).

It follows that very great care indeed is required whenever an original fund has been sub-divided, or a sub-trust has been created.

P SUMMARY WHERE NO INTEREST IN POSSESSION

The table on pages 336 and 337, which summarizes the position where there is no interest in possession, might be found helpful.

Q VALUATION RELIEFS

1 *Agricultural property*

a General Where the settled property includes agricultural land, agricultural valuation relief, or business assets, relief may be available. The general conditions which have to be satisfied in order to obtain these reliefs have been considered earlier (pp. 91 to 95, *ante*). Where, however, the property is settled property, the circumstances require close analysis.

b Concepts It will be convenient first to consider the concepts, often different, used for the purposes of the two reliefs.

  i *Transferor* Where there is an interest in possession the transferor is the beneficiary who has the interest in possession (FA 1975, Sch. 5, para. 4 (2); s. 51 (2)). If there is no interest in possession the transferor are the trustees (FA 1976, Sch. 10, para. 1; FA 1981, Sch. 14, para. 1 (1)).

VALUES TRANSFERRED AND RATES OF TAX PAYABLE

| Circumstance | Value Transferred | | | Rate | | Does pre-1983 concession apply | Any credit for amount of tax previously paid |
	Amount	Whether grossing up	Exceptions	Generally	Previous periodic charge		
1 Capital Distribution	Actual	Yes	i No GU where recipient pays (para. 6 (5)) ii Reduce where previous deemed capital distribution	Normal	Reduction in rate where CD within 20 years following PC (para. 13 (1))	Yes	—
2 Creation of IIP	Actual	Yes	Where tax paid out of property in respect of which IIP created	Normal	Reduction as above	Yes	—
3 Appointment to non-close company	Actual	Yes	Where tax paid out of property appointed	Normal	As above	Yes	—
4 Depreciatory Transaction	Amount by which value of settled property is reduced by transaction	No	—	Normal	As above	Yes	—

Circumstance	VALUE TRANSFERRED			RATE			
	Amount	Whether grossing up	Exceptions	Generally	Previous periodic charge	Does pre-1983 concession apply	Any credit for amount of tax previously paid
5 Conversion to Accumulation and Maintenance Settlement	Value of settled property in respect of which conditions satisfied	Yes	Where tax paid out of property in respect of which the conditions become satisfied	Normal	As above	Yes	—
6 Close Companies	The amount apportioned to trustees, less increase in value of settled property, other than increase in value of shares etc. in company	No	—	Normal	As above	Yes	—
7 Periodic Charge	Value of settled property in which no IIP	No	—	1 30% of normal 2 Reduction by 1/10th where property added to settlement; and where IIP existed	N/A	Yes	Credit for amount of tax paid under annual periodic charge
8 Annual Periodic Charge	As above	No	—	3% of normal	N/A	No	—

337

ii *Ownership* In two instances, the reliefs are available only where the property has been "owned" for a minimum period (FA 1976, Sch. 10, para. 4 (1) (a); FA 1981, Sch. 14, para. 3 (b)).

Capital transfer tax generally does not use the concept of "ownership," but that of property to which a person is beneficiary entitled, and what is treated as comprising a person's estate (FA 1975, s. 23; Sch. 5, para. 3 (1)). As a matter of general law, these concepts are different. Ownership of property (as contrasted with having an interest in property) may well denote holding the legal title, irrespective of where the equitable ownership lies. In general, therefore, no beneficiary will own settled property. However, if the beneficiary is a tenant for life for the purposes of the Settled Land Act, 1925, he will usually have the legal estate vested in him, and so he may be treated as the owner.

The Revenue practice, however, is to treat a beneficiary who has an interest in possession as being the "owner" for the purpose of the 1976 Act provision, and presumably it will also do so for the purpose of the 1981 Act provision (see further House of Commons Official Report, Standing Committee E, 24 June 1976, col. 1274).

iii *Business* A farming business comprises the land, the live and deadstock employed on it, and the total enterprise. Land in isolation will not be a business or part of a business, unless the transfer is of land of such extent that the transfer of the land necessarily causes a transfer of part of the business itself (*McGregor* v. *Adcock*, [1977] 3 All E.R. 65).

iv *Property, and interest in property* In the context of the agricultural relief, "property" is used both to indicate the physical land (FA 1981, Sch. 14, para. 2 (1) (*a*)) and, presumably, the freehold estate in the land (para. 3 (*b*)).

Where it is necessary to satisfy a condition depending on having an interest in property, it is necessary to consider the incidents both of the interest as an interest in real property, and the interest as an equitable interest.

c *The reliefs* There are four possible reliefs to be considered:

i 50% agricultural relief;

ii 20% agricultural relief;

iii 50% business asset relief; and

iv 30% business asset relief.

The general conditions for these reliefs have been considered earlier (p. 91, *ante*).

d Inter-relation of agricultural property and business asset reliefs
Where the conditions for agricultural property relief are satisfied, the relief does not have to be claimed, but it is granted automatically, and in priority to business asset relief (FA 1976, Sch. 10, para. 10; FA 1981, s. 96 (3) (d)). To the extent that agricultural property relief at either the 50% or 20% rates is available, business asset relief cannot be claimed. It will be seen in the context of business asset relief, however, that part of the value transferred by a transfer of value can attract agricultural property relief, and another part of the value transferred by the same transfer can attract business asset relief.

e 50% agricultural property relief

i *Essential requirements* The essential requirements for this relief are:

(*a*) the property must have been occupied by the transferor throughout the period of two years ending with the date of the transfer (FA 1981, Sch. 14, para. 3 (a)); and

(*b*) the interest of the transferor in the property must have carried the right to vacant possession (or the right to obtain vacant possession within twelve months) (para. 2 (2) (a)).

ii *Interest in possession* In principle, this relief is available where the agricultural property is settled property, and the life tenant is in occupation. The "transferor" is the life tenant (see p. 335, *ante*) and he must have been in occupation for the two year period. In strict law, the second condition involves considerable difficulty. Vacant possession is an incident of the legal estate, and denotes, *inter alia,* the right to possession which is good against third parties. This is contrasted with occupation, which is usually a more personal and less substantial right. Where the life tenant is in occupation of the settled property in which his beneficial interest subsists, he may occupy under a formal or informal licence from the trustees, or under a lease or tenancy which the trustees have granted to him. In the former case, the interest of the life tenant carries a right to occupation, but it is only in the latter case that his interest carried the right to vacant possession.

However, it seems that the Revenue will regard this condition as satisfied if it would be satisfied by treating the trustees and the life tenant for this purpose as an amalgam. Accordingly, if, apart from any right granted to the beneficiary, it could be said that the trustees by virtue of their legal estate have the right to vacant possession, then the transferor will be treated as satisfying the condition.

Further, it seems that the Revenue will leave out of account the arrangements between the trustees and the life tenant. Thus, if the life tenant has a lease or tenancy, the condition will still be satisfied, but the property will be brought into account at its vacant possession, and not tenanted, value, unless transitional relief is available (p. 92, *ante*).

iii *No interest in possession* If there is no interest possession, the relief will be available if both conditions are satisfied by the trustees.

f 20% agricultural property relief

i *Essential requirements* The essential requirements for this relief are:

(a) the property must have been owned by the transferor throughout the period of seven years ending with the date of the transfer (FA 1981, Sch. 14, para. 3 (b));

(b) the property must have been occupied throughout that period for the purposes of agriculture, whether by the transferor or by anyone else (*ibid*); and

(c) the conditions for the 50% relief must not be satisfied (para. 2 (2)).

ii *Interest in possession* In general, a life tenant will never "own" the property (see, p. 338, *ante*) so he will be incapable of satisfying the first condition. However, the Revenue will treat the condition as satisfied if he has had an interest in possession for seven years, but not any other type of beneficial interest. Suppose, for example, that a person is at first a beneficiary under an accumulation and maintenance settlement (p. 348, *post*), and later he takes an interest in possession in the settled property. The period during which he was interested under the accumulation and maintenance settlement cannot be taken into account.

Where there are successive interests in possession, periods of time for which other beneficiaries have had their interests also cannot be taken into account. Suppose that trustees hold agricultural property upon trust for Alan for life, with remainder to Brian for life, with remainder to Charles. Suppose also that Alan had his interest for thirty years, but that Brian's interest terminates four years after he took his interest. The condition will not be satisfied.

iii *No interest to possession* Where there is no interest in possession, the condition as to ownership must have been satisfied by the trustees. As "ownership" probably involves the holding of the legal title (see p. 338, *ante*), it seems that trustees will be able to satisfy this condition if the property has been in trust for the seven year period, even if during part of that period there was an interest in possession in it.

g 50% business asset relief

i *Essential requirements* The essential requirements for 50% business asset relief are:

(*a*) the property must consist of a business or an interest in a business (FA 1976, Sch. 10, para. 3 (1) (a)); and

(*b*) the property must have been owned by the transferor throughout the two years immediately preceding the transfer (para. 4 (1) (a)).

ii *Circumstances in which available* The relief applies to businesses in general, and is in no way confined to agricultural property. Indeed, where the conditions for both agricultural property relief and business asset relief are satisfied, the former relief is given (FA 1976, Sch. 10, para. 10). However, in certain circumstances, business asset relief will be available in respect of agricultural property, either where no agricultural property relief is available, or where agricultural property relief is available in respect of part of the value transferred, and business asset relief is available in respect of some other part of the value transferred by the same transfer.

The main circumstances in which business asset relief may be available in respect of the total value transferred are:

(*a*) where the land is outside the United Kingdom, the Channel Islands or the Isle of Man (FA 1981, Sch. 14, para. 1 (4)); and

(*b*) where the property is live and deadstock, and cut crops.

The main circumstance in which agricultural property relief may be available in respect of part of the value transferred, and business asset relief may be available in respect of the remaining value is where the land has development or hope value. Agricultural property relief is available in respect of the agricultural value only (para. 1 (3)), but as there is no such restriction in the case of business asset relief, that relief is available in respect of the value in excess of agricultural value.

iii *Interest in possession* The condition as to ownership is treated as satisfied if the beneficiary has had an interest in possession in the property for two years.

iv *No interest in possession* The condition as to ownership is treated as satisfied if the property has been trust property for two years.

h 30% business asset relief

i *Essential requirements* The essential requirements are:

(*a*) the property must be land or buildings, plant or machinery;

(*b*) the property must be used wholly or mainly for the purposes of a business carried on by the transferor;

(*c*) the property must be settled property; and

(*d*) the transferor must have an interest in possession in that property (FA 1981, s. 100).

ii *Circumstances in which available* The 50% business asset relief is only available where the trust property itself consists of a business or an interest in a business, and not merely assets which are used for business purposes. This 30% relief is intended to apply where the land, plant or machinery is trust property, but the business is owned by the life tenant on his own account.

As in the case of the 50% relief, the 30% relief will only apply in the case of agricultural property where agricultural property relief is not available. In many cases, where the settled property is agricultural property, and the life tenant occupies the land for the purpose of carrying on his business, 50% agricultural property relief will be available. Accordingly, this relief will only be available in those cases, of which the most important have been mentioned above, in which 50% business asset relief is available in respect of agricultural property.

2 *Business asset relief in other circumstances*

Business asset relief is available in respect of most other types of business or interests in business, as well as to other types of asset (see p. 90, *ante*).

R   MEASUREMENT OF DISTRIBUTIONS

1   *Actual values, not loss to estate*

In the case of an ordinary transfer of value, the amount of the value transferred is the amount by which the value of the transferor's estate is reduced (FA 1975, s. 20 (2)). Although, in effect, this approach is adopted in the case of depreciatory transactions, in other cases where there is an actual or deemed distribution payment, the amount of the distribution is that of the actual value of the property distributed (FA 1975, Sch. 10, paras. 9 (1), (2), (2A), 12, 15 (3)). If, therefore, there is a distribution of part of a shareholding which reduces the holding from a majority to a minority holding, the amount of the distribution will, nevertheless, be only the value of the holding which is itself distributed.

2   *Related property*

Property comprised in the estate of an individual, or his spouse, was related to that comprised in a settlement which was made by him or his spouse, if the settlement was created before 27 March 1974, there was no interest in possession in the settled property and the transfer of the individually owned property was made prior to 10 March 1981 (FA 1975, Sch. 10, para. 7 (2) (*b*); FA 1981, s. 105). This affected the value which was treated as being transferred by the individual. It did not affect the amount of value which was the subject of a distribution. Accordingly, if an individual owned 40% of the shares in a company, and the trustees of a pre-27 March 1974 trust which he created owned 20%, the related property provisions applied if the individual first transferred his shares. If, however, the trustees first distributed their shares, these shares could have been valued as a 20% holding (*supra*), and with no valuation disadvantage, the individual's shares could have ceased to have been related property.

S PROTECTIVE TRUSTS

1 Meaning of protective trusts

Protective trusts are trusts which are designed primarily to prevent family funds falling into the hands of a trustee in bankruptcy in the event of a beneficiary becoming insolvent. Where trustees hold a fund upon protective trusts for Andrew for his life, the trustees at the outset hold the fund upon trust to pay all the income which arises to Andrew, and Andrew is in the same position so far as income is concerned as if he had an ordinary life interest. If, however, Andrew does, or attempts to do, any act which would deprive him of the right to receive the whole of the income of the fund, his fixed interest automatically comes to an end, and a discretionary trust arises. The same result ensues if an event other than the advancement of capital occurs which deprives him of the right to receive the income. If, therefore, Andrew attempts to sell or mortgage his interest under the trust, or if he becomes bankrupt, a discretionary trust will automatically come into being. When the discretionary trust arises, the trustees hold the fund during the remainder of Andrew's life upon trust to distribute the income as they think fit between Andrew, his wife, his children and his remoter issue.

A protective trust arises either under s. 33 of the Trustee Act 1925, by the settlor using the expression "protective trusts" in the trust instrument, or by the trust instrument specifying in full the circumstances in which the discretionary trust will arise.

For capital transfer tax purposes, while Andrew is entitled to receive the whole of the income from the fund, he has an interest in possession, so that, were there no special provision, there would be a charge to tax when the discretionary trust arose, according to the rules relating to the termination of an interest in possession (p. 294, *ante*).

2 Capital transfer tax rules

The special capital transfer tax rules are:

a   where the principal beneficiary's fixed interest comes to an end, the coming to an end of that interest is ignored for capital transfer tax purposes (para. 18 (2) (a); FA 1978, s. 71). Although, therefore, for the purposes of the general law the fixed interest has come to an end, for capital transfer tax purposes the interest in possession is deemed to continue (para. 18 (2) (*b*));

b where, during the discretionary phase, a distribution payment is made to the principal beneficiary, no liability will result (para. 4 (3));

c where, during the discretionary phase, a distribution payment is made to anyone other than the principal beneficiary, there will be a notional termination of an interest in possession in that property (para. 4 (2)); and

d where the principal beneficiary dies, whether during the fixed interest phase or the discretionary phase, there will be a notional transfer of value of the whole of the settled property in which that interest subsisted (s. 22 (2)).

3 Use of protective trusts

If it is desired to create a trust which is a discretionary trust for the purposes of the general law, but which has an interest in possession for capital transfer tax, this can be done by creating a protective trust, with the principal beneficiary then purporting to assign his life interest.

T TRUSTS FOR BENEFIT OF DISABLED PERSONS

1 Generally

There are two entirely separate capital transfer tax codes which apply to trusts for the benefit of disabled persons. These codes apply not according to the circumstances at a current point in time, but according to whether the property was transferred into settlement before or after 10 March 1981.

2 Scope of pre-March 1981 code

The special provision applies to settled property where

a there is no interest in possession;

b the trusts of the settlement secure that if any of the property is applied during the lifetime of a mentally disabled person or a person in receipt of an attendance allowance, it is applied only or mainly for his benefit (para. 19 (1)); and

c the property was transferred into settlement prior to 10 March 1981 (FA 1981, s. 103).

For the purposes of this provision, a person is mentally disabled if he is suffering from mental disorder within the meaning of the Mental Health Act 1959, and as a result is incapable of administering his property or managing his affairs (para. 19 (4)). An attendance allowance is one payable under the Social Security Act 1975, s. 35.

3 Capital transfer tax privileges

Trusts coming within the scope of this provision have three privileges for capital transfer tax:

a   where the settlor is the disabled person, neither the making of the settlement nor the addition of further funds to the settlement is treated as as chargeable transfer, so that no tax is payable (para. 19 (2) (a)). This will also apply where the Court of Protection makes, or directs the making, of a settlement on behalf of and in the name of a mentally disabled person;

b   a distribution payment made for the benefit of the disabled person is not a capital distribution, and so is not taxable (para. 19 (2) (b));

c   the periodic charge is deferred until there is a capital distribution or until the disabled person dies (*infra*).

4 Deferment of periodic charge

a *Generally* Where, under the general rules governing the periodic charge, tax would have been payable on one or more tenth anniversaries of the creation of the trust during the period for which no interest in possession subsists, the charge is deferred until either:

i a capital distribution is made; or

ii the disabled beneficiary dies (para. 17 (5); 19 (3)).

The position differs according to which of these events occurs.

b *Where capital distribution* Although no capital transfer tax is payable on a capital distribution made to the disabled person, the making of a capital distribution either to the disabled person or to any other beneficiary causes the periodic charge to become payable if there has been a relevant anniversary (para. 17 (6)). If the whole fund is distributed, the charge will be on the whole fund, valued at the date when the distribution is made, and not at the date of the relevant anniversary (para. 17 (8), (9) (a)). The rate of tax is the rate which would have applied if the relevant anniversary had fallen on the date upon which the capital distribution was made (para. 17 (5) (a)).

c   Capital distribution of part of fund   Where only part of the fund is distributed, the deferred periodic charge is payable on a proportion of the value of the fund. This proportion is determined by applying the following formula (para. 17 (8), (9)):

$$\text{Value of whole fund at date of capital distribution} \times \frac{\text{Amount of capital distribution}}{\text{Value of whole fund at date of capital distribution}}$$

Where a capital distribution is made, then, unless the recipient pays the tax, the grossed up equivalent of the amount actually paid is to be used in the numerator of the fraction.

d   Death of disabled beneficiary   Where the disabled beneficiary dies, the deferred tax is chargeable on the value of the fund at the date of death, and at the rate which would have applied if the relevant anniversary had fallen on that date (para. 17 (5) (*b*), (6)).

e   Disabled person ceasing to benefit   If during his lifetime, the settled property ceases to be held on trust for the disabled beneficiary, the deferred charge becomes payable as if he had then died.

f   Deferment of more than one periodic charge   The period of deferment phase may last for a period which covers more than one relevant anniversary. In this case, when the deferred tax becomes payable the second amount of deferred tax is chargeable on the amount determined by the application of the formula in *c* above, less the amount of tax payable in respect of the first amount of deferred tax. The process is repeated for third and subsequent amounts of deferred tax (para. 17 (8)).

5   Scope of post-March 1981 code

The post-March 1981 code applies where:

a   the trusts of the settlement are such that no interest in possession will subsist during the lifetime of the disabled beneficiary;

b   the trusts of the settlement secure that not less than half of the settled property which is applied at all during the lifetime of the disabled beneficiary is applied for his benefit; and

c   the property was transferred into settlement after 9 March 1981 (para. 19 (1), substituted by FA 1981, s. 103).

The terms of the settlement will be treated as falling within *b* if the only circumstance in which more than half of the settled property which is in fact applied during the lifetime of the disabled beneficiary can be applied otherwise than or his benefit is in exercise of a statutory power of advancement (substituted para. 19 (3)).

6   Capital transfer tax rules

Where the post-March 1981 code applies, the disabled beneficiary is treated as being beneficially entitled to an interest in possession in the settled property (substituted para. 19 (2)). Accordingly:

a   there will be no liability on the making of the settlement if the disabled beneficiary is the settlor, and he is deemed to take an immediate interest in possession. In this case, there is no alteration to the value of his estate, and so no transfer of value (s. 20 (2); Sch. 5, para. 3 (1));

b   there will be no liability in respect of capital distributions made to or for the benefit of the disabled beneficiary (Sch. 5, para. 4 (3));

c   where a distribution payment is made to anyone other than the disabled beneficiary, there will be a termination of the notional interest in possession *pro tanto* (para. 4 (2)); and

d   when the disabled beneficiary dies, there will be a notional transfer of the whole of the property which is settled at that time (s. 22 (2)).

7   Overlap between codes

Where a settlement was created for the disabled beneficiary before 10 March 1981, and property was transferred to that settlement both before and after that date, the settlement will have to be treated as two settlements (para. 19 (1), p. 333 *ante*) with the appropriate code applying to each.

U   ACCUMULATION AND MAINTENANCE SETTLEMENT

1   Scope of provision

a   Statement of provision   There is an important provision which confers privileged status on accumulation and maintenance settlements where certain conditions are satisfied (para. 15 (1)). The basic conditions are that:

(a)   one or more persons, namely the beneficiaries

(b)   will

(c)   on or before attaining a specified age not exceeding 25

(d)   become entitled to either
  i the settled property, or part of it, or
  ii an interest in possession in the settled property or part of it, and

(e)   no interest in possession subsists in the settled property or part of it, and

(f)   the income is to be accumulated

(g)   so far as it is not applied for the maintenance, education or benefit of a beneficiary.

A number of these elements require elaboration.

b   "Will"   It is, of course, impossible to be sure that any beneficiary will himself inevitably become entitled to settled property or an interest in it at some time in the future. It seems that the expression means will *if he survives until the specified age,* so that it is thought that the provision will apply, if all the other conditions are satisfied, so long as the beneficiary is in fact living.

It also seems that the expression means *if the beneficiary does not himself do any future act which would operate to divest the interest, and if no other divesting event occurs.* The distinction is between an event which might deprive the beneficiary of his interest which occurs under the terms of the settlement, and an event which falls outside the settlement (*Lord Inglewood* v. *I.R. Comrs.* [1981] Simon's Tax Intelligence, 131). Thus, if a beneficiary will become entitled to settled property if he is living at the age of 25, the fact that he might be able to assign his interest before that age, or that it might be taken from him as a result of his bankruptcy, would not prevent the provision applying. On the other hand, if someone else has the power to defeat his entitlement, the provisions will not apply. This would in general be the case if the trustee, or someone else, has an overriding power of appointment, or a power to revoke the existing trusts and declare new trusts. If, however, the power can only be exercised in favour of a person under 25 who is a member of the class, the existence of the power would not, in the Revenue view, take the settlement out of the provision (Press Notice, 19 January 1976).

The existence of a statutory power of advancement is also not treated as taking the settlement out of the provision (Revenue letter, Law Society's Gazette, 8 October 1975).

c   The specified age   It seems that the trust instrument itself must specify the age as an age, so that if it specifies a date which in fact falls before the beneficiary's twenty fifth birthday, the provision will not apply.

d   Entitlement   It will be noted that the provision applies even if the beneficiary only becomes entitled to a life interest, or a lesser interest, on attaining the specified age.

349

e   The income   It will be noted that the trust instrument must impose an *obligation* to accumulate such income as is not *in fact* applied for the maintenance, education or benefit of the beneficiary. If, in breach of trust, income which ought to be accumulated is not accumulated, that would not appear to prevent the section from operating.

The Revenue practice is to regard this requirement as satisfied if the trust instrument imposes a primary obligation to maintain, with only a power to accumulate.

Where there has been a trust to accumulate, but this has expired, this condition as to income will cease to be satisfied.

2   Further Conditions

In addition to the basic conditions just discussed, it is necessary for one of two further conditions to be satisfied.

a   Maximum period of 25 years

In general, the settlement will only be privileged for a period of 25 years from its creation (FA 1976, s. 106 (1)). This period is calculated from the date when the settlement was created, if at that date it satisfied the basic conditions, or from the latest date upon which the basic conditions came to be satisfied. However, where the settlement was made before 15 April 1976, and the basic conditions were satisfied on that day, the 25 year period is calculated from 15 April 1976 (s. 106 (2)).

b   Common grandparent

As an alternative to the 25 year condition, the privileges will be afforded if and for long as it can be shown that all the persons who are or have been beneficiaries are or were the grandchildren of the same grandparent (s. 106 (1)).

In the case of settlements created after 14 April 1976, the condition as to relationship with a common grandparent must be satisfied throughout the period from the creation of the settlement. In the case of settlements created before 15 April 1976 the condition is treated as being satisfied if

    i   it was satisfied on 15 April 1976 and continuously thereafter, even if other persons were beneficiaries before that date; or

    ii   (a)   it was satisfied on 1 April 1977 and continuously thereafter; and

          (b)   either   (i)   there was no beneficiary living on 15 April 1976; or

  (ii) the only or oldest beneficiary living on 15 April
    1976 and all beneficiaries living on 1 April 1977
    were grandchildren of the same grandparent; or

iii (a) there is no power under the settlement whereby the condition could have become satisfied in respect of the period
   beginning on 1 April 1977;
  (b) the trusts of the settlement have not been varied at any
   time after 15 April 1976 (s. 106 (2)).

The relationship to the same grandparent can be established even
if a person is the illegitimate child, or adopted child, or step child of
his parent (s. 106 (2)).

3 *Living beneficiary*

Irrespective of the terms of the settlement, the conditions will only
be satisfied if there is a living beneficiary; or if there has been a living
beneficiary who has subsequently died (s. 106 (2)). In the latter case,
the settlement will retain its privileges even if there is no living
beneficiary for the time being.

4 *Capital transfer tax privileges*

Where at a particular time the conditions are satisfied, the settlement has the following capital transfer tax privileges:

a a distribution payment made to a beneficiary out of the settled
 property, or out of the part to which he is entitled, is not a
 capital distribution, and so is not taxable (para. 15 (2) (a)). It
 is, however, a distribution payment, and it will, therefore, be
 taken into account on any subsequent occasion on which a
 charge to capital transfer tax arises in respect of the settled
 property;

b when a beneficiary becomes entitled to an interest in possession
 in the settled property, or part, that is not treated as a capital
 distribution, so that it is not taxable (*ibid*);

c the periodic charge does not apply (para. 15 (2) (b)).

5 *Conversion to accumulation and maintenance settlements*

It has been seen (p. 329, *ante*) that where a settlement does not
satisfy the conditions, and the conditions subsequently become
satisfied, there is a deemed capital distribution at that time. This will
be so, for example, if following an appointment the conditions would
be satisfied but for the existence of a power of revocation, and that
power is subsequently revoked (*Lord Inglewood* v. *I.R. Comrs.*
[1981] Simon's Tax Intelligence, 131).

6   Where interest in possession

The capital transfer tax privileges apply only while all the conditions for an accumulation and maintenance settlement are satisfied, including the condition that at the point of time being considered there must be no interest in possession. In many cases, where a settlement at creation is an accumulation and maintenance settlement, an interest in possession will subsequently arise. At that time the privileges are lost.

V   ASSOCIATED OPERATIONS AND SETTLED PROPERTY

The question sometimes arises whether section 44, which deals with associated operations (p. 68, *ante*), can apply to settled property. That section has the effect of widening the concept of disposition, which is relevant to a transfer of value made by an individual (s. 20 (2)). The charges in respect of settled property, however, do not depend on the concept of disposition, with the result that section 44 cannot apply where there is a series of events designed, for example, to transfer property in which there is no interest in possession to a beneficiary.

However, a distribution of property by trustees is undoubtedly an operation, and that operation may be associated with other operations carried out by an individual. It is, therefore, possible for an individual to make a disposition by operations which are associated, even if one or more of those operations consists of a distribution of settled property.

W   CHARITIES

The capital transfer tax privileges conferred on charities are considered in a later chapter (p. 398, *post*).

X   OTHER PRIVILEGED TRUSTS

Capital transfer tax privileges are conferred on trusts governing superannuation schemes, trusts for the benefit of employees, newspaper trusts, and trusts governing compensation funds, but these are not considered in this book.

Y PAYMENT OF TAX ON CREATION OF SETTLEMENT

If on the creation of the settlement the settlor and the trustees agreed that the trustees would discharge the capital transfer tax out of the settled property, this will create an income tax disadvantage (see, p. 221, *ante*). There is, however, no disadvantage if the trustees pay the tax where there is no obligation in the trust instrument, or under a collateral agreement, upon them to do so.

Z PAYMENT OF TAX

1 *Due date of payment*

a Liability in respect of lifetime events Where the event which gives rise to the liability to tax occurs between 5 April and 30 September, both dates inclusive, tax is due on 30 April in the following year (Sch. 4, para. 12 (1)). Where the event occurs between 1 October and 5 April, the tax is due at the end of six months after the end of the month in which the event occurred (*ibid*).

b Liability due to death of beneficiary Where tax is payable as a result of the death of a beneficiary, it is due at the end of six months after the end of the month in which the death occurred, whenever that was.

2 *Payment by instalments*

a Where tax due in respect of lifetime events The tax payable can be paid by 8 yearly or 16 half yearly instalments provided certain conditions are satisfied. Where those conditions are satisfied the tax can be paid by instalments whether it is payable by the trustees, beneficiaries, or anyone else, the first instalment being due on the due date for payment ascertained according to the rules just considered (paras. 13 (6) (b), 14 (5) (a)).

The conditions are:

　i the event which gives rise to the liability to tax is one of the following:

　(a) the termination of an interest in possession;
　(b) the coming into existence of an interest in possession where none existed immediately before;
　(c) the periodic charge in respect of a trust with no interest in possession; or
　(d) where a settlement which does not comply with the conditions for an accumulation and maintenance settlement is made to comply with those conditions;

    ii the property is settled property immediately before the event giving rise to the liability occurs, and continues to be comprised in the settlement afterwards;

    iii the property is within one of the classes of property in respect of which the instalment option can be claimed on death (p. 132, *ante*). In the case of shares in an unquoted company where the market value does not exceed £5,000 (p. 88, *ante*) that value is calculated in the ordinary way, and no grossing up is made (para. 13 (6) (f)).

b   Where tax due in respect of death of beneficiary   The position is the same as in the case of property which the deceased owned outright at the date of his death (p. 132, *ante*).

3   Balance of tax becoming payable

Where the instalment option has been claimed, the outstanding balance of the tax may be paid at any time. It must be paid when the property ceases to be comprised in the settlement (paras. 13 (6) (b); 14 (5) (b)).

4   Interest

a   Rate   Where tax is payable as a result of the death of a beneficiary interest is payable at the rate of 9% p.a., and in every other case, it is payable at the rate of 12% p.a. (para. 19 (1); (Capital Transfer Tax (Interest on Unpaid Tax) Order 1979)). If an overpayment of tax is made, interest is payable by the Revenue to the trustees at the same rate (para. 19 (3)). It is not subject to income tax, and should be passed on to the beneficiaries without any deduction of tax (para. 19 (4)).

b   Where tax payable by instalments   If the option to pay the capital transfer tax by instalments is exercised, interest may be payable on the whole amount of the tax, or only on the amount of each instalment from the due date for payment. The position is the same as in the case of payment of tax following death (p. 134, *ante*).

5   Clearance

There is no provision under which trustees can obtain a clearance certificate from the Revenue in order to protect them against any future personal liability.

ZA   ACCOUNTABILITY

The trustees are responsible for paying capital transfer tax in respect of settled property (s. 25 (3) (a)). Trustees are liable only to the extent of the property which they have received, or which they would have received but for their default (s. 27 (2)).

To the extent that the trustees do not pay the tax on the due date, the Revenue may also recover the tax from:

1 Any person who is entitled to an interest in possession in the property, so far as the tax is attributable to that property (s. 25 (3) (b)). A person who is entitled in a fiduciary or nominee capacity is accountable in the same way as a person who is entitled beneficially.

2 Any person for whose benefit the property or any of the income from it is applied (s. 25 (3) (c)).

3 Where the event giving rise to the liability occurs during the lifetime of the settlor, then, if the trustees are not for the time being resident in the UK, the settlor (s. 25 (3) (d)).

Any money held on the trusts of a settlement may be used in paying the tax attributable to the value of any property comprised in the settlement and held on the same trusts (s. 28 (5)). Where a person is liable to pay the tax then even if the property is not vested in him, he may nevertheless sell or charge it for this purpose (s. 28 (3)).

ZB EVENTS WITHIN 3 YEARS OF DEATH

Where a beneficiary ceases to be entitled to an interest in possession in his lifetime, the tax will be calculated according to the lifetime scale of rates (p. 70, *ante*). If that beneficiary dies within 3 years of ceasing to be entitled to the interest, further tax will be payable to bring it up to the amount payable on the death-time scale (s. 37 (2)). In this case, the settlor can be under no liability to that additional tax (s. 25 (4)).

ZC REVERSIONARY INTERESTS

1 *Definition*

A reversionary interest is any future interest under a settlement, whether it is vested or contingent (s. 51 (1)). The expression covers interests in remainder, as well as reversionary interest strictly so called.

2 *The general rule*

The general rule is that a reversionary interest is "excluded property" (s. 24 (3)). Accordingly, *a*   no tax is in general payable where a reversionary interest is disposed of (s. 20 (3)); and

    b   the value of a reversionary interest is left out of account when calculating the liability to tax on the death of the beneficiary entitled to that interest (s. 23 (1)).

3 Special circumstances

In certain circumstances, and as exceptions to the general rule, transactions involving reversionary interests do have capital transfer tax consequences:

a Settlor or spouse entitled   In general, where the settlor or his spouse is beneficially entitled to the reversionary interest, it will not be treated as excluded property (FA 1975, s. 24 (3) (aa), added by FA 1976, s. 120 (1)). The gift of a reversionary interest arising under a settlement created by the settlor, or the passing of such an interest on death will be a transfer of value.

This general rule does not apply, however, where the interest is held by the settlor's widow; nor where the settlement under which the interest arose was made before 16 April 1976 (FA 1976, s. 120 (2)).

b Settlor or spouse previously entitled   If a person acquires a reversionary interest after 9 March 1981, that interest will not be excluded property if at any time previously the settlor or his spouse had been entitled to the reversionary interest (FA 1981, s. 104). This does not apply, however, if the settlement itself was made before 16 April 1976 (*ibid*).

c Purchase of reversionary interest   Where a person who has any interest in any settled property purchases a reversionary interest in that property, the amount paid for the reversionary interest is treated as a transfer of value, even though the price paid reflects the actuarial value of that interest (ss. 20 (2); 23 (3)). The result of this provision is that tax is not saved by, for example, a life tenant purchasing the reversionary interest. Suppose that a fund of £50,000 is held upon trust for Robert for life with remainder to Stanley. Suppose that Robert has a free estate of £70,000. Suppose also that the actuarial value of Robert's interest is £20,000 and Stanley's interest is £30,000. If there is no dealing with the reversionary interest, liability to tax will arise on the death of Robert on the whole sum of £50,000 (p. 121, *ante*), together with Robert's free estate of

£70,000, a total of £120,000. If Robert purchases Stanley's interest for £30,000, Robert's free estate will be reduced by £30,000 to £40,000, so that tax would be payable on the property which was previously settled, £50,000, and the remainder of Robert's free estate, £40,000, a total of £90,000. As a result of this special provision, however, at the time when Robert purchases the reversionary interest, he is treated as making a transfer of value of £30,000, and is taxable accordingly.

Where a person who does not have any interest in settled property purchases a reversionary interest, the value of the reversionary interest is taken into account, so that no capital transfer tax liability will arise where the price paid represents the actual value of the interest (*cf.* s. 20 (3)). Where the reversionary interest was purchased before 27 March 1974, the purchaser will not have to pay any tax when the interest falls into possession in excess of that which would have been payable by way of estate duty (FA 1975, Sch. 5, para. 23).

c Reversionary interest after purchase

i Where the property comprised in a settlement is situated outside the UK, and where the person entitled to the reversionary interest is domiciled outside the UK, the general rule, stated in paragraph 2, *supra,* applies, whether or not the reversionary interest had been purchased (s. 24 (2); Sch. 5, para. 2 (1) (b)). This is so whether or not the settlor was domiciled in the UK when the settlement was created.

ii In any other case, where a reversionary interest has been acquired for a consideration in money or money's worth, that interest is not excluded property (s. 24 (3) (a)). This is so even if the reversionary interest was acquired for value by a predecessor in title of the present owner of it. Accordingly, in this case:

(a) tax is payable if the interest is disposed of at less than its actuarial value (*cf.* s. 20 (3)); and

(b) the value of the reversionary interest is brought into account in calculating the tax payable on the death of the person entitled to it (*cf.* s. 23 (1)).

d Reversionary interest in respect of lease
In certain circumstances, the grant of a lease is treated as the creation of a settlement (p. 287, *ante*). Even where this is so, the reversionary interest under that deemed settlement is not excluded property, so that the position is as stated in para. *c* ii, *supra.*

357

ZD   OTHER INTERESTS

It has been seen that:

a   in effect, an interest in possession is not itself comprised in the estate of the beneficiary, so that the disposal of the interest in possession itself is not a transfer of value (para. 4 (1) (*a*)); and

b   special rules apply to reversionary interests.

In other cases, where an interest or inchoate right arises in settled property, that interest or right does, as such, form part of the beneficiary's estate. If, therefore, trustees held a fund upon discretionary trusts for Edward, Frank, George and Harry, if each of the beneficiaries themselves dispose of their interest, the same capital transfer tax results will ensue as in the case of a disposal of an ordinary asset.

Chapter 20

Tax on the Distribution of Trust Funds

In this chapter it is proposed to consider the tax position where trust money is distributed to one or more of the beneficiaries, either during the continuance of a trust, or on its determination. The situations to be considered are:

a   an "advancement" of capital to a beneficiary;

b   a distribution of accumulated income;

c   capital distribution upon determination of the trust in accordance with the terms of the trust instrument, for example, following the death of a person entitled to the income for life; and

d   capital distribution upon premature determination of a trust.

A   ADVANCEMENT

1   Powers of advancement

An "advancement" occurs when a capital sum is taken out of a trust, and paid to a beneficiary before the time when that beneficiary would normally be entitled to it. Trustee Act 1925, s. 32, confers upon trustees the power to advance to a beneficiary one half of the personal property he will definitely receive, or which he will receive if he attains a specified age or if a specified event, such as marriage, occurs. Where a person has a prior interest, he must give his consent to the advancement. Therefore, if a fund is held upon trust for Pauline for life, and on her death for Caroline, the trustees may, if they think fit, advance Caroline one half of the trust fund during the lifetime of Pauline, but Pauline must give her consent. This statutory power is often extended by the words of the trust instrument, and reference should always be made to the trust instrument (or will) to see whether there is in fact any special provision.

2   Income tax

Because advancement is a dealing with capital, there will usually be no income tax considerations, and, indeed, where the advancement is of cash, there will be no income tax problems at all. If, however, the advancement is of assets *in specie* there will usually be the need to apportion the dividends or other income, unless there is a provision in the trust instrument relieving the trustees from the need to apportion. This is discussed at p. 142, *ante*. However, this obligation to apportion income which may arise under the general trust law is not followed for income tax purposes, and the principles described previously (p. 20, *ante*) apply.

The position where an advancement is made out of income which has been accumulated is discussed at p. 239, *ante*.

3   Capital gains tax

a   Advancement of cash   Where an advancement is made in cash, that advancement in itself will not give rise to any capital gains tax liability, although there may be a liability where assets are sold in order to produce the cash (*infra*).

b   Advancement of specific assets   If the trustees propose to make an advancement by transferring particular assets to the beneficiary, for capital gains tax purposes the beneficiary is regarded as becoming the owner of those assets at the point of time when the trustees make their final decision. The trustees are, therefore, deemed to dispose of the assets at that point of time at their then market value and immediately to re-acquire them as nominees for the beneficiary (p. 254, *ante*). If as a result of that deemed disposal and re-acquisition a gain is realized, the trustees will be responsible for paying capital gains tax on that gain (CGTA 1979, s. 54 (1)). Should the asset rise in value between the date when the notional disposal and re-acquisition occurs and the date when the asset is transferred to the beneficiary, the beneficiary will be liable for tax on that gain at the time when he disposes of it.

If by virtue of the deemed disposal and re-acquisition the trustees realize a loss, and the trustees cannot offset that loss against gains accruing to them in that year, but before the deemed disposal and re-acquisition, the loss is treated as accruing at that time to the beneficiary (CGTA 1979, s. 54 (2)).

Where the assets are business assets, shares in a trading company, woodlands or agricultural property, roll-over relief may be available (see p. 274, *ante*).

4 Capital transfer tax

a Beneficiary having interest in possession Where the advancement is made to a beneficiary who has an interest in possession in the property advanced no capital transfer tax will be payable in respect of that advancement (FA 1975, Sch. 5, para. 4 (3); p. 295, *ante*).

b Other person having interest in possession If the advancement is made out of settled property in which an interest in possession subsists, but to a beneficiary other than the life tenant (or other person who has that interest in possession) in general capital transfer tax is payable as a result of that advancement (para. 4 (2); p. 294, *ante*). The tax is payable by the trustees out of the trust fund, but it is calculated by reference to the "CTT history" of the life tenant. Suppose that trustees hold a fund upon trust for Alison for life, with remainder to Bernice, and that during the lifetime of Alison an advancement of £10,000 is made to Bernice. The amount of tax payable will be that which Alison would have paid had she herself made a gift at that time of £10,000.

c No interest in possession Where there is no interest in possession in the property advanced, there will in principle be a liability to capital transfer tax on the grossed up equivalent of the amount advanced (para. 6 (1); p. 319, *ante*). There will, however, be no liability if the advancement is made out of an accumulation and maintenance settlement (para. 15 (2) (a); p. 245, *ante*) or to the principal beneficiary under a protective trust (para. 18 (2) (b); p. 242, *ante*) or, in certain circumstances, to a disabled beneficiary (FA 1981, s. 103; p. 348, *ante*).

B DISTRIBUTIONS OF ACCUMULATED INCOME

1 Occasions for distribution

Income will be accumulated under a trust either because the beneficiary who would otherwise be entitled to it is an infant, or because the trust instrument expressly directs accumulation. Where the beneficiary is an infant, Trustee Act 1925, s. 31, requires the trustees to accumulate all income which is not used for the maintenance of the beneficiary until he reaches the age of 21 in the case of a trust created before 1970, or the age of 18 in the case of a trust created after 1969. If thereupon the beneficiary has a vested interest in the trust fund, the accumulations are held upon trust for him absolutely, and he is entitled to call for them. In other circumstances the accumulations are added to the capital of the trust. The trust instrument itself may direct accumulations in a wide variety of cases (see, generally p. 237, *ante*).

2   Income tax

The trustees will have suffered tax year by year on the income which has been accumulated (p. 230, *ante*) so that generally no further income tax will be payable when the accumulations are transferred to the beneficiary.

It has been seen (p. 218, *ante*) that the only tax efficient method by which a high tax payer can provide for his own infant unmarried children is by settling property on trust to accumulate the income until his children reach the age of 18 or marry (TA 1970, s. 437). Provided the terms of the trust do not allow either parent to derive any benefit from it unless the child dies; do not allow any person to bring the trust to an end or to revoke it and provide that the beneficiary has no right to the income while he is under age, the income arising from his trust will not be regarded as the income of the parent. If when the child has attained the age of eighteen the accumulated income is paid to the child, that will not prejudice the position of the parent.

The circumstances in which a beneficiary may make a repayment claim when accumulated income is paid to him are discussed at p. 250.

Even if the trustees have suffered income tax at the additional rate as well as at the basic rate on the income accumulated (p. 230, *ante*) the general principle is that no repayment claim can be made where the payment made to the beneficiary is out of income which has been accumulated and so has become capital. The possible exception to the rule was noted at p. 239, *ante*.

3   Capital gains tax

a   *Beneficiary with vested interest in capital*   The liability to capital gains tax in respect of investments representing income accumulated during the infancy of a beneficiary will depend on whether that beneficiary has had during his infancy a vested or a contingent interest in the trust fund. As was mentioned earlier, a beneficiary has a "vested" interest if nothing can happen to take away the right of the beneficiary or, if he is dead, of his estate to receive the property either at once or in due course. A beneficiary has a "contingent" interest if some condition has to occur or some event happen before a definite interest arises. It has been seen (p. 282, *ante*), in effect, that where the beneficiary's interest is immediate and vested, the property subject to the trust is not considered as settled property for capital gains tax purposes.

Where the beneficiary has a vested interest in capital, CGTA 1979, s. 46, provides that for capital gains tax purposes, the infant is regarded as owning the trust property—which includes accumulations—and that transfers between the trustees and the beneficiary are disregarded. Thus, where income is accumulated during the infancy of the beneficiary, and the investments representing the accumulations are transferred to the beneficiary when he is 18, no capital gains tax is payable. The infant is regarded as having acquired those investments at the time when they were acquired by the trust. The same principle applies where under the provisions of the trust instrument income is accumulated from capital in which the beneficiary—whether an infant or not—has a vested interest.

b   Other cases   Where the beneficiary has not had a vested interest in capital, but he becomes entitled to have the investments representing the accumulations paid to him, it is necessary to identify the point of time at which he becomes so entitled. At that time, the trustees are deemed to dispose of the assets at their market value and to re-acquire them. They will be liable to capital gains tax on any gain. The notional re-acquisition figure becomes the base figure for the beneficiary. The essential point of time is when the beneficiary becomes *entitled* to have the assets transferred to him, not the time when they are in fact transferred to him (CGTA 1979, s. 54). Any dealings with the investments after that time effected by the trustees are treated for capital gains tax purposes as having been effected by the beneficiary.

Where the distribution was made in cash, no capital gains tax liability arises in respect of that cash, although if the trustees had sold investments to produce cash, there may have been a capital gains tax liability on the disposal of those investments on the ordinary principles.

4   Capital transfer tax

When income is accumulated it becomes capital for capital transfer tax purposes as well as for general purposes. The distribution of accumulated income will therefore give rise to a capital transfer tax liability in the same circumstances as would an advancement.

C   CAPITAL DISTRIBUTION UPON NORMAL DETERMINATION OF TRUST

We are here concerned with the situation where a trust fund comes to an end in the circumstances envisaged by the trust instrument.

363

The most usual circumstances will be upon the death of a person who was entitled to the income for life, or where the trust is a discretionary trust, and the trustees decide to bring it to an end.

1 Income tax

Only two points arise. First, the trustees will wish to ensure that liability to income tax in respect of the period to the date when the trust comes to an end is discharged before they part with all the trust property. The only other income tax point likely to arise is in respect of the apportionment of dividends, when the usual principles apply (p. 20, *ante*).

2 Capital gains tax

a Determination of trust in lifetime Where the trust comes to an end during the lifetime of the life tenant, the trustees are deemed to dispose of the assets at the date of determination at their market value, and to re-acquire them as nominees for the person or persons then absolutely entitled to them (CGTA 1979, s. 4 (1); p. 254, *ante*). If there is then any notional gain, the trustees will be liable to capital gains tax on that gain, unless roll-over relief in respect of business assets is available (p. 274, *ante*). If there is any loss which cannot be offset against other gains, the benefit of that loss is passed to the beneficiary (s. 54 (2); p. 275, *ante*). The notional re-acquisition figure is the base figure for the beneficiaries then entitled, and any dealings by the trustees on behalf of the beneficiaries will be treated as dealings by the beneficiaries themselves (s. 46 (1)).

It follows that no final distribution can safely be made by the trustees until any capital gains tax liability is satisfied.

b Determination of trust on death Where the trust comes to an end upon the death of a life tenant, the trustees are deemed to dispose of the assets of the trust at that date, and to re-acquire them at their then value (CGTA 1979, s. 55 (1)). However, no capital gains tax arises as a result of any uplift in value (s. 56 (1); p. 260, *ante*).

c Determination in other circumstances If a discretionary trust is brought to an end by a decision of the trustees to distribute the whole fund, they are deemed to dispose of the assets at the date of their decision and to re-acquire them at their then value s. 54 (1). Capital gains tax is payable on any gain realized as a result.

3 Capital transfer tax

The capital transfer tax position upon the normal determination of the trust has been described in Chapter 19. The position is summarized as follows.

D   PREMATURE DETERMINATION OF TRUST

1   *Generally*

It is not unusual for a trust to be brought to an end before the time envisaged by the trust instrument. By virtue of the decision in *Saunders* v. *Vautier* (1841), Cr. & Ph. 240, where a person is absolutely entitled to an interest in the capital of a trust, and no other person can in any circumstances have any interest in the trust property, the beneficiary who is absolutely entitled can, if he is over 18, demand that the trustees pay the trust money to him forthwith. Thus, if trustees are directed to hold £1,000 upon trust for Andrew absolutely, but not pay it to him until he is 35, as soon as Andrew reaches the age of 18 he can demand that the money is paid to him forthwith. The same principle applies if two or more people are of full age, and between them absolutely entitled to the whole of the beneficial interest in the trust property: they can require the trustees to transfer the trust property to them.

2   *Income tax*

The position is the same as considered at p. 364, *ante*.

3   *Capital gains tax liability of trustees*

a   Generally   In general the capital gains tax position on the premature determination of a trust is the same as a normal determination (p. 364, *ante*).

b   Retentions   In certain circumstances, notwithstanding the premature determination of a trust, trustees may wish to retain assets for a limited period by way of indemnity against possible liabilities which they incurred while acting as trustees. The fact that assets are retained does not prevent the beneficiaries from being regarded as having become the owners of the assets for capital gains tax purposes (CGTA 1979, s. 46 (2); p. 266, *ante*).

4 Capital gains tax liability of beneficiaries

A trust may be determined prematurely by means of a dealing by beneficiaries of their beneficial interests. If trustees hold a fund of £100,000 upon trust for Clifford for life with remainder to Denise, the trust may be brought to an end by, among other ways, Clifford transferring his life interest to Denise, so that she thereupon becomes absolutely entitled, or by Clifford and Denise transferring their respective interests to Edmund, so that he becomes absolutely entitled. So far as beneficiaries themselves are concerned, the rules are as follows.

a Generally The general rule applies where the beneficial interest was not created or acquired for a consideration in money or money's worth. Where the general rule applies no chargeable gain accrues where the beneficial interest is disposed of (CGTA 1979, s. 58). The general rule also applies where the beneficial interest was acquired in exchange for another interest under the settlement (*ibid*).

b Interest acquired for value Where a beneficiary acquired his beneficial interest for value, and as the holder of that interest becomes absolutely entitled as against the trustee to any settled property, a liability arises at that time. The liability of the trustees both to capital gains tax and to capital transfer tax is calculated first. The beneficiary is then liable to capital gains tax on the difference between the acquisition value of his beneficial interest and the net value transferable to him by the trustees (s. 58 (2)).

c Non-resident settlements Special rules apply where the beneficial interest is in a non-resident settlement (FA 1981, s. 88). These are considered later (p. 387, *post*).

d Insurance arrangements In certain circumstances, it is necessary for an insurance policy to be taken out as part of the arrangements for a premature determination of a trust. The premiums payable on such a policy will not normally be an allowable expense in the computation of any liability which attaches to the trustees (*Allison* v. *Murray*, [1975] 3 All E.R. 561).

5 Capital transfer tax: interests in possession

It will be helpful to consider the example previously given (*supra*) of a fund of £100,000 held upon trust for Clifford for life, with remainder to Denise. It will be supposed that the actuarial value of Clifford's life interest is £40,000, and that the actuarial value of Denise's reversionary interest is £50,000.

a Gift of life interest If Clifford gives away his life interest to Denise, or to anyone else, a liability will arise as if Clifford had himself given away at that time £100,000 (FA 1975, Sch. 5, para. 4 (2)). The actual amount payable will depend on his own CTT history. If, therefore, he had himself made previous chargeable transfers of £50,000, the tax payable would be £22,750. Although the amount of tax is calculated by reference to Clifford's CTT history, the trustees are responsible for ensuring payment out of the trust fund. If, therefore, Clifford gives his life interest to Denise, so that she becomes absolutely entitled to it, the trustees will retain thereout the capital transfer tax of £22,750, together with any capital gains tax, and they will account to Denise for the balance. However, if Clifford dies within 3 years of his giving away the life interest, the capital transfer tax liability will be adjusted to that applicable to the death-time rates (p. 79, *ante*), which, on these facts, would give rise to a further liability of £21,750. As the trustees are liable also for this additional tax (FA 1975, s. 25 (3), (4)), they will also retain the further £21,750 for a period of three years. While this appears to be the preferable course, it seems that if they do not retain this further sum, they will not themselves be liable for the further tax (s. 27 (4)) although the further tax would be a liability of Denise (s. 25 (3) (c)).

b Sale of life interest Clifford might sell his life interest to Denise for £40,000. In this case the capital transfer tax liability is calculated on the value of the settled property, less the purchase price received by Clifford, that is, on £60,000. Again upon the assumption that Clifford had made previous chargeable transfers of £50,000 the capital transfer tax payable would be (on the slices between £50,000 and £110,000) £11,750. Although the proceeds of sale are received by Clifford, the trustees are responsible for paying the tax. The trustees should, however, ask Clifford to provide evidence of payment to him of the purchase price, because it seems that they would not be entitled to rely merely upon his statement that payment had been, or would be, paid.

367

c Purchase of reversionary interest   Clifford might purchase Denise's reversionary interest for £50,000. In this case the value of the reversionary interest is ignored (s. 23 (3)) so that Clifford is treated as making a chargeable transfer of value of £50,000, which, where necessary, would have to be grossed up. The responsibility for paying the tax would be Clifford's, and there would be no liability on the part of the trustees (Sch. 5, para. 4 (3)).

d Gift of reversionary interest   Denise might give her reversionary interest to Clifford. In general, there would be no liability on Denise in respect of that gift (s. 20 (3)) and there would be no liability on the trustees (Sch. 5, para. 4 (3)). There would, however, be a liability on Denise if she had acquired her reversionary interest for value (p. 356, *ante*).

e Transfers of interests   Clifford might sell his life interest and Denise might sell her reversionary interest, to a third party, Edmund. There would be a liability in respect of the life interest to the same extent as if it had been sold to Denise (*b, supra*), but no liability in respect of the disposal of the reversionary interest by Denise.

f Partition   Clifford and Denise might partition the fund as to £45,000 to Clifford and as to £55,000 to Denise. Here there would be a liability in respect of the difference between the total trust fund, £100,000, and the amount received by Clifford, £45,000, that is, in respect of £55,000 (para. 4 (3), (10) (b)).

Chapter 21

Trusts with a Foreign Element

This chapter deals with the basic concepts of residence, ordinary residence, and domicile, and then with the situations of:

a a beneficiary under a trust situated abroad; and

b trustees of an English trust with beneficiaries abroad.

A DOMICILE AND RESIDENCE

1 *Generally*

The concepts of domicile, residence, and ordinary residence to some extent overlap. They have to be determined in the first instance according to the principles evolved by the general law. In some, but not all, cases, these principles are then modified by the legislation relating to the particular tax under consideration.

2 *Domicile*

Domicile is that place which a person intends to make his permanent home. Where a person is domiciled is in every case a question of fact, subject to three points:

a there is a strong presumption that a peron intends to retain his domicile of origin, that is, his domicile at the time of his birth. Clear evidence is, therefore, required before it will be accepted that a person has in fact acquired a new domicile.

b a married woman usually, but not necessarily, has the domicile of her husband.

c in any case other than retention of his domicile of origin, the surrounding facts must be consistent with the person's declaration of intention. Suppose, therefore, that a person has an English domicile of origin, that he goes to New Zealand, and says that he is going to live there permanently. His declaration of intention to live there permanently is far more likely to be

369

accepted if he has also severed his permanent ties with England, such as by selling his house and taking his money with him.

3   Residence

Residence is partly a question of law and partly a question of fact. If a person is present in the UK for over six months in one year of assessment, whether that is a continuous period or the aggregate of broken periods, he is regarded as resident here for income tax purposes, irrespective of his actual intention (TA 1970, s. 51). In any other case it is a question of fact whether he is resident here. To be resident it is not sufficient for a person actually to be here, but he must also live here and intend to live here either permanently or for a considerable time, or have a settled home here (*Levene* v. *I.R. Comrs.* (1927), 13 T.C. 486). A person must actually be within the UK for some part of the year of assessment if he is to be regarded as resident during that year.

Taking these two rules together, a visitor to the UK will be resident here if he is here for more than six months in the year of assessment, although if he chooses his time carefully, he can be here for a continuous period of just less than 12 months without becoming automatically resident. Thus, a person could be here for the period, say, 7 October 1979 to 4 October 1980 without becoming automatically resident, for he would not thereby be resident for six months in any one year of assessment. Whether he is resident in other cases will depend on how long he intends to remain here, and the length of time for which he has actually been here. Clearly the longer he has been here, the easier it is for the Revenue to establish that he has his settled home here.

Residence is not an exclusive concept, so that a person may be resident simultaneously in more than one country. Thus, an American businessman who has his permanent home in New York but works in England on a nine month engagement which falls within one year of assessment will be resident both in England, where he has been for more than 6 months, and in New York, where he has his permanent home.

4   Ordinary residence

A person is ordinarily resident in a country where he maintains a residence, in the sense just described, in the existing course of events (*Reid* v. *I.R. Comrs.* (1926), 10 T.C. 673). The essence of ordinary residence is that regard is had to the way in which a person usually conducts his life. If, therefore, a person has his main home abroad, but also keeps a house in England, or even, sometimes, if he just visits England as a regular event without making a home here, he may be ordinarily resident here (*Peel* v. *I.R. Comrs.* (1928), 13 T.C. 443). A person may be ordinarily resident here for a year of assessment even though he is not actually present here at any time during that year. If, therefore, a person who has his main home abroad, lived in his house in England for a holiday in each year from 1970 to 1980, except 1977 when illness prevented him from coming, he will probably be regarded as ordinarily resident here in each of these years, including 1977.

As in the case of the concept of residence, a person may be ordinarily resident simultaneously in more than one country.

The Revenue adopt two general principles in deciding whether a person who has his main home abroad is ordinarily resident in the UK. Though each case depends on its own facts, the general yardstick is that a person is regarded as being ordinarily resident here if he is here for three months or more in four consecutive years. Where habitual visits are made, even if they do not last for a total of three months, or if he maintains a place of abode here for his occupation, he will probably be regarded as being ordinarily resident. Where the general yardstick of visits of three months in each of four years is adopted, the person is regarded as ordinarily resident here from the beginning of the 5th year of assessment.

5 Husband and wife

Where in a tax year one spouse is resident in th UK, and the other is not, the same tax provisions apply as if they were permanently separated, and each is given the allowances and reliefs appropriate to a single person. If, however, there is no rupture in the matrimonial relationship, and total tax payable would have been lower had the husband been treated as a married man living with his wife, a reduction is made on the two assessments so that the amount payable is reduced to that total. The method of adjustment between husband and wife is in the discretion of the Revenue. Income from abroad arising to a wife is regarded as her own income and not that of her husband, so she will not be exempt merely because her husband is resident abroad.

6 Person leaving United Kingdom

Where a person is employed in full time employment abroad, and all the duties of that employment are performed outside the UK, the question of his residence is determined without taking into account any house which he maintains in the UK (TA 1970, s. 50). Strictly this rule applies only to the question of residence, and not to ordinary residence, but the Revenue practice is to extend it to ordinary residence. The rule applies to the taxpayer himself, but not to his wife, unless she also takes full time employment abroad. If, therefore, husband and wife spend some time abroad while he alone is in full time employment there, and a house is maintained for them in the UK, the wife may be treated as ordinarily resident in the UK.

Where a person who has been ordinarily resident in the UK goes abroad he is in general regarded at first as remaining ordinarily resident here for three years, and the position is reviewed at the end of that time. If he has not made visits to the UK exceeding three months in each year, he will then be treated, retrospectively, as ceasing to be ordinarily resident when he left, and the appropriate adjustment will be made. Where the taxpayer has quite clearly left England permanently, the Revenue may concede before the expiration of the three year period that he has ceased to be ordinarily resident. This is particularly so if he establishes a permanent place of abode abroad.

It is now possible to consider the two situations outlined at the beginning of this chapter.

B   BENEFICIARY UNDER FOREIGN TRUST: INCOME TAX

1   *Generally*

A person may be chargeable to United Kingdom income tax in respect of income of a non-resident trust in one of three circumstances:

a   the non-resident trust is a "settlement", within TA 1970, Part XVI;

b   the income arises to the non-resident trust as a result of a transfer to which TA 1970, s. 478 applies; or

c   the person is a beneficiary of a non-resident trust.

2   *"Settlements"*

The definition of "settlement" (TA 1970, ss. 444 (2), 454 (3)) is wide enough to include an ordinary foreign trust, and arrangements which are treated as constituting a settlement (see p. 187, *ante*). Whether or not income from a "settlement" in this sense will be subject to the Part XVI provisions depends on:

a   the place where the settlement was made; and

b   the residential status of the settlor.

a Place of making settlement The underlying principle appears to be that the Part XVI provisions do not apply to a settlement which is made abroad, unless the particular section so provides. There is no express provision to this effect, but the principle may be deduced from the fact that certain sections deal specifically with the place where the settlement is made. The following provisions contain express provisions under which they do apply "whenever" the settlement was made:

i   s. 437 (settlements for children of the settlor: s. 437 (2));

ii   ss. 445, 446 (revocable settlements: s. 445 (1), 446 (1));

iii s. 447 (settlements where settlor retains an interest: s. 447 (1));

iv   s. 448 (settlements where discretionary power to benefit settlor: s. 448 (1));

v   s. 450 (disallowance of deduction from total income: s. 450 (4));

vi   s. 451 (capital sums paid to settlor: s. 451 (8)).

The following provisions do not have any such provision, and do not, therefore, appear to apply where the settlement was made abroad:

i   s. 434 (short-term covenants); and

ii   s. 457 (excess liability).

b Residential status of settlor The settlement provisions cannot apply to make the income that of the settlor if under the law which governs the settlement the settlor has divested himself of the income, and the settlor is not chargeable to United Kingdom income tax. Thus, in *Becker* v. *Wright* (1966) 42 T.C. 591 a person who was not resident in the United Kingdom covenanted to make annual payments to a person who was resident. It was held that the forerunner of s. 434 could not apply to deem the income to be that of the non-resident covenantor, and the income was therefore held to be that of the covenantee.

If the settlor was resident at the time when the settlement was made, the provisions will cease to apply during any year in which he is not resident (s. 437 (5); s. 449 (1); s. 451 (6)).

c Where "settlement" provisions apply Where the settlement provisions apply, their effect is the same as in the case of a corresponding settlement which has no foreign element.

3 Section 478; FA 1981, s. 45

TA 1970, s. 478 and FA 1981, s. 45 are of wide application, and is not confined to trusts. They provide that if income becomes payable to persons resident or domiciled out of the United Kingdom, whether or not those persons are trustees, that income is deemed to be that of an individual resident in the United Kingdom if (*a*) the individual is ordinarily resident in the United Kingdom and (*b*) the income becomes payable to the non-resident trustees or other persons by virtue of, or in consequence of, a transfer of assets, including a payment of money.

It seems that if there is at least one trustee resident in the United Kingdom, it cannot be said that income becomes payable to persons who are (all resident abroad, and that therefore these provisions cannot apply.

While the possible operation of these provisions must be kept in mind, particularly where the individual in question is not named as a beneficiary, because they are of general application they are not considered further in this book.

4 Non-resident trusts

It is now possible to consider the ordinary case of a person who is resident in the United Kingdom and who is a beneficiary under a foreign trust.

a Relevance of foreign law If there is any question as to the nature of the rights of a beneficiary, that question is to be determined by the law which governs the settlement. However, when the nature of the beneficiary's rights has been determined, the taxation liability will be determined according to United Kingdom, and not foreign, tax laws.

The first proposition is illustrated by *Archer-Shee* v. *Garland*, [1931] A.C. 212. In *Baker* v. *Archer-Shee,* [1927] A.C. 844; p. 000, *ante,* the court had proceeded on the basis that the beneficiary was entitled to income from stock and securities. However, the settlement was governed by the law of the State of New York, and in *Archer-Shee* v. *Garland* further evidence was adduced that under New York law, the nature of the right of the beneficiary was only to see that the trust was properly administered by the trustees. The House of Lords held that the income of the beneficiary was that from a foreign possession other than stocks, shares or rents, and not from the stocks and shares themselves. *Archer-Shee* v. *Garland* illustrates the principle, although the particular distinction is not now material.

The second proposition is illustrated by *Inchyra* v. *Jennings,* [1966] Ch. 37. Under a settlement which was governed by the law of the District of Columbia, Lady Inchyra was entitled to a distribution of 1% of the capital of the fund each year. The nature of the payments to Lady Inchyra for the purposes of trust law was capital, but by virtue of the quality of recurrence they were treated for income tax purposes, but not for the purposes of general trust law, as income (see p. 241, *ante*). The fact that under the United States law the payments would have been treated as capital for taxation purposes was irrelevant.

b The source It may be necessary to determine the source of the income which the beneficiary receives or to which he is entitled. This will govern the Case under which the income is to be assessed, and so, in the case of commencement and termination, the particular provisions appropriate to that Case, and in some circumstances, such as where the trustees carry on a trade, the expenses which are deductible in computing the income.

The rule in *Baker* v. *Archer-Shee, supra,* will determine whether the source of the income is the underlying asset, or the trust itself. If it is the trust, it seems that where the beneficiary has a fixed interest, the source is the trust instrument itself (*Inchyra* v. *Jennings, supra*). If the trust is a discretionary trust, the source appears to be the decision of the trustees to confer the income benefit on the beneficiary.

c Basis of assessment The basis of assessment under Schedule D, Case V is:

a   for the first year in which the foreign income arises, the tax is assessed on the actual income of that year to 5 April;

b   for the second year in which the income arises, the tax is also assessed on the actual income of that year unless the income first arose on the preceding 6 April;

c   for the third year in which the income arises, the tax is generally assessed on the income of the preceding year, but the beneficiary can elect to be assessed on the income of the current year (TA 1970, s. 123). Notice of election may be given at any time within 6 years from the end of that year of assessment;

d   for the fourth and subsequent years, on the income of the preceding year;

e   for the penultimate year, the tax is charged either on the income of the preceding year, or, at the option of the Revenue, on the actual income of that year;

f   for the last year, on the actual income (TA 1970, ss. 121, 124).

In the exceptional case of a person who is not domiciled in the UK, or is not ordinarily resident here, he is assessed only on that part of the income which is remitted to the United Kingdom. The rules as to the basis of assessment are the same as just mentioned, except that the calculation is based on the amount remitted and not on that which arose.

d Delayed remittances   Where the laws of the country in which the income arises prevent the income being remitted to the United Kingdom, the beneficiary may elect that the charge to tax shall be postponed until it does become remittable (TA 1970, s. 418).

e Assessment   Foreign income is usually received gross, when the tax is collected by means of direct assessment, but where it is paid through an English agent, it will usually be paid subject to deduction of tax by him at the basic rate.

C FOREIGN TRUST: CAPITAL GAINS TAX: PRIOR TO 6 APRIL 1981

1 *Generally*

Where a trust is non-resident, it is necessary to consider separately the position of the trustees and that of the beneficiaries. One code applies up to 5 April 1981, and a different code thereafter.

2 *Liability of non-resident trustees*

Where the trustees of a trust are neither resident nor ordinarily resident in the United Kingdom in the year of assessment in which a gain is realised, the general rule is that the trustees cannot themselves be liable to capital gains tax (CGTA 1979, s. 2). This is so whether the asset is situated in the United Kingdom or abroad. In exceptional circumstances, a liability will arise where the asset is situated in the United Kingdom, but these will not usually affect trustees (CGTA 1979, s. 12; FA 1973, s. 38).

3 *Residence of trustees*

It is necessary to determine where the body of trustees as such is to be regarded as being resident and ordinarily resident. The question depends on:

a the residential status of the individuals who are themselves the trustees; and

b the place where the administration of the trust is ordinarily carried on.

The rules are:

a   as a general principle, all trusts (whether they have a foreign connexion or not) are regarded as resident and ordinarily resident in the United Kingdom (CGTA 1979, s. 52 (1));

b   as an exception to this general principle, if

  i the general administration of the trust is ordinarily carried on outside the United Kingdom; and

  ii the majority of the trustees are not resident or ordinarily resident in the United Kingdom

the trust is not regarded as resident or ordinarily resident in the United Kingdom (*ibid*).

c   Special provisions govern the position of a person such as a solicitor or a company such as an executor and trustee company of one of the banks, whose business consists of or includes the management of trusts, or of acting as trustees. Where such a person is acting as a trustee of a trust, that person is not regarded in relation to a trust as being resident in the United Kingdom if the whole of the trust property was derived from a person when he was not domiciled, resident, or ordinarily resident in the United Kingdom (s. 52 (2)).

If, taking into account the actual non-resident status of non-professional trustees, and the actual or deemed non-resident status of professional trustees, all or a majority of the trustees are regarded as being non-resident, the administration of the trust is deemed to be ordinarily carried on outside the United Kingdom even if it is actually carried on here (*ibid*).

The test of residence of a trust is broadly the same as that used for capital transfer tax (p. 332, *ante*) but with the burden of proof reversed.

4   Liability of beneficiaries in case of certain non-resident settlements

In view of the general exemption from capital gains tax of non-resident trustees, the Capital Gains Tax 1979, s. 17 provides that in certain circumstances, the gain which would have been chargeable in the hands of the trustees, had they been resident, was to be apportioned among those beneficiaries who were themselves domiciled and resident in the United Kingdom.

Section 17 applied to any "settlement" within the special Part XVI sense (see p. 186, *ante*; an example is *Chinn* v. *Collins,* [1981] 1 All E.R. 189, H.L.). Accordingly, it could apply to a wide variety of structures, such as a "arrangements, but it could not apply to an ordinary trust, or to a wider structure, if there is no element of bounty (*I.R. Comrs.* v. *Plummer,* [1979] 3 All E.R. 775, H.L.; p. 187, *ante*).

5 *Application only to certain* inter vivos *settlements*

Section 17 applied where (*a*) the trustees were not resident and not ordinarily resident in the United Kingdom when the gain was realised, and (*b*) either

- i the settlor was domiciled, and either resident or ordinarily resident in the United Kingdom at the time when the gain was realised; or
- ii the settlor was domiciled, and was either resident or ordinarily resident in the United Kingdom, at the time when the settlement was made (s. 17 (1)).

It is a general principle of law that where a disposition is made on death, it is treated as being made immediately *after* death. The capital transfer tax legislation contains the special provision which treats the transfer as being made immediately before death, but there is no such provision in the capital gains tax legislation, and the general rule applies (see *Larter* v. *Skone James,* [1976] 2 All E.R. 615). As a settlement which is made on death is treated for capital gains tax purposes as being made at the moment after death, when the settlor, by virtue of his death, can have no domicile, s. 17 could not apply to will trusts.

Further, if the settlement is an *inter vivos* settlement but the settlor was domiciled out of the United Kingdom, and was not resident or ordinarily resident in the United Kingdom when it was made, s. 17 could have no application after his death, whether or not he became domiciled or resident between making the settlement and when the death occurred.

On the other hand, if the settlor was domiciled and either resident or ordinarily resident in the United Kingdom at the time when the settlement was made, it remained potentially subject to s. 17 until 5 April 1981.

6 *Where life interest*

Where s. 17 could apply, the amount on which the trustees would have been chargeable had they been resident was apportioned among all the beneficiaries who had an interest in the settled property, the apportionment being made according the respective values of their equitable interests. In making the valuation, the fact that a life or similar interest was contingent was to be taken into account, but the fact that an interest was wholly or partially defeasible, as in the case of the potential reduction in the share of a child on the birth of further children to his parents, was ignored (s. 17 (2)). (*Leedale* v. *Lewis Pearson,* [1980] Simon's Tax Intelligence 515). Likewise, if a beneficiary had an interest which could be defeated by the future exercise of a power of appointment, that possibility was to be ignored (*ibid*).

Where amounts were apportioned to beneficiaries who were domiciled and either resident or ordinarily resident during the year of assessment in which the gain was realised, those amounts were treated in the hands of the beneficiaries as chargeable gains for that year (*ibid*).

7 Discretionary trusts

a Generally Even where the trust was discretionary, the legislation directed an apportionment of the gain to be made among beneficiaries according to the respective values of their interests. Even if the values of these interests are very small, they provided the basis for the apportionment. In *Leedale* v. *Lewis Pearson,* [1980] Simon's Tax Intelligence 515 the settlor transferred funds to non-resident trustees upon trust to hold capital and income on trust for such of her grandchildren born within the perpetuity period as the trustees should appoint. The trustees were given overriding powers to apply income to any of them, and to accumulate income. At the end of the perpetuity period, in default of appointment the funds were to be held on trust (for the grandchildren then living, with remainders over. The trustees had not made any distribution. The grandchildren had the right to procure proper administration of the trust, but the only "interests" which they had were their contingent interests in capital. It was accepted that the value of these interests was negligible. Nevertheless, the values of their interests were equal, and it was just and reasonable to apportion the gain equally between them. In this case no account was taken of the interests of others, which were said to be "microscopically remote."

b Income distributions If a beneficiary had received discretionary payments of income in the year of assessment in which the gain was realised, or in the two preceding years, he was treated as having an interest with a value equal to that of an annuity of a yearly amount equal to one-third of the income payments which he had received during the three year period (s. 17 (3) (*a*)). Income payments which were made after the end of the year of assessment in which the gain was realised were not taken into account.

379

c   *Capital distributions*   A further provision applied where at any time after the gain was realised a discretionary capital payment was made. If that capital payment "represented the chargeable gain in whole or in part", then except to the extent that the gain had been attributed to some other beneficiary who was domiciled and resident or ordinarily resident in the United Kingdom, the amount of the capital payment to the extent that it represents the gain was treated as if it was a chargeable gain in the hands of the recipient beneficiary in the year of assessment in which it was received (s. 17 (3) (*b*)). It seems that a capital payment can only "represent" an actual gain, so that the section cannot apply in the event of a gain on a deemed disposal. Further, while a payment which is made from the proceeds of disposal of an asset which was sold at a profit may be said to "represent" in whole or in part the gain, this provision would not appear to apply if the trustees remitted from some other source.

d   *Pre-6 April 1965 settlements*   If the settlement was made before 6 April 1965, no part of the gain could be apportioned to a beneficiary who had only a life interest, if he could not obtain any part of the capital (s. 17 (4) (a)). Further, the tax chargeable on a gain apportioned to a beneficiary who only had a reversionary interest could be deferred until his interest fell into possession, or until he could obtain any of the capital (s. 17 (4) (b)).

8   Losses

a   *Beneficiaries not directly entitled to benefit of losses*   Section 17 is stated not to apply in relation to a loss accruing to the trustees of a settlement (s. 17 (6)). This had the effect that if the only transaction which had occurred during the year of assessment had been the disposal of one or more assets at a loss, that loss could not be apportioned to the beneficiaries to give them loss relief.

b   *Net chargeable gains*   However, where there was a gain, the amount to be apportioned was "the amount, if any, on which the trustees would have been chargeable to capital gains tax under section 4 (1)". Had the trustees been domiciled and resident in the United Kingdom, the amount on which they would have been chargeable would have taken account of losses sustained in the year of assessment in which the disposal occurred, and in previous years to the extent to which they had not been used up. Thus, the amounts of these losses were taken into account in calculating the net chargeable gains which were apportioned to the beneficiaries.

9   Trusts and companies

It is very common to find that the sole asset of a non-resident trust is the whole of the issued share capital in a non-resident investment company; and that individual assets are acquired by the investment company. The question arises whether a gain which accrues to the underlying investment company can be attributed to the trust (under s. 15), and then further attributed from the trust to the beneficiaries. This attribution probably could not be made where the gain accrued to the company before 10 March 1981 (see FA 1981, s. 85).

10   Tax paid by trustees

If the trustees paid the capital gains tax which was chargeable on the beneficiary, the payment by the trustees is not for the purposes of taxation to be treated as a payment to the beneficiary (s. 17 (5)). The beneficiary would not, therefore, be under any income tax liability in respect of it.

D   FOREIGN TRUSTS: CAPITAL GAINS TAX: AFTER 5 APRIL 1981

1   Liability of non-resident trustees

The general rule is the same as that considered previously (p. 376, *ante*), namely that the trustees of a settlement which is neither resident nor ordinarily resident in the United Kingdom cannot themselves be liable to capital gains tax.

Likewise, the same rules which have been considered (p. 376, *ante*) to determine the residential status of a settlement apply.

2   Trust becoming non-resident

Where a trust which has been resident in the United Kingdom becomes non-resident, a liability can arise on the trustees in two circumstances.

a   Previous held-over gains   It has been seen (p. 192, *ante*) that where the settlor transferred assets into trust *in specie* after 5 April 1981, he could have elected for hold-over relief (FA 1980, s. 79; FA 1981, s. 78), but only where, at the time of transfer, the settlement was resident. If, thereafter, the settlement becomes non-resident, a chargeable gain is deemed to accrue to the trustees at the time immediately before the settlement becomes non-resident (FA 1981, s. 79 (1)). The amount of the chargeable gain is the held-over gain.

This does not constitute a deemed disposal and re-acquisition of the asset, but merely a clawback of the held-over gain.

The primary liability is that of the trustees. If, however, the trustees do not pay within twelve months of the date when the tax becomes payable, an assessment can be made on the transferor (s. 79 (7)). If the settlor pays the tax, he has a right of recovery against the trustees (s. 79 (9)).

b Following disposal of equitable interest In general, there is no liability to capital gains tax on the disposal by a beneficiary of his equitable interest under the settlement, provided that the trustees of the settlement are, at the time of the disposal of the equitable interest, resident and ordinarily resident in the United Kingdom (see p. 279, *ante*). A charge will arise on the trustees, however, if, at any time after the disposal by the beneficiary of his equitable interest, the trustees become neither resident nor ordinarily resident in the United Kingdom (FA 1981, s. 88).

In this case, a chargeable gain is deemed to have accrued to the trustees, immediately before they become non-resident. The amount of the deemed chargeable gain is equivalent to the gain which accrued to the beneficiary on the disposal of his equitable interest (s. 88 (2)).

Although the chargeable gain is deemed to accrue immediately before the trustees become non-resident, the position is in effect kept in suspense until the end of the year of assessment in which the trustees become non-resident. If by the end of that year the trustees dispose of all the assets which constituted the settled property at the time when the beneficiary disposed of his equitable interest, no chargeable gain is deemed to accrue under this provision, although there may be a liability under a different head (see p. 383, *post*).

There is a limit on the amount of the chargeable gain which is deemed to accrue. The amount can never exceed the market value as at the time when the trustees become non-resident of those assets which have not been disposed of by the trustees before the end of the year of assessment in which the trustees become non-resident (s. 88 (3)).

This provision applies only where the beneficiary disposed of his equitable interest after 9 March 1981 (s. 88 (7)).

3 *Liability of beneficiaries*

a Generally Although, in general, non-resident trustees are not liable to capital gains tax, in certain circumstances the gains which accrue to them can be attributed to the beneficiaries, and be treated as chargeable gains accruing to the beneficiaries (FA 1981, s. 80).

It will be convenient to consider separately settlements which have always been non-resident, settlements which have been resident but become non-resident, and settlements which have been non-resident but become resident.

b Settlements to which provisions apply The provisions apply to any settlement which:

i the trustees are at no time during the year of assessment in question resident or ordinarily resident in the United Kingdom (s. 80 (1)).

ii in the case of an *inter vivos* settlement, either

(*a*) the settlor was domiciled and either resident or ordinarily resident in the United Kingdom at any time during the year of assessment in which the settlement was made; or

(*b*) the settlor is domiciled and either resident or ordinarily resident in the United Kingdom at any time during the year of assessment being considered; and

iii in the case of a settlement created by will, or arising under the intestacy rules, the testator or intestate was domiciled and either resident or ordinarily resident in the United Kingdom at the time of death (s. 80 (7)).

It follows that, subject to what is said later (p. 386, *post*) the provisions do not apply:

i in the case of an *inter vivos* settlement, during the lifetime of a settlor who was not domiciled, or, if he was domiciled, was neither resident nor ordinarily resident, either when the settlement was created or at any time thereafter;

ii in the case of an *inter vivos* settlement which was created by a settlor who was not domiciled or was neither resident nor ordinarily resident at the time when the settlement was created, at any time after the death of the settlor; and

iii in the case of a settlement arising on death, where the deceased was not domiciled, or was neither resident nor ordinarily resident, at the date of death.

There is a "settlement" for the purposes of this provision if there is a settlement in the ordinary sense, and not in the special sense used in *I.R. Comrs* v. *Plummer* [1979] 3 All E.R. 775, H.L.; cf. p. 187, *ante*).

c Vulnerable beneficiaries A beneficiary becomes vulnerable to an assessment if at any time after 9 March 1981 he receives a "capital

payment", other than a capital payment which represents a chargeable gain which accrued to the trustees before 6 April, 1981 (s. 80 (8)).
A capital payment is treated as made when:

    i any payment is made which is not chargeable to income tax on the beneficiary, (or, in the case of a beneficiary who is neither resident nor ordinarily resident in the United Kingdom, is received by him otherwise than as income) (s. 83 (1));

   ii any transfer of assets not of an income nature is made (s. 83 (2));

  iii any loan is made, or any other type of benefit of a non-income nature is conferred (s. 83 (2)); or

  iv the beneficiary becomes absolutely entitled as against the trustees to any assets, or he would have become absolutely entitled to such assets but for being under a disability (see p. 255, *ante*).

A beneficiary is treated as receiving a capital payment if he receives it indirectly from the trustees, or if the trustees directly or indirectly pay it in discharge of a debt or otherwise for his benefit (s. 83 (5)). A beneficiary is also treated as receiving a capital payment if it is received by a third party at his direction, or by virtue of an assignment made by him (*ibid*).

A beneficiary who receives a capital payment in any of these senses jointly with another person is treated as receiving the payment himself (*ibid*).

    d Attributing the gains It is necessary to determine:

    i the amount of capital payments which each vulnerable beneficiary has received, and which are to be brought into account;

   ii the amount of so-called "trust gains"; and

  iii the extent to which the trust gains are to be attributed to the beneficiaries.

    i The amount of capital payments The value of capital payments which are made outright is the amount of the payment, or the value of the asset. In the case of any loan or other benefit, the value of the capital payment is the value of the benefit (s. 83 (4)). No formula is prescribed for determining the value of the benefit.

The total amount of capital payments which a beneficiary is treated as having received at any time is:

    (*a*) the amount of such payments received after 9 March 1981 (s. 80 (8));

(*b*) less:

   (i) the amount of such payments which represents chargeable gains which accrued to the trustees before 6 April, 1981 (s. 80 (8)); and

   (ii) in the case of years of assessement after 1981/82, the amounts of chargeable gains which are treated as having accrued to the beneficiary after 9 March 1981 (s. 80 (5)).

ii The amount of the "trust gains" The amount of the trust gains in respect of a year of assessment is the aggregate of:

(*a*) the amount on which the trustees would have been chargeable if they had been resident or ordinarily resident in the United Kingdom in that year (after deducting losses) (s. 80 (2));

(*b*) the amount of gains accruing to an underlying company which is attributed to the trustees (see p. 386, *post*); and

(*c*) (i) the amount on which the trustees would have been chargeable for all previous year of assessment from 1981/82 if they had been resident or ordinarily resident in those years; less

   (ii) the amount which has been attributed to the beneficiaries (s. 80 (2)).

iii The method of attribution The amount of the trust gains is provisionally attributed to all vulnerable beneficiaries in proportion to the amounts of the capital payments (as defined above) which they have received (s. 80 (4)). If, however, in the case of any beneficiary the amount provisionally attributed to him would exceed the amount of the capital payments which he has received, that excess is not attributed to any beneficiary during that year (*ibid*). It will, therefore, form part of the trust gains for the following year.

Each beneficiary is treated as realising chargeable gains to the extent to which the trust gains are attributed to him (s. 80 (3)).

iv Exempt beneficiaries The trust gains are attributed to all beneficiaries who have received capital payments, irrespective of the domiciliary or residential status of the beneficiaries. However, a beneficiary to whom gains have been attributed will only be chargeable to capital gains tax on them if he is domiciled in the United Kingdom at some time in the year of assessment in which the attribution is made (s. 80 (6)).

4 Resident settlements becoming non-resident

a Effect on liability of beneficiaries Where a settlement which has been resident becomes non-resident, there are, in principle, ignored payments made to beneficiaries while the settlement was resident in calculating the amount of the "capital payments" which they are treated as having received for the purposes just described (s. 81).

b Effect of trustees The effects on the trustees have been noted earlier (pp. 381, 382, *ante*).

5 Non-resident settlement becoming resident Where a non-resident settlement becomes resident, the amount of the trust gains for the last year of assessment in which the settlement is non-resident may not be fully attributed to the beneficiaries. In this case, the unattributed trust gains are attributed to the beneficiaries after the settlement has become resident to the extent to which capital payments are thereafter made from the settlement (s. 81 (2)).

Subject to this, the ordinary rules relating to resident settlements apply.

6 Transfers of assets to other settlements

Where assets are transferred from one settlement to another, the whole or a proportionate part of the trust gains of the transferring settlement are attributed to the transferee settlement (s. 82). The provisions just considered are then made to apply to the transferee settlement in respect of that amount, even if the transferee settlement would not otherwise be within the provisions. This would be so, for example, if the settlor of that settlement was not domiciled and not resident or ordinarily resident when the settlement was made (see p. 383, *ante*).

7 Gains accruing to companies underlying trusts

A very common form of arrangement is to have a non-resident trust owning the shares in a non-resident company, and for gains to accrue to that non-resident company. The rules governing the attribution to its shareholders of gains accruing to the company operate to enable those gains to be attributed to the trustees in the case of gains which accrue to the company after 9 March 1981 (s. 85). The gains which are attributed to the trustees form part of the trust gains for the year of attribution.

E DISPOSAL OF EQUITABLE INTEREST IN NON-RESIDENT SETTLEMENTS

1 Settlement non-resident at time of disposal

Subject to certain exceptions (see p. 279, *ante*), where a beneficiary disposes of his equitable interest under a settlement, no chargeable gain accrues on the disposal (CGTA 1979, s. 58). If, however, the trustees are neither resident nor ordinarily resident in the United Kingdom at the time of the disposal, and the disposal is after 9 March 1981, the disposal is one of a chargeable asset, and there will accordingly be a chargeable gain or an allowable loss (FA 1981, s. 88).

If the equitable interest disposed of is a life interest, it will usually be a wasting asset (CGTA 1979, s. 37 (1) (*d*)).

2 Settlement subsequently becoming non-resident

It has been seen (p. 381, *ante*), that if after 9 March 1981 a beneficiary disposes of his equitable interest under a resident settlement, and the trustees subsequently became non-resident, a liability arises at that time on the trustees (FA 1981, s. 88). If the trustees do not pay, the beneficiary may be assessed and charged to the tax (s. 88 (5)). The beneficiary is given a right of recovery against the trustees (s. 88 (6)).

F BENEFICIARY UNDER FOREIGN TRUST: CAPITAL TRANSFER TAX

1 Generally

The factors which govern liability to capital transfer tax in respect of a trust with a foreign element are:

a   the location of the settled property; and
b   the domiciliary status of the settlor at the time when the settlement was made.

It will be seen that if conditions as to location of the property and the domiciliary status of the settlor are satisfied, there may be an exemption from capital transfer tax, even if:

a   the trust is administered in the United Kingdom;
b   the trustees are resident in the United Kingdom; and
c   the beneficiary is resident in the United Kingdom.

It is therefore proposed to consider these conditions before the detailed rules.

Part VII: Administration of a Trust

2 Location of settled property

Type of property	Location
a Land, whether freehold, leasehold, or any other tenure	The country in which the land is situated
b Chattels	The country in which the chattel is situated
c Ships	The country of the port in which the ship is normally berthed (and not the country of registration: *Trustees, Executors and Agency Co. Ltd.* v. *I.R.C.,* [1973] Ch. 254).
d Stocks, shares, and other securities to bearer	The country in which the document of title is situated
e Registered stocks, shares and other securities	
i generally	The country in which the share, etc., register is required to be kept
ii UK company keeping a dominion register	In the case of shares, etc., registered on that register, the country in which that register is kept
iii Foreign companies keeping two registers, one being a principal register and the other a subsidiary register	The country in which the principal register is kept
iv Foreign companies keeping two principal registers, the security being registered on one register only	The country in which the principal register upon which the security is registered is kept
v Foreign companies keeping two principal registers, the security being registered on both	The country in which one of the principal registers is kept which can be identified as being the more appropriate country for location by virtue of other factors, such as the presence of the document of title
f i Currency	The country in which the coins or notes are physically situated
ii Bank accounts	The country in which the branch of the bank at which the money is payable is situated
g Debts	
i generally	The country in which the debtor resides
ii debts payable by virtue of a document under seal	The country in which the deed is situated
iii debts due from a Government, or payable by statute, where evidenced by document	The country in which the document is situated
iv judgment debts	The country where the judgment is recorded

Type of property	*Location*
v mortgage debts generally	As i or ii, according to whether or not the mortgage deed is under seal
vi mortgage debts where the mortgagor is not under a personal obligation to pay	The country in which the asset upon which the debt is secured is situated

3 Domicile of settlor

A person is domiciled in the United Kingdom for capital transfer tax purposes if either

a he is so domiciled for the purposes of the general law, under the rules stated earlier (p. 369, *ante*); or

b he is deemed to be so domiciled under special rules which apply only for capital transfer tax. These special rules are:

    i if a person was domiciled in the United Kingdom on or after 10 December 1974, and subsequently becomes domiciled in some part of the Channel Islands or the Isle of Man, he will be deemed to remain domiciled in the United Kingdom until he acquires another domicile outside the United Kingdom and outside the Channel Islands and the Isle of Man (FA 1975, s. 45 (1) (c)). This does not apply where the person had a domicile of origin or a domicile of dependence in the Channel Islands or the Isle of Man (s. 45 (2A); FA 1977, s. 49 (1).

    ii if a person was domiciled in the United Kingdom on or after 10 December 1974, and subsequently becomes domiciled elsewhere, (but not in some part of the Channel Islands or the Isle of Man) he is deemed to remain domiciled in the United Kingdom for a period of three years (s. 45 (1) (a)).

    iii if a person is not domiciled in the United Kingdom at a time which is relevant for capital transfer tax purposes, but was resident in the United Kingdom for income tax purposes in at least seventeen out of the twenty years of assessment ending with the year in which the relevant time falls he is treated as being domiciled in the United Kingdom at that time (s. 45 (1) (b) (2)).

4 Interests in possession

The position where there is an interest in possession is as follows:

    i if the settlement was created before 10 December 1974, there will be no liability to capital transfer tax in respect of the coming to an end (either in lifetime or on death) of the interest in possession in the settled property if:

(a) the property is situated outside the United Kingdom; and
(b) at the time when the settlement was made the settlor was domiciled outside the United Kingdom (FA 1975, Sch. 5, paras. 2 (1), 4 (11)).

ii if the settlement was created after 9 December 1974 there will be no liability to capital transfer tax in respect of the coming to an end of the interest in possession in the settled property if:

(a) the property is situated outside the United Kingdom; and
(b) at the time when the settlement was made the settlor was:
  (i) domiciled outside the United Kingdom; and
  (ii) not deemed to be domiciled in the United Kingdom for capital transfer tax purposes under the special rules already considered.

iii if the settlement was created before 10 December 1974, but property was added to the settlement on or after that date then the property which was settled before 10 December 1974 is dealt with under rule i and the property which was settled on or after that date is dealt with under rule ii.

If, therefore, the trust fund is invested outside the United Kingdom, and the settlor was not domiciled or deemed to be domiciled in the United Kingdom at the time when the settlement was made, there will be no liability in respect of an interest in possession under the settlement even if the beneficiary is domiciled and resident in the United Kingdom.

5 No interest in possession

If under the rules just considered there would be no liability to capital transfer tax, there will be no liability when a capital distribution is made or is deemed to be made out of settled property in which no interest in possession subsists (FA 1975, Sch. 5, para. 11 (11)).

6 Exempt Government securities

These rules are modified when the settled property consists of or includes, exempt British Government securities. These are considered later (p. 393 *post*).

7 Periodic charge

It will be recalled that where a trust in which no interest in possession subsists is, broadly, administered abroad, there will be liability to an annual periodic charge (p. 332, *ante*).

G FOREIGN BENEFICIARY OF ENGLISH TRUST

1 *Income tax*

Where the trustees of a trust are in the United Kingdom, the fact that a beneficiary may be resident abroad will, in general, make no difference to their income tax liability. In particular, all income which the trustees themselves pay to the foreign beneficiary must be paid subject to the deduction of income tax at the basic rate and, if appropriate (p. 232, *ante*) at the additional rate. However, where trustees hold on behalf of a foreign resident absolutely entitled, or where a foreign resident is entitled to the whole of the income, so that the trustees can properly direct that income payments are to be made to him direct, they might well wish to take advantage of the exemption from United Kingdom income tax on certain gilt-edged securities noted at pp. 393 and 405, *post*. They might also wish to direct payment of income derived from foreign sources to the non-resident beneficiary (p. 228, *ante*).

2 *Capital gains tax*

Liability for capital gains tax is governed primarily by the residential status of the trustees, but subject to the special rules noted earlier (p. 377, *ante*). Accordingly, where the trustees are resident in the UK, normal liability to capital gains tax will arise, even although one or more of the beneficiaries is abroad.

Where trustees resident in the United Kingdom hold assets as nominees for a foreign beneficiary who is neither resident nor ordinarily resident in the UK, they will not be under any liability for capital gains tax in respect of that asset (CGTA 1979, s. 46).

3 *Capital transfer tax*

Liability to capital transfer tax depends on the domiciliary status of the settlor at the time when the property became settled property (Sch. 5, para. 2) and on the location of the assets (p. 388, *ante*). It is only in those circumstances in which there would be no liability where the beneficiary is resident in the United Kingdom that there will be no liability where the beneficiary is elsewhere.

4 *Dividends*

Where non-resident trustees invest in United Kingdom equities, they are not entitled to a tax credit in respect of a dividend (FA 1972, s. 86 (1)), but no liability arises to income tax at the basic rate (s. 87 (5)).

5 Additional rate liability

Although no assessment can be made to income tax at the basic rate, where non-resident trustees of a discretionary or accumulating trust receive income from the United Kingdom, they are liable to income tax at the additional rate on that income, if they would have been liable had they been resident (*I.R. Comrs.* v. *Regent Trust Co. Ltd.*, The Times, 30 November 1979). The liability is on the actual dividends received, not on the grossed up equivalent of the dividends.

6 Payments to resident beneficiaries

It may be that non-resident trustees of a discretionary trust receive income from United Kingdom sources, and make income distributions to beneficiaries resident in the United Kingdom. The strict position is as follows:

a   the trustees will have suffered the additional rate liability on that income (*supra*);

b   so far as the beneficiary is concerned, the source of the income payment to him is the exercise by the trustees of their discretion;

c   FA 1973, s. 17 (p. 232, *ante*) does not apply, because the income of the beneficiary is chargeable under Case V, and not Case III, of Schedule D;

d   the payment which the beneficiary receives is treated as a gross payment, in respect of which he is not entitled to a credit for the tax suffered by the trustees.

The beneficiary is, therefore, at a disadvantage compared with what would have been his position had the trustees been resident. This is shown by the following examples, where it is assumed that the beneficiary is liable at the basic rate only.

		Trustees resident	Trustees non-resident
Trustees receive divident from United Kingdom company of		£70	£70
Trustees entitled to a tax credit thereon of	£30		
	=		
		£70	£70
Trustees liable to additional rate tax of		15	10.50
Leaving		£55	£59.50
Trustees make payment to beneficiary of		£55	£59.50

	Trustees resident	*Trustees non-resident*
Beneficiary treated as receiving a payment of	£100	£59.50
from which tax has been deducted of	£45	nil
Beneficiary can make repayment claim for	£15	
Beneficiary liable for		£17.85
Beneficiary's final position is:		
received from trustees	£55	£59.50
add: tax reclaimed	£15	
less: tax paid	—	17.85
	£70	£41.65

In some circumstances the Revenue allow, by concession, credit for the additional rate tax suffered by the non-resident trustees.

H EXEMPT GOVERNMENT SECURITIES

1 *The securities*

Certain Government securities are issued on the basis that neither the income therefrom nor the capital is liable to any form of taxation in the United Kingdom so long as they are in the beneficial ownership of persons neither domiciled nor ordinarily resident in the United Kingdom (F(No. 2)A 1915, s. 47; F(No. 2)A 1931, s. 22 (1); FA 1940, s. 60 (1)). In almost all cases, the exemption is subject to any present or future provisions of the law designed to prevent avoidance of tax by persons domiciled, resident, or ordinarily resident in the United Kingdom.

A list of the securities currently in issue is given in Appendix II.

2 *Income Tax*

Interest on 3½% War Loan is automatically paid without deduction of tax. In respect of other stocks, application for interest to be paid gross is made to:

The Inspector of Foreign Dividends
Lynwood Road
Thames Ditton
Surrey K77 OPD   Telephone 01 – 398 4242

If it should transpire that the recipient is not exempt from income tax on the interest, an assessment can be made under Schedule D, Case III (TA 1970, s. 101 (1)).

3 Capital transfer tax

a Generally The general terms on which Exempt Government Securities are issued do not by themselves confer exemption from capital transfer tax (*Von Ernst et Cie* v *I.R. Comrs.*, [1980] 1 All E.R. 677, C.A.). Accordingly, special exemptions are conferred, the conditions for which depending on whether there is an interest in possession.

b Interest in possession Where there is an interest in possession, the securities are excluded property if the beneficiary is neither domiciled nor ordinarily resident in the United Kingdom (FA 1975, Sch. 7, para. 3 (1) (*b*)). The relevant time to be considered is the moment before, and not the moment after, the interest in possession terminates (*Von Ernst et Cie* v. *I.R. Comrs., supra*). If the interest is directly owned by a close company, or a company which would be close if resident in the United Kingdom, the securities will only be excluded property if the participators are neither domiciled nor ordinarily resident in the United Kingdom (FA 1975, s. 39 (1) (*b*); Sch. 5, para. 24 (5); Sch. 7, para. 3 (2B); FA 1978, s. 72).

For this purpose domicile bears its ordinary meaning, and the concepts of deemed domicile do not apply (FA 1975, Sch. 7, para. 3 (3)).

c No interest in possession If there is no interest in possession, the securities are excluded property if all known persons for whose benefit the income or capital has been or might be applied are neither domiciled nor ordinarily resident in the United Kingdom (para. 3 (2)). In this context "benefit" denotes beneficial entitlement. Thus, in *Von Ernst et Cie* v. *I.R. Comrs.*, [1980] 1 All E.R. 677, C.A. where the possible beneficiaries were charities resident in the United Kingdom and individuals who were not domiciled or resident in the United Kingdom, it was held that the exemption applied. It was not necessary to take into account the possibility that payments might be made to the trustees of the charities, because these payments would not be for their "benefit".

As is the case where there is an interest in possession, domicile bears its ordinary, and not its extended, meaning, and where a close company, or a non-resident company that would be close, is involved, all participators must be neither domiciled nor ordinarily resident in the United Kingdom.

If by the same disposition property has passed from one settlement to another, the conditions must be satisfied in respect of both settlements (para. 3 (2A)).

d   Status of settlor irrelevant   It has been seen (p. 391, *ante*) that in general settled property can only be excluded property where the settlor was domiciled outside the United Kingdom when the settlement was made; and that the domiciliary and residential status of the beneficiary is irrelevant. These principles are reversed in the case of Exempt Government Securities. In this case, the exemption depends on the domiciliary and residential status of the beneficiary; and the status of the settlor is irrelevant.

Chapter 22

Charities

Charities enjoy many tax exemptions.

A INCOME TAX

1 Investment income

All sums received by way of interest, annuities, annual payments, and income from land such as rents and premiums on leases, are exempt from income tax provided that they are applied for charitable purposes only (TA 1970, s. 360).

To obtain the benefit of the exemption:

a the recipient must be a body of persons or a trust established for charitable purposes only; and

b the income must be applied to charitable purposes.

It was held in *I.R. Comrs.* v. *Helen Slater Charitable Trust Ltd.*, [1980] 1 All E.R. 785 that where a charity makes an outright payment to another charity, the charity making the payment applies its income to charitable purposes, even if the recipient charity merely accumulates it. It has not been decided whether a charity which receives income from non-charitable sources and accumulates it can be said to apply it to charitable purposes.

Much of the investment income of a charity may have been received subject to deduction of tax, and in this case a repayment claim can be made. Forms are obtainable from the Chief Inspector of Taxes (Claims), Magdalen House, Trinity Road, Bootle, Merseyside L69 9EB. Where the investment income consists of interest on Government securities, an application can be made through the Inspector of Taxes to the Bank of England for the interest to be paid without deduction of tax.

2 Trading income

The profits of a trade carried on by a charity are subject to curious tax rules. The profits of the charity will be exempt from income tax only if applied solely to its purposes and either
- (a) if the purpose, or one of the primary purposes, of the charity is to carry on that business; or
- (b) if the work in connection with that trade is mainly carried on by beneficiaries of the charity (TA 1970, s. 360 (1) (e)).

Otherwise the trading profits will be taxable. If, therefore, a charity is set up to provide assistance for the blind, and it carries on a trade in which the work is done by the blind, any profit applied solely for the purposes of the charity will not be taxable. If, however, the work is done by sighted people and the profits applied for the relief of the blind those profits will not be exempt.

3 Higher rates

Even where the income of a charity is subject to income tax, it is never subject to tax at the higher rates. Further, the additional rates of tax do not apply (FA 1973, s. 16 (2) (c)). This is so whether the income is actually applied to charitable purposes.

4 Deeds of Covenant

The position where income is payable to a charity has been described earlier (p. 200, *ante*).

B CAPITAL GAINS TAX

1 Disposals to a charity

Where an asset is disposed of to a charity by way of gift, or by way of sale at a value which does not exceed the cost to the disponor, the disponor is treated as making the disposal for a consideration which gives rise neither to a gain nor a loss (CGTA 1979, s. 146 (1), (2)).

2 Charity becoming entitled to settled property

Where a charity becomes absolutely entitled to settled property, the general rule (p. 256, *ante*) is displaced by one under which the trustees are deemed to dispose of the settled property for a consideration which gives rise neither to a gain nor a loss, and to re-acquire the property at that value as bare trustees for the charity (s. 146 (3) (a)). Likewise, if following the termination in lifetime of a life interest, the property is held on trust for the charity, the deemed disposal is for a no gain — no loss consideration (s. 146 (3) (b)). The latter rule does not apply in the case of the termination of a life interest on death, when the ordinary rule (p. 260 *ante*) applies.

The special rules apply only if the charity becomes entitled without any person receiving consideration.

3 Assets owned by charity

A gain which accrues to a charity, and is applied for charitable purposes, is not a chargeable gain (CGTA 1979, s. 145 (1)). If, however, property which has been held on charitable trusts ceases to be so held, it is deemed to be disposed of and re-acquired at its market value (s. 145 (2)). Any gain which thereby accrues is a chargeable gain to the extent that it represents the consideration for the disposal (*ibid*).

C DEVELOPMENT LAND TAX

In respect of disposals after 25 March 1980, development land tax is not chargeable on any development value which is realised on a disposal by a charity (DLTA 1976, s. 24 (1), as substituted by FA 1980, s. 111).

The amount of realised development value in respect of which a charity has obtained the exemption becomes chargeable if the disponor ceases to be a charity (s. 24 (2)).

D CAPITAL TRANSFER TAX

1 Transfers to charity

It has been seen (p. 79, *ante*) that provided certain conditions are complied with, there is a general exemption for transfers to charity (FA 1975, Sch. 6, para. 10). However, in the case of a transfer made by an individual within one year of his death, the transfer is exempt only up to an aggregate of £200,000 (para. 10 (1) (b), FA 1980, s. 86). The excess is taxable, but the charity and no other person is liable to pay that tax (s. 26 (3)).

It has also been seen (p. 321, *ante*) that a distribution payment made to charity out of settled property in which no interest in possession subsists is not a capital distribution, and so is not itself liable to tax (para. 10 (2); FA 1976, s. 111).

These exemptions are obtained if the property transferred becomes owned by a charity, or is held on trust for charitable purposes only (para. 10 (3)). It is not necessary to look to the application of the property thereafter. It is, however, necessary for certain conditions as to the gift itself to be satisfied (p. 108, *ante*).

2   *Transfers by charity*

Where settled property is held upon trust for charitable purposes there will usually be no interest in possession in that property. In that case none of the provisions imposing a charge to tax in respect of actual or deemed capital distributions apply (FA 1975, Sch. 5, para. 20).

E   OTHER TAXES

Charities enjoy certain other taxation advantages, for example, rates, which are not within the scope of this book.

Securities exempt from capital gains tax where held for more than one year

11½ %	Treasury Stock 1981
3½ %	Treasury Stock 1979–81
9¾ %	Treasury Stock 1981
8¼ %	Exchequer Stock 1981
9½ %	Exchequer Stock 1981
3%	Exchequer Stock 1981
Variable Rate	Treasury Stock 1981
12¾ %	Exchequer Stock 1981
8½ %	Treasury Loan 1980–82
3%	Treasury Stock 1982
11%	Treasury Stock 1982
2½ %	British Overseas Airways Stock 1977–82
Variable Rate	Treasury Stock 1982
8¼ %	Treasury Stock 1982
9¼ %	Exchequer Stock 1982
8¾ %	Exchequer Stock 1983
3%	British Overseas Airways Stock 1980–83
3%	Exchequer Stock 1983
12%	Treasury Loan 1983
12%	Treasury Loan 1983 "A"
Variable Rate	Treasury Stock 1983
9¼ %	Treasury Stock 1983
10%	Exchequer Stock 1983
13½ %	Exchequer Stock 1983

3%	Exchequer Stock 1983 "A"
5½%	Funding Stock 1982–84
3%	Exchequer Stock 1984
11¼%	Exchequer Stock 1984
12%	Treasury Stock 1984
14%	Exchequer Stock 1984
12¼%	Exchequer Stock 1985
12%	Exchequer Convertible Stock 1985
15%	Treasury Stock 1985
8½%	Treasury Stock 1984–86
3%	Treasury Stock 1985
12½%	Exchequer Stock 1985 "A"
3%	Treasury Stock 1985 "A"
11¾%	Exchequer Stock 1986
6½%	Funding Loan 1985–87
13¼%	Exchequer Stock 1987
12%	Treasury Stock 1987
7¾%	Treasury Loan 1985–88
3%	British Transport Stock 1978–88
5%	Treasury Stock 1986–89
11½%	Treasury Stock 1989
11½%	Treasury Stock 1989 "A"
13%	Treasury Stock 1990
8¼%	Treasury Loan 1987–90
11¾%	Treasury Stock 1991
11¾%	Treasury Stock 1991 "A"
5¾%	Funding Loan 1987–91
11%	Exchequer Stock 1991
13½%	Exchequer Stock 1992
12¾%	Treasury Loan 1992
10%	Treasury Stock 1992
12¼%	Exchequer Stock 1992
12½%	Treasury Loan 1993
6%	Funding Loan 1993
13¾%	Treasury Loan 1993
14½%	Treasury Loan 1994

13½%	Exchequer Stock 1994
12½%	Exchequer Stock 1994
9%	Treasury Loan 1994
12%	Treasury Stock 1995
10¼%	Exchequer Stock 1995
12¾%	Treasury Loan 1995
9%	Treasury Loan 1992-96
15¼%	Treasury Loan 1996
14%	Treasury Stock 1996
13¼%	Exchequer Loan 1996
13¼%	Treasury Loan 1997
10½%	Exchequer Stock 1997
8¾%	Treasury Loan 1997
6¾%	Treasury Loan 1995-98
15½%	Treasury Loan 1998
12%	Exchequer Stock 1998
12%	Exchequer Stock 1998 "A"
9½%	Treasury Loan 1999
10½%	Treasury Stock 1999
12¼%	Exchequer Stock 1999
12¼%	Exchequer Stock 1999 "A"
12¼%	Exchequer Stock 1999 "B"
9%	Conversion Stock 2000
13%	Treasury Stock 2000
14%	Treasury Stock 1998-2001
12%	Exchequer Stock 1999-2002
12%	Exchequer Stock 1999-2002 "A"
13¾%	Treasury Stock 2000-2003
13¾%	Treasury Stock 2000-2003 "A"
3½%	Funding Stock 1999-2004
11½%	Treasury Stock 2001-2004
12½%	Treasury Stock 2003-2005
12½%	Treasury Stock 2003-2005 "A"
8%	Treasury Loan 2002-2006
11¾%	Treasury Stock 2003-2007
11¾%	Treasury Stock 2003-2007 "A"

13½%	Treasury Stock 2004–2008
5½%	Treasury Stock 2008–2012
7¾%	Treasury Loan 2012–2015
2½%	Treasury Stock 1986–2016
12%	Exchequer Stock 2013–2017
2½%	Annuities 1905 or after
2¾%	Annuities 1905 or after
2½%	Consolidated Stock 1923 or after
4%	Consolidated Loan 1957 or after
3½%	Conversion Loan 1961 or after
2½%	Treasury Stock 1975 or after
3%	Treasury Stock 1966 or after
3½%	War Loan 1952 or after

Securities issued by the Treasury under Part II of the Tithe Act 1936

3%	Redemption Stock 1986–96

Securities issued by certain public corporations and guaranteed by the Treasury

4¼%	North of Scotland Electricity Stock 1974–79
4¼%	British Electricity Stock 1974–79
3½%	British Electricity Stock 1976–79
3½%	North of Scotland Electricity Stock 1977–80
3%	British European Airways Stock 1980–83
3%	North of Scotland Electricity Stock 1989–92
3%	British Gas Stock 1990–95

Securities exempt from taxation where held by persons domiciled and resident out of the United Kingdom

3%	Treasury, 1982
3½%	War Loan, 1952 or after
5½%	Funding, 1982-84
5½%	Treasury, 2008-12
5¾%	Funding, 1987-91
6%	Funding, 1993
6½%	Funding, 1985-87
6¾%	Treasury, 1995-98
7¾%	Treasury, 1985-88
7¾%	Treasury, 2012-15
8%	Treasury, 2002-6
8¼%	Treasury, 1987-90
8½%	Treasury, 1980-82
8½%	Treasury, 1984-86
8¾%	Treasury, 1997
9%	Conversion, 2000
9%	Treasury, 1994
9%	Treasury, 1992-96
9½%	Treasury, 1999
9¾%	Treasury, 1981
12%	Treasury, 1983
12½%	Treasury, 1993
12¾%	Exchequer, 1981
12¾%	Treasury, 1992

Index